To:

From:

Everyone's Time To Cook

HOW TO START A LOVE AFFAIR WITH COOKING

Robert L Blakeslee

SQUAREONE PUBLISHERS

The majority of recipes and information provided in this book are from Robert L. Blakeslee's award-winning gift book *Your Time to Cook: A First Cookbook for Newlyweds, Couples & Lovers.* The focus of this edition has been redesigned to include *anyone* who wants to learn the basics of cooking—old or young, male or female, married or single.

COVER DESIGNERS: Robert L. Blakeslee and Jeannie Tudor
COVER PHOTOS: Robert L. Blakeslee
INTERIOR PHOTOS AND GRAPHICS: Robert L. Blakeslee
EDITOR: Marie Caratozzolo
TYPESETTERS: Robert L. Blakeslee and Jeannie Tudor

Square One Publishers
115 Herricks Road
Garden City Park, NY 11040
(516) 535-2010 • (877) 900-BOOK
www.SquareOnePublishers.com

Library of Congress Cataloging-in-Publication Data

Blakeslee, Robert L.
Everyone's time to cook : how to start a love affair with cooking / by Robert L. Blakeslee.
pages cm
Includes index.
ISBN 978-0-7570-0379-0
1. Cooking. I. Title.
TX714.B5745 2013
641.5—dc23
2013000797

Printed at Nutech Print Services, India

10 9 8 7 6 5 4 3 2 1

Contents

Getting Started

1. Welcome to Your Kitchen

2. Stocking the Pantry

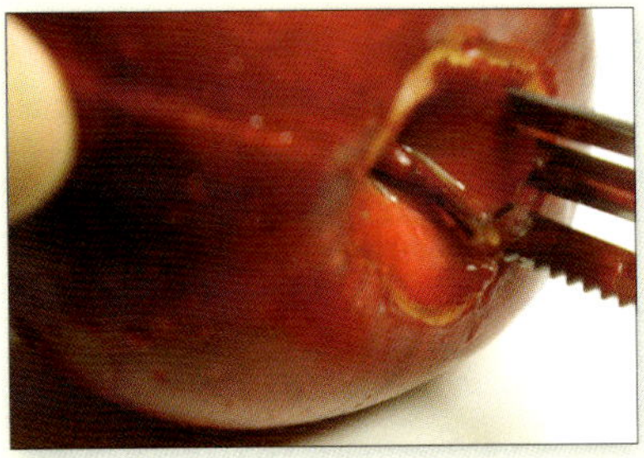

3. Terms and Techniques

4. That's Entertainment

The Recipes

5. I Love Breakfast!

6. Bottoms Up!

12. Everyone Loves Pasta!

13. Something Fishy

14. Chicken Tonight

Fun Food Trivia

15. What's Your Beef?

16. Pigs and Lambs

17. Holiday Feast

18. Just Desserts

This book is dedicated
in loving memory to the
Reverend Bruce Howes.
My cousin, my friend,
and an inspiring person
whom I will always
remember.

Acknowledgments

I would like to once again thank my pals at
Square One Publishers
for their support and dedication
to my cookbook series.
With a special shout out to my
totally cool publisher Rudy Shur,
sparring partner/editor Marie Caratozzolo,
graphics pal Jeannie Tudor,
and matchmaker/publicist Anthony Pomes.

I would also like to thank some people
who have supported me with my books
and related projects:
Brian (Big Bear) Bero,
Cassandra (the Rock) Barrows,
Lisa (Boca) Jenkins,
Linda and Ron (Cadillac) Fleetwood,
and Thomas (Dad) Blakeslee.

Words from the Author

Cooking, which began for me at age seven, has always been my passion. For as long as I can remember, the kitchen has been my classroom—a place of creativity and experimentation, of fun and frustration, of successes and failures. Over the years, I have prepared a countless number of dishes, and thrown hundreds of dinner parties to share my creations with family and friends. My guests have always bugged me for my recipes, which is where the idea of actually publishing them was born. I loved the idea, which took my passion for food and cooking to a new and exciting level.

Writing cookbooks, then having them published and sold internationally has been a dream come true. And for the icing on the cake, my first book, *Your Time to Cook,* received the Benjamin Franklin Award for "Cookbook of the Year" in a nationwide competition. Geared for beginners—*Your Time to Cook* was designed as a gift book for "newlyweds, couples, and lovers." The book you are holding now, *Everyone's Time to Cook,* is based on that award-winning title, but has been redesigned to include *anyone* who wants to learn the basics of cooking—old or young, male or female, married or single.

As you will see, I won't try to impress you with recipes that require exotic or expensive ingredients, or that involve difficult preparation techniques. You don't have to be a master of the culinary arts to be able to cook (and cook well). I believe I have a pretty good understanding of the best way to show the average person how to prepare food—simple, straightforward, and with lots of photos as visual guides. As far as the dishes themselves, I guarantee you'll enjoy the selection. Each kitchen-tested recipe (yep, really kitchen tested) has easy-to-follow step-by-step directions that are accompanied by full-color photos. These photos have not been retouched, nor has the food been altered in any way (known in the industry as "food styling"); so as long as you follow the directions, your completed dishes should look just as appetizing as they do in the finished shots.

I hope this book becomes your "go to" guide not only as a source for great dishes, but also as a handy reference. It offers so much more than simply recipes. I've included extensive food glossaries, guidelines for basic cooking and baking techniques, and helpful information on choosing and using kitchen utensils and appliances. There is even a table that lists lower-fat ingredient options and one that gives ingredient substitutions (just in case you discover you're missing one while in the middle of a recipe). Throughout the book, I've also shared lots of "Important Tips" that I've discovered over the years. These valuable bits of information are designed to prevent common mistakes when preparing certain dishes. In other words, they help ensure successful results.

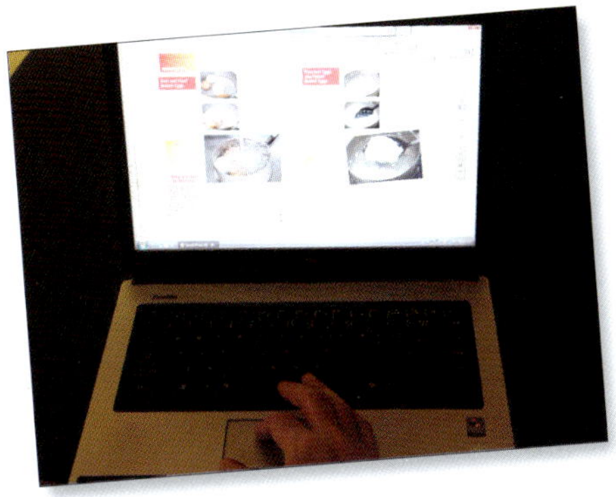

For further guidance, you can also check out my channel on You Tube called *Your Time to Cook*—named after my first book. On it, I've posted a series of instructional videos for many of my recipes. Each one begins with a humorous introduction that hopefully will give you a good laugh or two. I like to keep humor in my videos as well as in my cookbooks because I believe cooking should be fun.

So enjoy *Everyone's Time to Cook.* Through its simple instructions and visual guidance, you'll be sure to gain a solid cooking foundation—one that results in great culinary skill and confidence.

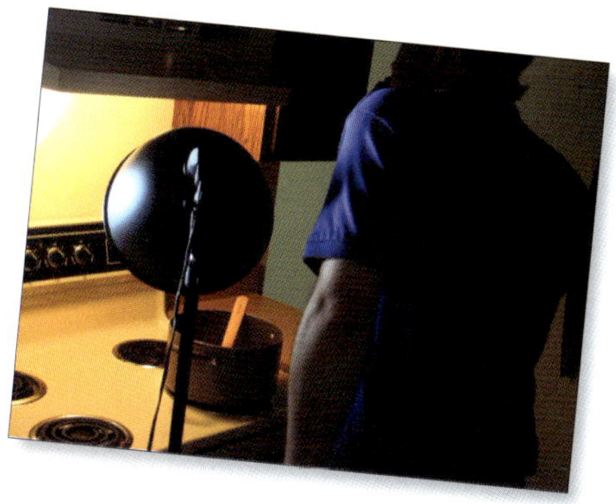

Bon appétit!

Robert L Blakeslee

Introduction

Welcome to the wonderful world of cooking! Don't be afraid. It's a lot easier than you may think.

Developing your skills in the kitchen (or improving your existing skills) is an adventure that anyone can enjoy . . . and *Everyone's Time to Cook* is the perfect starting place. It is a true "first" cookbook, packed with important kitchen essentials and cooking fundamentals, as well as a collection of basic, easy-to-prepare recipes.

One of the reasons this book is such a great choice for the novice cook lies in its unique visual approach. Cooking is an art, and it's no secret that most people tend to learn much better and quicker when they are guided visually rather than verbally. For this reason, throughout the book, you will find over a thousand full-color photos and illustrations to help make the information clear and accessible—whether it is the description of a cooking technique, a listing of kitchen staples, or directions on how to set the perfect table or brew the perfect cup of coffee. Photos also accompany each recipe's reader-friendly step-by-step directions that further guide you to perfect results every time.

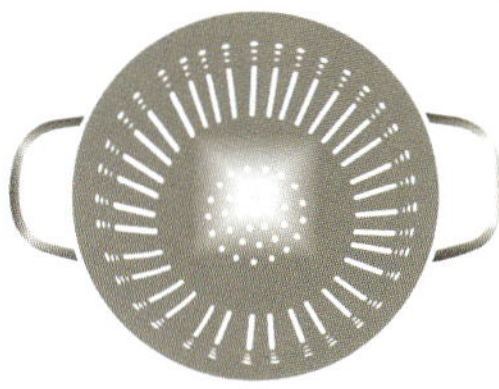

Although *Everyone's Time to Cook* is designed to build a solid foundation for the inexperienced cook, if your kitchen skills are better than basic, you will also find it beneficial. In addition to discovering some great new recipes, you are likely to come across a new technique, a helpful shortcut, or a better method for preparing certain foods.

No matter what your qualifications are as a cook, you will find *Everyone's Time to Cook* to be a valuable reference—one that will hopefully become the cornerstone of your cooking experience. May it help make your kitchen a happy place where you share good food, good times, and good memories.

Before You Cook, Read This

To help ensure that your cooking experience is an enjoyable one, especially if you're a novice in the kitchen, keep the following recommendations in mind:

Keep it clean

After preparing and enjoying a delicious meal, the last thing you'll want to face is a huge kitchen cleanup. But it doesn't have to be that way. While you are preparing a recipe, try to "clean as you go." Put away utensils and ingredients after using them—put dirty dishes in the sink or dishwasher, dry goods back in the pantry, and fresh items back in the fridge.

During any breaks in the preparation—while the soup is simmering or the cake is baking try to clean up as much of the kitchen as you can, especially before serving. No matter how delicious the food is, a big mess in the kitchen can take the fun out of cooking. So try not to let it get out of hand.

It's also important to clean dirty dishes and utensils as soon as possible. The longer the food remains, the harder it becomes to remove. If, however, the pot, pan, or casserole dish has a difficult-to-clean baked-on mess (such as from long oven-roasting), presoaking it in hot soapy water is recommended before you attempt to clean it.

Pay attention

Many people who say they cannot cook simply don't pay attention to what they're doing. Unless you are simmering a pot of soup or stew, cooking on a stovetop requires constant attention. Food that is cooked on the grill must be checked every few minutes. And baked goods should be checked a few minutes before the recipe's recommended cooking time, and then every minute or so until ready.

Give it a taste test

When you prepare a recipe, especially for the first time, let your taste buds test the dish before you serve it. Even if you have followed a recipe exactly as written and the dish looks and smells good, you might find—depending on your personal likes and dislikes—that it needs something more. You may, for example, find the food to be bland for your taste, so a pinch of salt or some other seasoning or herb may be needed. But no matter what you add, be sure to do so a little at a time. You can always put in more, but once you have added too much, the dish can be doomed.

Use suggested testing methods for doneness

Cooking times for most foods will vary depending on a few factors, including the type of oven and/or stovetop that are used, and even the altitude in which you live. For this reason, cooking times are approximate, not exact. Along with estimated cooking times, this book also includes recommended tests for doneness. For instance, you'll know that a cake is ready when a toothpick inserted in the center comes out clean. For roasts and large fowl, a meat thermometer, which reads internal temperature, will indicate doneness. And pasta is ready when it is soft yet firm to the bite. You'll discover many other methods for testing doneness throughout this book.

Follow baking directions exactly

Here is an important culinary fact—cooking is different from baking. With cooking, you can usually alter a recipe (throw an extra clove of garlic in the soup, add more salt to the casserole) and still have it come out tasting great. Baking, however, is more like chemistry. In order to ensure successful results, you have to measure the ingredients and follow the preparation methods exactly as written.

Take care in your presentation

I typically design my recipes to produce dishes that not only taste delicious, but also look delicious. Always take time to organize and present your food. Don't just fling it in a bowl (like the "slop on the gruel" technique you've seen in prison movies) or thoughtlessly dump it onto a platter. And consider adding a garnish or other finishing touch to give your delicious food even greater visual appeal. Keep in mind that when food looks good, it is always more appetizing.

Have Fun!

Cooking should be enjoyable. Once you understand cooking basics, feel free to use any of the recipes in this book as starting points—springboards to which you can add your own creative touches. And most important, remember to have fun. Revel in your successes and learn from (and laugh at) your mistakes.

How to Read the Recipes

The recipes in this book all contain common elements that are arranged for easy reading. The "Stuff You'll Need" box shows the utensils and cooking vessels you'll need to create the recipe. An ingredient list, yield information, and clear step-by-step instructions with photos are also included. Then all you have to do is follow the instructions. If you do it right, the finished product should look like the finished recipe photo. Many of the recipes also have helpful Important Tips—these pointers will help you make a better dish or save you from making mistakes that could ruin your meal. Be sure to read them!

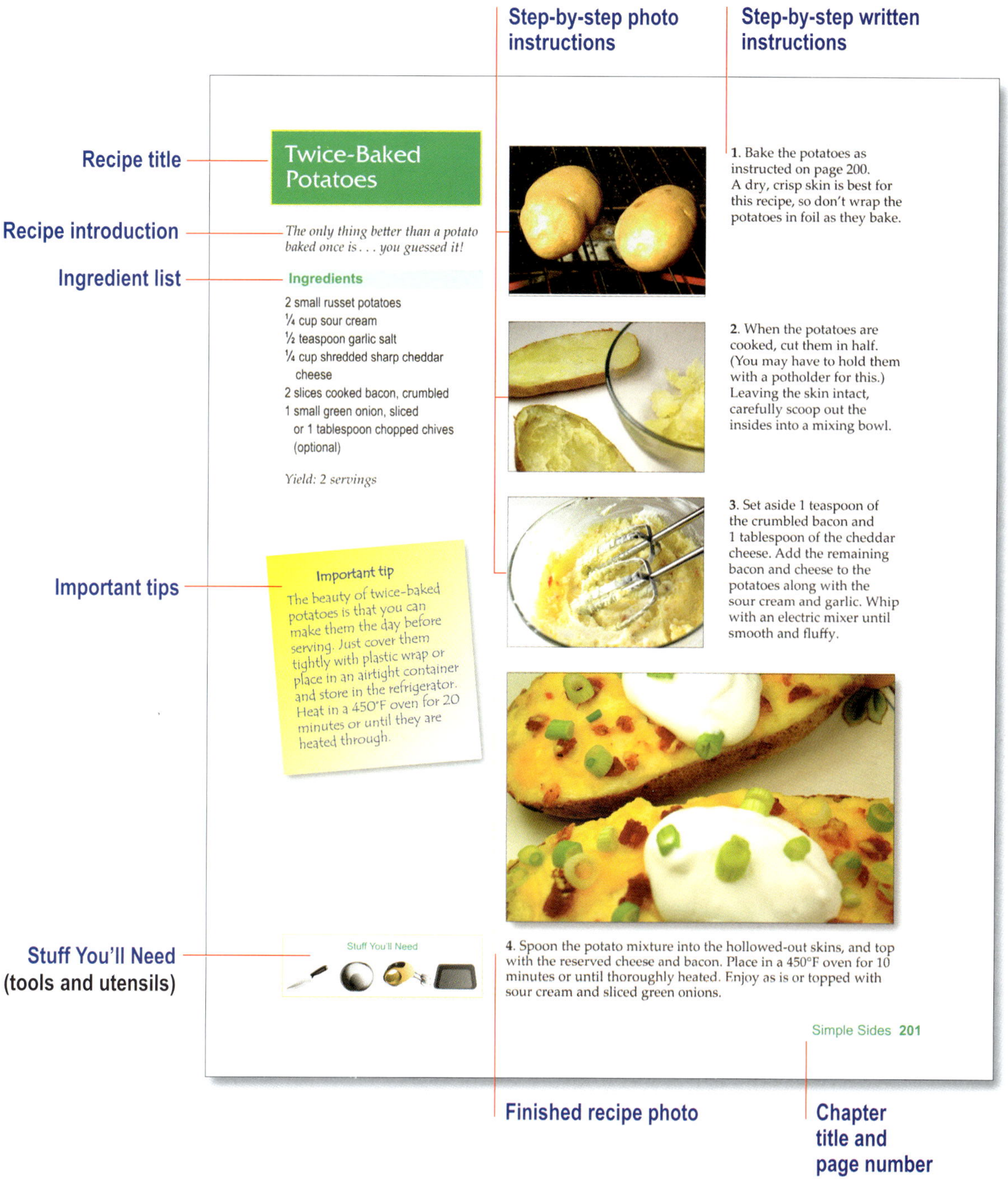

Twice-Baked Potatoes

The only thing better than a potato baked once is . . . you guessed it!

Ingredients

2 small russet potatoes
¼ cup sour cream
½ teaspoon garlic salt
¼ cup shredded sharp cheddar cheese
2 slices cooked bacon, crumbled
1 small green onion, sliced or 1 tablespoon chopped chives (optional)

Yield: 2 servings

Important tip
The beauty of twice-baked potatoes is that you can make them the day before serving. Just cover them tightly with plastic wrap or place in an airtight container and store in the refrigerator. Heat in a 450°F oven for 20 minutes or until they are heated through.

Stuff You'll Need

1. Bake the potatoes as instructed on page 200. A dry, crisp skin is best for this recipe, so don't wrap the potatoes in foil as they bake.

2. When the potatoes are cooked, cut them in half. (You may have to hold them with a potholder for this.) Leaving the skin intact, carefully scoop out the insides into a mixing bowl.

3. Set aside 1 teaspoon of the crumbled bacon and 1 tablespoon of the cheddar cheese. Add the remaining bacon and cheese to the potatoes along with the sour cream and garlic. Whip with an electric mixer until smooth and fluffy.

4. Spoon the potato mixture into the hollowed-out skins, and top with the reserved cheese and bacon. Place in a 450°F oven for 10 minutes or until thoroughly heated. Enjoy as is or topped with sour cream and sliced green onions.

Simple Sides 201

1. Welcome to Your Kitchen

It's the room with the refrigerator.

If you're tired of eating fast food or you've maxed out on frozen dinners . . . and if you're sick of making reservations at your local restaurant, maybe it's time to venture into that mysterious room in the house called *the kitchen.* You know the place, it's that room with the big cold box where you keep your drinks and deli meats. It's also home to that magical contraption called a microwave where you nuke your popcorn and reheat leftovers.

I must confess, the first time I looked at all of the dials and numbers on our stove and noticed those strange-looking gadgets lurking in the kitchen drawers, I was pretty intimidated (of course, I was only seven years old). But seriously, feeling comfortable in the kitchen and knowing how to use all of the gadgets and gizmos it has to offer is a very good thing—and an important first step in cooking basics.

This chapter is dedicated to teaching you everything you need to know to make your way around the kitchen. It kicks off with an overview of a basic kitchen layout along with some helpful recommendations on how to best organize your pantry, refrigerator, cabinets, and drawers. You will learn about the different types of stoves, ovens, and barbecues, and how to use them. You'll also find descriptions of standard kitchen supplies—cookware, knives, bakeware, and appliances—to help you get off to a good start. Take some time to become familiar with this information. Even if you've been cooking since you were a kid, I'm betting you may still learn a thing or two.

This photo is of a stand mixer I own that was manufactured by GS Blakeslee & Co. The company was started in 1870 by my great grandfather, who invented and manufactured the first commercial automatic dishwasher. The dishwasher, which was made out of wood, was considered a success because it washed more dishes than it broke. The company was sold after it had been in the family for 100 years and is still in operation today (but they don't make wooden dishwashers anymore).

An organized kitchen is a happy kitchen. Setting it up properly is a good idea if you want to have an efficient work flow while preparing recipes. If your kitchen isn't organized, you'll find yourself spending more time preparing to cook than cooking itself.

The Cooking Area

Let's start by taking a look at your cooking area. Most kitchens are designed with the"work triangle" concept in mind. As seen in the graphic below, this is the arrangement of your refrigerator, stove, and sink, which should be close to each other—this way, you won't have to take a lot of unnecessary steps while cooking.

Expanding on this triangle, you'll also need a place to cut food, use electric appliances, and store utensils, ovenware, pots, pans, and other cooking vessels.

Depending on how your kitchen is laid out, preparing food should be done next to the stove, or, as a second choice, next to the sink. You can use electric appliances anywhere; however, close to the stove is usually a good spot. This way, you can transfer the food easily to cooking vessels if necessary.

Try to keep your countertops clear of unnecessary items. It's amazing how much space you'll need when preparing a meal, so every inch is important. If you have appliances that you use only from time to time, store them on a shelf or in a cabinet rather than on the counter. The smaller the kitchen, the more important it is to conserve space.

Storing Stuff

Good organization in the kitchen helps make cooking enjoyable. Keeping your food organized, for example, will help you create good shopping lists because you'll easily notice when you're running low on an item. Keeping your cooking utensils organized will reduce the amount of time you spend uttering profanities when you can't find that wooden spoon or spatula you need at a crucial time.

The first step in creating a well-laid-out kitchen is examining the arrangement of the work triangle and the storage areas surrounding it. Then it's time for your common sense to take over . . . put the most frequently used items near the places you will be using them most—either within or close to your working triangle. Any areas outside the triangle are best for storing items that are used only once in a while.

In the graphic below, I have illustrated a basic kitchen layout along with some general storage recommendations. Of course, every kitchen is different, but by following a few logical guidelines, you'll find yourself doing a dance while cooking instead of running a marathon.

Refrigerator Area Cabinets

The upper cabinets in this area are best for storing dishes that you use occasionally, like gravy boats, serving platters, and crystal, while the easy-to-reach lower cabinets are good for storing items like plastic food containers, pitchers, and small electric appliances. Any cabinet over the refrigerator is hard to reach (even if you're tall). This makes it the perfect place to store those seldom-used dishes and appliances.

Sink Area Cabinets

The easily accessible areas near the sink are excellent for storing everyday dishes and glassware. If you have a dishwasher, there is a good chance that it will be located in this area next to the sink. The cabinet directly below the sink is typically used for storing dish soap and other cleaning products, and often a small garbage pail.

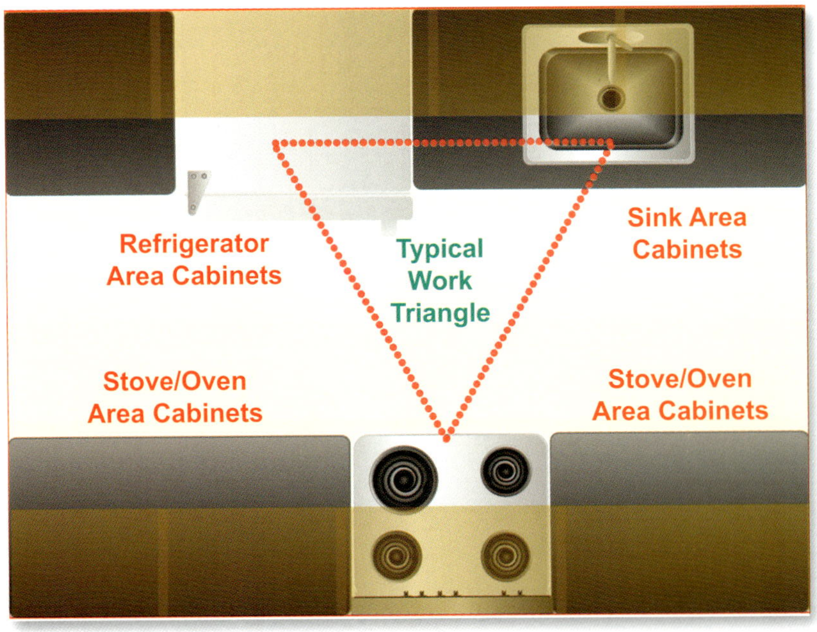

Stove/Oven Area Cabinets

The lower cabinets next to the stove are excellent for storing casserole dishes, baking pans, and other ovenware. They also tend to be fairly deep, so place the items you use most often toward the front. In the back, store bakeware and appliances that you don't use as often.

Upper cabinets in this area are good places to keep dry spices, as well as flour, sugar, and other baking supplies. If you have storage above the stove, it is often over a kitchen fan and almost as inaccessible as the spot above the refrigerator. It can be, however, a good spot for storing dry goods that are used occasionally, like pasta, rice, and certain canned goods.

Drawers

Drawers are often found next to the oven or sink. Top drawers are best for everyday cutlery and utensils that you use often, such as can openers and vegetable parers. Lower drawers are great for storing aluminum foil and other food wraps, storage bags, and utensils that you use occasionally like turkey basters and rolling pins.

Important tip

If you have children (or children who visit you often), be sure to keep dish soap, cleaning products, and other toxic items either out of their reach or in a cabinet with a childproof safety lock.

The Pantry

A pantry is great for storing nonperishable items like canned and bottled goods, and paper products, especially those bought in quantity at your local grocery or warehouse store. Buying in quantity can help stretch your food budget—typically, the more you buy, the less you pay per item. For things that you use on a regular basis like paper towels, your favorite peanut butter, or even those canned beets (yuck!), you can save big by buying big.

Some kitchens are not equipped with pantries, but don't let that stop you from creating your own. You can put up some storage shelves on the wall, or convert an unused closet or storage area into a pantry. Keep in mind that it is important to stock at least a one-week supply of food and water for every member in the household in case of an emergency.

The Refrigerator

A typical refrigerator is divided into two sections—the cold section, which is known as the refrigerator unit, and the really cold section, which is known as the freezer. Most people (even those who are clueless in the kitchen) know that fresh foods and many edible items that spoil easily are stored in the fridge. Many people, however, do not appreciate the importance of using the crisper shelves or drawers that are located near the bottom of the refrigerator. Because this area offers better moisture and temperature control, it is the best spot to store fresh fruits and vegetables for longer shelf life.

When freezing food, be sure it is stored in proper freezer containers or wrapped in freezer-quality paper. This will prevent the food from developing freezer burn, which compromises taste and texture.

Inside the refrigerator

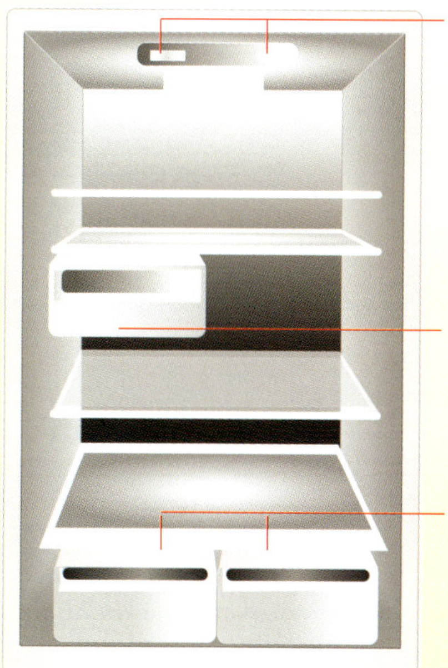

Climate control dials
There is usually one control dial for regulating the temperature of the freezer, and another for the refrigerator. To save on your electric bill, use the low-energy setting.

Deli and cheese compartment
This spot is for storing cold cuts and cheese.

Crispers
This area often has its own humidity control for keeping produce fresher, longer.

What's Cooking?

Most kitchen stoves/ranges are all-in-one units that have a stovetop or rangetop (for cooking food in pots and pans on top of the unit) and an oven (for baking or broiling food in an enclosed area). They are powered by gas or electricity. Standard stovetops have four burners, also called "elements." The temperature of both the burners and the oven is controlled by a panel of knobs on the stovetop.

Today, there are more types of stoves and ovens than ever before, with choices and options limited only by your pocketbook. But it doesn't matter how many buttons or dials or computer-aided functions your unit has, all are designed to do the same thing—cook food.

Stovetop Controls

Oven temperature dial: This dial allows you to set the oven temperature, which usually has a range of 150°F to 500°F. The highest setting is Broil.

Bake and broil dial: This dial lets you switch the oven temp to Bake, Broil, or Off.

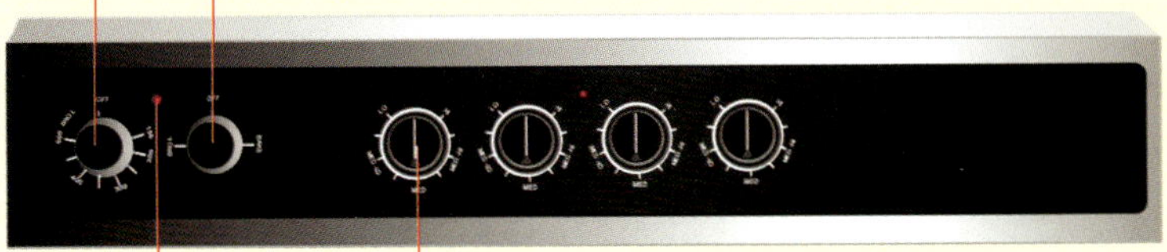

Burner controls: These dials are for turning the burners on and adjusting the heat level. Burner settings range from low to high with increments marked in between.

Warning lights: These let you know if you've left the oven on or if the burners (on electric models) are still hot.

Hot! Hot! Hot!

You'll need oven mitts or gloves to handle hot pans and to remove hot dishes from the oven. And don't forget that you will also need a safe place to rest the hot cookware—placing it directly on countertops or kitchen tables can cause damage. For this reason, be sure to have a few trivets of various sizes on hand. What are trivets, you ask? They are little stands or supports, usually made of metal, wood, ceramic, or silicone, on which hot pans or dishes are placed. They are designed specifically to protect the surface of tables and counters from heat damage.

Stovetops

Basically, there are two types of stovetop burners—gas and electric.

Gas

Natural or propane gas is the preferred method of stovetop cooking by most people, including chefs from around the world. This is because it offers several advantages over electric burners. The flame on a gas burner ignites instantly and its heat level is very easy to control.

Electric

All electric stovetops have the same drawback—the burners take time to heat up and cool down. Today's electric stoves, however, heat up faster and the temperatures are much more precise than they were in the past. The different types of electric stovetops include:

Electric coil burners

These are the most common of heating elements found on electric stoves. They are the least expensive, very durable, and easy to replace. One drawback of coil burners is that the drip pans below them can be hard to reach and difficult to clean.

Glass-ceramic cooktop

This flat, one-piece cooktop is heated from beneath by electric coils or infrared halogen lamps. The burner areas heat up and cool down quicker than coil burners, and because food cannot get underneath the elements, cleanup is a snap.

Induction cooktop

This unique type of cooktop creates an electromagnetic field that heats up special magnetic-based pans, not the cooktop itself. Because the cookware becomes the heat source and cooks the food, the cooktop remains cool to the touch.

Oven Types

With so many ovens to choose from, what's a person to do? Here is some basic information on the most common types of ovens.

Oven Features

Conventional Ovens

Conventional ovens are powered by gas or electricity. Gas ovens heat up faster than electric, but once the oven is preheated, there is little difference in how they cook food. The heat comes from elements located at the bottom of the oven.

Convection Ovens

Also known as a *fan oven*, a convection oven works the same way as a conventional unit, only with the addition of a high-temperature fan. The fan causes the air to circulate around the food, making it cook faster and at lower temperatures than in a conventional oven. The air circulation (convection) also tends to cook the food more evenly and eliminate any hot spots.

Toaster Ovens

Because of their reduced size, standard toaster ovens preheat faster and use less energy than conventional ovens. Convection toaster ovens are also available. They offer the same benefits as the larger models.

Microwave Ovens

Microwave ovens use microwave energy to heat or cook food in a fraction of the time it takes in a conventional oven. I don't recommend them for cooking most food because they tend to cook unevenly. They don't brown or crisp food, either. I like microwaves for heating up leftovers, soups, and beverages; for defrosting frozen foods; and for making popcorn.

Be aware that you cannot place any object containing metal in a microwave. This includes aluminum pans and foil, forks and other cutlery, dishes that are decorated with metal paint, and takeout containers with metal handles. These items can create an electric arc, cause sparks, and possibly result in fire.

Steam Ovens

This type of oven cooks food using superheated steam. It's like a pressure cooker without the pressured environment. Steam ovens make breads crisper, and meats and casseroles moister. Convection models are also available.

Important tip

Unless the recipe states otherwise, always begin cooking the dish in a preheated oven. (Cooking times are based on this.) Most ovens have a signal that indicates when the desired temperature is reached.

Often the terms "barbecue" and "grill" are used interchangeably—and sometimes together, as in "barbecue grill"—but there is actually a difference between them. Basically, a barbecue has a cover, while a grill does not. The ultimate question, however, is whether it is better to use charcoal or propane to fire up these units. I'm a propane man myself because I hate to clean up messes, and coals create a mess. I do agree that food tastes better when it's cooked over coals, but for that, I have a solution—I add wood chips to the grill for a wonderful smoky flavor. If you try this, be sure to soak the chips in water first, so they smolder rather than burn.

Building a Good Coal Bed

Once you get the hang of it, making a perfect coal bed will be easy.

1. Remove the metal food grill from inside the kettle. Begin with around twenty to twenty-five charcoal briquettes for a couple of steaks, and fifty or more for a few pounds of meat. Arrange them in a tall pile—don't spread them out.

2. Unless the coals have been pretreated, saturate them with charcoal lighter fluid. Do not use gasoline, kerosene, or any other liquid that is not designed for lighting charcoal. These products are dangerous and will make your food taste like the inside of your gas tank. Carefully light the coals with a long fireplace match.

3. Let the coals burn for twenty to thirty minutes (they should be red hot). With a long set of tongs or a metal spatula, carefully spread out the coals, arranging them so they are all touching each other and slightly overlapping.

4. Replace the metal food grill, and you're ready for some delicious *down home cookin'!*

Important tip

Be careful if you are not familiar with barbecues. These puppies get real hot and can be dangerous. The coals can smolder for days. Many home fires are started every year by people who throw the hot coals in the trash while they are still smoldering.

Charcoal Barbecues

Many barbecue experts swear by charcoal as the only way to barbecue. The major advantages are that coals can achieve a higher temperature than gas, and they have an inherent wood-smoke flavor. The major drawback is that charcoal is unpredictable as a heat source, and may take you a while to figure out how to control it. There is also the "mess" factor that comes with handling charcoal and ash.

How Big is Your Grill?

With most men, the size of their grill is a measure of their manhood. I remember when one of my best friends bought a bigger grill than mine and I had "grill envy." At one of his parties, I discussed my feelings with the other men who were there and discovered that they all felt the same way. Yes, we are insane.

Important tips

To clean the grill racks, once the cooked food has been removed:

- Leave the heat on and close the lid. Within 15 minutes, the heat will burn any baked-on food into ashes, which you can easily remove with a grill brush.
- Halve an onion, stick it on a long fork, and use it to rub the racks clean.

Gas and Propane Barbecues

While many cooks find charcoal to be the best for barbecuing, just as many swear by gas or propane as the only way to go. Gas creates fast, clean, even heat . . . and you don't have to keep running down to the store for charcoal. If you use propane, it's a good idea to always have a spare tank on hand. There is nothing worse than running out of fuel in the middle of grilling—especially when you have a yard full of hungry guests. And if you are able to connect your barbecue to a natural gas line, you won't ever have to worry about running out of fuel.

Basic Grilling Tips

Whether you grill with charcoal or gas, here are a few tips to help you get great results every time.

- Wait until your barbecue is hot before starting to cook the food—about thirty minutes for a charcoal grill and fifteen to twenty minutes for gas.
- The fat from meat or the oil from a marinade can drip onto the coals and create flames. If a fire starts in your charcoal barbecue, move the food away from the flames, close the lid, and close off the top and bottom vents. This will put out the fire. Remember to open the vents again, or the coals will go out. If a fire starts in your gas grill, turn down the heat and close the lid.
- Red meat cooks better over high heat, while poultry and fish do better over medium heat.
- To keep fish moist as it cooks, regularly brush it with oil and lemon or another oil-based marinade.
- After cooking steaks, let them rest at least five minutes before serving. This allows the juices (which move to the center of the steak as the outside is cooked) to be reabsorbed throughout the meat.

Potz 'n Panz

Most cookware is available in stainless steel, aluminum, cast iron, or copper. Cookware with nonstick surfaces is also available and often a good choice for the new cook.

Aluminum

Lightweight and an excellent conductor of heat, aluminum cookware is very popular. When purchasing aluminum cookware, choose pieces that are at least 1/8 inch thick (3.2 millimeters).

Cast Iron

The most durable cookware available, cast iron distributes and retains heat very well. It is also very heavy and needs to be seasoned (see "It's Pan Seasoning Time" on page 13).

Copper

Copper cookware is both beautiful and a good conductor of heat. It is also heavy and expensive.

Stainless Steel

Very durable and reasonably priced, stainless steel cookware was once the popular choice of most home cooks. Its biggest drawback is that it does not conduct heat as well as copper or aluminum.

Your needs . . .

These four items—three standard pots and one frying pan—will see you through most cooking experiences.

1-quart saucepan

For preparing sauces and heating up small quantities of food or liquid.

2- or 3-quart pot

For making dishes like rice and for steaming vegetables.

10- or 12-inch frying pan

This size frying pan (sometimes called a skillet or omelet pan) is good for browning, sautéing, and frying most foods. If you get one of these in a set, chances are the cover for the stockpot will also fit it.

4- to 8-quart stockpot or Dutch oven

For making soups and stews and for cooking pasta, you'll need at least a 4-quart pot. A larger stockpot or an oval-shaped Dutch oven are good for cooking casseroles, stews, whole chickens, and large cuts of meat such as roasts and spareribs.

And your wants . . .

7- to 10-inch sauté pan

Good for cooking an egg or two, or for sautéing small amounts of food.

Wok

Primarily for stir-frying, a wok can also be used for deep-frying, braising, and sautéing. It's also good for making soup.

Double boiler

A double boiler uses indirect heat to melt chocolate and to cook sauces and custards. It consists of two stackable pots—the bottom pot holds boiling water, which heats up the food in the upper pot.

Stovetop grill

These grills come in flat and ridged varieties. The flat grill is used like a large frying pan; the ridged grill is for cooking meat.

Fondue pot

This communal pot, which is set above a lit sterno, is for heating fondue—a dish often made of melted cheese and wine. Diners use long forks to dip bits of food, usually bread, into the pot to coat with the hot fondue.

Know Your Pans

Type	Average Size	Basic Uses
Sauté pan	7 to 10 inches	Sautéing small quantities of food.
Frying pan	10 to 12 inches	Frying, browning, and sautéing.
Wok	16 to 18 inches	Stir-frying, deep-frying, sautéing; making soup.
Stovetop grill	12-inch square	Frying and grilling.

Know Your Pots

Type	Average Size	Basic Uses
Saucepan	1 to 3 quarts	Cooking sauces; heating canned goods.
Dutch oven	4 to 8 quarts	Cooking soups, stews, roasts, casseroles.
Stockpot	4 to 8 quarts	Cooking pasta, soups, stews, roasts.
Double boiler	1 to 2 quarts	Melting chocolate; cooking sauces.
Fondue pot	1 to 2 quarts	For cheese, meat, and chocolate fondue.

It's Pan Seasoning Time!

Cast iron pots and pans need to be "seasoned," which gives them a nonstick surface. To season a pan, first rub the interior with cooking oil (peanut and canola are recommended because of their tolerance to high heat). Then place the pan on the stove over medium heat for about twenty minutes or until the oil begins to smoke. After the pan cools, wipe off any excess oil with a clean cloth or paper towel.

Gadgets from A to Z

For years during my "starving artist bachelor days," I got by with a few simple utensils—two pots and one frying pan. I had to be inventive back then. The lid from a pot became a strainer, a fork became a whisk, a cereal bowl doubled as a mixing bowl. I used hand-me-downs from various family members, so I had a very eclectic collection. Sometimes, a cook has to be inventive and adapt to what's available.

Later, when I got married, my wife and I got a large variety of kitchenware, plates, glasses, and a bunch of crystal. We also received a few fun toys that I won't mention here. (Oh what the heck, we also got an electric juicer and bread machine!) Personally, I had been cooking a long time. My bride, however, knew only how to microwave macaroni and cheese and warm up canned soup.

If you're anything like my wife, you're probably wondering what to do with all of those marvelous gadgets and gizmos that are found in the kitchen. Hopefully, it will all become clear to you in the next few pages.

Take Only What You Want

Although the utensils listed in this section are among the most useful ones for most cooks, it isn't necessary to own them all. Select the ones that are right for you and your particular needs. For instance, if you and your partner are vegetarians, you probably won't be needing a meat thermometer or a turkey baster. Nor should you feel the need to buy a timer if your stove already has one built in.

There are a couple of additional pointers I'd like to share with you about purchasing utensils and small appliances:

- I recommend investing in a good set of knives. With proper care, knives can last a lifetime. Also, choose varieties that work with your lifestyle. If you don't like having to sharpen them, get knives with serrated edges. Some are guaranteed to stay sharp (they even cut pennies). For more info on knives, see page 18.
- I tend to purchase good-quality small kitchen utensils like vegetable peelers and can openers. They cost only a few dollars more than cheaper ones, but the difference in the way they perform can be significant.
- Generally, I don't find it necessary to buy top-of-the-line small electric kitchen appliances like blenders and hand-held mixers. The moderately priced ones usually work well enough. For all the extra money you'll spend on some of the higher-priced items, there is often little difference in the jobs they do. (A twenty-speed blender, for example, will cost you more, when five speeds are all you really need.)
- Check to see if the items you purchase are dishwasher safe. Even if you generally wash dishes by hand, there may be times (like when you're cooking for several guests) that you may want to use a dishwasher.

Your Basic Gadgets

Apple corer/peeler

This semi-circular knife has a serrated edge for removing apple cores. Most models also have a peeler.

Can and bottle openers

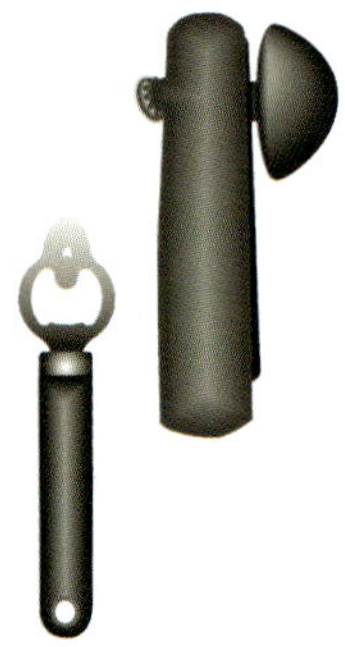

You'll need these to open bottles, remove can lids, and puncture the top of cans.

Chopper

Great for chopping a variety of fruits and vegetables, and it's easy to clean. It's also my favorite nonessential tool.

Citrus juicer

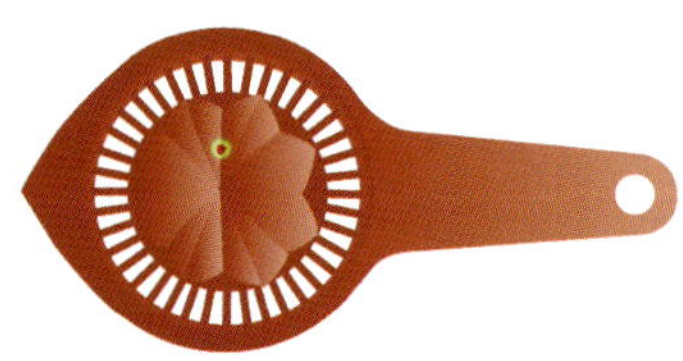

When juicing lemons, limes, oranges, and possibly grapefruits, this tool will be your "main squeeze."

Colander

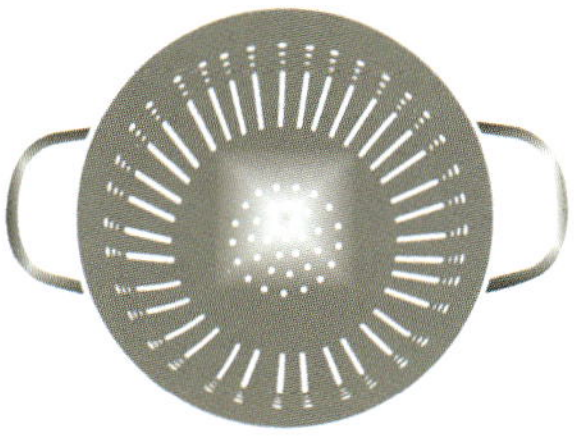

Used for straining pasta and washing vegetables and fruits, colanders are made of metal and plastic and come in various sizes.

Cookie cutters

Available in a variety of shapes, including gingerbread men and other holiday favorites, these molds are simply pressed onto rolled-out cookie dough.

Egg beater

Faster than a whisk or fork, this hand mixer is best for beating liquids, light batters, and eggs.

Fruit and vegetable peeler

An efficient tool for removing the skin from fruits and vegetables.

Funnel

Used for the spill proof transferring of liquids into bottles or jars.

Garlic press

For crushing garlic and mincing it through tiny holes.

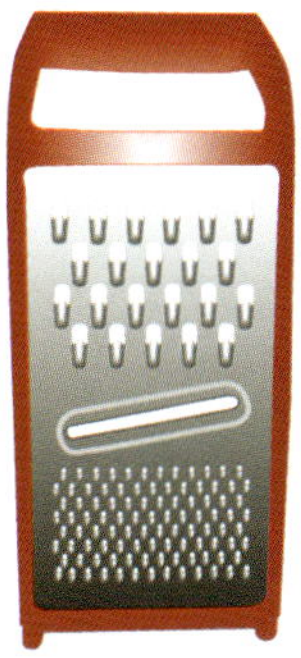

Grater or shredder

This tool has large holes for shredding and small holes for grating. It often has a hole for slicing as well.

Ice cream scoop

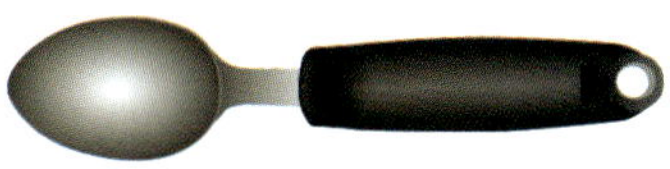

This very strong spoon is used for making nice round scoops of ice cream.

Kitchen scissors

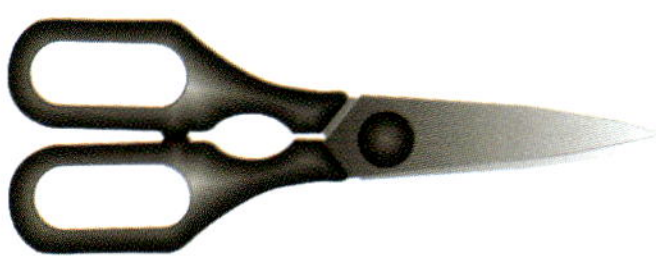

This multi-purpose tool is good for opening sealed bags and packages, as well as cutting herbs and vegetables.

Knives

Your main knife will be a chef's knife. I have a special one I call "ol' silver." For detailed information on knives, see page 18.

Ladle

This long-handled spoon with a deep bowl is for serving liquids like soup and stew.

Long fork or chef's fork

Perfect for picking up meat and for turning food on a grill, this fork is also used to hold a roast or poultry steady as it is being carved.

Measuring cups

For liquids a 2-cup measuring cup is recommended. For dry ingredients, a set that includes 1-cup, $^{1}/_{2}$-cup, $^{1}/_{3}$-cup, and $^{1}/_{4}$-cup measurements is standard.

Gadgets from A to Z

Measuring spoons

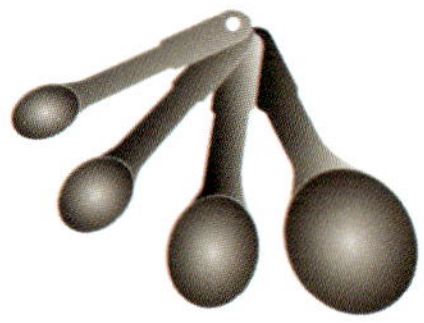

A set of four spoons with measurements of 1 tablespoon, 1 teaspoon, $\frac{1}{2}$ teaspoon, and $\frac{1}{4}$ teaspoon is all you'll need.

Meat thermometer

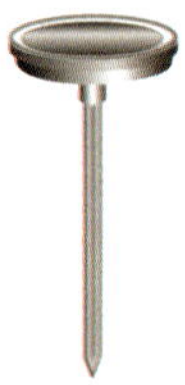

Used for testing the doneness of poultry and thick cuts of meat.

Mellon baller

Used to scoop melon or other soft fruit into round ball-shaped sections for a fruit salad. The unique shape of the fruit adds visual appeal.

Mixing bowls

A large mixing bowl is all you really need, but it is helpful to have a variety of sizes.

Nut or seafood cracker

For opening up nuts or cracking the shells of crabs and lobsters.

Pastry or barbecue brush

For spreading or basting butter, oil, glaze, or sauce on foods or baked goods.

Pastry dough blender

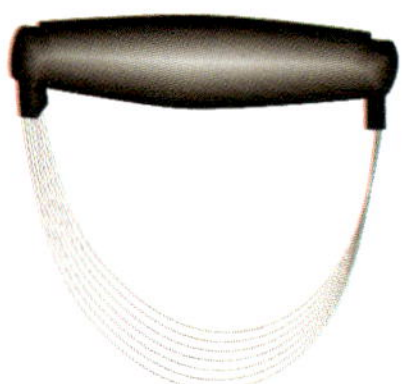

Used to "cut" butter or shortening into flour when making dough for biscuits, pie crusts, and other pastries.

Pie/cake server

A combination knife/server that is specially shaped for cutting and serving a slice of cake or pie.

Pizza cutter

This specialty knife—a circular blade mounted on a handle—rolls over pizza for easy cutting.

Potato masher

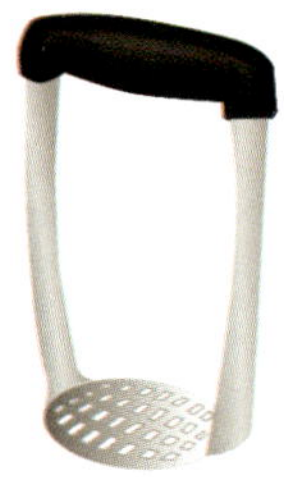

Used to mash boiled potatoes and softened fruits and vegetables.

Rolling pin

This cylindrical-shaped utensil, often made of wood, is used to flatten and shape dough.

Rubber spatula

This tool is used to scrape batter and soft foods from bowls and utensils.

Serving spoon

This long-handled, oversized spoon is for transferring food from a pot or casserole dish. It is also used for stirring ingredients.

Sifter

Tool for aerating flour, sugars, and other dry ingredients.

Skewer

A long metal or wooden stick on which food (often vegetables and cubed meat) is threaded.

Slotted spoon

Openings in the bowl of this spoon allow liquid to pass through. Slotted spoons are commonly used to remove food from a cooking liquid.

Spatula or pancake flipper

Used to flip food during cooking, spatulas are also used to serve food. You should have at least one plastic spatula for nonstick frying pans and a metal one for the barbecue.

Steamer

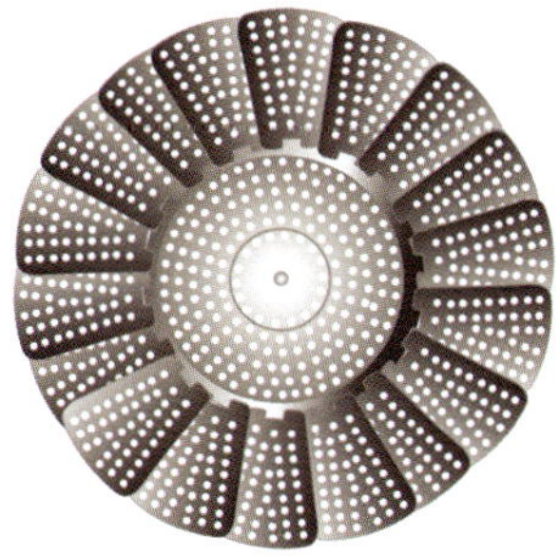

Food is steamed on top of this expandable metal basket, which is placed in a pot over boiling water.

Strainer

Similar to a colander, only with a mesh screen rather than larger holes, strainers are for separating solids from liquids.

Timer

This essential cooking gadget should have at least a one-hour capacity and an alarm.

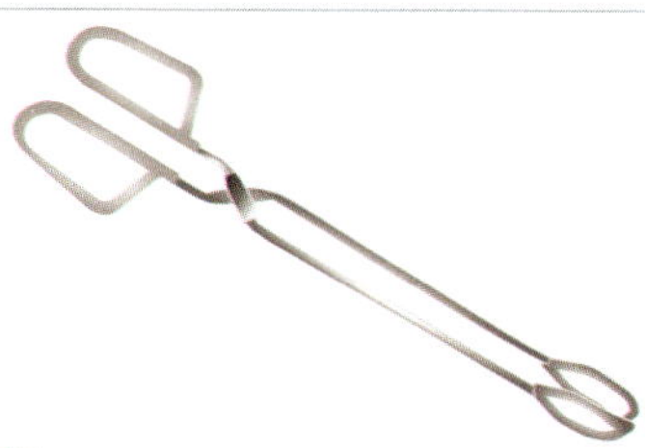

Tongs

This long-handled utensil is great for turning hot food in a pot, pan, or on the barbecue.

Turkey baster

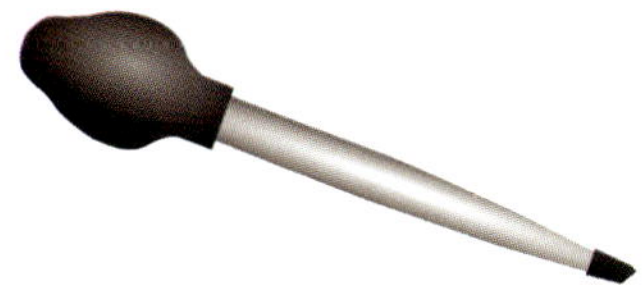

Resembling a very large eyedropper, a baster first sucks up the juices from a turkey, chicken, or roast as it cooks, and then releases the juice over the food to help it stay moist.

Whisk

Excellent for whipping and beating light batters and ingredients like cream, eggs, and egg whites.

Wooden spoon

Used for stirring, wooden spoons are good to use on nonstick pans. Get a few.

Zester

Used to scrape the outer layer (zest) of citrus fruits.

Careful with That Knife!

Watch out! When it comes to working with knives, you could really hurt somebody (including yourself). Knives are sharp, even if they are dull. Because of this, it's important to always cut away from yourself—never toward any part of your body that you may need later. Be especially careful of your fingers.

A sharp knife is actually safer than a dull knife. Dull blades make it more difficult to cut. They cause you to apply more force—and that can be dangerous. I suggest buying a knife sharpener and regularly sharpening the blades. Always respect your knives and be awake and alert when you cut anything, unless, of course, you like hanging around the emergency room.

As I mentioned earlier, if it's within your budget, buy good-quality knives. They're worth the investment. And with proper care, they can last a lifetime.

Important tip

Every kitchen needs a few good cutting boards, which can be made of wood, plastic, or tempered glass. To prevent bacterial cross-contamination, it is best to have more than one board for cutting different kinds of foods—one for veggies, one for meats, one for bread, etc. Opt for plastic or wood (treated compressed wood can go in the dishwasher), but avoid glass cutting boards. Glass may be easier to clean than plastic or wood, but it tends to dull or damage knives.

Your needs . . .

Chef's knife

Good for chopping, slicing, and mincing, the all-purpose chef's knife is the one you'll find most useful. Chef's knives are available with blade lengths of 6, 8, 10, and 12 inches. Keep this knife sharp at all times!

Paring knife

Resembling a smaller, thinner chef's knife, a paring knife has a 3- to 4-inch blade that tapers to a point. It offers more control than a chef's knife, making it good for peeling, slicing, dicing, and trimming small fruits and vegetables.

Serrated bread knife

With its 8- or 9-inch blade and serrated edge, this knife is designed to cut bread without squashing or tearing it. It's also good for cutting tomatoes and citrus fruits.

Utility knife

This multipurpose knife has a 4- to 7-inch plain or serrated blade. Good for jobs like cutting up vegetables and slicing through cheese.

And your wants

Carving knife

Generally used for slicing meats like turkeys and roasts, this knife has a long blade that allows you to make clean, even cuts for uniform slices.

Vegetable knife

The blade of a vegetable knife is flat on one side, making it good for slicing rounded vegetables such as carrots, mushrooms, and squash.

Boning knife

Used for removing meat from bones, this knife has a slender, somewhat flexible curved blade to get around tight spots.

Butcher's cleaver

Used to cut through meat and poultry bones with a downward chop, a cleaver can also slice through firm vegetables.

My Little Muffin Pan

Here is the essential bakeware you will need to prepare almost any recipe. Most are available in aluminum and glass; some come in ceramic as well. Glass cooks faster than aluminum, so you may have to adjust the cooking time depending on what you're using. Aluminum varieties often come with a nonstick coating—a big plus when it comes to cleanup. Most of these pans also come in disposable aluminum varieties that you can pick up in just about any grocery store.

Your Basic Ovenware

Cookie sheet
Good for baking cookies, oven potatoes, and other foods that need a large surface area, cookie sheets come in a variety of sizes. Most have shallow sides that prevent dripping.

13-x-9-inch baking pan
Ranging from 1 to 3 inches deep, this multipurpose pan is for making brownies and single-layer cakes, for cooking poultry and small roasts, and for roasting vegetables. I also use it for casseroles that don't need a cover.

Loaf pan
Great for baking bread and cooking meatloaves.

Cake pans/pie pans
You'll need two cake pans to make a double-layer cake. A pie pan is similar to a cake pan, but it has sloped sides. You can also purchase premade pie shells at most grocery stores.

Muffin pan
Used for making muffins and cupcakes. Unless the pan has a nonstick surface, I recommend using paper muffin cups to keep the muffins from sticking to the pan.

Roasting pan
This large, deep baking pan is big enough to fit a turkey, a roast, or a slab or two of spareribs.

Casserole Dishes

Although these dishes come in a variety of shapes and sizes (and often in sets), one with a 2- or 3-quart capacity is good for cooking most casseroles. Be sure they come with covers, even though you may not always need them. Also keep in mind that in addition to being cooking vessels, these dishes are used for serving—so choose ones that look good with your other dishes.

Electric Gizmos

Preparing your food with electric appliances can speed up your preparation time and improve your results. Three essential items—food processor, electric mixer, and blender—will help you prepare just about anything. From general preparation techniques like chopping, grating, and blending to whipping up beverages, sauces, and baers, these appliances can do it all.

Your needs . . .

Blender

Used for making smoothies, milkshakes, and yes . . . frozen margaritas and daiquiris. Make sure your blender has an ice-crushing blade. A glass container is more durable than plastic (unless you drop it).

Hand-held electric mixer

For the best consistency in batters and icings, you'll need an electric mixer. A handheld model with five speeds is all you'll need.

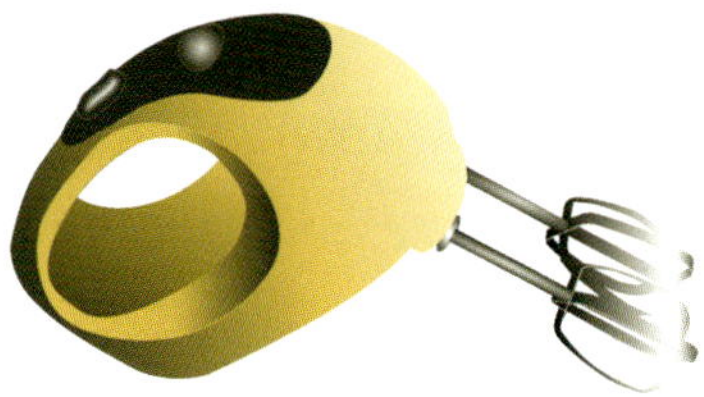

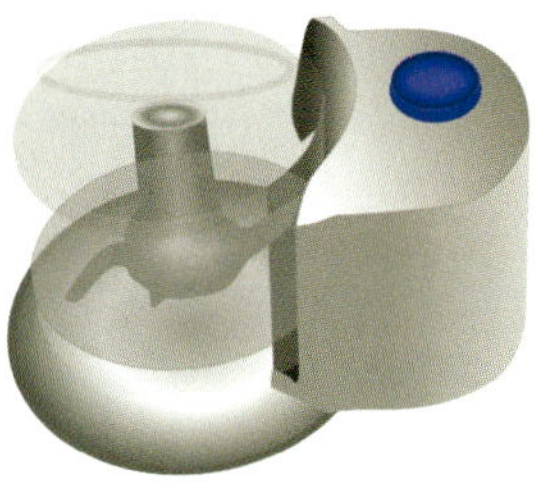

Food processor

A small to medium-sized food processor (2 to 4 cup capacity) that can chop, blend, and grate is my recommendation. I prefer a simple processor without a lot of parts.

Toaster

There are many types of toasters including wide-mouth, multi-slice, and toaster ovens. Pop-up toasters have at least one dial to control the darkness of the toast. This appliance is also good for toasting frozen waffles and pancakes, and toaster pastries.

And your wants

Bread machine

This appliance will do everything necessary to make a fresh loaf of bread, except add the ingredients. It kneads the dough, lets it rise, and bakes it with the touch of a button.

Coffee maker

Not only good for coffee, this appliance also heats up water for cocoa or tea.

Crockpot

Basically, an electric Dutch oven, a crockpot slow-cooks dishes like soups and stews over several hours.

Electric skillet

You can make just about anything in this versatile countertop skillet, which can range in heat from warm to 450°F. Especially good if you don't have a stove.

Ice cream maker

Homemade ice cream is the best! If you're willing to do the work, it's worth the reward. Available in electric and manual models.

Indoor grill

The countertop grill (made famous by George Foreman) cooks vegetables and meats while draining away any fat. Its biggest drawback is that it can be a little difficult to clean.

Pasta machine

This turns dough into long pasta of different widths and thicknesses, as well as specialty pasta like ravioli. Comes in electric and manual models.

Stand mixer

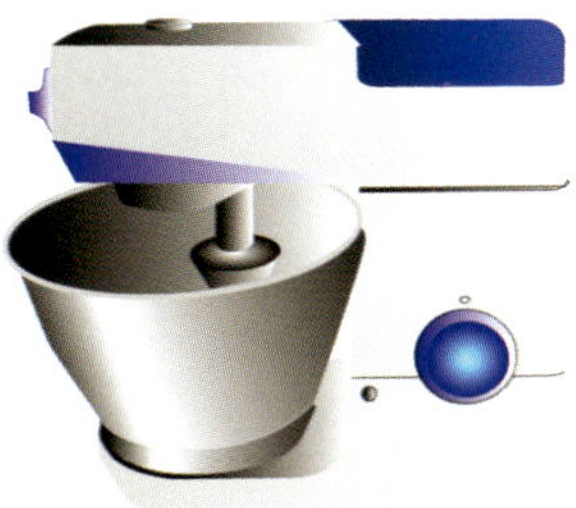

This heavy duty version of an electric hand mixer is attached to a stand and has a mixing bowl. Along with doing everything a hand mixer does, it can stir stiff batters and blend ingredients to form dough.

Waffle iron

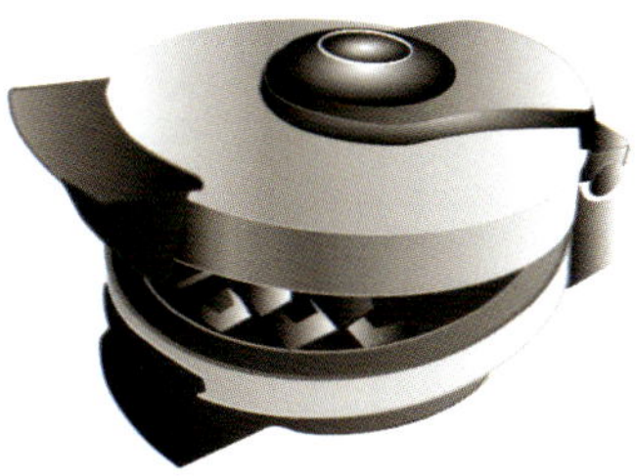

This appliance comes in two styles—one for American-style waffles and one for Belgian waffles.

Electric Juicers

Juicing machines fall into two main categories—citrus presses and mechanical juicers. A citrus press is only for juicing oranges, lemons, limes, and other citrus fruits.

With a mechanical juicer, you can juice vegetables and most fruits. The most common type is the centrifugal juicer, which sends chopped-up fruit and vegetables through a chute and into an internal basket. A high-speed spinning motion (like a washing machine spin cycle) separates the juice from the pulp.

Citrus press

Centrifugal juicer

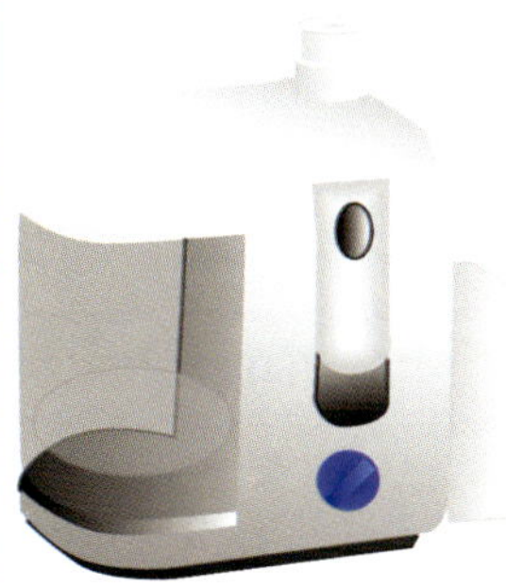

It Slices 'n Dices 'n Peels (oh my!)

Over time, as recipes and cooking techniques have become more complex, so have kitchen gadgets.

Veg-O-Satire

The Veg-O-Matic – a manually operated kitchen tool able to slice and dice vegetables in an instant – was one of the first "As Seen on TV" commercials. The heavily advertised gadget became a household name during the 1960s and '70s. Inspired by the commercials, comedian Gallagher created his "Sledge-O-Matic," a large wooden mallet he used to smash objects (especially watermelons). Dan Ackroyd also spoofed the commercials on *Saturday Night Live* with his "Bass-O-Matic" – an ordinary blender that turned fresh bass into a (revolting) drink.

How Long Will They Work?

On average, gas ovens last nineteen years, while electric ovens and refrigerators are good for about seventeen.

Tired of Being Pushed Around

In the 1930s, Sylvan N. Goldman invented and manufactured the first shopping cart. As the owner of Piggly Wiggly grocery stores, Goldman wanted a convenient way for his customers to carry their groceries as they shopped. He envisioned wheels on a folding chair with a basket on the seat and – voila! – the prototype for the first shopping cart was born. At first, customers didn't want to use these "basket carriers." Men felt they were a sign of weakness, while women didn't find them fashionable. And the elderly felt using the carts made them seem helpless. So Goldman hired models of both sexes and all ages to push the carts around the store and pretend to be shopping. That's all it took for the carts to catch on.

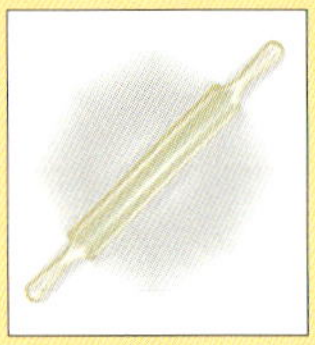

With or Without Handles?

Rolling pins come in two different styles – with handles and without. Americans typically prefer the handled version, while the French like theirs without or *sans manches.* When a Pennsylvania Dutch couple gets engaged, it is customary for the man to carve a rolling pin as a gift for his future wife.

How Things Got All Mixed Up

In 1908, engineer Herbert Johnson, who worked for the Hobart Corporation – a manufacturer of kitchen equipment – attempted to mechanically recreate the motion that bakers used when stirring dough. The result of his efforts was the first electric mixer. Initially, it had a giant 80-quart bowl and was used only commercially. In 1915, Hobart began manufacturing the first home models. Sunbeam introduced the first hand-held electric mixer in 1952.

Whisked Away

The first whisks were made of thin branches that were tied together in bundles. Often the branches, like those from peach trees, were aromatic and added flavor to the whipped ingredient. The French invented the modern whisk in the early 1900s.

Factory Bread

Before the 1920s, about 70 percent of bread in the United States was made in the home. By the late 1920s, over 80 percent was produced in factories. In the 1990s, the first automatic bread machines for the home were available.

2. Stocking the Pantry

I just want to make some pasta!

Sometimes shopping for groceries can be very confusing. I've often found myself overwhelmed by the sheer number of available choices for certain products. Take pasta, for example. Not only can you get lost trying to sort through all of the different shapes and sizes, you also have to decide on fresh or dried, short or long, and whole wheat or gluten-free. What about those varieties made with spinach, eggs, or rice? And then there's fresh produce. How do you know what to buy, how much to get, and how to store it once you're home?

In this chapter, you'll find pointers on how and where to shop, and which items to have on hand at all times. To help, I've provided shopping lists with popular kitchen staples, from dry goods and canned items to perishables like milk, fruits, and vegetables. With these items on hand, you'll always be able to make something good to eat. There are also helpful tips on food selection – how to pick the best and avoid the worst. And to help you avoid the "heebie-jeebies," I'll show you how to store and handle food properly.

Also within this chapter, you'll find a number of useful charts. One includes ingredient substitutions for those times when you are in the middle of following a recipe and discover you're missing something. Another chart offers lower-fat and/or calorie recommendations for lots of food items. And when it's necessary to know basic yield information, like how many carrots you'll need to make one cup of shredded, there is handy yield/equivalent chart.

So grab your coat and let's get started. It's time to go shopping.

Let's Go Shopping

There are many different places you can purchase food today—ranging from huge warehouse stores to local mom and pop shops. Here are some of them.

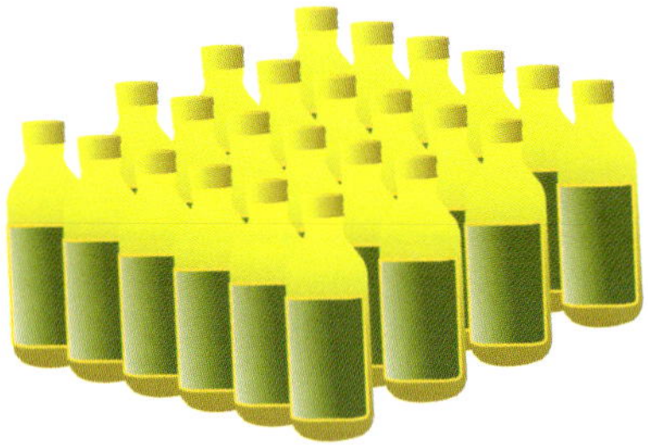

Warehouse Clubs

These retail giants are great for saving money, not only on food, but on all types of household items and general merchandise. Because the products are sold in large, wholesale quantities, and the format of the stores is "no-frills," warehouse clubs are able to keep prices low. They do, however, require annual membership fees. Before you join, make sure that you will be going to the store often enough to offset the membership cost. Also consider if you have significant storage space—like where you are going to put your thirty rolls of paper towels and case of peanut butter. If you're cooking for one or two and not throwing a lot of parties, this type of store won't be your first choice.

Major-Chain Grocery Stores

Major-chain grocery stores are where most people do their shopping. Located close to most homes, these stores offer a large variety of food at reasonable prices. Many include on-site bakeries, delis, fresh fish and meat departments, pharmacies, wine centers, and even bistro-type restaurants or coffee shops.

If there are several grocery stores in your area, take a trip to each one and explore their differences. Price, quality, and selection will vary from store to store, so find the one that best suits your tastes and budget. Also, be aware that most offer discount cards, which can save you hundreds, even thousands of dollars every year—and they're free! I strongly suggest signing up for one at every grocery store you frequent.

Independent Grocery Stores

Independently owned grocery stores vary in size from small mom and pop operations to larger establishments that rival the size of chain stores. Although they may have a reasonable selection of items, typically, their inventory is not as extensive as a chain's. They are also pricier because they don't buy items in large enough volume to compete with larger, corporate-owned giants. On the plus side, they tend to specialize, which means they may have a better selection of hard-to-find items, or they may offer superior quality products, such as produce or meat.

Big Box/Superstores

Superstores are often mass-merchandise stores (like Target or Wal-Mart) that also sell groceries. Generally, superstore prices are better than a grocery store's, but the quality and selection vary. Some places include a full line of grocery items, while others have only a few dedicated aisles. Fresh produce and baked goods, as well as choice meats are usually hard to find in superstores and the overall food quality tends to be mediocre.

Convenience Stores

A convenience store or mini-mart is usually located in a high-traffic area and opened for most of the day. Many are opened twenty-four hours, seven days a week. These stores typically sell items like candy, cigarettes, beer, and newspapers, but they also offer a small selection of food (usually prepackaged) and basic grocery items, like butter, eggs, and milk. Compared to grocery stores, their prices are clearly higher—store owners count on the fact that you are willing to spend extra money from time to time for the "convenience" of shopping at their establishments. And they're right. The stores are conveniently located, checkout lines move fast, and, let's face it, where else can you run out in the middle of the night to buy a gallon of milk or a cold six-pack of beer?

Ethnic Food Markets

Ethnic markets carry foods of a certain culture or nationality, such as Middle Eastern, Greek, Italian, and Chinese. They are often found in neighborhoods that are populated with people of such ethnic backgrounds. A growing number of grocery stores are beginning to carry some of the foods that were once found only in these neighborhood markets.

Farmers Markets

This type of public, often outdoor market is where farmers gather to sell their goods. Along with produce, which is freshly picked and locally grown, vendors may also sell meat, chicken, and eggs that come from animals that are raised on their farms. Homemade foods like bread, pies, and other baked goods; jams and preserves; cheese; and jars of golden honey are other common offerings. Foods sold at farmer's markets are often superior in quality and less expensive than what you'd find in a grocery store. Quality and selection varies greatly from market to market.

Drug Stores

Although this is not the first kind of store that comes to mind when you think of buying groceries, most chain drug stores now sell refrigerated and packaged foods. The prices are similar to a grocery store's, but the selection is very limited.

Speciality Markets

Before grocery stores came into being, everyone bought food at common street markets or specialty shops. You purchased your meat from the butcher, your fish from the fishmonger, and your bread from the baker. These places are still around, but harder and harder to find.

Butcher Shops

You'll usually find the best quality meat at a butcher shop. The prices are a little higher, but it's worth it if you want a special cut or meat that's fresher than what you'd find in most grocery stores.

Fish Markets

If you're looking for variety and freshness in your fish—and who isn't?—your best bet is a fish market. Most grocery stores offer just a few types of fish, and most are frozen or previously frozen. In coastal communities, many fish markets sell fish that was caught the same day. Some inland markets in large cities fly in fresh fish daily.

Bakeries

For a wide variety of freshly made breads and pastries, there is nothing better than a bakery. Most prepare personalized cakes and pastries for birthdays, holidays, and other special occasions.

Farm Stands

Roadside farm stands are usually found on highways in rural areas. They offer fresh produce grown by local farmers.

Produce Markets

Produce markets sell primarily fruits and vegetables. They offer a good selection at reasonable prices.

Online Groceries

With time at a premium, online grocery shopping is growing. Along with standard items, including dairy, kosher, frozen, and organic foods, many sites offer freshly baked goods, prepared foods, and health and beauty aids—often at competitive prices.

Gotta Have Food!

Time to go shopping! The following grocery lists contain some basic food items, which I recommend having on hand at all times. With these ingredients, you will always be able to prepare something good to eat.

Dry Goods

All-purpose flour
Baking powder
Baking soda
Breadcrumbs, plain
Brown sugar
Cereal
Confectioner's (powdered) sugar
Granulated (white) sugar
Nuts (walnuts or pecans)
Pancake mix
Rice

Breads
Sandwich bread
Flour tortillas
Pita bread

Herbs and spices
Basil
Black pepper
Chili powder
Cilantro
Cinnamon
Curry powder
Dill weed
Garlic powder or salt
Nutmeg
Oregano
Rosemary
Sage
Salt
Tarragon
Thyme

Pasta
Macaroni or elbows
Spaghetti

For the Fridge and Freezer

Dairy
Butter or margarine
Cheese (cheddar, Swiss, and/or mozzarella)
Cheese, grated (Parmesan, Romano, or Asiago)
Eggs
Milk
Yogurt

Meats and seafood
Bacon or breakfast sausage
Chicken, whole or cut up
Ground beef
Shrimp, frozen

Produce

Roots
Carrots
Onions
Potatoes

Fruits
Apples
Avocado
Bananas
Tomatoes

Vegetables
Bell peppers
Lettuce
Mushrooms
Yellow squash or Zucchini

Canned and Bottled Goods

Canned goods
Beans (black, kidney, chickpeas, and/or refried)
Broth (beef, chicken, and/or vegetable)
Cooking spray
Corn niblets
Olives, pitted
Tomato paste
Tomato sauce
Tomatoes, diced
Tuna fish

Bottled goods
Cooking oil
Honey
Ketchup
Maple syrup
Mayonnaise
Minced garlic
Mustard
Olive oil
Peanut butter
Salad dressing
Salsa
Soy sauce
Spaghetti sauce
Vanilla
Vinegar

You Need Some Staples

In the Can

Beans/legumes
Beans are so versatile! In my kitchen, black beans, kidney beans, and chickpeas are staples. I use them in soups, stews, salads, and rice and pasta dishes.

Broth
Available in beef, chicken, and vegetable flavors, as well as reduced-fat and low-sodium varieties, canned broth is a perfect base for soups and sauces, and a flavorful addition to many dishes.

Cooking spray
This spray form of various oils is used on cookware to prevent food from sticking. Only a spritz or two is needed, so it adds less fat than butter or oil.

Corn niblets
Heat up a can of these sweet kernels for a convenient side dish. You can also add them to salads and a variety of dishes.

Olives, pitted
Black and green olives make a tasty addition to salads and are used in many Greek, Mexican, and Italian-style dishes.

Tomato paste
This thick, concentrated tomato reduction is used to flavor soups, stews, and sauces without adding any liquid.

Tomato sauce
This sauce is made from briefly cooked, strained tomatoes. Used in many dishes and as a base for sauces.

Tomatoes, diced
Packed in juice, these chunks of plum tomatoes have more juice than diced fresh tomatoes.

Tuna fish
Tuna is great to have on hand for sandwiches and for tossing into salads and pasta dishes.

All Bottled Up

Cooking oil
Used in baked goods, this oil is also good for frying. Choose vegetable, corn, or canola.

Honey
An excellent sugar substitute, honey is added to tea and used in dressings and glazes.

Ketchup
What's a burger and fries without the sweet "tomatoey" goodness of ketchup?

Maple syrup
This classic pancake topper is a favorite in cookies and other baked goods. The "real" stuff is more expensive than processed, but the taste is superior.

Mayonnaise
This creamy condiment is used as a spread for sandwiches, a base for sauces and dressings, and an ingredient in salads like tuna, egg, and chicken.

Minced garlic
Packed in water or oil, minced garlic takes the work out of crushing the garlic yourself, but it is not quite as strong as freshly minced cloves.

Mustard
Whether mild and yellow or brown and spicy, mustard is a popular sandwich condiment and hot dog topper.

Olive oil
Not for frying, olive oil adds flavor to salads and many Mediterranean dishes. Extra-virgin, cold-pressed varieties are the richest in flavor.

Peanut butter
Whether a sandwich spread or an ingredient in sauces, cookies, and other baked goods, peanut butter is a true kitchen staple.

Salad dressing
Keep a variety of these dressings on hand to prevent salad "boredom." Many can double as marinades.

Salsa
Ranging from mild to fiery hot, this tomato-chile based sauce is essential in many Mexican dishes and a great dip for tortilla chips.

Soy sauce
This dark, salty sauce, made mostly from soybeans, is an Asian cooking staple.

Spaghetti sauce
Available in tomato, cream, and pesto flavors, this sauce is ready to use straight from the jar.

Vanilla
Extract from the vanilla bean is used to flavor beverages and baked goods. The pure extract is superior to imitation varieties.

Vinegar
Red wine and balsamic vinegars have a range of uses in the kitchen, especially salad dressings. Pungent balsamic is preferred for most vinaigrettes.

How Sweet It Is!

Once called "white gold" because it was so scarce and expensive, sugar was a luxury only the wealthy could afford. Today, this ingredient staple, which comes primarily from sugar cane and sugar beets, is neither scarce nor expensive. There's a lot more to sugar than meets the eye. Used to sweeten both foods and beverages, it also adds tenderness to doughs and gives baked goods a warm golden hue.

Sugar needs to be stored in an airtight container and kept in a cool, dry place. Leaving it exposed to the air will cause it to clump, especially brown sugar, which forms into rock-hard lumps.

Granulated white sugar

This most commonly used sugar, made from sugar cane or sugar beets, gets its white color from the refining process. It dissolves easily and lends sweetness to beverages, as well as most baked goods and other dessert items.

Confectioner's sugar

The superfine crystals of this "powdered" granulated sugar have a little added cornstarch to prevent clumping. Because it dissolves so easily, this sugar is often used for icings. It's also used to decoratively "dust" the top of some desserts.

Brown sugar

This is white sugar combined with molasses, which gives it a soft texture. Light varieties contain less molasses and are more delicate in flavor than dark varieties. Store in a sealed plastic bag to keep it soft.

Raw sugar

This is the crystallized juice that has been extracted from sugar cane. It has a coarse texture and a flavor similar to brown sugar. It also dissolves slowly, making it a good choice for coffee and other hot drinks.

Important tip

To soften hardened brown sugar, place it in a plastic storage bag with an apple wedge and seal it tightly for a day or two. For a quick fix, place the open bag in the microwave next to a cup of water, and heat on high for two to three minutes.

What's the Deal with Sugar Substitutes?

If you're watching your calories or are diabetic and need to control your blood sugar, it's nice to know you can still have your sweet zone activated. Sugar substitutes, both natural and artificial, are available. The most popular of these sweeteners include aspartame (Equal, NutraSweet), saccharin (Sweet'n Low), and sucralose (Splenda). They are used like sugar, only without the calories. Aspartame, however, loses its sweetness when exposed to high heat for long periods, so it is not good for cooking or baking. Stevia—the extract from the leaves of the stevia plant—is gaining popularity as a natural sweetener. Available in powder or liquid, stevia is 200 to 300 times sweeter than sugar.

You're Really Milking It!

Back when I was a child, there were still milkmen that delivered milk, cream, and cheese from local dairies right to your door. The milk came in a glass quart bottle with a foil cap. My brother bears a striking resemblance to our old milkman, but I've never said a word to him about it.

Calcium-rich milk commonly refers to cow's milk, which is the most popular kind. It is enjoyed as a beverage, added to coffee or tea, poured over cereal, and used in smoothies, shakes, sauces, baked goods, and so much more.

Remember the Following:

- Milk has a short shelf life, so be sure to inspect the "good to" date on the container.
- Always refrigerate your milk and never leave it out for more than a minute or two.
- Milk absorbs flavors, so keep the container closed when storing it in the refrigerator.
- The higher the milk's fat content, the quicker it sours. Skim milk lasts longest, cream the shortest.
- If milk is past its expiration date, just throw it out. If you want to have some fun, have your partner smell it first.

Important tip

Milk is a good barometer for how cold your refrigerator is. If it develops frost, you will know your fridge is too cold. If it spoils before the expiration date, the refrigerator may be too warm.

Whole milk

Rich and creamy, whole milk contains at least 3.25-percent fat.

Reduced-fat milk

This milk contains 2-percent fat. Most contain added vitamins A and D, which are removed during the fat-reducing process.

Low-fat milk

Containing only 1-percent fat, low-fat milk is generally fortified with added nutrients.

Skim milk

Considered "nonfat," skim milk has as much fat removed as possible (it must contain less than 0.5 percent). It's also thin and watery with a bluish cast, and has half the calories of whole milk.

Cream

This rich layer of milk fat is skimmed from the top of milk before it is homogenized. It is light or heavy, depending on the amount of fat. Light cream is often added to coffee; heavy cream is used for whipping and as an ingredient in cream-style sauces and desserts.

Half-and-half

Equal parts whole milk and cream, half-and-half is a lower-fat version of cream (although it still contains 10- to 12-percent milk fat). Neither half-and-half nor light cream can be whipped.

Buttermilk

Buttermilk was the slightly thick, tangy flavored liquid that remained after butter was churned. Today, it is made commercially. Excellent for pancakes, biscuits, and many baked goods.

Lactose-free milk

People who cannot digest lactose (a sugar found naturally in milk) are able to tolerate lactose-free milk. This milk has an added enzyme that breaks down the lactose.

Soymilk

This milky-flavored nondairy liquid, pressed from cooked soybeans, is cholesterol-free and low in calcium, fat, and sodium. It's a good choice for those who are lactose intolerant or have a milk allergy.

Rice milk

Cholesterol and lactose-free, this "milk" made from rice, is available plain or flavored, and can be used in many recipes in place of cow's milk. It's a good alternative for those who are allergic to dairy and soy.

Goat's milk

A creamy rich alternative to cow's milk, goat's milk contains more easily digestible fat and protein. Many people who are lactose intolerant or allergic to dairy are able to enjoy this milk.

Flour Power

That which we call "flour" by any other name would smell as sweet (to loosely quote Shakespeare).

Just about any grain, as well as certain seeds and legumes, can be ground into flour; wheat, however, is the most popular. One of the reasons for its popularity is due to its gluten-forming capability. (Gluten is a necessary component for baked items to rise properly.) Here are some of the most popular flour varieties.

All-purpose flour

As its name implies, this flour, which comes in bleached and unbleached varieties, works in just about any recipe for bread and other baked goods; as a coating for foods that are fried or sautéed; and as a thickener for gravies, sauces, and stews. Bleached flour is whiter than unbleached and has a longer shelf life; however, the chemicals used in the bleaching process can affect the strength of the gluten. For this reason, some bakers prefer unbleached flour, especially for making bread.

Bread flour

Milled specifically for the purpose of making bread, this flour, sometimes sold as "bread machine flour," has a very high gluten content, which causes bread to rise into larger, lighter-textured loaves than it would with other flours.

Cake flour

This flour's low gluten content results in cakes and other baked goods that are very light and tender.

Cornmeal

A coarse yellow flour milled from corn and used for making tortillas and cornbread.

Pancake flour

This mix contains all of the dry ingredients needed for making pancakes, waffles, and biscuits.

Potato flour

Made from cooked potatoes that are dried and then ground, this flour enhances the flavor of potato-based recipes, like potato pancakes. It's also used as a thickener for gravies, soups, and sauces.

Self-rising flour

Already sifted, this light all-purpose flour contains a leavening (rising) agent in the form of baking powder or soda.

Whole wheat flour

All parts of the wheat berry are contained in this nutritionally superior flour that is brownish in color. Because it usually results in heavy, dense baked goods, whole wheat flour is usually combined with other white refined flours. It offers nutrition (especially protein and fiber), texture, and body to the finished product.

Whole wheat pastry flour is more finely milled than whole wheat flour. It is rich, light, and used in many baked goods.

Rice Is Nice . . . Especially with Some Spice

Rice—one of the world's staple foods—is classified mostly by grain size. Long-grain rice is long and slender. When cooked, its fluffy grains make a perfect side dish. Medium-grain rice is shorter, plumper, and stickier when cooked, making it a good choice for paella and risotto. Short-grain rice is very round and sticky when cooked—perfect for rice pudding and rice balls. Most varieties are sold as either brown or white. You can find the following popular varieties at most grocery stores.

For a rice cooking chart and recipes, see pages 206-211 in Chapter 11.

Brown Rice

Chewy, nutty-flavored brown rice comes in long-, medium-, and short-grain varieties. It is what white rice was before it was "refined." This means it's a whole grain, still retaining its nutritious germ and natural bran covering. It takes longer to cook than white rice, but is also available in instant varieties.

White Rice

To extend its shelf life, white rice, which comes in different grain varieties, has had all or part of its bran and germ removed. It is less nutritious than brown rice, but many brands are enriched with vitamins and other nutrients. White rice has a light flavor that easily absorbs spices and sauces, making it a great base for many dishes. Instant white rice is also available.

Speciality Rice

Basmati
This fragrant, nutty-flavored long-grain rice is used in many Indian and Middle Eastern-style recipes.

Jasmine
This long-grain scented rice has a slight jasmine flavor and is very popular in Asian cooking.

Red rice
A variation of brown rice, often with the bran removed, red rice has a slightly stronger flavor than white rice and comes in various grain sizes.

Texmati
Grown in Texas, this rice is an American version of basmati.

Wild rice
Actually a seed from a water grass, wild rice comes in long-, medium-, and short-grain varieties. It is chewy and dark brown in color with a distinct nutty flavor.

You Don't Know Beans!

Pinto beans, chickpeas, kidney beans, lentils . . . what are they and how do you use them?

Rich in protein and fiber, low-fat beans (legumes) have long been a staple food throughout the world. A great choice for vegetarians, beans, when combined with rice, create a protein similar to meat. And talk about versatile. Enjoy beans as a side dish; add them to soups, stews, and salads; combine them with vegetables and grains; or mash them into dips or spreads.

I usually buy canned beans because they're already cooked—it's a lot quicker than preparing them from scratch. Dried beans are, however, a better value!

Black beans

Often enjoyed in soup or served with rice, these sweet, mild-tasting beans are popular in Mexican, Caribbean, and Latin American dishes.

Kidney beans

These medium-sized red beans have a firm, meaty texture, which makes them a great addition to soups, salads, chili, stews, and wraps.

Black-eyed peas

Often enjoyed in soup or served with rice, these slightly sweet, mild-tasting beans are popular in soul food dishes and Cajun cuisine.

Lima beans

Lima beans are soft and creamy and nearly melt in your mouth. They are delicious on their own or when added to salads, soups, or stews.

Chickpeas/Garbanzo beans

Typically added to salads and soups, these sweet-tasting, nutty flavored beans are also ground and used as the main ingredient in hummus.

Navy beans

These small, soft-textured white beans are the ones used for baked beans. They are also a popular addition to soups, stews, salads, and pasta.

Pink beans

The popular choice in canned chili, firm-textured pink beans are also a common addition to soups and salads.

Pinto beans

You can't make real Mexican refried beans without pinto beans, which are also popular in Latin American, Southwestern, and Caribbean dishes.

Red beans

Smaller and milder-tasting than kidney beans, red beans also cook faster. They are classically paired with rice in a popular Southern dish.

Quick-Cooking Legumes

Legumes are the pods of certain plants like peas, peanuts, and beans. Unlike most dried legumes, the following varieties don't need to be presoaked and they cook up quickly—in only about thirty minutes. They are the perfect base for soups and stews.

Lentils

Available in brown and red varieties, lentils are ideal choices for tomato-based soups and stews. Red lentils are a classic ingredient in traditional Indian cooking.

Split peas

Very small and flat on one side, split peas (actually dried beans without the skin) soften and dissolve when they are cooked, resulting in creamy-textured soups and sauces.

For a bean cooking chart and recipes, see pages 214-219 in Chapter 11.

Along with the kitchen staples just presented, a variety of fresh fruits and vegetables—like potatoes, tomatoes, apples, and peppers—are also commonly found in many kitchens.

I Think That Potato Has Its Eyes on Me

The potato is an American staple. We bake 'em, boil 'em, fry 'em, and mash 'em. We enjoy them for breakfast, lunch, dinner, and sometimes in between. When cooking unpeeled potatoes, be sure to scrub them thoroughly. If you're boiling potatoes, peel them first. Store in a dry cool place and use them before they start to sprout roots (commonly referred to as "eyes"). The starchier the potato, the lighter and fluffier it is. Here are some popular varieties.

Red potato

These small, round, waxy potatoes are firmer and lower in starch than russets. Good for boiling and roasting. Use in stews, soups, and potato salads.

Sweet potato

Pale-skinned varieties have a light yellow flesh that is dry and not sweet. Dark-skinned varieties have a bright orange flesh that's moist and sweet.

Russet potato

These popular guys, sometimes called *baking potatoes,* are high in starch, making them a good choice for mashing, frying, roasting, and baking.

White potato

With less starch than russets but more than reds, this potato is good boiled, baked, fried, and roasted. Use for mashed potatoes and in potato salads.

Yams Are Not Sweet Potatoes

Many people think these two potatoes are one and the same, but yams aren't even distantly related to sweet potatoes. Yams have dark brown skin that almost looks like tree bark, and their flesh is purple or red. And believe it or not, yams are sweeter than sweet potatoes.

She's a Real Tomato

Although we tend to know it as a vegetable, the tomato is actually a delicious, nutritious fruit. We enjoy tomatoes raw, cooked, and even dried. They are added to salads and sandwiches, made into soups and sauces, and enjoyed as a juice. What's there not to like? Tomatoes come in different colors, shapes, and sizes, but for the most part, they are similar in taste.

Grape tomato

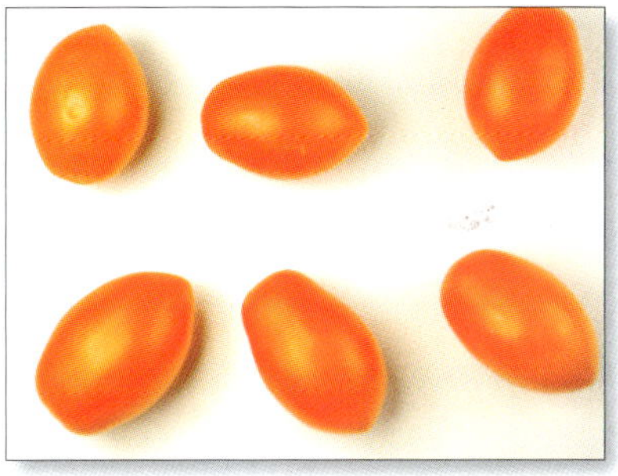

Resembling grapes in shape and size, these intensely sweet tomatoes are a hybrid fruit. Good for snacking or adding whole to salads.

Russo brown tomato

The rich, robust flavor of this reddish-brown tomato makes it a delicious choice for salads and sandwiches.

Cherry tomatoes

These bite-sized tomatoes are perfect for tossing whole into salads. They are also great for snacking, and often found on raw vegetable platters.

Plum/Roma tomato

Less flavorful than globes, plum tomatoes have a low water content, firm flesh, and few seeds, making them good for sauces and canning.

Tomatillo

Also known as *husk tomatoes*, spicy tomatillos are popular in salsas and Mexican sauces. Don't confuse them with green tomatoes, which are unripened globes.

Globe tomato

This popular medium-sized tomato is firm and juicy with a sweet acidic flavor. Globes are best enjoyed raw in salads and sandwiches.

Beefsteak tomato

The large, meaty beefsteak tomato holds together well when sliced, making it a good choice for adding to sandwiches. Beefsteaks also cook down well for sauces.

There's Some Fungus Among Us

Mushrooms have a distinctive fresh earthy flavor that adds depth and texture to dishes. Available fresh or dried, they can be grilled or sautéed, simmered in sauces and stews, roasted with vegetables and grains, and added—cooked or raw—to many dishes. Some mushrooms, like black truffles, cost more by weight than gold! Here are just a few of these amazing fungi.

Crimini

Often called *baby portabellas*, these small brown mushrooms are similar in size to white buttons, only denser and more flavorful. Good in soups, sauces, and stews.

Enochi

These long-stemmed slender mushrooms have small caps and a mild, faintly sweet flavor. They are used in many Asian-style dishes.

Oyster

These odd-looking mushrooms with their fluted caps range in color from light beige to oyster white. Mild-flavored and velvety textured, they are a popular choice in a number of Asian-style dishes. Also delicious sautéed and added to soups or sauces.

Shiitake

Ranging in color from tan to dark brown, shiitake have umbrella-shaped caps and inedible woody stems. Their rich earthy flavor works well in stir-fries and in pasta and egg dishes. Also good raw in salads and simmered in soups, sauces, and stews.

Portabella

White button

Portabella: These jumbo mushrooms are known for their deep woodsy taste and meaty texture. Portabellas are delicious grilled, roasted, and sautéed, or simmered in soups and stews.

White button: The most common of all cultivated mushrooms, all-purpose white buttons have a mild woodsy taste that intensifies when cooked. Enjoyed raw or cooked, these mushrooms can be added to just about any type of dish.

I Love Onions So Much, They Make Me Cry

Onions come in a variety of shapes and sizes. Some are tart and sharp, others are mild and sweet, but they all taste like onion. Thicker-skinned storage varieties, like yellow and white, can last a long time when stored in a cool dry place. Fresh, thin-skinned onions, like green onions and leeks, should be stored in the refrigerator where they can last up to four or five days.

Green onions and leeks

Green onions or *scallions* are good in salads, soups, and dishes requiring mild onion flavor. Leeks look like giant green onions and are used in soups and stews.

Mexican onion

This bulbous variation of a green onion has a medium-onion flavor. It works with just about any recipe that benefits from a mild onion flavor.

Pearl onion

Strong and sweet-flavored, tiny pearl onions are tossed whole into soups and stews. They are also grown for pickling as cocktail onions.

Red onion

Best raw, red onions have a mild sweet flavor that is perfect in salads and on burgers. Cooking dulls their color to an unappetizing shade.

Shallots

These bronze-skinned bulbs have a hint of garlic and are best in mild-flavored dishes, which showcase their delicate sweet taste.

Vidalia onion

Resembling slightly flattened globes, these mild onions are delicious raw and delicately sweet when cooked. Ideal in sauces, sautés, and soups.

White onion

Although they can be used interchangeably with their yellow cousins, white onions have a sharper, cleaner, more robust flavor.

Yellow onion

The most common onions used in cooking, all-purpose yellow onions have a biting hot flavor that becomes sweet and mellow when cooked.

Squash, Anyone?

Squash is a favorite vegetable in many households. Thin-skinned summer varieties, like zucchini and yellow squash, can be eaten cooked or raw, skin and all. Winter squash, like acorn, butternut, and spaghetti, have thick inedible skins and require cooking. Here are some common squash varieties that are carried in grocery stores most of the year.

Butternut

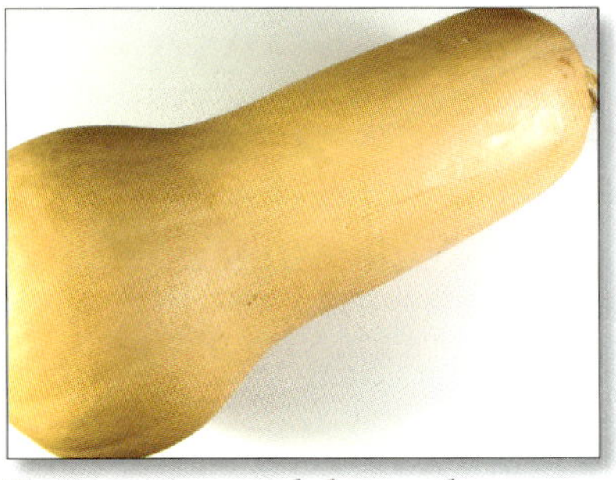

Butternut squash has pale, yellow skin and a bulbous end. Its deep orange flesh has a sweet, nutty taste that is similar to a sweet potato.

Spaghetti

This fibrous squash has a spaghetti-like consistency and subtle flavor. Serve it with sauce (just like spaghetti) or season with olive oil and spices.

Acorn

With a shape that resembles an acorn, this sweet, delicious squash is usually steamed, sautéed, or baked. You can also toast the seeds.

Chayote

This native Mexican plant has a crisp, somewhat bland-tasting flesh that is best when added raw to salads. When cooked, it needs to be well-seasoned.

Yellow

This mildly sweet squash can be eaten raw in salads or with dips. It can also be grilled, steamed, or sautéed.

Banana

Banana squash has a sweet, buttery bright-orange flesh. Because it can grow as long as two feet, it is often sold in pieces that are wrapped in plastic.

Mexican

Similar to zucchini, this beautiful speckled squash has a mild, slightly sweet flavor. Good in casseroles, stews, and stir-fries.

Zucchini

This versatile squash is good raw or cooked in just about any way. Enjoy it alone, mixed with other vegetables, or added to casseroles and stir-fries.

Ay Yi Yi Chili Peppers!

Although the Mexican word "chili" refers to both sweet and hot peppers, in the United States, it refers to hot varieties only. Chili peppers can really add some spice to your dishes, just be careful of the kind you use, as they range from mildly hot to insanely hot. With over a hundred varieties, this small, powerful vegetable comes in many shapes and lengths, but all add distinct character to any dish. Most peppers are available fresh and dried—store fresh ones in the refrigerator and dried ones in a cool dry place. Here are some of the most commonly used and readily available types.

Banana

Also called a *yellow pepper*, this mild to medium-hot chili gets its name from its color and shape. It is often pickled and added to salads.

Poblano

Slightly flat and dark green, this chili ranges in flavor from mild to medium-hot. It is the pepper used for the popular Chili Rellenos.

Habanero

Available fresh and dried, the habanero is orange to dark red in color and one of the most intensely hot chili varieties.

Serrano

Slightly longer and narrower than jalapeños, serranos have a much hotter taste. As they ripen, their dark green color turns red, orange, or yellow.

Anaheim

With a taste that ranges from mild to medium-hot, this pepper is a popular choice for many recipes. It is available both fresh and dried.

Jalapeño

Dark green, orange, or red in color, jalapeños range from medium-hot to hot and are popular in sauces, salsas, and even on pizza. Dried jalapeños are called *chipotle.*

Red cayenne

This long, extremely hot chili has a red to deep-red, thick, waxy skin and tapers to a point. It is available in both fresh and dried forms.

Get Fresh!

How Do You Like Them Apples?

A favorite of ancient Greeks and Romans, apples, of which there are thousands of cultivated varieties, are one of the world's most popular fruits. You can eat them fresh or baked, include them in pies and cakes, and use them to make juice, wine, vinegar, butter, and jelly. Here are a few common varieties.

Gala

The skin of these small, mildly sweet apples are red with shades of yellow-gold. They are excellent for eating and baking.

McIntosh

Sweet and slightly tart, this is the most popular choice for apple pies. It is also good for making applesauce and cider.

Ambrosia

With its crisp texture and sweet flavor, this is a good eating apple. It is also good in salads.

Golden Delicious

This yellow-skinned apple is crisp and sweet, and delicious raw. When cooked, it becomes even sweeter.

Pink Lady

This sweet-tasting apple has a beautiful pink blush. It is juicy and crisp, but not hard. Delicious cooked or raw.

Fuji

Best eaten raw, this apple has a mild sweet flavor and fine texture.

Granny Smith

Tart and crisp, this delicious eating apple is also a good choice for pies and applesauce.

Red Delicious

Best eaten raw, this is the most widely grown apple in the world. It is crisp and juicy with a deep red skin.

Berry, Berry Nice!

Berries, which can be berry, berry nice, can also be berry, berry delicate, especially raspberries, blackberries, and strawberries. Make sure you inspect them before buying. Keep an eye out for mold, which forms very quickly, especially on damaged berries. To keep berries fresher longer, refrigerate or freeze them.

Blueberries

This summer fruit is often baked into pies and added to pancakes and smoothies.

Raspberries

Sweet and tart, this delicate berry is added to cereal, fruit salads, and smoothies.

Blackberries

Added to fruit salads or used in pies or other pastries, this berry has tiny edible seeds.

Gooseberries

Available during the summer, this tart fruit can be eaten fresh or used in pies.

Strawberries

America's favorite berry. Great in pies, smoothies, fruit salads, and shortcake.

Check Out These Melons!

Watermelon

Canary

Casaba

Cantaloupe

Crenshaw

Honeydew

Santa Claus

During the summer, many melon varieties are available—from popular choices like watermelon to less familiar types like Santa Claus melons. With the exception of watermelon, the melons listed here are closely related in taste and texture. They have firm, juicy flesh that ranges in color from pale green to bright orange. You can tell these melons are ripe if they smell sweet. They should also give slightly when pressed at one end. A ripe watermelon sounds hollow when tapped.

Let's Spice It Up!

Flavorful herbs and spices are great food enhancers. For the most part, fresh herbs are superior to dried; however, most dried varieties can be used with good results. When figuring equivalents, keep in mind that 1 tablespoon of a chopped fresh herb is equal to 1 teaspoon dried.

Allspice
With a cross in flavor between nutmeg and cinnamon, allspice is used in baked goods, as well as gravies and marinades.

Anise seed
This sweet spice has a strong, distinct flavor similar to black licorice. It is sprinkled on rolls, added to cookies, and used as a pickling spice.

Basil

A key ingredient in classic pesto, this sweet herb is strong enough to enhance hearty stews and sauces, yet delicate enough to use in salads or sprinkle on freshly sliced tomatoes. Fresh basil is far superior to dried.

Caraway seeds
Available whole or ground, these nutty licorice-flavored seeds add a flavorful crunch to breads, cheese, and vegetables. Also good in soups and stews.

Cardamom
Essential in Indian curry, cardamom has a sweet pungent flavor. Used in baked goods, as well as some coffees and teas.

Cayenne pepper
This red hot chili pepper is typically ground and used in spicy dishes. Popular in Mexican, Chinese, and Thai cuisines.

Celery salt
This mixture of fine-grained salt and ground celery seeds adds flavor to vegetables, potatoes, and tomato or vegetable juices.

Chervil
The peppery licorice flavor of this spice is great with fish, vegetables, cream soups and sauces, and egg dishes.

Chili powder
A ground blend of chili peppers, cloves, coriander, cumin, garlic, and oregano.

Chives
This herb adds a subtle onion flavor to egg dishes, salads, and soups.

Cilantro/Coriander

Pungent cilantro leaves and seeds are used in dishes all over the world. (The seeds are called *coriander*.) Especially good with spicy dishes, cilantro is used in a wide range of foods from salsas, soups, and dips to burritos and meat dishes.

Cinnamon
This sweet spice comes from the bark of a tree and is sold in sticks or powder. Often used to flavor fruits, breads, and rolls.

Cloves
Sweet and pungent, cloves are available in dried buds or powder. They are used to flavor meats as well as baked goods and fruit dishes.

Cumin
This slightly bitter, pungent spice adds depth to savory dishes. It is a main ingredient in curry and chili powders.

Curry powder
This blend of spices, which is an Indian cuisine staple, often includes cinnamon, cloves, cardamom, chilies, turmeric, and red and black peppers.

Dill

The fresh, clean flavor of dill is perfect sprinkled on fish and potato dishes, and mixed with sour cream or yogurt. The seeds are used to flavor dill pickles.

Fennel seeds
The slight licorice flavor of fennel seeds works well in breads, coleslaw, and sausage.

Garlic
The cloves of this fragrant bulb are pungent and spicy when raw, and deliciously mellow when cooked. Garlic was once available only in fresh and powdered forms. Today, it comes chopped or minced in jars. Store fresh bulbs in a cool dry spot with good ventilation.

Ginger
Available as a fresh root, ginger is also sold in crystallized, dried,

and powdered forms. A staple in Asian and Indian cooking, ginger is also used to flavor cookies and other baked goods.

Mustard
Available in dried or prepared forms, mustard lends pungent flavor to many foods, sauces, and marinades.

Nutmeg
The strong nutty taste of this spice is used in many desserts and sauces. It is an essential ingredient in eggnog (especially if you leave out the rum!).

Oregano

This potent lusty herb is a staple in Mediterranean dishes. A traditional flavoring in tomato sauces, oregano is equally popular in salad dressings and marinades, as well as bean, grain, and pasta dishes.

Paprika
Fiery-orange in color, paprika ranges from mild to hot. It adds flavor to savory foods and is used as a colorful sprinkling on dishes like deviled eggs and potatoes.

Parsley
A popular garnish, parsley (flat-leafed and curly) also adds a subtle fresh flavor to many foods.

Pepper
Available in whole peppercorns or ground, pepper is available in black and white varieties. White pepper is milder.

Poppy seeds
These crunchy nutty seeds are often used in breads, salad dressings, and pastry fillings.

Rosemary

The slight lemony-pine flavor of this herb is excellent with grilled meats, roasted potatoes, and marinades. When using fresh, use only the leaves and discard the woody stems.

Saffron
Pricey orange-colored saffron "threads" add deep yellow color and distinctive flavor to rice dishes, sauces, and soups.

Sage

This pungent herb has a musty, slightly minty taste. It is a good choice for flavoring poultry and game stuffings, as well as dishes containing pork, fish, or beans.

Salt
Used mainly in cooking, fine-grained *table salt* contains additives to keep it from clumping. *Iodized salt* is table salt with added iodine; coarse-grained *kosher salt* contains no additives; *sea salt* comes from evaporated sea water and is available in fine grains or larger crystals.

Savory
This herb has a minty, thyme-like flavor that is good with hearty soups, and meat, fish, and bean dishes.

Sesame seeds
The nutty, slightly sweet flavor of these tiny seeds is used in breads, cakes, and other baked goods, as well as marinades and salad dressings.

Tarragon

The slight licorice flavor of tarragon goes well with meat, fish, and egg dishes. It is also a popular flavoring for vinegar.

Thyme

Used extensively in French cuisine, thyme has a light lemony flavor that goes well with meat, fish, poultry, soups, and stews.

Turmeric
Popular in Indian cooking, turmeric has a distinct yellow color. It is an essential ingredient in curry powder and prepared American-style mustard.

Food Safety

Be a Chicken When It Comes to Handling Chicken

Always use common sense when handling any food. Just remember, even though you can't see the germs and bacteria, they've got their eyes on you (and your food)!

When it comes to food safety, follow these simple rules:

- If it looks bad, smells bad, and tastes bad, guess what . . . It *is* bad!
- Wash all fruits and vegetables. You don't know where they've been or what they've been sprayed with. You can make a fruit-veggie wash by mixing 1 tablespoon white vinegar with a liter of water. Keep it in a spray bottle near the sink.
- Inspect food carefully. We have all heard horror stories about people finding foreign objects in their canned or packaged food. If you spot anything that looks suspicious, throw it out or return it to the store for a refund.
- Don't leave cooked food out of the refrigerator more than two hours.
- Don't eat leftovers that are more than three days old.
- Eat frozen foods within three months. (This is why marking the freeze date on storage bags is important.)
- Wash your hands before and after handling raw meat, poultry, or seafood. Also, use hot soapy water to clean every surface the food has touched, including plates, platters, and utensils.
- When marinating raw meat, poultry, or seafood for just ten or fifteen minutes, it can remain at room temperature. But when marinating longer, keep it in the refrigerator until you're ready to begin cooking. And if you want to use the marinade as a baste or a sauce, first boil it over high heat for a minute or two. This will destroy any bacteria it may have picked up from the raw food.
- Always check the packing date on meats and poultry, and follow cooking instructions carefully.
- Pay attention to the news regarding food warnings or recalls. Discard these items or return them to the store for a refund.

As a General Rule . . .

As a general rule, always check the expiration dates on everything you buy—especially perishable items. Also check the seals and safety devices on canned, bottled, and other packaged goods to be sure they haven't been tampered with. I've only been fooled once in the last few years. I bought a can of potato chips and days later discovered that someone had already opened the can and scarfed down half the chips!

Packaged Goods

Be sure to check the package for rips or tears.

Canned Goods

Don't buy cans that are dented or punctured. The tiniest bit of air can cause deadly botulism bacteria to form. Also wash the lids with soap before opening the can, which may have been sitting in a warehouse or on a truck and covered with dirt, pesticide residue, and/or other unwanted foreign matter. Better to be safe than sorry.

Bottled Goods

Check the cap to make sure the seal hasn't been tampered with. If it's a vacuum-sealed item, there is usually a button on the top that you can press to check the seal.

Meats, Fish, and Poultry

Contaminated meat is the number-one cause of illness and death caused by food. When possible, buy fresh meats and poultry from a reliable, busy butcher. The faster the turnover, the fresher the meat is likely to be. When buying packaged, be sure to check the dates. Avoid meat that is discolored or smells funny.

It is best to buy fresh fish from a reliable fish store. All seafood should smell fresh and clean, not fishy. When buying fish whole, select those with firm flesh and eyes that are bright and clear, not cloudy or sunken. The gills should be bright pink or red, not dull. And if the tail is dried out, the fish is probably not fresh. When buying fillets, they should be firm, moist, and dense. The flesh should be translucent, not opaque. When buying packaged fish, avoid packages that contain liquid, which encourages bacterial growth. As for shellfish—fresh shrimp should be firm and dry (not slimy); the shells of clams and mussels should be firmly closed; and scallops should be firm and sweet-smelling.

Dairy Products

Because of their short shelf life, it is extremely important to check expiration dates on all dairy products. If they are in your refrigerator and close to their expiration, give them a quick smell to make sure they haven't spoiled.

Vegetables

In general, check vegetables for firmness and uniformity in color. Avoid those with cuts, bruises, or soft spots.

Corn
Peel away the top of the husk to inspect the corn. (Don't worry people do it all the time.) The kernels should be firm and plump.

Lettuce and other greens
Inspect all greens for browning. The leaves should be firm, not wilted. For greens with solid heads like cabbage and iceberg lettuce, lightly squeeze them to make sure they're firm.

Peppers
Avoid peppers that are soft, bruised, or wrinkled, unless, like some chili peppers, they are supposed to be dry and wrinkled.

Tubers and roots
Avoid onions that are soft or have moldy areas. The outer skin should be intact. Choose carrots that are crisp and firm and potatoes that don't have sprouting "eyes."

Fruits

Typically, color and smell are good indicators of the ripeness and quality of most fruit. It's also important to inspect for bruises, cuts, and worm holes.

Apples
After checking an apple for worm holes and bruises, orchestrate a 360-degree squeeze to make sure it is firm all over.

Avocados
Check for ripeness by squeezing gently. Avocados should be slightly soft (and give a little), yet uniformly solid.

Bananas
Bananas bruise easily, so avoid those with brown spots. They also ripen quickly, so unless you plan on using them right away, it's best to buy them when they're still a little green.

Berries
Choose berries with good color and watch for bruised spots (especially on strawberries) and mold, which develops quickly on these very perishable items.

Grapes
Avoid grapes with bruises or those that are dried out, off-color, or turning brown near the stems.

Melons
Ripe cantaloupes, honeydews, and other melons actually smell like melons. When applying gentle pressure to the stem side of a ripe melon, it should give a little.

Oranges
Make sure the skin has no rips, bruises, or dry patches, and the orange is relatively firm when squeezed. Thin-skinned, heavy oranges are usually the juiciest.

Peaches
Give your peaches a little squeeze (they actually like it) to make sure they are firm and not too soft.

Pineapples
Picking a ripe pineapple is a little tricky. The skin should be brown and it should have a faint pineapple smell. If you can pull out one of its leaves easily, the fruit is ripe. If the leaf comes out too easily, there is a good chance that it's overripe.

Tomatoes
The depth of a tomato's color is usually a good indicator of ripeness, and a gentle squeeze will tell if it's firm and tender, or soft and overripe.

Let's Wrap This Up

If you cook more than you eat, you have created "leftovers." One of the great things about leftovers is that you can have the same delicious meal you just ate at a later date. To do this, it's important to know how to store the food properly and know how long to keep it. I have to admit that there are often foods that have been in my refrigerator way too long—and they kinda frighten me. Sometimes they are in containers that I would like to keep, but I am afraid to open them up to see (and smell) the poor unrecognizable food that lies within. Hopefully, you are little more organized than I am and will do what I say rather than what I do.

There are a variety of ways to store food. Depending on what you're storing, the food will have different requirements for air, temperature, and the size and shape of the containers. Here are some basic food-storing methods, materials, and containers.

Aluminum foil

This short-term storage wrap, also acts as a barrier, preventing light and outside odors from reaching the food.

Plastic wrap

Along with wrapping up certain foods, plastic wrap is also used to "seal" the tops of bowls and plates that contain food. Use for short-term storage only.

Glass and ceramic jars

Glass jars and cannisters with airtight lids are great for storing dry goods like rice and pasta. Mason jars are also used for storing homemade jams, preserves, pickles, and stewed vegetables.

Tupperware/plastic containers

These containers, which come in a variety of shapes and sizes, are great for storing everything from dry cereal and cookies to leftover soups, sauces, and entrées. Most are microwave and dishwasher safe.

Vacuum-seal systems

These food-storage systems seal food in special plastic bags or containers after removing the air. This helps keep the food fresher longer.

Wax paper

Although not good for storing food, wax paper prevents layers of stored items like cookies and brownies from sticking together.

Zipper bags

Great for day-to-day storage, these bags come in various sizes and thicknesses. If you are going to freeze the food, be sure to use bags that are designed specifically for the freezer. Before sealing the bag, try to remove as much air as possible, which will keep the food fresher longer. When freezing food, I recommend writing what you are freezing along with the date on the bag itself. Don't freeze items longer than three months.

Wraps and Containers . . .
A Thousand and One Uses!

In addition to storing food, the following items have many other uses in the kitchen and around the house!

Aluminum foil
Because it is made of metal and has a high resistance to heat, foil is very useful in the kitchen. You can bake, grill, or broil food on it; use it to cover bakeware as it cooks in the oven; or line cookware or ovenware with it for easy cleanup.

Plastic containers and jars
These containers are great for storing just about anything. I don't think there is anyone in the world who doesn't have at least one container for storing "stuff." The penny jar, for example, is as common as a cookie jar. Many plastic containers are also good for reheating food in the microwave.

Vacuum-seal systems
When I started working on this book, I bought one of these puppies and soon discovered that they are also good for marinating food and preparing full "boil-in-bag" meals.

Zipper bags
Whenever I travel, I always store my cologne and other liquid items in these bags before packing them into my suitcase (even before it was an airline requirement). If you've ever had a bottle of shampoo leak all over your luggage, you probably would have figured that out, too. Anyway, these bags are also great for storing all kinds of small things like nuts and bolts, and for protecting precious items, such as your loose family photos.

When You're Outta Dis, Use Dat

If you are getting ready to prepare a recipe (or you're in the middle of preparing one), and you discover that you're missing an ingredient—don't worry. Here is a list of some common items you can use as ingredient substitutes if you ever find yourself "in a pinch."

Ingredient Substitutions

Ingredient	Amount	Substitution
Baking powder	1 teaspoon	⅓ teaspoon baking soda plus ½ teaspoon cream of tartar.
Breadcrumbs, dry	1 cup	3 slices bread, dried or toasted.
Butter	1 cup	⅞ cup oil plus ¼ teaspoon salt.
Buttermilk	1 cup	1 cup milk plus 1 tablespoon lemon juice (let stand five minutes).
Corn syrup	1 cup	1 cup granulated or packed brown sugar plus ¼ cup water.
Cornstarch	1 tablespoon	2 tablespoons all-purpose flour.
Eggs	1 whole	2 egg whites plus 2 teaspoons oil, or ¼ cup egg substitute.
Flour (for thickening)	2 tablespoons	1 tablespoon cornstarch or 4 tablespoons arrowroot.
Flour, cake	1 cup	1 cup less 2 tablespoons sifted all-purpose flour.
Garlic, fresh	1 small clove	⅛ teaspoon garlic powder.
Herbs, dried	1 teaspoon	1 tablespoon minced fresh variety.
Honey	1 cup	1¼ cups granulated sugar plus ¼ cup water.
Lemon juice	1 teaspoon	½ teaspoon vinegar.
Molasses	1 cup	1 cup honey or maple syrup, or 1 cup brown sugar and ¼ cup water.
Mustard, dry	1 teaspoon	1 tablespoon prepared mustard.
Pumpkin pie spice	1 teaspoon	¼ teaspoon allspice, ¼ teaspoon nutmeg and ¼ teaspoon cinnamon.
Sour cream	1 cup	1 cup plain yogurt.
Sugar, brown	1 cup, packed	1 cup granulated sugar plus 2 tablespoons molasses.
Sugar, granulated	1 cup	½ cup plus 1 tablespoon granulated sugar.
Sugar, powdered	1 cup	1 cup firmly packed brown sugar, or 1¾ cups powdered sugar.
Tomato juice	1 cup	½ cup tomato sauce plus ½ cup water.
Vinegar	1 teaspoon	2 teaspoons lemon juice.
Wine, red	1 cup	1 cup beef broth for savory dishes; 1 cup cranberry juice for desserts.
Wine, white	1 cup	1 cup chicken broth for savory dishes; 1 cup white grape juice for desserts.
Yogurt, plain	1 cup	1 cup buttermilk or sour cream.

More Food, Less Guilt!

Did you ever wish you could lose a few pounds and not have to sacrifice eating delicious food? Here are some easy substitutions you can make that taste almost as good as their full-flavored, calorie-rich cousins. Some brands are better than others, so if at first you don't succeed . . .

Lower Fat / Calorie Choices

Ingredient	Substitution
Bacon	Turkey bacon, bacon bits, Canadian bacon.
Broth, chicken or beef	Lower-fat, lower-sodium, or fat-free broths.
Butter	Vegetable oil, cooking spray.
Cheese	Nonfat or reduced-fat varieties.
Chicken	Skinless breast cuts.
Chocolate chips	Carob chips.
Cream	Half-and-half (regular or nonfat).
Coconut milk	Light coconut milk.
Cottage cheese	Nonfat or reduced-fat varieties.
Cream cheese	Nonfat or reduced-fat varieties; Neufchatel cheese.
Eggs	Egg whites, egg substitute.
Ground beef	Ground sirloin, ground turkey.
Ice cream	Reduced-fat varieties.
Lard	Vegetable oil, shortening.
Margarine	Vegetable oil, cooking spray.
Mayonnaise	Nonfat or reduced-fat varieties.
Meat, red	Lean cuts with fat trimmed off.
Milk	Reduced-fat, low-fat, or skim milk.
Oil	Cooking spray.
Peanut butter	Reduced-fat varieties.
Salad dressing	Nonfat or reduced-fat varieties.
Sugar	Sugar substitutes.
Sour cream	Nonfat or reduced-fat varieties.
Whipped cream	Nonfat or reduced-fat whipped topping.
Yogurt, fresh or frozen	Nonfat or reduced-fat varieties.

How Many Apples in a . . . ?

How many apples will yield a cup of slices? How many sticks of butter in a pound? Here is a chart of common ingredients and their approximate weight or volume equivalents.

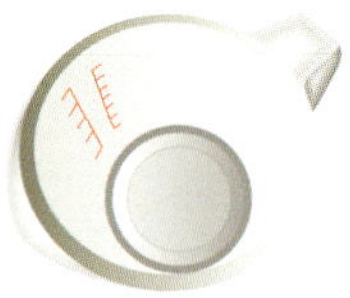

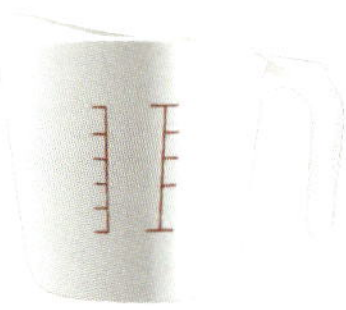

Ingredient Yields

Ingredient	The Recipe Needs . . .	You Will Need . . .
Apples	1 cup slices	1 medium apple
	1 pound	3 or 4 medium apples
Asparagus	1 pound	16 to 20 medium stalks
Bacon	½ cup crumbled	8 slices
Bananas	1 cup mashed	2 medium bananas
Beans (legumes)	6 cups cooked	1 pound dried
Beans, green	1½ cups (1-inch pieces)	8 ounces
Bread (white)	1 cup soft crumbs	1½ slices
	1 cup dry crumbs	5 fully toasted slices
Broccoli	1 cup flowerets	3 ounces
Butter	1 cup	2 sticks or 8 ounces
Cabbage	2 cups shredded	8 ounces
Carrots	1 cup grated	1 large or 1½ medium carrots
Celery	1 cup chopped	2 medium stalks
Cheese	1 cup grated	4 ounces
Corn	1 cup kernels	2 medium ears
Cottage cheese	1 cup	8 ounces
Crabmeat	1 cup	1 to 1½ pounds cooked
Cranberries	1 cup whole	4 ounces
Cream	2 to 2½ cups whipped	1 cup (½ pint) heavy cream
Cream cheese	1 cup	8 ounces
Cucumbers	1 cup chopped	1 medium cucumber
Eggs	1 cup	4 large eggs
Egg whites	1 cup	8 large eggs, separated
Eggplant	5 cups cubed	1 pound
Flour	3½ cups	1 pound

Ingredient Yields (continued)

Ingredient	The Recipe Needs . . .	You Will Need . . .
Garlic	1 teaspoon minced	2 medium cloves
Leeks	2 cups sliced	1 pound
Lemon	2 to 3 tablespoons juice	1 medium lemon
Lettuce	2 cups shredded	5 ounces
Lime	2 tablespoons juice	1 medium lime
Melons	2 cups cubed	1 pound
Mushrooms	3 cups sliced	8 ounces
Onions	½ cup chopped	1 medium onion
Orange	¼ to ½ cup juice	1 medium orange
Pasta, long	5 cups cooked	8 ounces uncooked
Pasta, short	4 to 4½ cups cooked	8 ounces or 3 cups uncooked
Peaches	1 cup sliced	8 ounces or 2 medium peaches
Pears	1 cup chopped	8 ounces or 2 medium pears
Peas	1 cup shelled	1 pound
Peppers, bell	1 cup chopped	1 medium pepper
Potatoes	1 cup chopped	1 medium potato
Rice, brown	4 cups cooked	1 cup uncooked
Rice, white	3 cups cooked	1 cup uncooked
Shortening	2¼ cups	1 pound
Spinach	12 cups	1 pound
Strawberries	3 cups whole or 2 cups sliced	1 pound
Sugar, brown	2¼ cups packed	1 pound
Sugar, granulated	2 cups	1 pound
Sugar, powdered	4 cups	1 pound
Tomatoes	1 cup chopped	1 large tomato

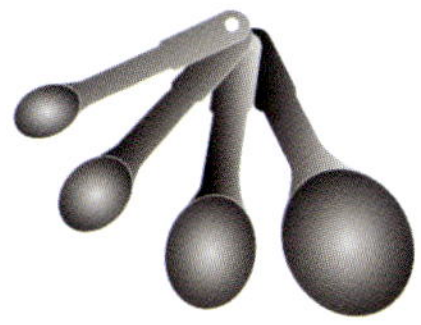

Food, Glorious Food

Check out the following little-known food facts!

1,500 Miles

Produce in the United States travels an average of nearly 1,500 miles from the farm where it was grown to grocery store shelves. For the freshest fruits and veggies, buy locally grown.

What a Gas!

Want to speed up the ripening of fruits like peaches, pears, and avocados? Place them in a brown paper bag with an apple or two, then close the bag and leave it on the counter for a day or so. The apples release ethylene gas, which triggers the ripening process.

The Oldest and the Biggest

Established in 1791, the historic French Market, located in New Orleans' famous French Quarter, is the oldest public market in the United States. Originally a Native American trading post, the landmark site has evolved into a six-block stretch that is home to restaurants, retail stores, a farmer's market, a flea market, and more.

2 Million Flowers = 1 Pound

It takes bees visiting about 2 million flowers to produce just one pound of honey. Due to its high sugar concentration and low moisture content, honey doesn't spoil. Once the jar is opened, however, it can get dry and crystallize – but it's still safe to use.

Soapy Herb

Some people have an enzyme in their saliva that causes cilantro to taste like soap.

Milking It

Check out these interesting facts about milk:

- Just about every large mammal is milked, including camels, buffalos, reindeer, donkeys, sheep, goats and yaks. (The donkey's milk is one of the closest to human's.) Pigs, whose milk is very similar to human's, are never milked!
- The average cow produces 7 gallons of milk a day – and it takes about 350 squirts to make 1 gallon.
- Currently the record amount of milk produced by a cow in one year is 72,170 pounds. That's roughly 8,400 gallons at an average of 23 gallons per day!
- Did you know that it take 21 pounds of whole milk to make 1 pound of butter?
- Know why milk is white? It's due to a calcium-rich protein called *casein*. Also, the cream in milk contains fat, which is white. The more cream in milk, the whiter it is. Because low-fat and fat-free milk contain less cream, they are more grayish in color.
- There is evidence that the Britons were milking cows more than 6,000 years ago.
- The milk of a reindeer contains 22.5 percent milkfat, while the cow's milk has only 5.5 percent.

Expending Energy

Did you know that only 10 percent of the fossil fuel energy used in the world's food system goes toward production? The remaining 90 percent is spent on packaging, transportation, and marketing.

3. Terms and Techniques

It's time to mix it up a little . . .

It's amazing how many cooking terms have made it into our vocabulary. Your blood could "curdle." You can be "half-baked" or "fried" or "stewed." You can also be "whipped" or "beaten," yet still have a "zest" for life. When it comes to food preparation, it's important for you to know what these terms (and lots more) mean. You don't want to come across a recipe instruction that stops you in your tracks.

During my early days as a novice cook, I was following a recipe when suddenly it instructed me to "fold" two mixtures together. My mind went into an instant state of panic. How could I fold something that isn't solid? I mean, I knew I could fold a piece of paper and fold my laundry, but how the heck was I supposed to fold two liquidy mixtures? What the heck did "fold" mean?

That experience is what prompted me to spend so much valuable time writing and photographing this chapter — to help you avoid any cooking panic attacks like I had. I know how beneficial it is for the good cook to understand the terms of the trade and know how to execute food-preparation basics properly. In this chapter, you'll find it all — from illustrated steps for standard cooking and baking techniques, to helpful guidelines for common food preparations, and a comprehensive A-to-Z glossary of cooking terms, complete with reader-friendly definitions.

So sit back, kick off your shoes, and start turning the pages. It's time for some background basics . . .

Boiling and Simmering

When you're cooking with liquids, it's important to know the difference between a simmer, a soft or medium boil, and a rapid or rolling boil.

Simmer

A liquid simmers when it is heated just enough to cause tiny bubbles—a few at a time—to rise to the surface. Simmering is typically used for sauces, soups, stews, and other "liquid" recipes that need to be cooked slowly over low heat.

Soft or Medium Boil

For a soft or medium boil, the liquid is set over medium to medium-low heat until a steady stream of pea-sized bubbles rise to the surface. This boil is a controlled one with very little splashing and a modest amount of steam.

Important tip

If a recipe requires a rapid boil, keep an eye on the pot. If there is any starch or protein in the water (from pasta or meat, for example) the rising bubbles won't burst at the surface. This can cause a "boil over" and create a huge mess.

Rapid or Rolling Boil

Also called a *hard boil*, this rollicking frolicking boil is commonly used for cooking pasta. It is also called for during the early cooking stage of many other foods, such as rice, sauces, and soups. To prevent the boiling contents of the pot from splashing onto your stovetop, don't fill the pot more than three-quarters full. To reach and maintain a rapid boil, the heat should be set on medium-high to high.

Scald

A scalded liquid, usually milk, is briefly heated just below the boiling point until tiny bubbles form around the edge of the pan and a thin skin (similar to the skin on pudding) forms on top. Scalded milk is sometimes called for in bread recipes to help increase the volume of the bread as it rises and bakes.

Chopping, Grating, and More . . .

The following basic cutting techniques are commonly called for in recipes. Learn them and you will be a real cut-up in the kitchen. (Sorry. I know that was lame, but I couldn't help myself.)

Shredding

Shredding is a method for cutting foods—often potatoes, cabbage, and firm or semi-firm cheese—into long, thin uniform strips. To shred an ingredient, either cut it by hand or simply slide it over the large holes of a grater. Be careful not to keep shredding the food if it gets too small (less than a half-inch) or you'll risk shredding your fingers!

Grating

Similar to shredding, grating, which is done by passing food over the very small holes of a grater, cuts the food into very fine strips. Chocolate and hard cheeses like Parmesan and Romano are often grated.

Chopping

To chop an ingredient, cut it into small pieces that are not necessarily uniform in shape. A "coarsely" chopped item is cut into bite-sized pieces, while a "finely" chopped ingredient is cut much smaller.

Slicing

To slice an ingredient, cut it into pieces that are fairly similar in width. This is a way to cut an item (a mushroom, a carrot, a loaf of bread) into smaller pieces while still maintaining some of its shape.

Mincing

To mince an ingredient, cut it into very tiny pieces that disperse evenly throughout the dish. Herbs and spices, like fresh parsley and garlic, are often minced for this very reason.

Julienne Cutting

To julienne-cut an ingredient, cut it into long, narrow strips. Potatoes, peppers, and carrots are sometimes cut this way. French fries, for instance, are julienned potatoes that have been deep-fried.

Cubing

As the term implies, to cube food, simply cut it into pieces with six equal sides ("cube shaped" in other words). Cubed foods, which are often used for stews, soups, and kebobs, usually range from ¼ to 1 inch in size.

Preparation Techniques

Have you ever skinned and cored a pineapple or prepared an artichoke? The next few pages present a number of common preparation techniques for a variety of foods.

Coring a Pepper

Hold the pepper stem-side up. With a sharp knife, cut from top to bottom, slicing off one of the pepper's flat sides. Continue cutting the remaining sides. Toss away the core, which will be attached to the stem.

Seeding an Avocado

After cutting an avocado in half and twisting the halves to separate them, use a sharp knife to give a firm but quick chop to the center of the seed. Twist the knife and the seed will easily pull out without tearing up the avocado.

Tearing Lettuce

Tear lettuce leaves gently by hand to create bite-size pieces. You can also cut lettuce with a knife. Contrary to an earlier belief, using a knife will *not* cause the leaves to wilt and turn brown faster.

Peeling Fruits and Vegetables

I usually do my peeling over a lined garbage bag, but you can use the kitchen sink as well. Hold the food firmly and peel away from yourself, removing the outer skin. Don't let the blade of the peeler get close to your hands; it is, after all, a knife and very sharp.

Chopping Onions

To chop an onion into small uniform pieces, try the following:

1. Cut off and discard the top of the onion with a sharp knife.

2. Make a shallow cut down the length of the outer skin and then peel the skin down to the bottom.

3. Make parallel cuts through the onion (as shown), close to but not all the way through to the bottom.

4. Turn the onion on its side and slice through the cuts. Discard the bottom of the onion along with the peeled outer skin.

Trimming Broccoli and Cauliflower

Use a sharp knife to cut off the tops of broccoli and cauliflower along with a small section of the stems. Although the thicker, bottom portion of the stem is edible, it is often reserved for soups.

Skinning a Garlic Clove

Lay the garlic clove on a flat surface. Place the wide handle of a large knife on top of the clove and hold it steady. Make a fist with your other hand and give the handle a quick hit. The skin will separate from the clove and peel off easily.

Using a Garlic Press

To use a garlic press, just place a peeled clove into the press and squeeze the handles together to force the garlic through the holes. Use a knife to scrape off any garlic that is clinging to the press.

How to Core an Apple

There are many utensils designed for coring apples. Some remove just the core, others remove the core and cut the fruit into sections, and still others core, slice, and peel the fruit all at once. My personal favorite is an apple corer/peeler. Simply insert the corer into the top of the apple (about ¼ to ½ inch from the stem) and push it through to the bottom. Next, use the serrated side of the corer to cut a circle around the stem, and then push out the core. *Now you're ready for peeling!*

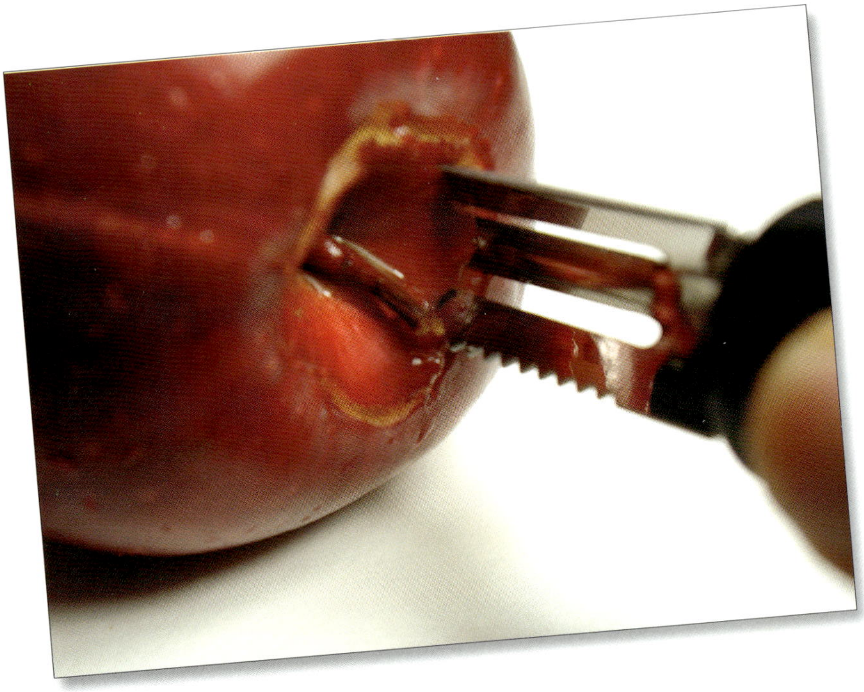

How to Core a Really Large Apple—the Pineapple

The first thing to remember when handling a pineapple is that it has spikes, so you need to be careful when handling it. To cut away the pineapple's tough outer skin, I find that using a slight sawing motion with a serrated knife works well.

1. Lay the pineapple on its side on a cutting board and cut off the crown and the base—about a half inch below the crown and a half inch above the base.

2. Stand the pineapple up and carefully cut away the skin, cutting from top to bottom.

3. Inspect the fruit and cut out any remaining spikes with a paring knife or fruit corer.

4. If you are cubing or slicing the pineapple, simply cut the edible fruit from around the hard core. If you are cutting the pineapple into spears, first cut the fruit in half lengthwise, and then cut each half further into the desired number of spears. Using a sharp knife, cut away the core, which is easy to differentiate from the fruit.

Sectioning Citrus Fruit

Using your thumbnail, carefully pierce the skin of an orange or grapefruit. Peel away the skin and as much of the white outer membrane (the pith) that surrounds the fruit as possible. Carefully pull apart the sections with your thumbs. Be gentle or the fruit will break apart.

Preparing Artichokes

Watch out for those thorny leaves when preparing an artichoke! First, pull off any small tough outer petals and discard them. Turn the artichoke on its side and trim about an inch off the top. Also cut off the stem so that it can stand on its own. With kitchen shears, snip off the thorny spikes (if any) from the tips of the leaves.

Husking or Hulling Corn

Before cooking fresh corn on the cob, you'll have to remove the outer leaves (the husk), as well as the stringy, silky fibers that surround the ears. First, cut off the top inch or so from the corn, then peel away the leafy husk along with as many strands of fiber as possible. Place the ears under running water to remove any remaining fibers with your hands. If the stem is long, you may want to trim it.

Preparing a Grapefruit

1. Cut the grapefruit in half horizontally. Remove the seeds from each half with a knife.

2. With a small paring knife, cut each segment between the membranes. Cut against the membranes so you don't damage the fruit.

3. Cut around the inside of the peel to separate the sections. *If your grapefruit isn't sweet, you can sprinkle on a little granulated sugar!*

The Egg Yolk and Egg White . . . A Marriage Made in Heaven

Is there a more harmonious union than that which exists within the egg? But sometimes, even perfect couples have to separate. I once knew a yolk and a white that were separated to become part of a lemon meringue pie. Here's part of their story . . .

After the egg white and yolk separated, they changed because of their different experiences. The white was whipped and set aside. The yolk was beaten and then thrown together with a bunch of fruits. The yolk simmered for a while after that. Happily, when they were reunited, the white was stiffer but more beautiful; the yolk tasted better and had learned to blend in with others. They had become a more delicious and attractive couple.

Separating Eggs

To separate the egg yolk from the white, crack the egg against the edge of a bowl and break the shell in half. Do this over the bowl. The two half shells will form "cups" that are large enough to hold the yolk.

Pass the yolk back and forth from one cup to the other, letting the white fall into the bowl. Place the yolk in a separate bowl.

Greasing Bakeware

To prevent certain foods from sticking to pans or dishes while cooking, a recipe may instruct you to first "grease" the pan. Either spray the inside of the dish with cooking spray, or take a dab of butter or margarine and spread it around the dish. Use the butter wrapper or a paper towel to do this.

Flouring Bakeware

To keep breads, cakes, and other baked goods from sticking to baking pans or dishes, recipes often suggest that in addition to greasing the pan, you should also "flour" it. Once the pan is greased, place a handful of flour in the middle. Shake the pan to shift the flour around until it coats the entire surface. If there is excess flour, toss it out.

Whip It Good!

There are a number of different ways to combine ingredients. Folding is the gentlest technique, requiring just a few easy strokes. Whipping (as the word suggests) is the most vigorous and is usually done with a high-speed electric mixer.

Stirring/Mixing

Stirring or mixing involves combining ingredients—usually with a spoon or fork—until they are evenly distributed. Often the ingredients need to be only loosely combined and the mixture does not necessarily have to be completely smooth.

Beating and Blending

Briskly combining ingredients with a spoon, fork, whisk, or an electric mixer, beating incorporates air into the mixture, which becomes smooth and well combined. Blending is similar, but refers to combining liquids in an electric blender.

Whipping

Usually done with an electric mixer (or by someone with good whisking skills and great endurance), whipping involves vigorously beating ingredients, such as cream or egg whites, until they are light and airy.

Folding

Folding lightens a dense batter by combining it with a whipped, airy mixture. Part of the whipped mixture (typically half) is placed on top of the batter. With a rubber spatula and starting from the bottom of the bowl, one ingredient is brought up and gently mixed with the other.

How Do You Measure Up?

Measuring ingredients accurately with the right type of equipment is key to achieving successful recipe results—especially when it comes to baked goods like breads and cakes. No matter what you are making, if you are following a recipe for the first time, it's best to prepare it exactly as written. I recommend making adjustments only after you've tasted the dish.

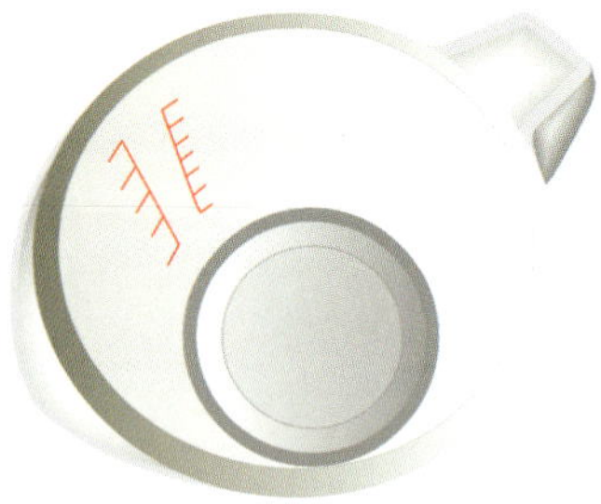

Glass Measuring Cup

Common sizes:
1 cup
2 cup (most common)
4 cup

Proper usage:
Place the cup on a flat, level surface. Pour the ingredient to the desired mark, and then check it at eye level. If there is too much, pour it out. If you need just a little more, add it with a spoon.

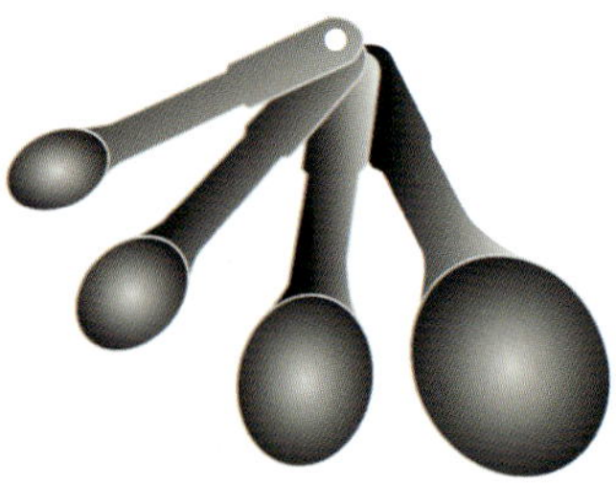

Measuring Spoons

Common sizes:
¼ teaspoon
½ teaspoon
1 teaspoon
1 tablespoon

Proper usage:
Most recipes require level spoon measurements. After filling the spoon, level it off with the back of a knife. For a heaping amount, overfill the spoon and let the ingredient round off the top in a small mound.

Dry Measuring Cups

Common sizes:
¼ cup
⅓ cup
½ cup
1 cup

Proper usage:
Use the proper cup for the proper measurement. If, for example, you need ¼ cup of a particular ingredient, use a ¼ dry measuring cup. For an exact measurement, slightly overfill the cup, then use the back of a knife to level the surface and scrape the excess back into the original container.

Metric Conversions

Unlike the United States, which uses a system for measuring ingredients based on cup and spoon amounts, most countries use the metric system. During your culinary adventures, if you happen to run across a recipe that uses metric amounts, don't automatically give up on it. Instead turn to page 392. There, you will find a convenient, easy-to-use metric conversion chart to help you translate those unfamiliar ingredient amounts into familiar ones.

Important tip

If you have a semi-solid ingredient like shortening or a lumpy ingredient like brown sugar you'll have to "pack" it into the measuring cup. First, overfill the cup. Then press the ingredient into the cup with your hand or a rubber spatula.

Abbreviations Used in Some Cookbooks

- **t or tsp** . . . . teaspoon
- **T or Tbsp** . . . . tablespoon
- **c** . . . . cup
- **oz** . . . . ounce
- **pt** . . . . pint
- **qt** . . . . quart
- **gal** . . . . gallon
- **lb or #** . . . . pound

Butter and Margarine

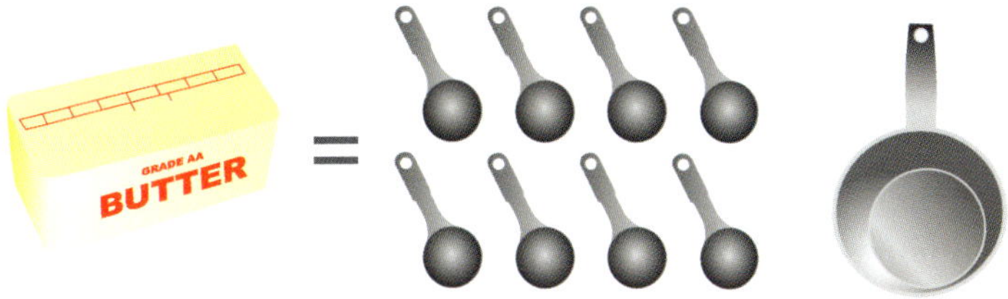

1 stick (¼ pound) *equals* 8 tablespoons *or* ½ cup

2 sticks (½ pound) *equal* 1 cup

Conversions

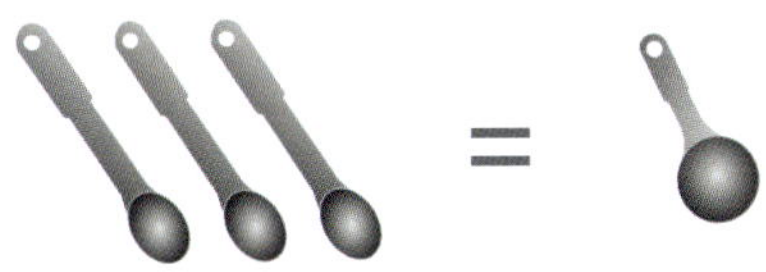

3 teaspoons *equal* 1 tablespoon

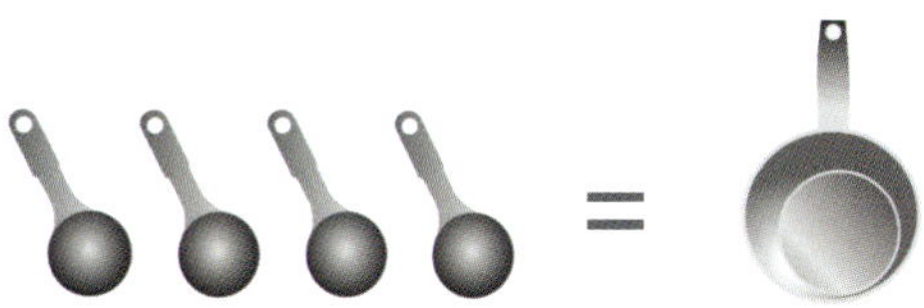

4 tablespoons *equal* ¼ cup

2 cups *equal* 1 pint

2 pints *equal* 1 quart

4 quarts *equal* 1 gallon

16 ounces *equal* 1 pound

Cooking Terms from A to Z

Don't worry if you come across an unfamiliar cooking term. Simply turn to this glossary for an easy, concise definition. I'll bet you already know some of them!

A

Aerate
To incorporate air into an ingredient to make it lighter. Sifting a dry ingredient like flour is an example of this process, as is whipping cream or butter.

Al dente
Term used to describe the degree of doneness for pasta; it means tender, yet firm and chewy, but not undercooked.

Au gratin
A dish, often potatoes, that is topped with breadcrumbs, butter, and cheese, and then heated in the oven or under the broiler until brown and crisp.

B

Bake
To cook using dry heat, usually in an oven.

Baste
To moisten meat with liquid (usually fat or juice from the meat) as it cooks to prevent it from drying out. Basting is done with a spoon or a baster.

Batter
A pourable mixture of flour and liquid, often with the addition of eggs and shortening. Batters are used for pancakes, cakes, and other baked goods.

Beat
To combine ingredients by mixing them briskly with a spoon, whisk, or an electric mixer until smooth and well combined.

Bind
To thicken a sauce, soup, or other hot liquid by stirring in an ingredient such as eggs, flour, cheese, or cornstarch.

Blacken
Cooking method in which fish, meat, or poultry is coated with spicy seasonings and then seared in a very hot skillet or on a grill. The spices partially burn (blacken) on the surface of the food.

Blanch
To briefly cook food, usually a vegetable, in boiling water before plunging it into ice water to stop the cooking process. This helps maintain the vegetable's color and crispness. Blanching is also a way to loosen the skin of fruits and vegetables, such as peaches and tomatoes, for easy removal.

Blend
To mix together ingredients, often liquids, with a spoon or blender until smooth and well combined.

Boil
To heat liquid to the point that it bubbles.

Bone/debone
To remove the bones from a cut of meat, poultry, or fish.

Boullion. *See* Broth.

Braise
A slow-cooking method for tenderizing tough cuts of meat or poultry. The meat is first browned, and then placed in a pan and partially submerged in liquid. The pan is covered and placed in the oven where the meat simmers until tender.

Bread
To coat food, usually meat or vegetables, with bread-crumbs. The food is first dipped into beaten eggs, milk, or other liquid, and then into the crumbs, which stick to it.

Broil
To cook directly under a high heat source.

Broth
Flavorful liquid made by gently simmering meat, fish or vegetables, in water that may also contain herbs and spices.

Brown
To lightly sear the exterior of meat to enhance its texture, flavor, or visual appeal.

Brush
To use a pastry or barbecue brush to coat food with a liquid, such as melted butter, sauce, or glaze.

Butterfly
Cutting method in which food, such as shrimp and thick cuts of meat, is sliced down the center, but not all the way through. The two halves are spread apart and flattened, and the food resembles a butterfly.

C

Caramelize
The process of cooking sugar over medium heat until it melts and begins to brown. When some vegetables, such as onions, are slow cooked, their natural sugars are released and they will caramelize and turn brown.

Chiffon
This is generally a puréed pie filling that is made light and fluffy by adding beaten egg whites or gelatin.

Chop

To cut food into small, often irregular pieces.

Clarify
To remove the impurities from melted butter or the solids from stock by using a strainer.

Coat
To evenly cover food with batter, oil, flour, breadcrumbs, or herbs.

Coddle
To simmer slowly and gently in liquid that is just below the boiling point. A coddled egg may be cooked in its shell or cracked into a special container that is set over boiling water.

Combine
Term for mixing two or more ingredients together.

Confit
Term for various types of meat that are slowly cooked in their own fat and juices. Pork, turkey, and duck are popular choices for confit.

Core

To remove the inedible center of certain fruits such as apples, pears, and pineapples.

Cream
To beat together butter, margarine, or shortening with sugar until somewhat smooth and creamy.

Crimp
To pinch the edge of a pie crust to give it a decorative finish. Crimping also seals together the two edges of a double-crust pie.

Crumble
To break apart food, such as cheese or bacon, into small pieces with your fingers.

Crush
To smash food or ice into smaller pieces.

Cube
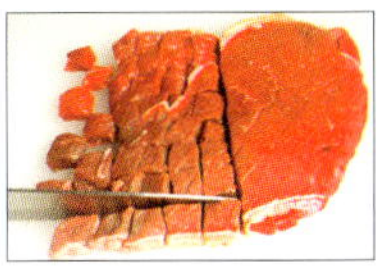

To cut foods like meats and vegetables into pieces with six equal sides—usually ranging from ¼ to 1 inch in size.

Curdle
To coagulate or thicken a liquid —typically milk, cream, a cream-based sauce, or egg whites—either through overheating or by adding an acidic ingredient.

Cut-in
To work a semi-solid ingredient like shortening or soft butter into a dry ingredient like flour.

D

Dash
Measurement of $^{1}/_{8}$ teaspoon.

Deep-fry

To cook food by submerging it in hot oil.

Deglaze
To add broth, wine, or other liquid to a skillet or roasting pan to remove and/or dissolve the seasoned bits of food and juices that are stuck to the bottom. The resulting liquid can be used to make gravy or a sauce.

Devil
To add hot or spicy ingredients to a food.

Dice
To cut food into small cube-shaped pieces.

Dilute
To thin a liquid by adding water or another liquid.

Divide
To separate an ingredient into portions for multiple uses in a recipe.

Dot

To add small pieces of an ingredient, usually butter, over a food to ensure even distribution during cooking.

Dredge
To lightly coat food with flour, cornmeal, or other dry ingredient before it is cooked.

Drizzle
To pour a liquid over food in a very thin stream.

Cooking Terms from A to Z

Drippings
The juices and melted fat that are left in the bottom of a pan in which meat or other food has been cooked. Drippings are often used as a base for gravies and sauces.

Dust
To sprinkle a food, usually a baked good, with a dry ingredient such as powdered sugar or cinnamon.

E

Egg wash
A glaze made of beaten egg (yolk, white, or both) and a little water or milk. Breads and other baked goods are sometimes brushed with egg wash, which gives them a glossy shine and color when baked.

Emulsion
A smooth mixture of two liquids, such as oil and water, that normally do not combine well. Mayonnaise and vinaigrettes are examples of emulsions.

F

Filet
To cut away the bones from a piece of meat or fish.

Filter
To remove the solids or impurities from a liquid by running it through a fine strainer or paper filter.

Flake
To pull or break apart delicate foods, such as fish, usually with a fork. This technique is also used to determine if a fish is fully cooked.

Flambé
Cooking technique in which a dish, usually a dessert, is sprinkled with liquor and set aflame just before serving.

Fold
Technique used to gently combine a whipped, airy mixture with a dense batter to make the batter lighter.

Frizzle
To fry thin slices of meat, such as bacon, over high heat until it is crisp.

Fry
To cook food in oil or butter over medium to high heat until browned or cooked through.

G

Garnish
To decorate a dish with an edible item, such as a parsley sprig or a radish rosette, for added visual appeal.

Glaze
To give food a shiny coating by brushing it with thin layer of frosting or sauce.

Grate
To finely shred food.

Grease
To spread a thin layer of butter, oil, margarine, or shortening on a cookware surface to keep food from sticking to it.

Grill
To cook food on a rack over direct heat, usually a charcoal or gas grill.

Grind
To cut food into fine pieces with a food processor, blender, or grinder.

H

Husk/hull
To remove the inedible outer covering of certain nuts, seeds, fruits, or vegetables.

I

Ice
To cool food by placing it on ice or in ice water. Also refers to spreading a frosting or glaze on cake or other baked goods.

Infuse
To extract the flavor of certain ingredients—coffee, herbs, tea—by steeping them in heated liquid in a covered pan. The resulting liquid is called an infusion.

J

Jell
To cause a liquid to become firm or solidify, usually by adding gelatin.

Jerk
A dry mixture of hot spices used to season meat for Jamaican-style barbecuing. Also describes your partner when he or she forgets to replace the cap on the toothpaste.

Julienne
To cut food into long, thin strips.

K

Knead
To work dough with the heel of your hands in a folding motion until it becomes smooth and elastic.

L

Larding
The insertion of strips of fat into meat before braising. This helps keep the meat moist as it cooks.

Leavening agent
An ingredient, such as baking powder, baking soda, or yeast, that causes breads and other baked goods to rise.

Line
To place wax paper, parchment paper, or foil on the bottom of a baking sheet or pan to prevent food from sticking to it.

M

Marbling
The gentle swirling or folding of two different colored mixtures (usually cake batters) into one another to create the look of marble. Marbling also refers to the thin streaks of fat that run throughout a piece of meat, adding to the meat's flavor and tenderness.

Marinate
To steep raw food, usually meat or veggies, in a seasoned liquid (marinade). This helps make the food tender and more flavorful.

Mash
To press or mix food, such as bananas or boiled potatoes, until smooth and free of lumps.

Medallion
A small round or oval-shaped piece of lightly pounded meat or poultry.

Meringue
A mixture of stiffly beaten egg whites and granulated sugar that is used as a topping for pies, puddings, and other desserts such as Baked Alaska.

Mince
To chop a food (often a spice or herb) very finely so that it disperses evenly throughout the dish.

Mix
To stir ingredients together, usually with a spoon or fork, until they are evenly distributed.

Moisten
To add enough liquid to a dry ingredient to just dampen it.

Mull
To flavor a beverage, usually wine or cider, by slowly heating it with ingredients such as herbs, spices, sugar, and fruit.

N

Nicen
To make something nicer by adding love. (I made that up because I couldn't think of any term that started with N.)

O

Open
To take the top, bottom, or side off a container that holds good food that you want to eat. (Did I have to tell you that?)

P

Pan-broil
To cook meat or fish over high heat in an uncovered skillet without oil. As the food cooks, any fat that accumulates in the pan is removed.

Pan-fry
To cook food in a little oil or butter in a frying pan over medium-high to high heat, turning the food only once or twice.

Parboil
To partially cook food by briefly boiling it in water.

Pare
To remove the thin outer skin of a fruit or vegetable with a knife or vegetable peeler.

Peaks
Mounds that form on a whipped ingredient or mixture when it has become thick and stiff.

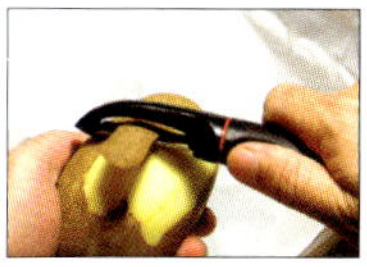

Peel
To remove the rind or skin from a fruit or vegetable with a knife or vegetable peeler. The skin of some foods, like oranges and bananas, can be peeled with your fingers.

Pinch
Measurement of $^1/_{16}$ teaspoon.

Pipe
To squeeze icing or a semi-soft food through the tip of a pastry bag.

Pit
To remove the seed or stone from a fruit.

Poach
To cook food gently in simmering liquid.

Pound
To flatten meat with a mallet.

Purée
To grind or mash food in a blender or food processor until it is completely smooth.

Q

Quell
To pacify and quiet your family and guests while they are waiting for your food.

R

Reconstitute
To bring a dehydrated item (such as powdered milk or instant coffee) back to its original consistency by adding water or another liquid.

Reduce
To boil a liquid, such as a sauce, stock, or stew, until it is reduced in volume due to evaporation. This makes the liquid thicker and more flavorful.

Render
To cook fat or lard to make drippings, which can be used to flavor other dishes.

Roast
To cook food in the oven in an uncovered pan.

Roux
A cooked mixture of melted butter, flour, and water that is used as a thickener for sauces, gravies, and stews.

S

Sauté
To briefly cook food in oil or butter in a skillet or sauté pan over medium to medium-high heat.

Scald
To briefly heat a liquid, usually milk, just below the boiling point until tiny bubbles form around the edge of the pan and a thin skin forms on top.

Score
To make shallow diagonal cuts in the surface of foods. This is often done to tenderize certain cuts of meat and help them absorb more flavor while marinating. Scoring some foods, such as bread before it is baked, adds a decorative touch.

Sear
To brown meat quickly over high heat, usually in a frying pan, to seal in the juices. After it is seared, the meat is often braised or stewed.

Season
To flavor food by adding herbs and/or spices. Seasoning also refers to preparing a pan for cooking, usually a cast iron skillet, by coating the interior with vegetable oil and then heating it. The oil is absorbed in the pan, which prevents food from sticking to it.

Shred
To cut food into long, thin, uniform strips, either by hand or by running it over the larger holes of a grater.

Sift
To pass a dry ingredient, such as flour or powdered sugar, through a fine mesh screen or sifter to make it lighter and airier. This is also done to remove any large pieces.

Simmer
To cook food gently in liquid that is heated just below the boiling point.

Skewer
To thread pieces (often cubes) of meat, chicken, and/or vegetables on a stick (skewer), usually before grilling or barbecuing.

Skim
To remove the top layer from a liquid, such as fat from a sauce or foam from a pot of soup.

Slice
To cut food into pieces of uniform thickness.

Steam
Method of cooking food by placing it on a rack or in a steamer basket that is set above boiling water in a covered pan.

Steep
To soak herbs, spices, or tea in a hot liquid to extract their flavor.

Stew
Cooking method in which food —typically chunks of meat, vegetables, and seasonings—is covered with broth and slowly simmered in a Dutch oven or tightly covered pot. Stewing tenderizes tough pieces of meat.

Stir-fry
To quickly fry small pieces of food in a wok or other large pan over very high heat while rapidly stirring. This cooking method requires very little oil.

Stuff
To fill poultry, meat, fish, or vegetables with a mixture—often seasoned bread cubes—before cooking.

Stock. *See* Broth.

T

Thin
To reduce the thickness of a mixture by adding liquid.

Toss
To gently mix together ingredients like the fruits and vegetables in a salad.

Truss
To secure meat or poultry with string or skewers to maintain the food's shape or to prevent stuffing from falling out during cooking.

U

Unleavened
Term that describes bread or other baked good that does not contain a leavening (rising) agent—yeast, baking powder, or baking soda.

V

Vinaigrette
A combination of oil and vinegar, often with added spices, and generally used to dress salad greens.

W

Whip
To briskly beat an ingredient, typically cream or egg whites, until it is light and fluffy.

Y

Yummm
The sound that guests makes when they like your cooking.

Z

Zest
To remove the outermost colored rind of a citrus fruit, usually an orange or lemon, with a fine grater, zester, or knife.

Enjoy the Adventure

Once you venture past basic cooking and attempt more challenging recipes, chances are you'll come across an instruction, technique, or term that you've never seen before. The terms in this chapter are fairly basic. They're the ones you will find in most cookbooks, but by no means is this list complete—there are hundreds and hundreds more terms.

During your culinary adventures, if you come across an unfamiliar word or instruction, don't let it stop you from trying the recipe. Just look it up (with the Internet at your fingertips, information is just a moment away). The procedure may be easier than it sounds.

Who would imagine, for example, that to cook food *en papillote* simply means to wrap it first in parchment paper? Besides, even if the instruction is more difficult than anything you've done before, go for it! Each dish you prepare—every success and failure—adds to your experience, and with experience comes confidence. Enjoy the adventure.

For the Love of Food!

The art of cooking has been around since man discovered fire.

Put It in a Large Pot, and Turn the Laser to Low . . .

Molecular gastronomy is a modern process for cooking food. It uses unconventional ingredients, methods, and tools, like helium, lasers, ion particle guns, centrifuges, and liquid nitrogen.

A Tongue Tastes Good

Our sense of taste can distinguish four basic flavors – sweet, salty, sour, and bitter. Most scientists also agree that there is a fifth "savory" flavor called *umami,* which was identified by a Japanese scientist. At one time, it was believed that each area of the tongue (front, back, sides) was responsible for sensing one specific flavor. But this "tongue mapping" has been disproved. In fact, the entire tongue is able to sense *all* of these tastes pretty much equally.

Acid Tears

Most people cry when cutting onions. This is because onions release enzymes and acids that produce fumes. The fumes irritate the tissues of the eyes, causing them to burn and tear. Here are some popular methods for avoiding this:

- Wear "onion goggles" specifically designed for this purpose. (Ski goggles work, too.)
- Chill the onion for 30 minutes in the refrigerator or 10 minutes in the freezer before cutting.
- Cut the onion next to running water (or stick out your wet tongue) to draw the fumes.
- Place a small fan or a lit candle next to the cutting board.

Cookbook Poetry

The first known cookbook was written by the ancient Greek poet (and foodie) Archestratus around 350 BC. Called *Hedypatheia* ("Life of Luxury"), the work was actually a long humorous poem that contained the ingredients, cooking techniques, and banquet favorites of the time.

Fit for a King

Haute cuisine, the elaborate preparation and artful presentation of food, began in the palaces of seventeenth- and eighteenth-century France. After the French Revolution, the palace chefs made their way into the general public and began sharing their secrets of "high dining" with the rest of the world.

Pinching Dough

In England, before people had ovens in their own homes, housewives would bring dough they had prepared to a baker, often their landlord, who would bake it for them. Some bakers had secret trap doors in the back of their ovens so an apprentice could pinch off some of that dough, which the baker would then use to make other baked goods to sell. This unethical practice and others like it led to the enactment of the "Assize of Bread and Ale" – the first law in England, written during the thirteenth century, to regulate practices in the sale of food and beverages.

Horse-Drawn Diner

In 1872, Walter Scott of Providence, Rhode Island, came up with the idea of serving meals from the back of his horse-drawn wagon to people who worked the night shift. He is credited for creating the first diner.

4. That's Entertainment

C'mon play-ya, let's par-tay!

When I was younger and threw a party, especially during my college days, nobody really expected much. A couple of six packs and a bag of cheese puffs were usually enough to satisfy my guests as a "cocktail party." And if I had a pizza delivered, my "dinner party" was a smashing success. But now that I'm a mature adult (okay, maybe "mature" is stretching it a bit), I've upped my game. And although I still enjoy throwing casual affairs like beach parties and barbecues, I also like hosting parties with real food served on actual dishes along with silverware, napkins, candles . . . the works!

In this chapter, I'll show you how to set a proper table (you'll never again have to wonder if the fork goes to the right or left of the dinner plate!). I've also thrown in a few suggestions that will give your table greater visual appeal, including some of my magic napkin folds to dazzle and amaze your guests, as well as pointers on centerpieces, tablecloths, and the use of candles. There's even a section on how to "do" a buffet.

When you're ready to throw a ragin' cocktail party or prepare a four-course dinner that (like) totally rocks, you'll find lots of menus with various suggested food and beverage combinations — true gastronomic delights.

So let's crank up some tunes and pop a few corks. Time to get this par-tay started! Whoop, whoop!

Table for Two (or More)

When I was single, I rarely sat down at the table to eat. Only when I had guests over would I pull out the tablecloth and actually sit down to a meal. If you've never set a table before, it's helpful to first know the basic rules . . . after that, you can be creative and really dress up the table for special occasions.

Setting the Table

Place settings include dinnerware (plates, bowls), flatware or cutlery (knives, forks, spoons), glassware, and napkins.

- The dinner and salad forks go to the left of the plate.
- The knife always goes to the right of the plate with the sharp side of the blade facing the plate.
- The soup spoon goes to the right of the knife.
- Dinner plates are always centered. Soup bowls and salad plates can be put on top of the dinner plate if they are going to be used for a first course.
- When using multiple flatware items, like a salad fork and a dinner fork, for example, place them in the order of their use, from the outside in.
- Set flatware an inch from the edge of the table.

Formal Place Setting

- For formal settings, the napkin goes to the left of the fork(s) or on top of the dinner plate. For casual, informal settings, it can go under the fork.
- The bread plate goes to the left of and slightly above the dinner plate.
- A butter knife goes on top of the bread plate.
- The salad plate can be set to the left of the fork(s) or on top of the dinner plate, if salad will be served as a separate course.
- Glassware is set to the right of the dinner plate, above the knife. The water glass is at the top of the knife and any added drinkware (like wine goblets) should go to the right of the water glass.
- When using chopsticks, place them diagonally across the dinner plate or to the left of it.
- If you are serving seafood in shells, place a seafood fork to the far right of the setting, next to outermost spoon.
- Coffee cups and saucers can go to the right of the setting. They can also be brought out when dessert is served.
- Placemats and tablecloths are put under the plates, flatware, and glasses. (Just checking to see if you're paying attention.)

Keep in mind that form should follow function when setting the table. You shouldn't "decorate" the table with plates, glasses, or other items that you won't be using. (If you're not serving soup, don't set a soup spoon!) You should, however, put out all of the items needed for the different types of food and beverages that you will be serving.

Accessorize It, Dar-link!

The following items can help enhance the look of your table. A simple online search will give you an eye-opening look at the variety and availability of these suggested table accessories.

Placemats

Along with helping protect your table, placemats—which come in a variety of shapes, colors, and fabrics—can help set a mealtime mood, from everyday casual to ultra formal. They also provide quick table cleanup. Depending on the material, placemats are generally easy to clean. Disposable varieties are also available.

Tablecloths

Whether made of cotton, linen, or vinyl, and whether a solid color or bold print, tablecloths always make a statement. They are welcome table coverings for casual gatherings, elegant dinners, and even outdoor meals. Always make sure the tablecloth is big enough to hang at least six to eight inches over the edge of the table.

Napkin rings

These decorative napkin holders add the perfect finishing touch to any table setting. Simple or fancy, napkin rings come in many different materials, including wood, cloth, leather, and more. Some are designed specifically for holiday tables and special occasions.

Centerpieces and candles

Flowers, plants, cornucopias, and fruit bowls are just a few items you can use to help dress up a table. And, of course, nothing helps set a mood better than candles. (For more info, see page 76.)

Name cards or place cards

You can have a lot of fun with place cards, which come in a variety of styles. Personalized seating is also a great (and clever) way to keep your most unruly guests separated!

Napkin Magic

*Okay, napkin folding isn't exactly magic, but it **will** have a magical effect on your guests when they realize the extra effort that you put into setting such a lovely table! Specially folded napkins add a creative, often dramatic or playful touch to any table—and they're also useful for wiping stuff off your filthy gob.*

I usually use lightly starched linen or cotton napkins, but I can even do some folds with paper napkins if they are large and sturdy enough. To make the following folds, the napkins have to be square (18-inch squares are recommended).

Important tip

For easier folding and better presentation, use lightly starched cotton or linen napkins that are thick enough to stand on their own when folded.

Triangle Fold

1. Fold a square napkin in half to form a triangle with the point at the top.

2. Fold the left and right corners up to the top.

3. Turn the napkin over, then bring the bottom point up to the top to form another triangle.

4. Lift the napkin up by the bottom so that it stands on its own.

5. Place the napkin on top of the plate.

A Napkin Flower?

You can fold napkins into a variety of organic shapes, including flowers, plants, and even birds! If you don't believe me, do a simple Internet search—you will be amazed at the number of different creations you can make with a napkin.

The Lily (shown on this page) is only one of many really neat freestanding napkin designs. Freestanding means the napkin will stand on its own and you can place it anywhere, including the top of a plate or even in a wine glass. Are we having fun now or what?

Lily Fold

1. Fold a square napkin in half to form a triangle with the point at the top.

2. Fold up the left and right corners so they are slightly to the right and left of the top point.

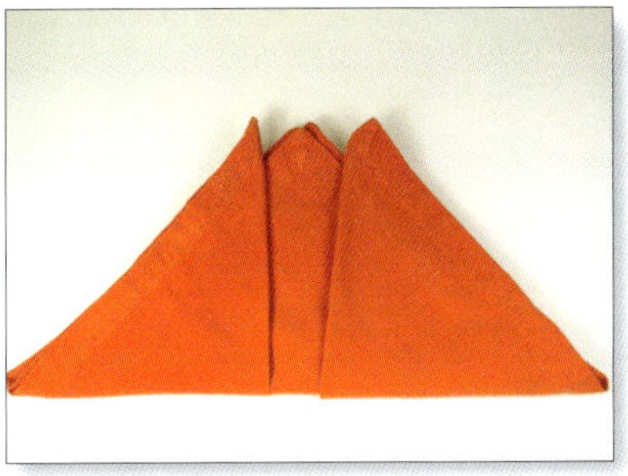

3. Fold the bottom half of the napkin under.

4. Turn the napkin upside down. Tuck the right corner deep into the left-hand fold to form a circular base.

5. Stand the napkin up and pull down the outer "petals" to form the lily.

Candles and Centerpieces

To create the right mood for a romantic dinner or special get together, nothing dresses up a table better than a beautiful centerpiece and/or some candles. Just keep in mind that you and your guests will be conversing between bites of your delicious food, and most people like to look in each others eyes when talking—as opposed to talking to an arrangement of daisies. For this reason, it is important to select centerpieces based on their height as well as their beauty.

Feel free to use silk flowers or even small flowering plants. Often simplicity is the ticket, and a single rose in a bud vase can do the trick, especially if the table is being set for an intimate dinner for two.

Candles can also enhance the beauty of your table and there are many different varieties from which to choose. Tall tapered candles are typically used for more formal functions like special-occasion or high-end dinner parties. Pillar candles, which are less formal, come in various heights and thicknesses. Whether they are used alone or clustered together in a multi-level grouping, pillars offer a dramatic effect. Small votive candles and even smaller tea lights are also growing in popularity as decorative table accessories.

When using candles, just be aware of a couple things. Never use scented candles, which will clash with the wonderful smells of your food. (You might love the smell of lavender, but not while you are eating stuffed mushrooms!) Also, be careful of candle placement on the table. Many fires have been started by candles that were set too close to centerpieces or freestanding napkins. And finally, keep in mind that candles should be used to provide ambiance and supplemental lighting—do not rely on them as your only source of light. People like to actually see the food they are eating. I have a dimmer switch in my dining room to control the lighting for my dinner parties.

From left to right: Pillar candle on a round glass plate, tea light in holder, tapered candle in holder, tea light, and votive candle.

How to Buffet

If you are having a large party or you have a limited amount of table space, you might consider serving your guests buffet (pronounced boo-fay) style. It is also a nice way to let people serve themselves and choose the foods (and the amount) they want. There is less wasted food and people are happy.

From left to right: Dinner plates, main course with serving spoon or fork, side dish, and salad. Be sure to include serving utensils with each dish.

Dinner Table or Lap?

There are a couple different ways to set up a buffet. It all depends on where you want your guests to eat once they have filled their plates. Are you planning to have them sit down to a somewhat formal setting around a dinner table? Or will it be an informal gathering where people can eat anywhere?

For more formal occasions, set the dinner table as you normally would, only right before you are ready to serve the food, collect the dinner plates and stack them on the buffet table. The rest of the buffet table should be set as shown in the illustration above.

For informal occasions, like barbecues and picnics, you'll also need to include cutlery and napkins on the buffet table. I usually place these items at the end of the table (after the last of the food). This way, people don't have too much to hold while they are busy filling their plates.

Beverages and desserts should have separate setups. Most people will drink before they eat, and dessert is served after the meal.

The Super Silverware Napkin Roll

If you're not seating people at a table, you'll need to provide them with eating utensils and napkins. The best way to do this is by wrapping up the cutlery in the napkin. This way, your guests don't have to fumble around for these items and can concentrate on filling their plates. Here's a simple way to do it.

1. Fold the napkin in half to form a triangle with the point at the top

2. Place the cutlery near the bottom. Fold the left side of the napkin over the utensils, followed by the right side.

3. Fold the bottom of the napkin over the cutlery and roll it up.

4. Voilá! A perfect utensil packet.

Ragin' Cocktail Parties

Sometimes it's nice to have people over and just nosh on some appetizers and have a few drinks. On those occasions, you will need some special treats to keep your partygoers happy and the party rockin'.

When possible, try to preplan your menus and serve food and beverages that go well together. The following appetizer-and-beverage combinations, which I've arranged thematically, are guaranteed to make your party a ragin' big hit!

Mexican Theme

Appetizers

Macho Nachos (page 143)
Holy Guacamole (page 129)
Killer Quesadillas (page 142)

Suggested beverages

Mexican beer, margaritas, and/or sangria.

Italian Theme

Appetizers

Mini Pizzas (page 141)
Basil 'n Cheese Twirlies (page 138)

Suggested beverages

Red and white wine.

French Theme

Appetizers

Brie en Croute (page 139)
Mussels au Currie (page 279)
Sliced baguette and Camembert cheese

Suggested beverages

White wine and/or champagne.

Greek Theme

Appetizers

Hummus (page 133)

Suggested beverages

Uzo, red wine, and/or white wine.

American Theme

Appetizers

Clam Dip (page 130)
Devilish Eggs (page 134)
Veggie Dip (page 131)
Stuffed Mushrooms (page 137)

Suggested beverages

Perfect Lemonade (page 120), soda, and/or beer.

Rockin' Four-Course Dinners

Part of planning a successful meal is picking the right dishes that go together along with the right beverages. To make it easy for you, I've prepared the following menus, which include tried-and-true four-course meals that are bound to please even the most demanding guest.

It is not necessary to make every recipe from scratch or prepare them that day. For example, for the "Mexican Fiesta 1" on page 81, I would probably use canned refried beans unless I really wanted to "go large" for my mother-in-law or my boss (my two harshest critics). If I decide to make the beans from scratch, I would prepare them a day or two ahead of time. I would certainly make the Mexican Wedding Cakes the day before. And I would prepare the cheese and vegetables for the Tacos earlier that day and store them in sealed plastic containers in the refrigerator. I would even make the taco filling ahead of time, so it needed only to be warmed before serving.

Get the idea? The more you can do ahead of time, the more time you can spend with your charming guests. Don't worry, you'll have plenty to do after they leave, and you're faced with the cleanup!

Menu for Burger Night

Appetizer
Veggie Dip (page 131)

Main course
Cheeseburgers or Swiss Mushroom Burgers (page 150)

Side dish
Hungarian Fries (page 203)

Dessert
Chocolate Chip Cookies (page 372)

Suggested beverages
Perfect Lemonade (page 120), soda, and/or beer with dinner.
Milk and/or coffee with dessert.

Mexican Fiesta 1

Appetizer
Killer Quesadillas
(page 142)

Main course
Me Gusta Tacos! (page 320)

Side dish
OMG! Refried Beans
(page 218)

Dessert
Mexican Wedding Cakes
(page 374)

Suggested beverages
Ice water, beer, sangria, and/or margaritas with appetizers and dinner. Milk and/or coffee with dessert.

Mexican Fiesta 2

Appetizer
Macho Nachos (page 143)

Main course
Chicken Fajitas (page 296)

Side dish
Spanish Rice (page 210)

Dessert
Hot Fudge Sundae
(page 366)

Suggested beverages
Ice water, beer, sangria, and/or margaritas with appetizers and dinner. Coffee and/or ice water with dessert.

Italian Night 1

Appetizer
Mini Pizzas (page 141)

Main course
Penne with Pesto (page 244)

Side dish
Minestrone! (page 190)

Dessert
Coconut Custard (page 369)

Suggested beverages
Sparkling water, red wine, and/or white wine with appetizers and dinner. Coffee and/or cappuccino with dessert.

Italian Night 2

Appetizer
Basil 'n Cheese Twirlies (page 138)

Main course
Tortellini with Roberto Sauce (page 246)

Side dish
Caesar Salad(page 171)

Dessert
Chocolate Almond Torte (page 388)

Suggested beverages
Sparkling water, red wine, and/or white wine with appetizers and dinner. Coffee and/or cappuccino with dessert.

Nuit Français

Appetizer
Brie en Croute (page 139)

Main course
Rowbear's Cordon Bleu (page 289)

Side dish
Asparagus with Mustard Dressing (page 225)

Dessert
Chocolate Cream Puffs (page 370)

Suggested beverages
Sparkling water, white wine, and/or champagne with appetizers and dinner. Coffee with dessert.

Greek Night

Appetizer
Hummus (page 133)

Main course
Bob's Kabobs (page 342)

Side dish
Opa! Greek Salad (page 170)

Dessert
Almond-Poppyseed Muffins (page 387)

Suggested beverages
Uzo, sparkling water, red wine, and/or white wine with appetizers and dinner. Coffee and/or tea with dessert.

Steak Night 1

Appetizer
Salmon Toast (page 140)

Main course
Steak with Mushroom 'n Onion Topping (page 312)

Side dish
Asparagus with Mustard Dressing (page 225)

Dessert
Carrot-Pineapple Cupcakes (page 386)

Suggested beverages
Sparkling water, red wine, and/or white wine with appetizers and dinner. Coffee and/or milk with dessert.

Steak Night 2

Appetizer
Mussels au Currie (page 279)

Main course
Filet Mignon with Béarnaise Sauce (page 313)

Side dish
Green Beans and Mushrooms (page 224)

Dessert
Strawberry Shortcake (page 367)

Suggested beverages
Sparkling water, red wine, and/or white wine with appetizers and dinner. Port and/or sherry with dessert.

Fish Night

Appetizer
Clam Dip (page 130)

Main course
Pan-Fried Sole Almondine (page 265)

Side dish
Mixed-Up Salad (page 169)

Dessert
Apple-Blueberry-Walnut Pie (page 379)

Suggested beverages
White wine, beer, and/or water with appetizers and dinner.
Tea, port, and/or sherry with dessert.

Barbecue Night

Appetizer
Veggie Dip (page 131)

Main course
BBQ Ribs (page 335)

Side dish
Corn on the Cob (page 221)

Dessert
Pecan Pie (page 380)

Suggested beverages
Red wine, beer, and/or water with appetizers and dinner.
Tea and/or milk with dessert.

Where Would We Be Without Manners?

A civilized society is measured by its manners. Codes of conduct have changed over the years, and vary from country to country.

Table Manners

Check out these interesting table manners from around the world:

- In China, when taking food from a communal serving dish, diners must select the closest piece (and not choose one they prefer).
- When eating a bowl of hot noodles in Japan, it is polite (even encouraged) to slurp them, which signifies a "thumbs up" to the cook.
- In India, Pakistan, and many Middle Eastern and African countries, food is eaten with the hand – but only the right hand.
- Finishing all the food on one's plate in places like Egypt, the Philippines, and Korea, is an insult – a sign that your host didn't give you enough.
- In Turkey, Saudi Arabia, and many other Middle Eastern countries, burping after a meal is a sign of satisfaction (and a compliment).

Fork It Over

Americans eat with the tines of their forks facing up. Throughout Europe, the "continental style" is to eat with the tines facing down.

Take It or Leave It

When you have finished eating in a restaurant, place your knife and fork together in the center of the plate at a slight angle. This signifies to the server that you are done.

That's 511 Hours a Year

According to the U.S. Bureau of Labor Statistics, in 2011, the average American spent eighty-four minutes a day eating and drinking.

Who Made Up the Rules?

Today's rules of etiquette had their origin in the royal courts of France beginning in the 1600s. The nobles drew up the social customs and behaviors that were to be followed by the upper class. Emily Post was the most notable American to publish a book on the subject. Her 1922 bestseller, *Etiquette in Society, In Business, In Politics, and At Home,* continues to be updated to reflect the changing times.

Wipe This Off With That

The first napkins were actually chunks of dough that the ancient Spartans customarily used to wipe their mouths and hands. They then squeezed and kneaded the pieces, and popped them into their mouths at the end of the meal. (Talk about a quick and easy cleanup!)

How Versatile!

In ancient Rome, it was customary for dinner guests to bring their own squares of cloth to use as napkins. At the end of the meal, the fabric would serve as a pouch for carrying home leftovers – the first doggy bags!

Dinner Is Over!

At a formal dinner party, when the host puts his napkin on the table, it means the meal is over. (So put down your fork and stop eating!)

May I Serve You?

Over 40 percent of all Americans have worked in a restaurant at one point in their life. (At fifteen, my first job was as a busboy!)

5. I Love Breakfast!

Breakfast for dinner?

As a rule, if I'm not hungry, I don't eat. And since I'm usually not hungry until the late morning or early afternoon, I often skip breakfast. The problem, however, is that breakfast is my favorite meal, and I don't like missing it. One day, when I was in my early twenties, I decided to have breakfast for dinner. (After all, nobody was looking.) So that night, I broke with tradition and made myself some French toast with a side of sausage. Deeelish! From that point on, I've often found myself enjoying traditional breakfast fare in the evening. And why not?

If you're like most people, your day will begin with breakfast — which may be nothing more than a quick cup of coffee (or *cawfee* if you live in the Northeast) and a bowl of cereal or a donut. However, on those wonderful lazy mornings when you actually have time to sit down to a leisurely breakfast, you'll want to whip something up to fit the occasion. I'll show you just how easy it can be.

This chapter will show you how to make all types of egg dishes, including a variety of delicious omelets. You'll also learn to prepare home fries, breakfast meats, pancakes, waffles, and my famous French toast, which is out of this world. And wait until you see how easy it is to make specialty dishes like Eggs Benedict and Huevos Rancheros!

So let's heat up the coffee and fire up the griddle — it's time for breakfast!

Boiling Eggs 101

Soft and Hard Boiled Eggs

The length of cooking time will determine whether your egg is soft or hard boiled. Soft boiled eggs are served in egg cups, over toast, or in a bowl. To open the egg, crack the shell with a small spoon about a ¼-inch below the top, then remove just enough of the top so that you can fit an entire teaspoon inside the shell to scoop out the contents. To remove the shell from a hard boiled egg, start peeling at the larger end, where there is an air pocket. This will make it easier to peel away the shell.

Important tip

Eggs cook differently at different altitudes. If you live in a high-altitude area, add 2 minutes cooking time for soft boiled eggs and 4 minutes for hard boiled.

Make Your Eggs Do the Twist!

Always check your eggs before buying. Those thin shells can crack during transport or when the cartons are stacked on store shelves. The contents of a cracked egg will leak into the carton and corrupt the eggs closest to it. It will also cause the shells to stick to the carton. That's why it's so important to do the "twist test." Just open up the carton and give the eggs a spin. Don't worry, people do it all the time. *Go ahead—nobody's looking!*

1. Place the eggs in a 1- or 2-quart pot with enough water to cover. Do not overcrowd the eggs—make sure there is space between them. Place the pot over high heat and bring to a boil.

2. Once the water begins to boil, reduce the heat a bit to maintain a steady boil without splashing.

3. **Cook soft boiled eggs for 3 to 4 minutes.** Place the pot in the sink under cool running water to stop the eggs from cooking any further. Serve immediately.

3. **Cook hard boiled eggs for 9 to 10 minutes.** Let them cool completely before removing from the water. Store the eggs in the refrigerator where they will keep for about a week.

Poached Eggs *aka* Naked Boiled Eggs

Poaching an egg—gently boiling it in water without the shell—is a healthy preparation method because no oil or butter is used. It does, however, require your attention. The water temperature must stay at a slow boil (simmer). If the water isn't hot enough, the egg will separate before it's cooked; if it is boiling too hard, the whites will be tough and the yolk will be overcooked. And—unless you are using special poaching cups—you must place the eggs in the water very carefully so that they hold their shape. Poached eggs are excellent served over toast or English muffins. Be sure to try the EZ Eggs Benedicts on page 101.

1. Fill a 1- or 2-quart pot (depending on the number of eggs you are poaching) with 3 inches of water and place over high heat. As soon as the water begins to boil, reduce the heat to medium or medium-low to maintain the simmer.

2. Crack the eggs over the pot and gently drop them into the water. The water temperature will drop and the water will stop boiling, but don't change the heat setting. Gently separate the eggs with a slotted spoon.

3. Simmer for 3 to 5 minutes, or until the whites are thoroughly cooked but the yolks are still runny. Remove the eggs from the water with a slotted spoon and serve immediately. Add salt and pepper to taste.

Important tip

If you'd rather not break the eggs directly into the simmering water, crack them into a teacup or on a saucer and then gently slide them into the pot. And if you break a yolk, make scrambled eggs instead!

Stuff You'll Need

Sunny Side Up, Basted, and Eggs Over Easy

These are three of the four basic ways to fry eggs (the fourth is "scrambled" and is found on the next page). They all start out the same way—by cracking some eggs into a hot buttered pan.

Important tip

Eggs cook quickly, so they will need your constant attention for about a minute or two. Don't let the pan get too hot or you'll burn the eggs.

Stuff You'll Need

1. Melt a tablespoon of butter or margarine in a frying pan over medium heat and spread it around a little with a spatula. To cut down on fat and calories, you can lightly coat the pan with cooking spray instead.

Sunny side up eggs

2. Gently crack the eggs into the heated pan and let them fry until the whites are thoroughly cooked and the yolks are still runny.

Basted eggs

2. Gently crack the eggs into the heated pan, cover with a lid, and cook for 1½ to 2 minutes. Covering the pan creates steam, which will cook the top of the eggs as well as the bottom.

Eggs over easy

2. Gently crack the eggs into the heated pan and let them fry as for sunny side up. Once the bottom of the eggs are solid, use a spatula to gently flip them over. Cook another minute.

Scrambled Eggs

If you know how to make scrambled eggs, you don't have to be a rocket scientist to make an omelet. Raw scrambled eggs are also used to make French toast.

Important tip

If you use butter, don't let the pan get too hot or you'll end up burning the butter as well as the eggs. If you accidentally burn the butter, throw it out and start over. Margarine and nonstick cooking spray tend not to burn as easily.

1. Crack eggs into a bowl and add about 1 teaspoon of milk or water per egg. Beat with a whisk or fork until the mixture is well-blended and uniform in color.

2. Melt a tablespoon of butter or margarine in a frying pan over medium heat and spread it around a little with a spatula. To cut down on fat and calories, you can lightly coat the pan with cooking spray instead.

3. Pour the beaten eggs into the hot pan. Stir gently with a spatula or wooden spoon for a minute or so, or until the eggs are completely cooked.

Stuff You'll Need

Cheese Omelet

Omelets start out the same way as scrambled eggs; but instead of stirring the eggs as they cook, let them form a solid egg "disc," which you will fold in half over your choice of fillings.

Use the steps of this basic cheese omelet to create any type of omelet your heart desires. The sky's the limit when it comes to filling variations! Be sure to check out the delicious recommendations that appear on the next page.

Ingredients

4 large eggs
4 teaspoons milk or water
1 tablespoon butter
½ cup shredded cheddar cheese

Yield: 2 servings

Important tip

When added to the pan, the egg mixture should be between ¼ and ⅜ inches deep. The thicker the mixture, the more you'll have to fluff (Step 2). This is so the eggs on the top and bottom of the omelet cook evenly (and the bottom doesn't burn). If the liquid is thinner than ¼ inch, you will need to fluff only once or twice.

Stuff You'll Need

1. Crack the eggs into a bowl and add the milk (1 teaspoon per egg). Beat with a whisk or fork until the mixture is well blended and uniform in color.

2. Melt the butter in a pan over medium heat. Add the eggs, let them cook just a bit, then push in the edges with a spatula to let the uncooked eggs flow to the bottom. This also fluffs up the omelet.

3. When the eggs are mostly solid, add the cheese to one side.

4. Use a spatula to fold the half without the cheese over the half with the cheese.

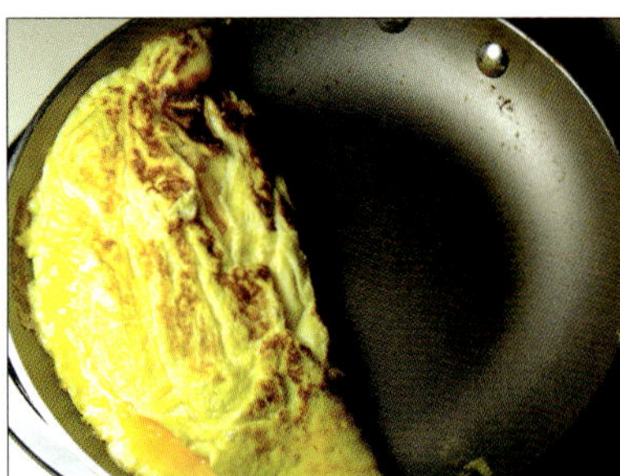

5. Cook for about another minute, then serve it up!

Try These Variations!

The following omelets are among my favorites. You can make them by following the steps for the Cheese Omelet on the previous page and adding a few extra ingredients to the cheese filling.

Spanish Omelet

¾ cup chopped canned potatoes
1 tablespoon chopped red bell pepper
1 tablespoon chopped green bell pepper
1 tablespoon chopped green onion

Top with 2 tablespoons salsa and a sprinkling of grated cheese.

Western Omelet

2 tablespoons chopped ham
2 tablespoons chopped red bell pepper
1 tablespoon chopped green onions

Italian Omelet

2 tablespoons cooked chopped Italian sausage
2 tablespoons chopped mushrooms
2 tablespoons chopped mild onion
2 tablespoons diced tomato

Top with some grated cheese.

Veggie Omelet

½ cup sliced mushrooms
2 tablespoons chopped tomato
2 tablespoons chopped green onion
2 tablespoons zucchini
½ teaspoon minced oregano

Try this with Monterey Jack cheese intead of cheddar.

Potato/Bacon Omelet

¼ cup cooked crumbled bacon
¼ cup cooked diced potatoes
2 tablespoons chopped green onion
1 tablespoon minced parsley

California Omelet

5 or 6 avocado slices
3 or 4 tomato slices

Try this with Monterey Jack cheese instead of cheddar, and top with 1 tablespoon chunky salsa.

California Omelet (my favorite)

You Silly Sausage!

Precooked breakfast sausage, which comes in patties or links and is found in the freezer section of your grocery store, needs only to be warmed up in a pan or the microwave. Uncooked varieties can be pan-fried or baked. To bake, place the sausage in a baking pan, and cook in a 350°F oven for 15 to 20 minutes, or until golden brown. For more even browning, turn the sausage after it has been cooking for about 10 minutes.

In addition to regular breakfast sausage, feel free to cook any type of sausage for breakfast. When using thick hot dog or bratwurst-sized links, simply slice them up and cook as you would regular breakfast sausage.

Stuff You'll Need

1. To pan-fry, place the sausage in a frying pan over medium heat. Keep links together for easier turning.

2. **Links.** Try to cook the links on all sides. Every 30 to 40 seconds, use a spatula to roll the links together as a unit. Continue to cook and roll until there is no pink in the center of the sausage.

2. **Patties.** Cook patties about 2 minutes or so on each side, or until golden brown and thoroughly cooked.

Makin' Bacon . . .

You probably already know all about makin' bacon. If you don't, ask your parents. I'm sure they'll be glad to tell you all about it.

The length of time you cook bacon depends on how you like it—from soft and limp to stiff and burned to a crisp (the way Elvis Presley liked it).

Important tip

The biggest mistake people make when cooking bacon is trying to cook it too fast over high heat. Bacon should be cooked slowly over medium heat. Although this takes more time, the bacon is less likely to burn—or splash you with hot grease.

Stuff You'll Need

1. Lay the slices side by side. If your pan is a little too small for the amount of bacon you want to cook, you can overlap the slices slightly.

2. You will need to turn the bacon several times—four times or more. Use tongs or a fork to carefully flip the slices.

3. Once the bacon is cooked to your desired level of doneness, remove it from the pan and place it on paper towels to absorb the excess fat.

Pancakes to Flip You Out

Although I usually use packaged pancake mix, occasionally I make my own batter from scratch. When making pancakes, keep in mind that they will be fluffier if the batter is a little lumpy. (Strange, huh?) If you use homemade batter, it also helps if you let it sit an hour before cooking the pancakes.

Ingredients

1 cup flour

1 teaspoon baking powder

½ teaspoon baking soda

Pinch of salt

½ to ¾ cup milk

1 egg

Yield: 6 to 8 pancakes

1. Combine the dry ingredients in a mixing bowl. Add the milk and egg, and gently stir with a whisk or fork until thoroughly mixed but still a little lumpy.

2. Heat up a frying pan over medium-high heat (see the "Important tip" below). Add a tablespoon of butter and spread it around a bit. (If the pan is nonstick, you won't need butter.) Pour or ladle the batter in the hot pan, using about ¼ cup for each pancake.

3. Cook about 2 minutes or until bubbles form and begin to break on the surface of the pancakes and the bottoms are golden brown. Flip and cook another 30 seconds or until both sides are golden brown. Serve them hot, topped with your favorite syrup.

Important tip

When making pancakes, the frying pan should be very hot but not too hot. To determine if the pan is the right temperature, drop some water on it. If the drops sputter and dance across the pan, it's perfect. If the water instantly evaporates, the pan is too hot.

Stuff You'll Need

Make 'em Extra Special!

For pancakes and waffles that are extra delicious, check out the following variations:

Blueberry. Add ¼ cup blueberries to the batter.

Banana-nut. Add 2 tablespoons chopped nuts and 2 tablespoons chopped bananas to the batter.

Pecan or walnut. Add ¼ cup chopped nuts to the batter.

Chocolate chip. Add ¼ cup chocolate chips to the batter.

Holey Waffles!

You'll need a waffle iron to make this breakfast favorite, which is delicious topped with maple syrup, jam or jelly, fresh fruit, or even a sprinkling of powdered sugar. The homemade Berry Good Syrup on page 104 is another good choice.

When making batter from scratch—rather than from a prepared mix—try this recipe. It will produce waffles that are light and fluffy. To make them even fluffier, first separate the eggs, beat the whites, then fold them into the batter (see page 61 for folding instructions). And don't forget to try the batter variations on the previous page.

Ingredients

1½ cups flour
1 teaspoon baking powder
½ teaspoon baking soda
Pinch of salt
1 cup milk
2 eggs

Yield: 2 to 3 waffles

Stuff You'll Need

1. Combine the dry ingredients in a mixing bowl. Add the milk and eggs, and gently stir with a whisk or fork until thoroughly mixed but still a little lumpy.

2. Pour or ladle about ½ cup of batter onto a preheated waffle iron, not quite to the edges. (It is better to use too little than too much.) Lower the top of the iron onto the batter.

3. The waffle will rise initially and then start to steam. Let it cook 4 to 5 minutes, or until the steam stops.

4. Open the lid and use tongs or a fork to remove your golden brown waffle from the iron. Serve immediately with your favorite topping.

Hash Browns

If you want to make homemade hash browns or home fries, it's best to first precook the potatoes until they are slightly tender. This recipe provides a foolproof way to do that.

Ingredients

1 or 2 small russet potatoes, shredded
2 tablespoons canola oil
Salt and pepper to taste

Yield: 2 to 3 servings

1. Peel the potatoes.

2. Fill a large pot with enough water to cover the potatoes and bring to a rapid boil over high heat. Let the potatoes boil for 1 minute, then turn off the heat and let them sit in the pot for 45 minutes.

3. Shred the potatoes.

4. Heat the oil in a frying pan until it is very hot, but not smoking. Spread the potatoes over the bottom of the pan, and gently flatten with a spatula. Cook 4 minutes, then lift up a corner with a spatula and peek at the bottom. If it's golden brown, flip the potatoes over as you would a pancake.

5. Continue cooking the potatoes another few minutes until the other side is golden brown. Cut into wedges, season with salt and pepper, and serve.

Important tip

You can precook the potatoes (Step 2) and keep them in the water for many hours. You can also store them in an airtight container in the fridge for a couple of days.

Stuff You'll Need

Home Fries

These flavorful potatoes are often served alongside eggs and bacon. They are also wonderful for soaking up the Hollandaise sauce that tops Eggs Benedict.

Ingredients

2 medium russet potatoes
½ cup chopped onions
½ cup chopped bell pepper
¾ cup canola oil
Salt and pepper to taste

Yield: 2 to 3 servings

Important tip

Be sure to dice the potatoes into very small pieces so they cook through. Because the potatoes will take longer to cook than the onions and peppers, don't add these ingredients until the potatoes are light brown and partially cooked.

Stuff You'll Need

1. Precook the potatoes as in Steps 1 and 2 for Hash Browns on the previous page. Dice the potatoes into small cubes.

2. Chop the onion.

3. Chop the bell pepper.

4. Heat the oil in a frying pan until it is very hot, but not smoking. Add the potatoes and let them cook about 10 minutes while stirring frequently. Add the onions, bell pepper, salt, and pepper, and cook another 5 minutes or until the potatoes are golden brown. Serve hot.

Toast Français

You can't order French toast in France—they've never heard of it. This popular breakfast dish works best with French bread, or just about any bread that you can cut into thick slices. The bread can even be stale, which is actually better for French toast.

Ingredients

4 large eggs
1 tablespoon milk
2 tablespoons butter or margarine
6 slices (1 inch thick) French or Italian bread, or 8 slices sandwich bread

Yield: 2 servings

Important tip

The pan must be hot when making French toast, so the outside of the egg-coated bread gets crisp. And keep in mind that the butter can soak into the bread, so the pan may become dry. Because of this, sometimes I add more butter to the pan after I flip the slices.

Stuff You'll Need

1. Place the eggs and milk in a bowl and beat with a whisk or fork until the mixture is blended and uniform in color. Set aside. Heat up the butter in a frying pan over medium-high heat.

2. Dip both sides of the bread in the egg mixture, then place the slices in the hot pan.

3. Cook the bread about 2 or 3 minutes on each side, or until golden brown. Top with a little butter and your favorite syrup, such as the Berry Good Syrup on page 104.

EZ Eggs Benedict

For this traditional egg dish, you can use a commercial Hollandaise sauce mix, or you can choose to make the real thing (see page 105). The main advantage to the mix is that it is quicker and easier to make, although it doesn't taste as good as homemade.

Ingredients

4 eggs
2 toasted English muffins
4 slices Canadian bacon
1 package Hollandaise sauce mix, or EZ Hollandaise Sauce (page 105)

Yield: 2 servings

1. Poach the eggs (see page 89).

2. Prepare the Hollandaise sauce.

3. Top each English muffin half with a slice of Canadian bacon. Place a poached egg on top, then spoon 2 to 3 tablespoons of Hollandaise sauce over the eggs. Serve immediately.

Stuff You'll Need

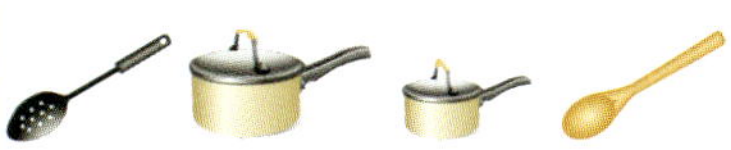

Huevos Rancheros

"Huevos" is Spanish for eggs; but in slang, it means "big balls." If a man says to another man, "You've got some huevos," it's a compliment. Try not to think of that while eating this delicious Mexican dish.

Ingredients

4 large eggs

1 tablespoon chopped fresh cilantro

$\frac{1}{4}$ cup enchilada or ranchero sauce

$\frac{1}{2}$ cup shredded Monterey Jack cheese

2 small flour tortillas

Yield: 2 servings

Stuff You'll Need

1. Poach the eggs (page 89), or fry them sunny side up (page 90).

2. Chop the cilantro.

3. Place the enchilada sauce and cilantro in a small pan over medium heat and simmer for 3 to 4 minutes.

4. Place the tortillas on two plates. Top each with two eggs. Spoon half the sauce over the eggs, followed by half the cheese. Repeat. Serve while hot. *Aye, me gusta!*

Ole! Breakfast Burritos

Here's a chance to put your cooking skills to the test. If you've mastered the art of making scrambled eggs and bacon, this recipe will be easy. If you want to eat these burritos with your hands, wrap the bottom in a paper towel or it will drip on your clothes (trust me).

Ingredients

- 4 slices bacon
- 1 sliced avocado
- 4 eggs
- 1 tablespoon milk
- ½ cup shredded Monterey Jack or cheddar cheese
- 4 tablespoons hot or mild salsa
- 4 small flour tortillas

Yield: 4 burritos

1. Cook the bacon, and drain on paper towels (page 95).

2. Slice the avocado.

3. Beat the eggs and milk until the mixture is uniform in color.

4. Scramble the eggs (page 91).

Stuff You'll Need

5. On one half of each tortilla, place 1 slice of bacon, 1 or 2 slices of avocado, 1 tablespoon salsa, and equal amounts of the eggs and cheese. Starting at the filled half, roll up the tortillas and serve immediately.

Berry Good Syrup

This syrup adds fresh fruit flavors and visual appeal to your pancakes, waffles, or French toast. It's even good over ice cream.

Ingredients

1 banana
4–5 large strawberries
½ cup maple syrup
1 tablespoon butter or margarine

Yield: About ¾ cup

Try These Variations!

Apple-Banana Syrup
Substitute 1 peeled, sliced apple for the strawberries.

Mixed Berry Syrup
Substitute ½ cup raspberries or blackberries for the banana (but don't slice the berries!)

Stuff You'll Need

1. Slice the banana.

2. Slice the strawberries.

3. Place all the ingredients in a 1- or 2-quart pot over medium heat. Stirring frequently, bring to a slow boil and simmer 3 or 4 minutes. Enjoy hot or warm.

EZ Hollandaise Sauce

Be sure to double up on your cholesterol medication (and plan to spend an extra day at the gym) after eating this sinful delight. Not only is Hollandaise sauce classically enjoyed on Eggs Benedict (see page 101), it's excellent over steamed asparagus, broccoli, and many other vegetables, as well as on boiled or oven-browned potatoes.

Ingredients

4 egg yolks
1 stick (½ cup) butter
Juice of 1 medium lemon

Yield: About 1 cup

Important tip

It is crucial that the butter is bubbling hot when adding it to the blender. It must also be added in a slow, steady stream. If the butter is just warm or you pour it too quickly, the sauce will not thicken properly.

Stuff You'll Need

1. Separate the eggs (see page 60). Discard the whites and place the yolks in a blender.

2. Juice a lemon and add the juice to the blender.

3. Heat the butter in a small pan until it is bubbling, but not burning. Be ready to use it immediately. (I usually transfer it to a measuring cup at this point, which makes the next step easier.)

4. Run the blender on medium speed to blend the egg yolks and lemon juice. Pour the hot butter into the opening at the top of the blender in a thin steady stream. The sauce will begin to thicken right away. Best if used immediately.

America's Favorite Meal

I love breakfast so much, I could have it for breakfast, lunch, and dinner.
Wait . . . is that actually possible?

Two Cackleberries and Wreck 'em!

Walk into any diner for breakfast, and you are likely to hear your order shouted out with the following unconventional lingo:

- ▶ *Two cackleberries and wreck 'em!* Two scrambled eggs.
- ▶ *One cowboy and sweep the kitchen.* Western omelet and a side of hash.
- ▶ *Two deadeyes on a raft.* Two poached eggs on toast.
- ▶ *Short stack with motor oil and side of logs.* Pancakes with maple syrup and sausage links.
- ▶ *Checkerboards and grunt.* Waffles with bacon.
- ▶ *Elephant dandruff with moo juice.* Corn flakes with milk.
- ▶ *Shingles with axle grease.* Toast with butter.
- ▶ *Sinkers and java.* Donuts and coffee.
- ▶ *Cup of Joe and make it moo.* Coffee with milk.

Sweet Trees

It takes forty to fifty gallons of sap from maple trees to produce just one gallon of syrup! The sap is boiled for several hours until it becomes thick and concentrated. Canada produces about 85 percent of all maple syrup. Much of the maple syrup found on grocery store shelves is not pure, but rather an imitation product made primarily of high-fructose corn syrup, maple flavoring, and colorings.

The World of Doughnuts

Doughnuts are known throughout the world by many different names. They are called *tortas fritas* in Argentina, *puff-puffs* in Camaroon, *gravy rings* in Ireland and Scotland, *chin-chins* in Nigeria, and *dough rings* in England. And they are *delicious* in any language!

God Bless Our Hens

▶ There are over 240 million laying hens in the United States that produce over 50 billion eggs. The average hen lays anywhere from 300 to 325 eggs per year. That is about one laying hen and one egg per day for every person in the country.

▶ The largest egg on record weighed one pound. It had a double yolk and a double eggshell. That hen must have been the size of a goose!

Nobody Doesn't Like Sara Lee

In 1935, Charles Lubin and his brother-in-law bought three Chicago bakeries called Community Bake Shops. Lubin named one of the cakes he sold after his daughter, Sara Lee. He also changed the name of his business to Kitchens of Sara Lee, which eventually expanded to seven bakeries. In 1956, the Consolidated Foods Corporation bought the Kitchens of Sara Lee, and in 1985, changed the name to Sara Lee Corporation. The company became known for its advertising jingle, "Everybody doesn't like something, but nobody doesn't like Sara Lee," which was often incorrectly sung as ". . . but nobody does it like Sara Lee."

Why We ♥ Bacon

"When in doubt, add bacon." This standard joke among most cooks is a tribute to bacon's incomparable flavor and "deliciousness." Current research also indicates that bacon may actually trigger a pleasure center in the brain, making it somewhat addictive.

6. Bottoms Up!

I love to drink all day long!

For many of us, nothing starts the day better than a hot cup of freshly brewed coffee — also known as java, Joe, jungle juice, morning mud, bean juice, rocket fuel, brain juice, wakey brew, go-go juice, black gold, jitter juice, and a myriad of other names. Coffee is certainly popular, but it isn't the most consumed beverage on the planet. That honor goes to tea. In this chapter, you will find helpful tips on how to brew the world's best cup o' coffee and make a lovely cup o' tea. You'll read about the different types of pots and how to steep, drip, perk, and more.

But this chapter isn't just about coffee and tea. It includes all sorts of popular beverages for your drinking pleasure. Since just about everyone enjoys smoothies, I've shared a few of my favorites along with some easy guidelines for creating your own. One of the great things about smoothies is that they're so simple to make — all you really need (at the very least) is some fruit, a little liquid, and a blender. A breakfast smoothie is a delicious way to greet the morning; and during the day, you can enjoy one for a quick energy boost or even as an occasional light meal.

Also included in this chapter are a couple of tasty choco-licious beverages, followed by some fresh and fruity drinks like lemonade and punch, complete with "spiked" options. Then it's time for wine! You'll learn how to select, uncork, and serve a bottle for your gastronomic pleasure. You'll even learn which glass to serve it in.

So 'ave a drink on me, Gov'ner.
Cheers!

Have a Cup of Joe

Regardless of whether you like your coffee strong or mild, you certainly want it to be fresh and flavorful. Although coffee beans are grown all over the world, those that are grown in Columbia are rated the best by coffee experts. In addition to where the beans are grown, a few other factors—roasting, grinding, brewing, and the type of coffeepot used—contribute to their flavor and quality.

Keeping It Fresh

Coffee is highly perishable. Whether you buy your beans whole or already ground, try to purchase small amounts—ideally, only as much you can use in a week. Then store the coffee in an airtight moisture-proof container in your freezer. The container will protect the coffee from the air, and the freezing will help it stay fresh tasting. Stored this way, whole beans will stay flavorful for four weeks; ground coffee will stay about two weeks. Do not store coffee in the refrigerator. It will develop moisture, which will have an adverse effect on flavor.

Instant Coffee

Although instant coffee (freeze-dried coffee crystals) lacks the full flavor and character of a freshly brewed cup, it is very convenient. Just stir a spoonful of the dry crystals into freshly boiled water. Some instant coffees are available in flavors, but be aware that many contain lots of artificial ingredients and very little coffee.

Coffee Tips

- When possible, use fresh beans and grind them to the proper consistency just before brewing the coffee.
- Start with fresh cold water. If your tap water is not drinkable, use bottled spring water. Do not use distilled or softened water, which lack the minerals needed to bring out the natural flavors of the coffee.
- Make sure the coffeemaker is clean. Wash it after each use with warm, soapy water. Otherwise, the coffee oils will build up, turn rancid, and give the coffee a bad taste.
- Use the right amount of coffee. For every six ounces of water, two level tablespoons of ground coffee is recommended. Then adjust these proportions to taste as desired.
- Brew only as much coffee as you will be consuming at a sitting.
- Stir the pot of coffee before serving. Heavier oils tend to sink to the bottom of the pot. Also, the coffee brewed at the beginning of a drip cycle is generally stronger than the coffee brewed at the end.
- Serve your coffee as soon as it is brewed, and finish the pot within thirty minutes. Coffee that sits longer than thirty minutes becomes stale and tastes bitter.

Roasting Them Beans

The length of time coffee beans are roasted will affect the color and flavor of the brew. The lighter the bean, the shorter the roasting time; the longer the roasting time, the stronger the flavor. The different types of roasts—from very light to very dark—are listed below. Each type is known by different terms (many of which are included below).

Type of Roast	Bean Color	Coffee Characteristics
Light Roast (Cinnamon Roast, Institutional Roast, New England Roast, Half-City Roast)	Light brown or cinnamon	Undeveloped flavor and body due to very short roasting time. Also high in undesirable acids.
Regular Roast (Medium Roast, American Roast, British Roast)	Medium-brown	Flavor and body are more developed than Cinnamon Roast, but acidity is high.
City Roast (Full City Roast, High City Roast, Special Roast)	Deep chestnut brown	Fully developed flavor; good balance of sugars and acids.
Dark Roast (High Roast, Double Roast, Continental Roast)	Very dark brown and shiny	Smooth, rich, and full-bodied.
French Roast (Espresso Roast, French Roast)	Almost black and very shiny	Strong, heavy-bodied, and low acidity. Has a "burnt" flavor.

Coarsely ground coffee in an electric blade grinder.

Choosing the Best Coffee Grind

The type of coffeemaker you use is an important factor in choosing a grind. The less time the grounds will be in contact with the water, the finer the grounds must be to allow the flavor of the beans to be fully extracted. For information on the different types of coffeemakers, see page 110.

Type of Coffeemaker	Recommended Grind
Percolators; commercial urns.	Coarse (Fully ground, but in fine pieces.)
Electric drip pots; plunger pots.	Medium (A little grainier than sand.)
Manual drip pots; espresso pots/machines.	Fine (Almost powdery.)

Hey! Hot Stuff!

Makin' da Coffee

The following information will help guide you to a coffeemaker that best suits your needs—and show you how to use it.

The Single-Cup Coffeemaker

The coffee for this type of machine generally comes premeasured in tiny pods (often plastic cups sealed with foil). The pod is placed in the machine, which pierces the seal. The water in the reservoir quickly heats up and is then forced at high pressure through the coffee in the pod and into the cup below.

The Electric Drip Pot

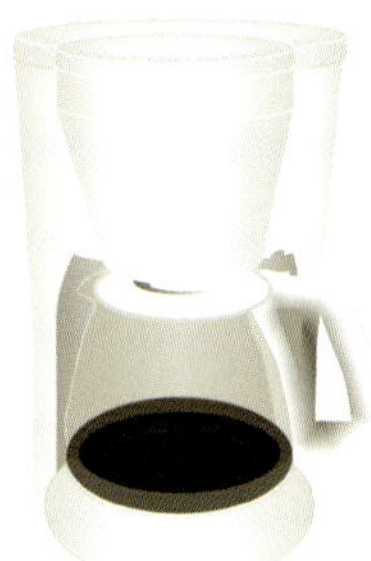

For this pot, coffee grounds are placed in a filter above the coffeepot, and the water is poured into the unit's reservoir. When the water heats to the correct temperature, it drips through the grounds and into the pot below, which sits on a warming plate. Some models include a coffee bean grinder.

The Percolator

Water is poured into the pot of a percolator. (The sides of these pots have water-level markings for the number of cups.) The coffee grounds are spooned into a metal basket that sits on top of a long hollow stem. The stem and basket are placed in the pot and the lid is added. Then, whether the unit is powered by electricity or the heat of a stovetop, the water begins to boil and is forced up through the stem and sprayed over the grounds. The water then drips slowly through the grounds into the pot below, where it is again heated and forced upwards, over the grounds. The sound of the water shooting up the stem is called "perking." When the perking stops, the coffee is done.

The Plunger Pot

The plunger pot is also called a *French press*. It consists of a cylinder-shaped glass pot with a metal rod that extends through the center of both the pot and the domed lid. Protruding from the top of the rod is a handle. Adhered to the bottom of the rod is a disc with small holes (the plunger) that fits snugly inside the glass cylinder.

The lid and plunger are removed from the pot and the coffee grounds are added. Freshly boiled water is poured slowly into the pot over the grounds. After four to five minutes, the plunger is pushed slowly down to the bottom of the pot, separating the grounds from the liquid.

Brewing the Perfect Cup

Coffee Strength	Level Tablespoons (per 8-ounce cup)
Strong	2½ tablespoons
Moderate	2 tablespoons
Weak	1½ tablespoons

The Skinny on Espresso

Because of its intensely strong bitter flavor, espresso is typically served in 1 to 1½-ounce "shots," which are served in small demitasse cups. Although stovetop espresso coffeepots are available, espresso "machines" have become the more popular choice. The base is filled with water, and the filter container is filled with specially ground coffee. Steam and water are then forced under high pressure through the pot to the grounds. The black espresso streams from the machine, closely followed by the *crema*—the dark honey-colored froth.

The following coffee favorites are made from espresso and/or regular brewed coffee. Prepare each cup individually.

Caffè Latte (Café au Lait)

4 ounces espresso or strong coffee
4 ounces hot or steamed milk

Iced Coffee

6–8 ounces cooled coffee
2 ounces cream (optional)
1–2 ice cubes

Kahlua and Coffee

7 ounces strong coffee
1 ounce Kahlua liqueur

Cappuccino

3 ounces espresso
3 ounces steamed milk
2 ounces foamed milk
Cinnamon garnish

Irish Coffee

7 ounces strong coffee
1 ounce whiskey
Whipped cream garnish

Mocha Latte

6 ounces espresso or strong coffee
2 ounces hot milk
1 tablespoon sweetened cocoa
½ teaspoon vanilla extract

Steaming Milk

If you want rich, creamy froth for topping a cappuccino, a caffè latte, or even a plain cup of coffee, consider buying a milk steamer. Most work by expelling steam through a nozzle, which is inserted in a pitcher of cold milk. As the steam mixes with the milk, cream-like foam is created—a foam that you can easily spoon or pour onto the beverage of your choice. You can also froth milk with a hand-held electric frothing machine, although the foam won't be heated.

Tea for Me

There are nearly 3,000 tea varieties available today. Believe it or not, all are derived from one plant—the Camellia sinensis.

There are only four "true teas"—black, green, oolong, and white. These four teas can be blended together or with other ingredients. They can also be scented and flavored.

True Tea Varieties

Black
This hearty, full-bodied tea is the most popular in the Western world. In the US, it accounts for over 90 percent of all the tea consumed, often in the form of iced and ready-to-drink teas.

Green
Green tea has a light, delicate, sometimes pungent or grassy taste. It is the most popular tea in Asia, although it is gaining popularity in the US due to its health benefits.

Oolong
A cross between black and green tea, oolongs have a delicate orchid-like fragrance, but are more full-bodied than green tea and require a longer steeping time.

White
White tea is the rarest and least processed tea. It is made from very young tea leaves or buds and has a light, delicate taste.

Important tip

Good filtered water will make the best tea. Pay attention to the steeping times and water temperature (see "Take Your Time, Brew It Right" on page 114). If tea is not prepared properly, you can actually burn it, especially green and white varieties.

Tea Blends

Blended teas are a mixture of tea leaves from different origins and of similar size that are brought together to create a specific flavor. Flowers, spices, or flavoring oils may also be added to the mix. Because very few teas have the quality and character to stand alone, most teas are blends.

Scented and flavored teas
Scented and flavored teas are dried with fruits or flowers, or they are infused with aromatic oils of spices, fruits, flowers, or nuts.

Earl Gray, for example, is a popular blend of black tea and oil from bergamot oranges.

Chai tea
Although there are many variations of chai tea, the traditional Indian version is a sweet combination of milk, black tea, and ground spices that include cloves, star anise, cinnamon, cardamom, ginger, and peppercorn. The spices are brewed with black tea, then strained and combined with milk and sweetener.

Herbal Teas

Contrary to what you might think, herbal teas are not teas at all. They are "infusions" made from the leaves, flowers, roots, bark, berries, bulbs, and seeds of various plants, but they do not contain tea. Many are reported to have health benefits. The following ingredients are found in many herbal teas, as well as real teas and tea blends:

- *Chamomile blossoms*
- *Ginger*
- *Hibiscus flowers*
- *Lemon juice and rind*
- *Orange blossoms and rind*
- *Peppermint leaves*
- *Raspberry leaves*
- *Rose petals*

Storing Tea

Tea absorbs surrounding odors, so it is best to keep it in an airtight jar or container. And to keep tea fresh, store it in a cool dry spot that is out of direct sunlight. When stored this way, tea will stay fresh about six months

Coffee or Tea?

Tea has more than twice as much caffeine per pound than coffee; however, a pound of tea makes 200 cups, and a pound of coffee makes about 40 to 60 cups. This means there is much less caffeine in your cup of tea than there is in a cup of coffee.

Caring for Your Teapot

It is recommended that you don't wash unglazed teapots with soap or in a dishwasher. They should be rinsed out with hot water and turned upside down to dry. If you generally make a variety of teas, you may want to purchase several pots to maintain the quality of each tea's flavor. The natural tannin residue in your teapot over time will enhance the flavor, so don't worry about washing it out.

I'm a Little Teapot Short and Stout

So what's the difference between a teapot and a tea kettle? And isn't a plunger pot just for coffee?

Teapot

Available in many styles and made of various materials, teapots are specifically designed for brewing tea. Loose tea leaves or bags are placed in the pot, and then hot water is added. Loose tea can be put directly in the pot or in a special holder called an infuser. (See "Have a Ball" on page 115.) Some pots have built-in infusers or strainers.

Tea Kettle

Usually made of metal, tea kettles are containers for heating up water on the stovetop. The water is then poured over the tea in a cup or teapot. Some kettles have spouts with lids, which start to whistle when the water starts to boil—a sort of low-tech timer. Electric tea kettles are also available.

Tea Press

The tea press is a type of plunger pot used for brewing loose tea leaves. Heated water is poured into the pot over the tea leaves. After the appropriate steeping time, the plunger is pushed slowly to the bottom of the pot, separating the tea leaves from the liquid and holding them at the bottom of the pot.

A Better Brew

Brewing tea is pretty basic. Just steep the leaves in hot water a few minutes. You can enjoy it as is or with the addition of a sweetener, lemon, and/or milk. Very little equipment is required—all you need is a way to heat the water. Most people use a kettle or teapot, but you can heat the water in a microwave or a pot on the stove. If you are brewing loose tea leaves, rather than tea in a single-serve tea bag, you'll need a strainer or tea infuser. (See "Have a Ball!" on page 115.)

It's in the Bag

The most convenient way to make tea is with a teabag. Place it directly in a teacup and add hot water, or use several teabags to make larger quantities of tea. After the tea has finished steeping, simply throw out the bag(s)—no muss, no fuss.

Brewing Tips

- Use the correct proportion of tea and water. As a general rule, for every cup of water, use one tea bag. For loose tea, use one to two rounded teaspoons, depending on the size of the leaves (use less if the leaves are small).
- Start with fresh cold water.
- Preheat the teapot (or teacup for single serving) with hot water, then discard before adding the tea and fresh hot water.
- Make sure the temperature of the steeping water, as well as the steeping time are correct. Follow the guidelines in the chart below.

Tea and C-C-C-Caffeine

All tea contains c-c-c-caffeine. (Even decaffeinated tea has some.) The amount in a cup varies depending on certain factors, such as the amount of dry tea used, the temperature of the water, and how long the tea steeps. The hotter the tea water and the longer the leaves steep, the more caffeine will be released into the cup.

You can also significantly decaffeinate tea yourself as it brews. Simply let the tea steep for one minute, then discard the liquid and re-steep the leaves. Up to 80 percent of the caffeine will be lost by doing this. If, however, you want to avoid caffeine completely, consider herbal "teas."

Take Your Time, Brew It Right . . .

The best brewing temperature depends on the type of tea. Delicate green and white teas are best brewed with water that has not yet begun to boil, the more robust oolong tea requires water that is just beginning to boil, while black tea should be steeped in water that has come to a rolling boil. (See page 54 for water-boiling guidelines.) Steeping time also depends on the type of tea.

Tea Variety	Water Heat	Steeping Time
Black	Rolling boil	3 to 4 minutes
Green	Simmering	1 to 3 minutes
Herbal	Rolling boil	3 to 4 minutes
Oolong	Gentle boil	2 to 3 minutes
White	Simmering	2 to 3 minutes

Have a Ball!

Tea infusers are small, mesh, basket-like containers, often in the shape of a ball or an egg, for holding loose tea leaves as they brew. Because the leaves are held in the infuser, they can't spill into the cup when the tea is poured. Infusers come in various sizes for brewing a single cup or a full pot. A chain or handle is attached for easy removal from the pot or cup.

Another way to keep loose leaves from spilling into the cup is with a mesh tea strainer. The strainer is placed over the cup and catches any leaves as the tea is poured.

Cold Brews

Tea doesn't have to be heated to be brewed. Many can be brewed very successfully in cold water, which is ideal for making iced teas. In one popular method, the tea is brewed outdoors in the sun. Another method has the tea brewed in the refrigerator. For both, be sure to start with fresh cold water.

Sun Tea

Fill a 2-quart clear glass pitcher with cold water. Add 4 to 5 teaspoons loose tea or 2 to 3 tea bags. Cover the pitcher and place in full sunlight for 3 to 4 hours, depending on the desired strength. Strain the leaves or remove the tea bags and refrigerate until cool. Serve over ice.

Fridge Tea

Fill a 2-quart clear glass pitcher with cold water. Add 4 to 5 teaspoons loose tea or 2 to 3 tea bags. Cover the pitcher and place in the refrigerator for 8 to 12 hours, depending on the desired strength. Strain the leaves or remove the tea bags and serve as is or over ice.

Hot Chocolate

Nothing warms me up more than a cup of hot chocolate on a cold winter day. Here's my creamiest version. If you don't want whipped cream, try marshmallows instead . . . or just drink it "au natural."

Ingredients

1 cup milk
2 tablespoons granulated sugar
2 tablespoons unsweetened cocoa
½ teaspoon vanilla extract
Whipped cream for garnish
Grated chocolate for garnish (optional)

Yield: About 10 ounces

Important tips

- Do not boil the milk or a film will form.
- Add the cocoa to the milk gradually. Use a wooden spoon to break up the powdery cocoa against the sides of the pot and help it dissolve in the milk.

Stuff You'll Need

1. Heat up the milk in a small pot.

2. Add the sugar, then gradually stir in the cocoa. Continue stirring until fully dissolved.

3. Pour the cocoa into a mug, top with some whipped cream, and sprinkle with grated chocolate. *Mmmmmmmmmmm.*

Chocolate Milkshake

Milkshakes should really be called ice cream purées. They require just a little milk (to thin out the ice cream), and you don't have to actually shake it. You can use any type of ice cream for milkshakes, but it's best to avoid those that contain large solids, like Rocky Road or Rum Raisin. The little bits and pieces tend to get stuck in the straw.

Ingredients

2 large scoops chocolate ice cream
¼ cup milk

Yield: About 12 ounces

1. Pour the milk into a blender and add the ice cream.

2. Blend on medium speed for 2 to 3 minutes or until smooth.

3. Pour the milkshake into a tall glass, grab a straw, and enjoy.

Important tips

- Let the ice cream thaw 5 to 10 minutes for smoother blending.
- When you start blending, air bubbles may form and stop the blending process. If that happens, turn off the blender and pop the bubbles with a spoon. Then continue blending.

Stuff You'll Need

Real Smoothie!

Delicious shakes that you can whip up in your blender, smoothies are healthy, satisfying ways to enjoy your fruit!

Important tip

To prevent large pieces of ice in your smoothie, either use a blender that has an ice crushing blade or pre-crush the ice.

Super Special Tip

Instead of using ice to cool down your smoothie, use frozen fruit instead. You can purchase fruit that is already frozen, or freeze your own fresh fruit. Simply wash the fruit, dry it well, and place it in a zip-lock freezer bag. Berries in particular will spoil quickly and they are not always in season. Frozen, they can last for months.

Smoothie Essentials

The foundation of any smoothie is fruit or fruit juice that is often thickened with ice. But there are lots of ingredients that can turn a basic smoothie into a delicious smoothie drink with added richness, flavor, and nutritional value.

Juices

- *Apple*
- *Carrot*
- *Cherry*
- *Cranberry*
- *Grape*
- *Grapefruit*
- *Mango*
- *Orange*
- *Pear*
- *Pineapple*
- *Pomegranate*

Whole fruits (pitted/peeled)

- *Apricots*
- *Bananas*
- *Blackberries*
- *Blueberries*
- *Cantaloupes*
- *Honeydews*
- *Kiwis*
- *Mangoes*
- *Nectarines*
- *Peaches*
- *Plums*
- *Raspberries*
- *Strawberries*
- *Watermelon*

Thickeners

- *Bananas*
- *Cream*
- *Ice cream*
- *Ice cubes*
- *Sherbet*
- *Sorbet*
- *Yogurt*

Added twists

- *Chocolate syrup*
- *Cocoa powder*
- *Coconut milk*
- *Coffee*
- *Ginger**
- *Ginseng*
- *Milk*
- *Mineral supplements*
- *Peanut butter*
- *Protein powder*
- *Tea*
- *Vitamin supplements*
- *Wheatgrass juice*

** Fresh ginger is very potent. A scant half-teaspoon of grated ginger per 12-ounce smoothie is recommended. Adjust the amount as desired.*

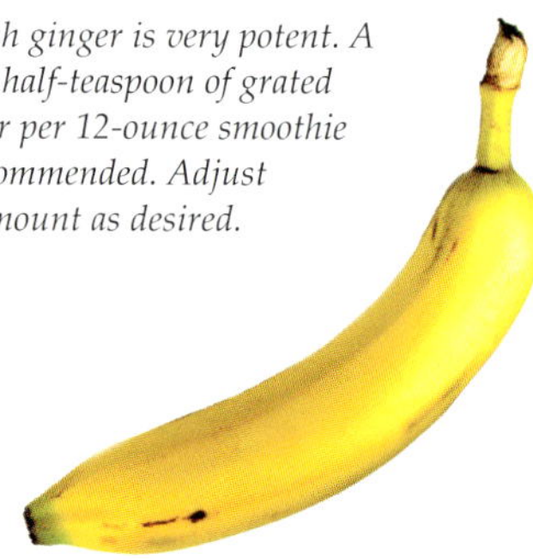

Banana-Berry Smoothie

I don't usually eat fruit; I drink it instead. Smoothies are the best! And there are so many ways to make them. This is one of my favorite smoothie recipes and a few recommended variations. Have fun creating your own!

Ingredients

4 or 5 large strawberries, tops removed
1 large banana
1 cup fresh orange juice
½ cup crushed ice or 4 large ice cubes

Yield: About 16 ounces

Try These Variations!

Melon Smoothie

Half a honeydew melon or a whole cantaloupe, cut into small chunks
7–10 ice cubes (depending on the amount of melon)

Yield: About 16 to 24 ounces

Yogurt Berry Smoothie

1 cup raspberries, blackberries, and/or strawberries
1 cup apple juice
½ cup plain yogurt
½ cup crushed ice or 4 large ice cubes

Yield: About 16 ounces

1. Remove the tops of the strawberries with your fingers. (You can also use a knife, but you will run the risk of cutting away some of the berry.)

2. Put all the ingredients in a blender. Blend on high speed for 2 to 3 minutes, or until the ice is well crushed (you won't hear it clicking against the glass).

3. Pour into a large glass and enjoy as is or garnished with fresh fruit.

Stuff You'll Need

Perfect Lemonade

*What makes this drink perfect is dissolving the sugar in the lemon juice **before** adding the water. This traditional method keeps the lemonade from being sour on the top and sweet on the bottom.*

Ingredients

3 large lemons ($\frac{1}{2}$ cup juice)
$\frac{1}{3}$ cup sugar
3 cups cold water
1 cup ice (optional)

Yield: About 4 cups

Important tip

Lemonade is mostly water, so the better tasting the water—the better tasting the lemonade.

Stuff You'll Need

1. Juice the lemons.

2. Mix the sugar and lemon juice together until almost all of the sugar has dissolved.

3. Pour the sweetened lemon juice into a pitcher, add cold water, and serve as is or over ice.

Healthy Fruity Soda!

Want to make your own fruit soda? Simply mix equal parts carbonated sparkling water and your favorite juice. Grape juice for grape soda, orange juice for orange soda . . . you get the idea. For lemon soda, mix 1 part of the concentrate in Step 2 (above) with 3 parts sparkling water. It's a great way to drink low-calorie soda without a lot of chemicals and additives. I prefer it over regular soda in a heartbeat.

Who Spiked the Punch?

The perfect party drink, punch is simply a mixture of juices and often a carbonated beverage—sometimes spiked with alcohol, sometimes not. It is generally served in a bowl from which guests ladle the drink into their own glasses. The recipes on this page can be easily doubled or tripled for larger crowds.

Yield: About 6 or 7 servings (8 ounces each)

Basic Fruit Punch

Mix together in a punch bowl:

2 cups sparkling mineral water
1 cup cherry juice
1 cup pineapple juice
1 cup apple juice
1 cup orange juice
Ice cubes
Orange and/or lemon slices

Spiked: Add 1 cup vodka

Tropical Fruit Punch

Mix together in a punch bowl:

2 cups pineapple juice
2 cups orange juice
2 cups mango or papaya juice.
Ice cubes
Orange slices

Spiked: Add 1 cup dark rum

Hot Christmas Punch

Simmer 20 minutes and serve in a heatproof serving bowl or crockpot:

1 quart (4 cups) apple juice
1 cup orange juice
¼ cup lemon juice
½ cup granulated sugar
2 cinnamon sticks
½ teaspoon ground cloves
Orange slices

Spiked: Add 1 cup vodka

Sangria

Mix together in a punch bowl or large pitcher and chill 8 hours:

1½ cups orange juice
¾ cup lemon juice
½ cup frozen lemonade concentrate
3 cups dry red wine
¼ cup granulated sugar
Lemon, lime, and/or orange slices
Maraschino cherries

What's Your Favorite Whine?

The French take their wine so seriously that they have specific wines for specific foods. I once drank white wine with a cheese course in France and my French friend felt it necessary to explain to the others at the table that I was American and didn't know any better.

Although certain wines are traditionally paired with certain foods, there are no right or wrong choices. Let your palate decide—eat and drink what you enjoy!

What's in a Name?

The true names of wines come from the regions in which they are grown, or the type of grape (or mixture of grapes) they contain. For instance, Burgundy (which can be red or white) refers to the region in France where it is produced, not a specific type of wine. In this section, I will be using the names as they are commonly displayed in liquor and grocery stores in the United States.

White Wines

White wine is sometimes made from the same grapes as red, only the skins are removed before fermenting. White wine can be sweet or dry and is generally lighter in taste than red. Dry whites are typically preferred with lighter meats like poultry, veal, and fish, and anything with a cream sauce. Sweet white wines, often paired with fruit or spicy foods, may be described as fruity. White wine is traditionally served chilled, but not with ice.

Red Wines

It is the primarily the color of the grape skins that give red wine its hue, which ranges from light red to deep maroon. Red wines are generally more complex than whites; they are also "dry," which refers to their sharp, acidic, low-sugar taste. They are the preferred choice with stronger flavored foods like red meats, stews, full-flavored cheeses, and pasta dishes with hearty meat and/or tomato sauces.

Rosé and Blush Wines

Crisp and light, rosé or blush wines are made from dark grapes. The grape skins are allowed to steep with the juice for only a short period—this produces their pinkish color. (Some rosés are actually white wine with some red added.) Like reds and whites, rosés can be sweet or dry, dark or light. Dry rosés are paired with light dishes, like summer soups and salads. Rosés are also a popular, refreshing summer drink.

Champagne and Sparkling Wines

Champagne and most other sparkling wines are made from a double-fermentation process. True champagne is produced in the Champagne region of France. Any bubbly wine made outside that region is called "sparkling wine," even if the identical production method was used. Most champagne is made from a blend of Pinot Noir and Chardonnay grapes. There are several classifications for champagne, which refer to the type of grape or the production method used, including:

Blanc de noirs
Variety made exclusively from black grapes, usually the Pinot Noirs. Literally means "white from blacks."

Blanc de blancs
Variety made exclusively from white Chardonnay grapes.

Brut
Process that produces a very dry sparkling wine called "modern" champagne.

Rosé
Variety made with Pinot Noir grapes and their skins, which steep with the juice for a short time to produce a pink color.

Aged Wine

Wine is dated to indicate its vintage, which is the year the grapes for the wine were grown. If stored properly, many wines, particularly reds, benefit from some aging. Most wines, however, are best consumed shortly after their production—within a year or so.

Letting Wine Breathe

For red wine, it is best to open the bottle a few hours before serving to let the wine mingle with the air. This aerating process—also known as letting the wine "breathe"—makes the wine smoother and helps bring out more of its subtle flavors.

Wine Serving Chart

Light, Medium, or Full Bodied?

A wine's "body" refers to its depth of flavor and fullness. A light-bodied wine is delicate in flavor, while a full-bodied wine is stronger and more concentrated.

Serving Temperature

The serving temperatures in the chart below are recommended by connoisseurs, but you can serve red wine at room temperature as well.

Very chilled = 41–50°F   Chilled = 50–54°F   Slightly chilled = 54–65°F

Wine Name	Description	Body	Serving Temp
White Wines			
Chardonnay	Buttery, dry but not sharp.	Full	Chilled
Chablis	Intense dry wine	Full	Chilled
Chenin Blanc	Light and dry	Light	Very chilled
Pinot Grigio	Dry and light	Light	Chilled
Reisling	Semi sweet and fruity	Light	Very chilled
Sauvignon Blanc	Complex and dry	Full	Slightly chilled
Red Wines			
Beaujolais Nouveau	Fresh and fruity	Medium	Slightly chilled
Bordeaux	Dry and fruity	Full	Slightly chilled
Burgundy	Dry. fruity and complex	Full	Slightly chilled
Cabernet Sauvignon	Dry and complex	Full	Slightly chilled
Chianti	Dry and light	Medium	Slightly chilled
Merlot	Dry and fruity	Medium to full	Slightly chilled
Pinot Noir	Rich and slightly dry	Full	Slightly chilled
Syrah/Shiraz	Complex and strong	Full	Slightly chilled
Zinfandel	Rich and dry	Full	Slightly chilled

Let's Get Glassy

Glassware for wine comes in a variety of shapes and sizes, but most are made of three parts—a bowl, which holds the wine; a foot, which is the glass's base; and a stem, which attaches the bowl to the foot and is the part held by the hand. Aside from adding to the beauty of a wine glass, the stem serves an important purpose—holding it prevents the heat of your hand from warming the wine in the bowl. As you will see, the shape and size of the bowls also serve a purpose, with some better suited to certain wines than to others.

Is This My Glass or Yours?

Ever set your wine glass down at a party, and then get it mixed up with someone else's? Wine charms are the perfect solution. Great for gatherings both large and small, these charms provide a unique and fun way for your guests to personalize their wine glasses. Each individual charm clips around the stem of a glass, making it easy for your guests to always know which glass is theirs.

Wine Glass Varieties

Red and white wine glasses are similar. Most are long-stemmed with oval bowls that narrow somewhat at the top. This shape concentrates the fragrance or "nose" of the wine. And because the flavor of red wine improves when it is exposed to the air, the bowl of a red wine glass is slightly wider than the bowl of a white wine glass. Stemless wine glasses are also available. They were first used by the restaurant industry, which saw them as a solution to the high wine glass breakage rate.

Champagne and sparkling wines are often served in long-stemmed flutes, which have a long, narrow bowl to keep the bubbles bubbly. Brandy, a wine that is distilled from grapes, is served in a snifter—a short-stemmed, pear-shaped goblet with a narrow opening. The proper way to hold a snifter is by cupping one's hand under the bowl. The warmth of the hand will cause the brandy to evaporate a bit, which helps release its flavor and aroma. The bowl's narrow opening traps the aroma within the glass.

Wine varieties like port and sherry are fortified with another type of alcohol (often brandy). They are very strong flavored and have a high alcohol content. Because of this, they are usually served in stemmed glasses with small one-ounce bowls.

White and red wine glasses

Stemless wine glass

Champagne flute

Brandy snifter

Sherry glass

Port glass

Open Up!

There is a vast assortment of wine bottle openers on the market. Most have a pointed metal helix or "worm" (which screws into the cork) and a lever system. Shown below are three of the most popular manual openers with instructions on how to use them.

Butler's Helper

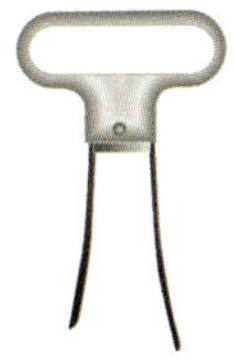

This simple opener has two metal prongs that are squeezed between the cork and the bottle. The prongs prevent the cork from breaking and fragmenting into the bottle.

1. Insert the longer prong between the cork and the bottle. Push the handle down until the shorter prong is inserted as well, then push both prongs all the way down.

2. Gently twist the handle while pulling up to remove the cork. The prongs will hold the cork in place.

Wing or Butterfly Corkscrew

This is the easiest of the manual corkscrews.

1. Place the corkscrew base on the lip of the bottle. Twist the handle until the "worm" is screwed into the cork and the arms of the opener are extended in the up position.

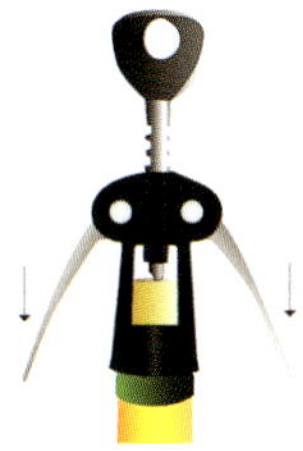

2. Push down on the arms. As you push, the cork will slowly lift up and out of the bottle.

Waiter's Friend

This is the most popular of all the manual corkscrews. It usually includes a retractable foil cutter.

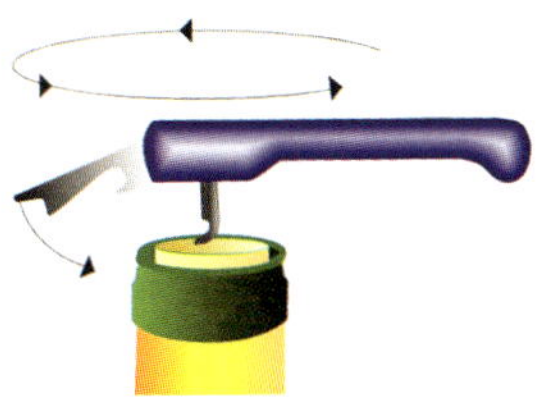

1. Twist most of the "worm" into the center of the cork until the hinged arm can swing down and reach the lip of bottle.

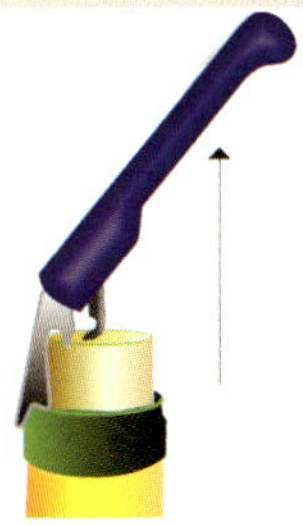

2. Position the notched part of the arm on the lip of the bottle (for leverage) then pull up on the handle to remove the cork.

I'll Drink to That!

We've got coffee and tea to wake us up and wine to put us to sleep. Then it's coffee and tea to wake us up again!

Tiny Bubbles

Technically, for a sparkling wine to be called Champagne, it must be produced exclusively in the Champagne region of France through a strictly controlled double-fermentation process. Bubbly wines made outside that region are called *sparkling wines,* even if the identical production method was used. Did you know that the average bottle of "champers" contains over 49 million tiny bubbles?

Serve Responsibly

In some states, the host of a party is held responsible for the actions of any guest who has had too much to drink and subsequently causes an accident that results in injuries or death.

A Toast to Toast!

Toasting is an expression of good will that varies from country to country. Americans and Canadians typically toast with the word "Cheers." The French are partial to *Santé* (to health), Italians say *Salute* (to health), and those who are Jewish say *L'Chayim* (to life). My favorite toast is *Skoal* (skull), which comes from the ancient Norse custom of drinking from the skull of an enemy.

Holy Spirits!

During the 1920s and early 1930s, when the manufacture and sale of alcohol was prohibited in the U.S., priests, rabbis, and other members of the clergy were allowed to have sacramental wine.

Trillion-Dollar Secret 4 Sale – Cheap!

In 1887, pharmacist John Pemberton sold the Coca-Cola formula he created to Asa Cander, another pharmacist and businessman, for the grand sum of $2,300. Within just a few years, Coke, which was originally sold as a tonic and contained extracts of cocaine and kola nut, became one of America's most popular fountain drinks.

I Love C-C-C-Coffee

Even though Americans consume over 400 billion cups of coffee a day – more than any other nation – they rank only twenty-second on consumption per capita. Finland takes the number-one spot with an average consumption of twenty-four pounds per person, per year. (Americans average nine pounds.)

It's Nice to Be Popular

Tea is the most consumed beverage in the world, second only to water. More tea is drunk than all other drinks combined – that includes soft drinks, coffee, and alcoholic beverages. China is the largest tea producer, followed by India, Kenya, Sri Lanka, and Turkey. India is the largest tea-drinking nation with the average person consuming 1.5 pounds per year.

Starbucks

Did you know that the Starbucks coffee shop chain is named after the loyal first mate in the novel *Moby Dick*? Today, the name pretty much reflects the kind of money it makes – Starbucks serves as many as 40 million customers worldwide each week!

7. Appeteasers

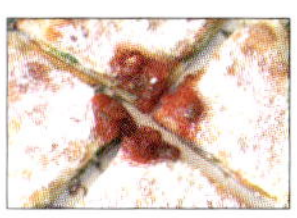

Sometimes it's nice to be teased.

Appetizers are supposed to tease your taste buds and make you hungry for the main course . . . which is why I call this chapter appe*teasers.* The word *appetizer* is actually defined as "a small portion of a food served before or at the beginning of a meal to stimulate the desire to eat." Before dinner in France and throughout much of Europe, it is also quite common to serve an *apértif* — a small alcoholic drink — to stimulate the appetite. Personally I don't need anything to stimulate my appetite, but I sure do love appetizers (and apértifs).

Serving appetizers is also an excellent way to keep hungry guests at bay while you're trying to get the meal ready for dinner. Years ago, a friend and I made up the word "hangry" to describe the feeling of being hungry and angry at the same time. Put a bunch of hungry people in a room filled with the aroma of a delicious meal being prepared, but without any appetizers to munch on, and you will see the definition of hangry in action! Personally, I prefer to play it safe and at the very least offer my guests some chips with a dip or two to keep things from getting ugly. And I recommend that you do the same!

So in this chapter, I'll be sharing recipes for a wide variety of taste-tempting appeteasers that are bound to please. There are a bunch of amazing dips — including one that is served in a bowl you can actually eat! You'll also find a couple flaky treats, some "mushroomy" bites, a few toasty delights, and the perfect 'teasers for a Mexican fiesta.

Like *Gone with the Wind's* Scarlett O'Hara, your satisfied guests will *"never be hangry again."*

Can You Salsa?

Salsa is Spanish for "sauce." In the United States, a Mexican type of chunky dipping sauce has also come to be known as "salsa." But if you want to salsa in Spain, you have to dance. Did I just confuse you?

This recipe uses hot and spicy pico de gallo sauce for this chunky Mexican-style salsa. Once you try this dip, you'll be spoiled by the freshness of its ingredients—and never look at store-bought salsa the same way again.

Ingredients

1 cup diced tomatoes
1 tablespoon fresh chopped cilantro
¼ cup minced onion
1 tablespoon lemon juice
½ cup pico de gallo sauce

Yield: About 2 cups

Stuff You'll Need

1. Dice the tomatoes into ¼-inch cubes.

2. Chop the cilantro.

3. Mince the onion.

4. Juice the lemon.

5. Mix together all of the ingredients in a bowl and serve with crisp tortilla chips.

Holy Guacamole

There's nothing better than guacamole made with fresh ingredients. It goes well with all kinds of Mexican food (except maybe sweet churros). Enjoy it as a topping on fajitas, tacos, burritos, and even burgers.

Ingredients

1 tablespoon minced onion
2 tablespoons diced tomato
2 large avocados, pitted and skinned
2 tablespoons salsa
1 tablespoon chopped fresh cilantro

Yield: About 2 cups

Stuff You'll Need

1. Mince the onion.

2. Dice the tomato.

3. Mash the avocados in a bowl. Add the onion, tomato, salsa, and cilantro, and stir well.

4. Surround with tortilla chips and serve.

Clam Dip

My mother used to make this clam dip for parties and it was always a big hit. I always made sure to get a good seat next to the dip.

Ingredients

2 tablespoons minced onion
8-ounce package cream cheese, softened
1 tablespoon Worcestershire sauce
⅓ cup heavy cream
6-ounce can minced clams, with 2 tablespoons juice reserved

Yield: About 1½ cups

Stuff You'll Need

1. Mince the onion.

2. Place the cream cheese, Worcestershire sauce, and cream in a bowl and mix with a hand-held electric mixer until smooth.

3. Add the clams, clam juice, and onions, and stir well.

4. Serve with sturdy ridged chips or raw vegetables.

Veggie Dip

Here's a dip that calls for cut-up raw veggies—instead of chips—to do the dipping. This type of raw vegetable appetizer is also known by the French term "crudites" (croo-dih-TAY).

Ingredients

1 tablespoon minced onion
1 tablespoon minced fresh basil
2 tablespoons diced bell peppers
½ teaspoon minced garlic
½ cup mayonnaise
½ cup sour cream

Yield: About 1½ cups

Serve with any or all of the following veggies:

Bell pepper strips or squares
Broccoli flowerets
Carrot slices or sticks
Cauliflower flowerets
Celery sticks
Cherry or grape tomatoes
Mushroom slices
Pea pods
Yellow squash slices
Zucchini slices

Important tip

Certain raw vegetables, like broccoli and cauliflower, can be a little difficult to digest. Steaming or blanching them for a minute or two can help alleviate this problem. (Be sure to cool before serving.)

Stuff You'll Need

1. Mince the onion.

2. Mince the basil.

3. Dice the bell pepper.

5. Place all of the ingredients in a bowl and mix well. Place the bowl on a platter and surround with your choice of raw vegetables.

Spinach Dip in a Bread Bowl

Serving dip in a bread bowl is especially great for parties. Once you've eaten half the dip, you can start tearing apart the bowl and eating it as well (yum). Is that fun or what?!

Ingredients

8- or 9-inch bread round (rustic variety or sourdough is best)
10-ounce box frozen chopped spinach, thawed
1 cup sour cream
½ cup mayonnaise
1 packet dry onion soup mix
Black pepper to taste

Yield: About 2 ½ cups

Important tip

For the best flavor and consistency, it's important to drain the thawed spinach thoroughly. It should be as dry as possible.

Stuff You'll Need

1. With a long serrated knife, cut a circle around the top of the bread that extends to (but not through) the bottom crust. Remove the circle of bread, then use your hand to pull out any remaining bread from the interior, leaving a 1-inch thickness along the sides.

2. Place the thawed spinach in a colander and press out as much water as you can. Set the spinach on some paper towels, and blot any excess moisture with more paper towels.

3. Add the spinach, sour cream, mayonnaise, soup mix, and pepper to a medium bowl. Stir until well combined.

4. Spoon the dip into the bread bowl and serve with pieces of bread from the interior of the round.

Hummus

This classic Middle Eastern dip is easy and inexpensive to make.

Ingredients

15-ounce can chickpeas, drained
1 tablespoon olive oil
1 tablespoon fresh lemon juice
1 teaspoon minced garlic
4 small pita rounds
1 teaspoon tahini sauce (optional)

Yield: About 1½ cups

Try These Variations!

Black Bean Hummus

Substitute half the chickpeas with 1 cup black beans. At the end of Step 1, stir 9 or 10 coarsely chopped, pitted Greek olives into the mixture.

Curried Hummus

Add 1 tablespoon curry powder to the ingredients.

Zucchini Hummus

Sauté 1 small chopped zucchini in 1 tablespoon olive oil, and use it to replace half the chickpeas.

Jalapeño Hummus

Add 2 tablespoons canned jalapeño peppers (or finely chopped fresh) to the ingredients. For a super spicy version, also add ½ teaspoon cayenne pepper.

Stuff You'll Need

1. Place all of the ingredients in a blender or food processor and blend until smooth. (You can also use an electric hand mixer.)

2. Cut the pita into triangles.

3. Transfer the hummus to a bowl and surround with pita triangles.

Egg-ceptional Starters

Devilish Eggs

Here's one of my Gran'ma's specialities . . . and a pick-i-nic favorite.

Ingredients

6 large hard boiled eggs, chilled
2 tablespoons mayonnaise
1 teaspoon Dijon mustard
¼ teaspoon paprika
2 or 3 green and/or black pitted olives, sliced
Dill sprigs for garnish

Yield: 12 little devils

1. Cut the eggs in half lengthwise and remove the yolks.

2. Place the yolks in a bowl along with the mayonnaise, mustard, and paprika. Mix together until smooth.

Stuff You'll Need

3. Using a teaspoon, fill the egg halves with the yolk mixture. Top some with an olive slice and others with a sprig of dill. Sprinkle with paprika before serving.

Quiche Me!

Real men ***do*** *eat quiche. Although I must confess, the day after I have it, I usually "man up" my meal choices with a thick steak or platter of spicy Buffalo wings.*

Ingredients

9-inch frozen deep-dish pie crust, thawed
1 tablespoon butter
$\frac{1}{3}$ cup onion, thinly sliced and cut in quarters
3 eggs
1 $\frac{1}{2}$ cups milk
1 tablespoon flour
1 tablespoon minced parsley
1 teaspoon dried oregano
1 cup cubed ham
8 ounces shredded sharp cheddar cheese

Yield: 9 to 12 servings

Try This Variation!

Quiche Lorraine

Substitute Swiss cheese for the cheddar and $\frac{1}{2}$ cup crumbled bacon for the ham. (See Makin' Bacon on page 95.)

Stuff You'll Need

1. Poke holes in the pie crust with a fork. Place in a preheated 375°F oven for 7 to 9 minutes or until lightly browned.

2. Heat the butter in a small pan over medium heat. Add the onions and cook 5 minutes or until soft. Let cool.

3. In a large bowl, add the eggs, milk, flour, parsley, and oregano, and beat well. Stir in the onions, ham, and cheese.

4. Pour the filling into the crust. Bake in a preheated 325°F oven for 35 to 40 minutes or until the center has set.

5. Allow the pie to cool about 15 minutes before cutting.

Marinated Mushrooms

Not only is this appetizer easy to make, it keeps for about a week or so in the refrigerator. The mushrooms are "cooked" by the vinegar in the salad dressing.

Ingredients

1 pound small white button or brown crimini mushrooms
2 cups Caesar or Italian salad dressing

Yield: 6 to 8 servings

1. Trim the stems of the mushrooms so only a small part protrudes from the cap.

2. Place the mushrooms in a medium-sized resealable container. Add the dressing, cover, and refrigerate at least 8 hours. Occasionally shake the container as the mushrooms marinate.

3. Transfer the chilled mushrooms to a serving bowl. Use toothpicks to spear the tasty morsels.

Stuff You'll Need

Stuffed Mushrooms

Look for the biggest mushrooms you can find for this recipe. Many grocery stores carry "stuffers"—large mushrooms that are specifically for stuffing.

Ingredients

⅓ pound ground sausage
¾ cup breadcrumbs
¼ cup grated Parmesan cheese
1 tablespoon minced garlic
2 pounds large white button mushrooms, stems removed
½ cup olive oil

Yield: 20 to 24 stuffers

Stuff You'll Need

1. Brown the sausage in a frying pan and drain the excess fat. Set aside to cool a bit.

2. Place the sausage, breadcrumbs, cheese, and garlic in a bowl and mix together.

3. Fill the mushroom caps with the sausage mixture and place in a baking dish or on a cookie sheet. Drizzle the olive oil (use all of it) over the stuffing.

4. Bake uncovered in a preheated 350°F oven for 20 minutes. Let the mushrooms cool a few minutes before serving.

Basil 'n Cheese Twirlies

Loaded with flavor, these appetizers are light and crisp and so very easy to make! Guaranteed to impress your guests.

Ingredients

1 sheet frozen puff pastry dough
1 egg, beaten
½ cup grated Parmesan cheese
¼ cup sliced green onions
15–20 fresh basil leaves
2 teaspoons minced garlic

Yield: Approximately 18 twirlies

Stuff You'll Need

1. Defrost the pastry dough per package instructions. Unfold it on a sheet of wax paper, flatten with your hands, and brush both sides with the beaten egg.

2. Sprinkle the cheese on the top of the dough, then add the basil, onions, and garlic.

3. Roll up the dough over the filling.

4. Cut the roll into ½-inch slices and place on a baking sheet. Don't worry if there are gaps within the rolls; they will fill up as they bake.

5. Bake in a preheated 400°F oven for 15 minutes or until golden brown. Serve hot or warm.

Baked Brie en Croute

The first time I tried this, it was with a bubbly glass of vintage Champagne—I thought I had died and gone to heaven. Although it's perfect when made with Brie, this delectable appetizer also works well with Camembert.

Ingredients

3 to 6-ounce round of Brie
1 sheet frozen puff pastry dough, thawed
1 egg, beaten
2–3 tablespoons blackberry or raspberry jam

Yield: 4 to 8 servings (depending on size of cheese)

Stuff You'll Need

1. Find a plate that's about 3 or 4 inches wider than the round of Brie. Place it on top of the pastry sheet and cut around the edge of the plate to form a circle of dough.

2. Place the round of Brie in the middle of the dough. Fold the dough onto the center of the round as shown.

3. Place the round in a baking pan and brush the top with egg. Bake in a preheated 375°F oven for 20 to 25 minutes, or until golden brown.

4. Spoon jam over the top and let set for 15 minutes. Cut out slices of warm Brie and spread on buttery crackers or baguette slices.

Salmon Toast

Here's a little treat I dreamed up one night before a dinner party.

Ingredients

3 large slices sourdough bread
¼ cup olive oil
1 teaspoon garlic
½ teaspoon minced dill
4 ounces cream cheese with chives, softened
3 ounces sliced lox
Dill springs for garnish

Yield: Approximately 12 pieces

1. Cut the bread into 2-inch squares with a serrated knife.

2. Mix together the olive oil, dill, and garlic, then sprinkle over both sides of the bread. Place the bread in a frying pan over medium heat and fry until both sides are toasted.

Stuff You'll Need

3. Spread the cream cheese on the toast while it is still warm. Top with a slice of lox, garnish with a sprig of dill, and serve.

Mini Pizzas

These fun, easy-to-make pizzas lend themselves to a wide variety of tastes. Real crowd pleasers!

Ingredients

1 loaf French bread
1 cup pizza sauce
8 ounces shredded mozzarella cheese

Topping suggestions

Pepperoni
Cooked sausage
Cooked chicken
Chopped bell peppers
Sliced tomatoes
Sliced olives
Chopped onions
Pineapple cubes

Yield: 12 mini pizzas

Stuff You'll Need

1. With a serrated knife, cut the loaf in half lengthwise. Discard the top half or reserve it for another use. Cut the bottom half into quarters. Next, score each quarter into thirds, cutting down to (but not all the way through) the bottom crust.

2. Reassemble the quarters on a baking sheet. Cover the top with sauce, then sprinkle with mozzarella.

3. Add your choice of toppings.

4. Bake in a preheated 400°F oven for 20 minutes, or until the cheese is melted. Separate the quarters with a spatula, then cut or break them apart where scored. Transfer the mini pizzas to a platter and serve.

Killer Quesadillas

The addition of fresh tomatoes and avocados, plus the special touch of Parmesan cheese makes these quesas "killer."

Ingredients

1 teaspoon butter
2 large flour tortillas
½ cup shredded cheddar cheese
5–6 avocado slices
1 small tomato, chopped
2 tablespoons grated Parmesan cheese
1 tablespoon salsa

Yield: 2 to 4 servings

1. Heat the butter in a pan over medium heat, then add a tortilla. Cover with cheddar cheese, then add the tomato and avocado. Cook for 3 to 5 minutes or until the cheese is mostly melted.

2. Place the remaining tortilla on top and gently press it into the filling. Flip with a spatula and cook another 2 minutes, or until the bottom is golden brown.

Stuff You'll Need

3. Transfer to a platter, sprinkle with Parmesan cheese, and place a spoonful of salsa in the center. Cut in quarters or eighths and serve.

Macho Nachos

These nachos are the real McCoy—not the melted cheese product they sell in stadiums and movie theaters. If you like 'em hot, toss on some sliced jalapeño peppers!

Ingredients

3 ounces tortilla chips
¼ cup refried beans, heated
1 cup shredded sharp cheddar cheese

Topping suggestions

Chopped fresh cilantro
Holy Guacamole (page 129)
Salsa
Sour cream

Yield: 4 to 6 servings

Important tip

When this dish is placed in the oven, the cheese will melt before the refried beans heat up. Because of this, I recommend heating the beans before adding them to the dish.

Stuff You'll Need

1. Place the chips in a casserole dish and top with the beans.

2. Sprinkle the cheese on top.

3. Place in a preheated 350°F oven for 7 to 10 minutes, or until the cheese is fully melted. Top with guacamole, sour cream, or whatever topping suits your fancy. Enjoy hot!

Fancy Snackin'

Once you get to a certain age, a bag of cheese puffs won't satisfy or impress your more discriminating guests.

Out of Work?

The French phrase *hors d'oeuvres* could be literally translated to mean "out of work" or "apart from work." In this case, however, the word *hors* means "before" and the *oeuvre* refers to a main course. So it translates as "before the main course." The Italian word *antipasto* (or the plural *antipasti*) has the same meaning – "before the meal."

Appetite Stimulants

To stimulate their appetites, the ancient Greeks and Romans were said to eat bits of fish, seasoned vegetables, cheese, and olives before meals. The Greeks were also known for enjoying wine as an appetite opener.

Move Over, Ketchup!

Salsa now reigns as the number-one tomato-based condiment sold in grocery stores, pushing ketchup – the former long-time reigning champion – into second place.

Super Foods

If you guessed the number-one food served at Super Bowl parties is pizza, you'd be right. Sub sandwiches and buffalo (chicken) wings are next. Over 1 billion chicken wings are eaten during the telecast, which accounts for 5 percent of the annual consumption for Americans.

A Poppin' Good Favorite

During World War II, when sugar rationing made it hard to get candy, popcorn became the number-one snack sold at movie theaters. Movies and popcorn still go hand in hand. Did you know that the average American eats 70 quarts of popcorn a year?

Spam Sushi

In Hawaii, where Spam is a kitchen staple, a sushi-style snack called Spam Musubi has gained recent popularity. Basically, it's a slice of pan-seared Spam that is placed on a "block" of rice, then wrapped in a strip of nori seaweed. The Japanese are *not* impressed!

American Hors D'oeuvres

In the United States, the idea of "cocktail" appetizers – tasty nibbles served with drinks before sitting down to a meal – didn't become popular until the mid 1900s with the publication of legendary chef James Beard's *Hors D'oeuvre & Canapes.* Beard, who filled his book with recipes ranging from the plain and simple to the elegant and elaborate, believed the idea of cocktail appetizers evolved from the free tibits that were customarily set out at bars.

Tasty Fingers

The English custom of serving "afternoon tea" between lunch and dinner originated during the mid-1980s. Served with a light snack, often scones or muffins, this tea break was meant to curb one's hunger without ruining the appetite for dinner. Finger sandwiches are other traditional accompaniments. These dainty two- or three-bite sandwiches with light fillings are usually crustless and cut into small squares or rectangles. They are also picked up with the fingers – hence, their name.

8. You're My Hero!

Is the sandwich the ultimate meal or what?

According to most accounts, the story behind the invention of the sandwich goes as follows:

The Earl of Sandwich was a lover of playing cards for long periods of time. So much so that he didn't want to have to stop to eat, especially if he was having a streak of good luck. Placing meat and cheese between two pieces of bread allowed him to hold the food in one hand, while continuing to play cards.

This means the sandwich was the first meal designed for multi-tasking. We do all sorts of things while eating sandwiches like talking on the phone, watching TV, or even reading cookbooks.

During my younger days, I created what I called a "mouth sandwich." I'd take a bite of cheese, a bite of ham, and a bite of bread, and then chew it all together in my mouth. Not only was this a quick way to make a meal, it didn't require plates, cutlery, or even cleanup. It also turned out to be a great way to save on food expenses because none of my friends wanted to come to my place for "mouth sandwiches." Since then, I've certainly kicked my sandwich repertoire up a notch (or two or three or . . .). One of the greatest things about sandwiches is that they lend themselves to creativity. The choice of fillings, breads, condiments, and garnishes are practically limitless.

In this chapter, I'm going to take you on a thrill ride of cosmic sandwich delights. There are lots of new takes on classic favorites, as well as a few of my more innovative creations. There's even a sandwich that you can dip!

*That's right. I said **dip**!*

For the most part, a sandwich consists of two slices of bread with a filling between them. What can you put between the two slices? Plenty!

Gimme Some Bread!

Bread, the basis or foundation of any sandwich, comes in a wide variety of tastes, shapes, and textures—ranging from uninspired slices of commercial white bread to nutritionally superior whole grain loaves. There are hearty ryes and dark pumpernickels, twisted Italian loaves with sesame seed crusts, dense potato breads, sweet Jewish challahs, crusty French baguettes, tangy sourdoughs, and much more. Bread comes in long loaves—either whole or sliced—as well as rustic rounds and smaller biscuits and rolls. When it comes to making sandwiches, the choices are practically endless. Here are some favorites:

- *Bagels*
- *Baguettes*
- *Challah bread*
- *Ciabatta bread*
- *Croissants*
- *English muffins*
- *Focaccia bread*
- *Flour tortillas /wraps*
- *French bread*
- *Italian bread*
- *Kaiser rolls*
- *Onion rolls*
- *Pita bread*
- *Potato bread*
- *Pumpernickel bread*
- *Rye bread*
- *7-grain bread*
- *Sourdough bread*
- *Wheat bread*
- *White bread*

Getting to the Meat of It.

After bread, the next important sandwich component is the filling, which is often some type of cold cut or deli meat. Hot dogs and other sausage varieties, burgers, and meat spreads are also popular choices. Typically salty and flavored with spices, sandwich meats are often made from pork, beef, or poultry and are boiled, cured in brine, roasted, or smoked. Here are some varieties that you will find at most deli counters:

- *Bologna*
- *Canadian bacon*
- *Capicolla*
- *Chicken breast*
- *Corned beef*
- *Frankfurters*
- *Ham/Deviled ham*
- *Liverwurst/Braunschweiger*
- *Lox/Smoked salmon*
- *Mortadella*
- *Olive loaf*
- *Pastrami*
- *Prosciutto*
- *Roast beef*
- *Salami (hard, Genoa, kosher)*
- *Summer sausage*
- *Turkey breast*

Who Cut the Cheese?

From mild American and buttery Gouda to creamy Brie and tangy provolone, cheese is both a popular filling as well as flavorful addition to many sandwiches (it's probably my favorite part). Cheese is usually sliced for sandwiches, although some types, like Parmesan and mozzarella—which are often added to hot sandwiches—are grated or shredded.

- *American*
- *Blue*
- *Brie*
- *Camembert*
- *Cheddar*
- *Colby*
- *Gouda*
- *Goat (chèvre)*
- *Gruyère*
- *Havarti*
- *Monterey Jack*
- *Mozzarella*
- *Muenster*
- *Parmesan*
- *Pepper Jack*
- *Provolone*
- *Swiss/Baby Swiss*

Healthy Additions

Let's not forget our vegetable friends. Without them, our sandwiches wouldn't have any crunch or juicy surprises. Be creative. Think of veggies as the salad you are eating along with your sandwich. Consider the following popular veggie additions:

- *Alfalfa sprouts*
- *Avocado slices*
- *Bean sprouts*
- *Bell peppers, roasted or raw*
- *Carrots, grated*
- *Celery, chopped*
- *Cucumber slices*
- *Lettuce*
- *Mushroom slices*
- *Olive slices*
- *Onions, chopped or sliced*
- *Pepperoncini*
- *Pickle wedges, chips, or slices*
- *Sauerkraut*
- *Spinach leaves*
- *Sun-dried tomatoes*
- *Tomatoes, sliced or chopped*
- *Watercress*
- *Zucchini slices*

Tasty Toppers

The condiments, seasonings, herbs, and other sandwich toppers listed below offer an additional spark of flavor to sandwiches. (Without tasty condiments, our sandwiches wouldn't drip onto our clothes.) Many condiments, like ketchup and mayonnaise, also come in reduced-fat and low-sodium varieties. Mustard, which is made from the ground seeds of the mustard plant, comes in a wide range of strengths and flavors, including mild yellow, robust Dijon, and grainy whole-seed varieties.

- *Barbecue sauce*
- *Black pepper*
- *Butter*
- *Celery salt*
- *Horseradish*
- *Italian dressing*
- *Ketchup*
- *Mayonnaise*
- *Mustard*
- *Ranch dressing*
- *Relish*
- *Salt*
- *Tabasco sauce*
- *Thousand Island dressing*

Hot Dog!

Hot dogs are a type of sausage made from beef, pork, turkey, or chicken. Most are precooked, so you just need to heat them up before serving. There are many methods you can use for cooking hot dogs, including one in which you hold them over an open campfire on sticks. In case you don't have a campfire handy, you can boil, broil, grill, microwave, or steam them as well.

There are many different types of hot dogs. My favorites are those made with pure beef—like kosher varieties—not the ones that contain "fillers." Be sure to check the ingredient labels. Bratwurst, a thick German-style sausage, is a popular hot dog alternative. Cooking methods for "brats" and other thick sausages are the same as for hot dogs, only they need to be cooked about twice as long due to their size.

Boil

Bring a pot with several inches of water to a boil. Add the hot dogs and cook 2 to 3 minutes. Because some of the flavor is boiled away, this is my least favorite method. If this is your only option, try boiling the dogs in beer, which will give them a better taste.

Broil

Place the hot dogs on a baking sheet lined with foil (for easy cleanup) and set under the broiler about 2 or 3 minutes. Then turn them over and continue cooking another 2 minutes.

Grill

I think grilling makes the best hot dogs—smoky and crisp with those wonderful grill marks. Place the dogs on a preheated grill over high heat and turn every minute or so until they are browned on all sides. Takes 2 to 4 minutes.

Microwave

Simply wrap the hot dog in a paper towel, place on a microwave-safe dish, and cook approximately 30 to 60 seconds. Time depends on the oven as well as the thickness of the hot dog. Cooking two or more dogs takes longer.

Steam

Place a steamer basket in a pot with an inch of water. Bring the water to a boil, place the hot dogs on the basket, and cover the pot. Cook for 2 to 3 minutes.

Try These Variations!

Chicago Hot Daag

Place a cooked hot dog in a bun and top with chopped onions, relish, yellow mustard, and ketchup. Add two tomato wedges on one side of the dog and a pickle spear on the other. Top with marinated hot green chili peppers and a sprinkling of celery salt.

Coney Island Chili Dawg

Place a cooked hot dog in a bun and top with heated chili, some minced onion, yellow mustard, and a dash of Tabasco sauce.

Polish Sandwich

Top a slice of rye bread with a thick slice of Swiss cheese. Cut a cooked hot dog in half and place it on top of the cheese. Add some sliced pickles, onions, and mustard. Finish with another slice of rye bread.

To Top It All Off!

Every good dog could use a little dressing up.

Condiments

Barbecue sauce
Ketchup
Mustard
Relish
Tabasco sauce

Toppings

Bell peppers, marinated or fresh
Cheese, shredded
Chili (with or without beans)
Onions
Pepperoncini
Pickle slices
Sauerkraut
Tomatoes

The Perfect Cheeseburger

Although most of the world associates hamburgers with America, let's not forget that this beef patty was named after a town in Germany. "You liken der hamburger, Frauline?"

Ingredients

4-8 ounces ground beef
1 hamburger bun
1-2 ounces cheddar cheese

Yield: 1 cheeseburger

Hamburger Cooking Times

The cooking time for a hamburger is determined by thickness not by weight. The following times are for a burger cooked over medium heat to medium doneness. For rarer burgers, reduce the time on each side by a minute or so; for well-done burgers, add a minute or two.

Thickness	Time Per Side
1 inch	8 minutes
$\frac{3}{4}$ inch	5 minutes
$\frac{1}{2}$ inch	3 minutes

Stuff You'll Need

1. Form the beef into a patty and place it in a heated frying pan over medium heat.

2. Flip the patty when halfway cooked (see time chart at left) and cook to desired doneness.

3. Place the cheese on top of the burger about a minute before the burger is done cooking. If the cheese hasn't melted thoroughly, cover it with the lid of a pan for a minute or so.

Try These Variations!

Bacon Cheeseburger

Add 2 or 3 strips of cooked bacon to the cheeseburger.

Mushroom-Swiss Burger

Sauté $\frac{1}{4}$ cup sliced mushrooms and $\frac{1}{4}$ cup chopped onions in butter or margarine about 5 minutes over low heat. Top the burger with a slice of Swiss cheese and top with the hot mushroom-onion mixture.

Guacamole Burger

Make a cheeseburger using Monterey or pepper Jack cheese. Spoon some store-bought guacamole or Holy Guacamole (page 129) on top, and add lettuce and tomato. Make sure you have plenty of napkins!

How to Make the Perfect Burger

- Buy fresh ground beef and avoid prepackaged varieties. The best place to find the fresh stuff is behind the meat counter at your grocery store. The fresher the beef, the better the burger.
- When forming patties, handle the beef as little as possible and don't make them too firm. This will help keep the fat from breaking down in the meat, and result in a moist, juicy burger.
- Because burgers naturally shrink and thicken during cooking, make the patties flatter and wider than you want them for the serving size.
- Before cooking, make sure the pan or grill is heated.
- If using a pan, cook the burgers over medium heat (don't crowd the pan). If using a grill, use high heat.
- Never flatten the burgers with a spatula as they cook. This will press out the juices and result in dry meat.
- Flip the burgers once when they are halfway cooked, then cook the other side.

Grilled Cheese

This is the most basic of all the grilled sandwiches. Although it's delicious on its own, try adding some ham, tomato slices, or cooked bacon for a tasty change. Also experiment with different types of bread.

Ingredients

2 teaspoons butter
2 slices bread
3 ounces cheddar cheese, sliced

Yield: 1 sandwich

1. Butter one side of a slice of bread and place it buttered side down in a hot frying pan over medium heat. Add the cheese, cover the pan, and cook for 2 minutes or until the cheese starts to melt and the bread is golden brown on the bottom.

2. Butter a second slice of bread and place it buttered side up on top of the cheese.

3. Flip the sandwich over and cook for another minute or until the bread is golden brown on the bottom.

4. Remove the sandwich from the pan and let it sit a minute before serving.

Important tips

- If using processed cheese, be aware that it will melt quickly, so you won't need to cover the pan to get it to melt.
- After removing the sandwich from the pan, let it sit a minute before serving.

Stuff You'll Need

Grilled PB&J

I've never seen anyone else make this and I don't know why! It's so good, sometimes I enjoy it as dessert. Be sure you have plenty of cold milk in the fridge!

Ingredients

2 slices bread
2 tablespoons peanut butter
1 tablespoon jelly or jam
2 teaspoons butter

Yield: 1 sandwich

Try These Variations!

PB&H
Substitute honey for the jelly.

PB&B
Substitute sliced banana for the jelly. Place the slices on top of the peanut butter and top with the second slice of bread.

Important tip

This sandwich needs to be browned quickly so the peanut butter doesn't melt too much. Use medium-high heat and flip the sandwich the second the bottom of the bread is toasted golden brown.

Stuff You'll Need

1. Spread the peanut butter on one slice of bread and the jelly on the other. Then put the slices together to form a sandwich. Spread half the butter on the top slice of bread.

2. Melt the remaining butter in a hot pan set over medium-high heat. Place the sandwich in the pan buttered side up, and cook for 1 minute or just until the bread on the bottom is golden brown.

3. Flip the sandwich over and cook for another 30 seconds or until the bottom is golden brown.

4. Remove from the pan and serve immediately.

Club Sandwich

The name of this sandwich comes from the fact that it was originally served at country clubs. So put on your fancy duds and use your country club manners when you eat this 'mitch.

Ingredients

4 slices bacon
1 medium tomato, sliced
3 slices white or wheat bread, toasted
2 romaine or iceberg lettuce leaves, torn into sandwich-sized pieces
4 ounces sliced chicken or turkey breast
2 slices cheddar cheese
1–2 tablespoons mayonnaise

Yield: 1 fat sandwich

1. Cook the bacon until crisp (page 95).

2. Thinly slice the tomato.

3. Toast the bread and spread mayonnaise on one side of each slice.

4. To make the sandwich, start with a slice of toast (mayo side up). Stack half the lettuce on top of the bread, then add half the tomato, bacon, chicken, and cheese. Top with another slice of bread and repeat the layers. Cover with the last slice of bread (mayo side down). Secure with toothpicks and cut into quarters.

Stuff You'll Need

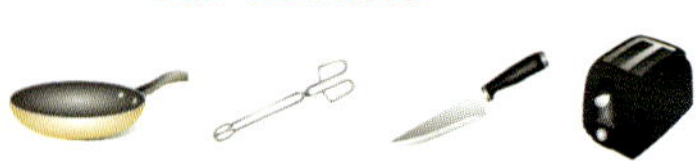

Italian Deli Sub

This sub is definitely Italian, but use whatever fillings you like best—the sky's the limit!

Ingredients

12-inch-long roll
4 slices ham
4 slices Genoa salami
4 slices capicolla
4 slices provolone cheese
1 tablespoon olive oil
1 teaspoon balsamic vinegar
Salt to taste
Pepper to taste

Suggested Additions

Lettuce
Tomatoes
Onions
Pitted olives

Yield: 1 sandwich

Stuff You'll Need

1. Cut the bread lengthwise, but not all the way through. Layer with the ham, salami, capicolla, provolone, and any desired additions.

2. Whisk together the oil and vinegar, then drizzle over the sandwich fillings. Add a couple shakes of salt and pepper if you like.

Great American Heroes

In addition to being called subs (short for submarine), these long sandwiches, which originated in the Northeast, are regionally called by other names, including:

Grinder—New England, the Midwest, and southern California.
Hero—Downstate New York, northern New Jersey, and the eastern United States.
Hoagie—Philadelphia, Pittsburgh, and southern New Jersey.
Poor boy or Po' boy—Southeastern United States, especially the Gulf Coast.
Spuckie—Boston, Massachusetts.
Wedge—Yonkers, and parts of the Bronx and New York City.

Portabella Pocket

Portabella mushrooms have a very meaty flavor and texture when cooked. Tuck them into a pita pocket, add some provolone cheese and marinated peppers, and you've got an incredibly delicious sandwich.

Ingredients

1 large portabella mushroom, sliced
1 tablespoon olive oil
Dash garlic salt
4 slices marinated, roasted red peppers
4 slices provolone cheese
1 tablespoon mayonnaise
1 teaspoon Dijon mustard
2–3 romaine lettuce leaves
2 pita pockets

Yield: 2 pocket sandwiches

Stuff You'll Need

1. Cut the mushroom into ¼-inch-thick slices.

2. Heat the oil in a pan over medium heat. Add the mushrooms and sauté 2 to 3 minutes, occasionally flipping the slices. Add a couple shakes of garlic salt.

3. Mix the mustard and mayonnaise in a small bowl. Using a rubber spatula, coat the inside of the pitas with this mixture.

4. Place a slice of provolone cheese on the bottom of each pocket, then fill with the hot mushrooms, marinated peppers, and lettuce.

Chicken Caesar Salad Wrap

When they first made the scene, wraps were all the rage. Although their popularity has calmed down a bit, wraps are definitely here to stay. Here's a recipe for my favorite, which goes a little somethin' like this . . .

Ingredients

1 green onion, chopped
½ avocado, sliced
1 burrito-sized flour tortilla
2 slices Muenster cheese
3 ounces sliced chicken breast
1–2 romaine lettuce leaves (preferable from the heart)
1 tablespoon Caesar salad dressing

Yield: 1 wrap sandwich

Stuff You'll Need

1. Chop the green onion.

2. Slice the avocado.

3. Place the cheese, chicken, lettuce, and avocado slices on the tortilla (don't cover more than two-thirds of the surface area). Drizzle the salad dressing over the filling ingredients.

4. Tightly roll up the filling in the tortilla. When you've finished "wrapping," secure the roll with toothpicks and cut in half.

Tuna Melt

This sandwich was a specialty of my Grandfather Blakeslee. I think it's the only thing he ever cooked for my brother and me (Grandma was the cook). I jazzed up the recipe over the years, but I still think of him when I eat this.

Ingredients

1 small green onion, sliced
6-ounce can albacore tuna, drained
2 tablespoons mayonnaise
½ teaspoon Dijon mustard
2 slices firm bread
2 tomato slices
2 thick slices cheddar cheese

Yield: 1 sandwich

Important tip

Before toasting the sandwich, place a piece of aluminum foil or a pan below the rack to catch any dripping cheese.

Stuff You'll Need

1. Slice the green onion.

2. Mix together the tuna, mayonnaise, mustard, and scallions in a bowl.

3. Spread the tuna mixture on the bread slices, add the tomatoes, and top with the cheese.

4. Place in a toaster oven or the middle rack of the oven, using the broiler setting. (Place directly on the wire rack.) Toast for 3 minutes or until the cheese melts. Serve immediately.

French Dip

Here's another "French" recipe that the French have never heard of. Ask for a "French dip" in France and they will either give you a funny look, or start to tango with you.

Ingredients

1 tablespoon minced shallot

1 cup beef broth

3 ounces thinly sliced rare roast beef

1 long French or Italian deli roll

Yield: Makes 1 dipper

1. Mince the shallot.

2. Place the broth, shallots, and roast beef in a pot over medium heat. Cook for 2 minutes.

Stuff You'll Need

3. Remove the beef and most of the shallots with a slotted spoon and place in the roll. Pour the broth into a bowl and dip away!

Lox and Bagel Plate

This is like having a mini buffet just for you (or someone you love). You've got the bread, cheese, salad, and seafood all on one plate.

Ingredients

1 large bagel halved lengthwise
2 slices red onion
2 tomato slices
3 ounces lox
2 ounces cream cheese
1 romaine lettuce leaf
1 teaspoon capers (optional)

Yield: 1 bagel sandwich

1. Cut 2 thin slices from a red onion.

2. Cut 2 thick slices from a tomato.

3. Arrange all the ingredients on a plate. On one side, place the lettuce leaf and top with the tomato and onion slices. Garnish with capers, if using. On the other side of the plate, put the bagel and lox. Serve with cream cheese.

Stuff You'll Need

OMG! Deli Reuben

This sandwich is to die fawr! What makes a good Reuben, Dar-link, is good lean, tenda cawned beef. It should melt in your mouth like a big stick of butta.

Ingredients

2 slices rye bread
4 teaspoons Thousand Island dressing
5 ounces sliced lean corned beef
1–2 slices Swiss cheese
3 tablespoons sauerkraut
1 tablespoon butter

Yield: 1 sandwich

Important tip

If you don't have Thousand Island dressing, you can make your own by mixing together:

1 tablespoon mayonnaise
1 teaspoon ketchup
$\frac{1}{2}$ teaspoon sweet pickle relish

Stuff You'll Need

1. Spread one side of each slice of bread with half the Thousand Island dressing.

2. Place the sauerkraut on one slice, the corned beef and cheese on the other, then put them together to form a sandwich.

3. Melt the butter in a frying pan over medium heat. Add the sandwich and grill 2 minutes or until the bread is golden brown on the bottom. Flip and continue to cook another 2 minutes or until the bottom is golden brown.

4. Remove from the pan and serve immediately.

The Pride of Philadelphia

Philly Cheesesteak

Here's an East Coast sandwich with attitude. The traditional recipe calls for shaved steak and American cheese (or Cheese Whiz). I prefer to use provolone cheese and thinly sliced rare roast beef (it's easier to find and tastes just as good). Try 'em both!

Ingredients

2 tablespoons olive oil
2 onion slices (1/4 inch thick)
1/3 cup julienned red bell peppers
2 large mushrooms, sliced
4 ounces thinly sliced very rare roast beef
Dash garlic salt
2 slices provolone cheese
1 long Italian or French deli roll
1 tablespoon pizza sauce

Yield: 1 sandwich

Important tip
If you're making a traditional cheesesteak with Cheese Whiz, don't add the cheese to the pan. Spread it inside the bun instead.

Stuff You'll Need

1. Cut 2 thick (1/4 inch) slices from a medium onion, then cut each slice in half and break apart.

2. Cut the pepper into julienne strips.

3. Slice the mushrooms.

4. Place the oil in a frying pan over medium heat. Add the mushrooms, peppers, and onions, and cook 5 to 8 minutes or until soft. Add the roast beef and cook 1 minute while stirring frequently. Sprinkle with garlic salt.

5. With the spatula, push the ingredients together in the center of the pan. Place the provolone slices on top and cook another minute or until the cheese has melted.

6. Use the roll to scoop up the filling from the pan.

7. Top with pizza sauce and enjoy. Be careful, though . . . this sandwich is guaranteed to drip.

Meal in Hand

The sandwich – an entire meal you can hold in your hand.
What a great concept!

Lunch Order – Diner Style

Here's some diner slang referring to sandwiches, sandwich ingredients, and popular sandwich sides. Have fun using them in your own home!

- *Bloodhounds in the hay.* Hot dogs with sauerkraut.
- *Hockey pucks.* Hamburgers well done.
- *Mouse trap.* Grilled cheese sandwich.
- *Cow feed.* Salad.
- *Frog sticks.* French fries.
- *Run it through the garden and put a rose on it.* Add lettuce, onions, and tomato.

Big Dog

The world's longest hot dog to date was made by the Empacadora Ponderosa meat products company in Monterrey, Mexico. Longer than an American football field, the 375-foot frank was displayed before hundreds of spectators, who were then served pieces of the edible treat.

Frizzled Beef

The beloved Philadelphia Cheesesteak was created in the 1930s by brothers Pat and Harry Olivieri, who owned a hot dog stand. One day, tired of eating hot dogs for lunch, Harry bought some beef, sliced it up, and grilled it with onions. After loading it into rolls, the brothers were about to take a bite when a cabbie smelled the sandwiches and bought one. After downing it, he told the brothers they should start selling them instead of hot dogs. The sandwich was an instant hit and became so popular, the Olivieris opened up a restaurant to sell them. Pat's King of Steaks is still in operation today.

Deal Me In

The eighteenth century aristocrat John Montagu, Earl of Sandwich, is generally credited for inventing the sandwich. An avid poker player, Montagu loved to eat while playing cards. By tucking the meat and cheese he was eating between two pieces of bread, he was able to hold the food in one hand, while continuing to play cards with the other. Actually, the practice of placing food between bread had been done before, but it was the earl who is credited with giving the sandwich its name.

Reubenesque?

Was it Arnold Reuben or Reuben Kolakofsky who created the Reuben sandwich? Arnold Reuben claimed to be the first to serve the deli classic – grilled corned beef on rye with Swiss cheese, sauerkraut, and Russian dressing – at his Manhattan restaurant in 1914. According to another account, Nebraska grocer Reuben Kolakofsky supposedly invented the sandwich during his weekly poker game at Omaha's Blackstone Hotel. At the games, the men would make their own sandwiches from a tray of meats and cheeses supplied by the hotel kitchen. Kolakofsky came up with the combination that everyone loved.

How Much for That Grilled Cheese?!

Diane Doyser found a live one on Ebay in 2004. She sold a ten-year-old grilled cheese sandwich with a bite taken out of it for $28,000. The sandwich, which had no mold growth, supposedly resembled the Virgin Mary.

9. Salad Days

The salad days of youth . . .

The expression "salad days" comes from the play *Antony and Cleopatra* by William Shakespeare. It refers to a period of youthful inexperience. During my salad days, the only "salad" I ate was on top of a burger or a sandwich. Thankfully, over the years, I have come to appreciate this course as an exciting mixture of interesting tastes, textures, and colors.

Salads are *so* versatile. Depending on how it's made, a salad can be an appetizing side dish, a light snack, or a substantial main course. In some countries, like Italy, it is served at the end of the meal. With a wide choice of lettuce varieties, colorful vegetables and fruits, flavorful fresh herbs, and an endless array of dressing choices, the salads you can create are limited only by your imagination and personal preferences.

This chapter offers a great opportunity to flex your creative culinary muscles, and I hope you have fun with it. It begins with an introduction to some of the more popular salad greens and lettuce varieties that are readily available in your local supermarket. Next come some easy-to-make classic dressings, followed by the recipes, which include a number of sensational green salads like Caesar and Greek, as well as a bunch of non-green salad choices like egg, potato, and macaroni.

So "lettuce" get started . . .
or as Cleopatra would say, "♋☪❍♒♒♎♐."

Let Us Eat Lettuce

Did you ever wonder what all those different types of lettuce and greens are in the produce section of your grocery store? Pictured here are some of the more popular ones. Packaged lettuce and salad blends, which are often prewashed and cut into small pieces, are also available.

For longer shelf life, store lettuce in a loosely sealed plastic bag, and keep it in the crisper drawer of the refrigerator. Dense varieties like iceberg and romaine should last a week or more, while more delicate types like butter and leaf will keep about four or five days.

When washing lettuce, rinse the leaves well under cold water, then pat or spin dry. Tear them into bite-sized pieces when using them for a salad. If you plan to store the lettuce for later use, after drying, wrap it in fresh paper towels, store in a plastic bag, and place in the crisper drawer of the refrigerator.

Q. Ever hear of the Newlywed Salad?

A. Lettuce alone with no dressing!

Important tip

To prevent green salads from becoming limp, never dress them ahead of time. Either serve the dressing on the side or add it to the salad just before serving.

Belgian endive

This rocket-shaped green has a compact head and pleasantly bitter taste. Its creamy-white slender leaves are often tossed whole into salads or used for scooping up dips.

Bibb or butter lettuce

The tender green leaves of this lettuce are soft and have a mild buttery taste. Excellent in salads, bibb leaves are also a good for lettuce wraps.

Cabbage

Available in red and green varieties, cabbage ranges in flavor from mildly sweet to strong and pungent. Red cabbage adds a flavorful crunch to salads, while green cabbage is the main ingredient in coleslaw.

Chicory (curly endive)

This green's frilly dark-green leaves are coarse and somewhat bitter. Chicory should be added in small amounts to salads along with more delicate-flavored greens.

Escarole

This variety of endive has ragged broad leaves and a tangy, mildly bitter taste. It is often torn into small pieces and mixed with other milder greens in a salad.

Iceberg lettuce

Clean, crisp, and mild-flavored, iceberg lettuce has a longer shelf life than most salad greens. This popular salad choice also offers a welcome cooling crunch when served with tacos and other hot dishes.

Leaf lettuce

Available in red or green varieties, this curly loose-leaf lettuce has a mild, delicate flavor. It also has a very short shelf life, so be sure to use it shortly after buying.

Radicchio

This rose-colored endive has a tight compact head and looks like a small red cabbage. It offers color and a somewhat crisp, slightly bitter taste to salads.

Romaine lettuce

The long green leaves of this lettuce are mild and sweet with a lasting crunchiness. Romaine is a perfect salad green and a welcome addition to most sandwiches.

Spinach

Delicate-textured spinach comes in curly and flat-leaf varieties. Raw spinach has a mild, refreshing taste that makes it a great choice for salads (baby spinach is best).

Watercress

The crisp, mild-tasting watercress leaves have a slightly peppery flavor. They are often mixed with other greens in a salad, and are also a popular sandwich addition.

Greens

Hearty greens like collards and kale have coarse leaves that are often tough and sometimes bitter. Because of this, they are usually served cooked, which releases much of the bitterness. When raw, they can be chopped or shredded and added to salads . . . sparingly.

Collards

This soul food staple (pictured above) is a type of cabbage with very tough dark-green leaves. The traditional Southern way of cooking collards is to boil them with a chunk of bacon.

Dandelion greens

The bright green leaves of this common weed have a slightly bitter, tangy flavor that adds interest to salads. They can also be cooked like spinach.

Kale

The tough frilly leaves of this cabbage family member come in a variety of colors. They are cooked like spinach, added sparingly to salads, and often used as an edible garnish.

Mustard greens

Typically steamed or sautéed, these peppery leaves of the mustard plant are popular soul food ingredients.

Dressing It Up

There are dozens of different types of salad dressing available at your local grocery store. They may be convenient, but dressings you make yourself taste a heck of a lot better. All you need are a few ingredients, a bowl, and a spoon or whisk— it's that easy! You can even buy bottles with measurements marked on the side that are specifically for making dressing. Just add the proper ingredients, put the cap on the bottle, and shake it . . . but don't break it.

Directions

To make any dressing on this page:

1. Place all of the ingredients in a bowl.
2. Stir with a spoon or blend with a whisk. (You can tell which method to use by looking at the pretty pictures.)

Yield: About 1¼ cups

Important tip

If you want to thicken the Sour Cream Ranch or Blue Cheese dressing to serve as a dip, use only half the buttermilk.

Vinaigrette

¾ cup olive oil
¼ cup balsamic vinegar
¼ teaspoon salt
¼ teaspoon black pepper
¼ teaspoon minced garlic (optional)

Italian

¾ cup olive oil
¼ cup white wine vinegar
1 teaspoon minced fresh oregano
½ teaspoon minced garlic
½ teaspoon sugar
¼ teaspoon dry mustard
¼ teaspoon salt
¼ teaspoon black pepper

Sour Cream Ranch

⅓ cup buttermilk
⅓ cup mayonnaise
⅓ cup sour cream
1 tablespoon minced onion
1 garlic clove, minced
½ teaspoon minced fresh dill
¼ teaspoon salt

Blue Cheese

½ cup buttermilk
½ cup crumbled blue cheese
1 teaspoon white wine vinegar
½ teaspoon lemon juice
½ teaspoon dry mustard
½ teaspoon black pepper

Thousand Island

⅔ cup mayonnaise
⅓ cup ketchup
2 tablespoons sweet pickle relish

More Than Just for Salads

Although salad dressings are made specifically for flavoring salads, many varieties can be used as marinades and dips, as well as appetizing sandwich toppers.

Mixed-Up Salad

The best salad is one that is made exactly the way you like it. Imagine that your grocery store is a salad bar. Think of all the delicious ingredients you can choose to make your salad special . . .

Basic Starters

- Lettuce(s) of choice, torn into bite-size pieces
- Dressing, homemade or store-bought

From the Veggie Department

- Avocado, sliced
- Bell peppers, chopped or julienned
- Carrots, sliced or grated
- Celery, sliced
- Cucumbers, sliced
- Green beans, whole or halved
- Mushrooms, whole, sliced, or chopped
- Onions (red, yellow, white, green), minced, chopped or sliced
- Pea pods
- Radishes, sliced
- Tomatoes (cherry or grape), whole or halved
- Tomatoes (globe), sliced, halved, or chopped
- Yellow squash, sliced

Fruits and Nuts

- Berries (strawberries, raspberries, blueberries, blackberries)
- Fresh fruits (apples, pears, oranges, mangoes), whole, sliced, or chopped
- Dried fruits (raisins, craisins, strawberries)
- Nuts (cashews, walnuts, almonds, pine, hazelnuts, pecans), whole, halved, or chopped

Bottled and Canned Goodies

- Anchovies and sardines
- Artichoke hearts
- Asparagus
- Beans (kidney, black, garbanzo, refried)
- Beets
- Chili
- Corn niblets, pickled baby corn
- Roasted peppers
- Tuna
- Salmon

Meats and More

- Bacon or bacon bits
- Cold cuts (ham, turkey, salami, roast beef), sliced or cubed
- Grilled or poached chicken, salmon, tuna
- Shrimp
- Sliced steak

And the Finishing Touches

- Basil leaves, whole or chopped
- Capers
- Cheese (American, goat, Parmesan, Swiss), crumbled, cubed, grated, shaved, or shredded
- Chili peppers, chopped
- Croutons
- Eggs (hard boiled), sliced, halved, or chopped
- Olives (green or black), whole, sliced, or chopped
- Sesame or sunflower seeds
- Sprouts (alfalfa, bean, radish)

Opa! Greek Salad

I was engaged to a full-blooded Greek woman for a few months, but we never got married. Her family disapproved of me because I wasn't Greek or wealthy. I can relate to the movie ***My Big Fat Greek Wedding*** *because I lived it (except for the wedding, of course).*

Ingredients

1 cucumber, sliced
1 red bell pepper, julienned
1 tomato, sliced
1 red onion, sliced
1 large head romaine lettuce, torn into bite-size pieces
4 ounces crumbled feta cheese
⅓ cup pitted black or Greek olives
Pinch salt
Pinch black pepper

Yield: 4 servings

For the dressing, whisk together in a bowl:

¼ cup olive oil
2 tablespoons balsamic vinegar
½ teaspoon minced garlic
Pinch salt
Pinch black pepper

Stuff You'll Need

1. Slice the cucumber.

2. Julienne the bell pepper.

3. Slice the tomato, then cut each slice in half.

4. Thinly slice a red onion. Cut each slice in half, then peel them apart.

5. Place the lettuce in a salad bowl along with the remaining ingredients, including the dressing. Toss and serve.

Caesar Salad

Back in the 1920s, Cesare Cardini created the Caesar salad in Tijuana, Mexico. So this salad is actually Mexican, not Italian.

Ingredients

1 large head romaine lettuce, torn into bite-size pieces

1 cup croutons

¼ cup grated Parmesan cheese

Dressing

¼ cup olive oil

2 tablespoons Worcestershire sauce or balsamic vinegar

Juice of 1 large lemon

1 egg (optional)

1 teaspoon anchovy paste (optional)

Pinch salt

Pinch black pepper

Yield: 4 servings

1. Place all the dressing ingredients in a blender or food processor and blend for 30 seconds on medium speed.

2. Place the lettuce in a salad bowl along with the croutons and Parmesan cheese.

3. Add the dressing and toss the ingredients together well.

4. Serve with some fresh Italian bread.

How to Coddle Eggs

Raw eggs, a traditional ingredient in Caesar salad dressing, can contain salmonella bacteria, so many people (and restaurants) omit them. If, however, you want to use a raw egg, you can coddle it to kill any possible bacteria.

1. Place the egg in a pot with lukewarm water and bring to a boil.
2. Boil the egg 30 seconds, then run the pot under cold running water.
3. The egg is now ready to crack open and use.

Stuff You'll Need

Warm Spinach Salad

I discovered this salad at the rehearsal dinner for my wedding. The dressing has a wonderful combination of sweet and salty flavors that complement the spinach.

Ingredients

3 cups baby spinach leaves
2 shallots, finely minced

Dressing

4 strips bacon
¼ cup olive oil
2 tablespoons balsamic vinegar
2 tablespoons honey

Yield: 4 servings

1. Cook the bacon until brown and crisp (page 95), then drain and let cool on paper towels.

2. Mince the shallots.

3. Crumble the bacon with your hands and place in a small bowl along with the olive oil, vinegar, and honey. Whisk until well blended.

4. Place the spinach in a salad bowl and sprinkle with the shallots. Heat the dressing in a microwave or a saucepan until very warm but not hot. Pour the warm dressing over the spinach, which will cause it to wilt slightly. Toss and serve immediately.

Chef Salad

You can use any type of lettuce, cheese, or sandwich meat for this salad. I chose to go with ham, but you might prefer turkey, roast beef, or chicken. To cube the meat properly, have the person behind the deli counter cut it into half-inch slices.

Ingredients

1 head iceberg lettuce
4 ounces cheddar cheese, cubed
4 ounces ham, cubed
4 hard boiled eggs, sliced
10 cherry tomatoes, halved (optional)
2 tablespoons sliced black olives
¼ cup Vinaigrette (page 168), or your favorite salad dressing

Yield: 2 main-course servings

1. Tear the lettuce into bite-size pieces.

2. Cut the cheese into ½-inch cubes.

3. Cut the ham into ½-inch cubes.

4. Slice the eggs.

Stuff You'll Need

5. Place all the ingredients except the eggs in a salad bowl and toss until well mixed. Arrange the sliced eggs on top of the salad before serving.

Tuna in a Salad?

During my starving artist days, a few of my friends and I often scoured our pantries and pitched our meager funds together to make a community salad. One of us would bring the lettuce, someone else would kick in a can or two of tuna, another an onion, and so on. Thankfully, there was always some extra money for a loaf of bread and a few bottles of cerveza!

Ingredients

½ head iceberg lettuce, torn into bite-size pieces
½ large bell pepper, chopped
1 small onion, chopped
6-ounce can tuna, drained
⅓ cup mayonnaise

Yield: 2 servings

1. Chop the onion.

2. Chop the bell pepper.

Stuff You'll Need

3. Place all the ingredients in a salad bowl and toss until thoroughly mixed.

Gourmet Chicken Salad

I discovered this chicken salad years ago at a gourmet shop in Miami, where it was selling for nearly five times what it would have cost me to make it. I must admit, though, the pineapple and walnuts really made it special.

Ingredients

8 ounces boneless, skinless chicken breasts
14.5-ounce can chicken broth
8-ounce can chopped pineapple, drained
1 cup walnut halves
¼ cup mayonnaise

Yield: 2 servings

Important tip

When draining the canned pineapple, don't throw out the juice. Either save it for later use or pour it over ice and drink up!

Stuff You'll Need

1. Place the chicken and broth in a pot and bring to a boil. Reduce the heat to medium-low and simmer the chicken 20 minutes or until it is no longer pink inside when cut with a knife.

2. Remove the chicken from the broth and refrigerate 30 minutes or until cool. Cut into bite-size pieces and place in a large bowl.

3. Place the remaining ingredients in the bowl and mix thoroughly. Cover and refrigerate at least 1 hour before serving.

4. Enjoy as is or served on a bed of lettuce.

Egg-ceptional Egg Salad

Here's an old favorite, but taken to a flavorful egg-streme. Simple to make and also great for sandwiches.

Ingredients

4 hard boiled eggs
1 teaspoon dry mustard or 2 teaspoons prepared
2 tablespoons mayonnaise
¼ teaspoon paprika
Pinch salt
Pinch black pepper
2 tablespoons sliced black olives (optional)
½ cup chopped celery (optional)

Yield: 2 servings

1. Place the eggs in a medium bowl and chop with a fork into small pieces (they don't have to be uniform).

2. Add the remaining ingredients and stir until thoroughly mixed.

3. Enjoy as is or served on a bed of lettuce.

Stuff You'll Need

Macaroni Salad

To my knowledge it isn't against the law to use pasta other than elbow macaroni for this salad. It may, however, be a good idea to check out your local pasta regulations (just to be on the safe side).

Ingredients

1 pound elbow macaroni
1 tablespoon cider vinegar
1 ½ cups mayonnaise
¼ cup buttermilk
3 hard boiled eggs, chopped
½ cup minced onion
½ cup chopped dill pickles
6-ounce can pitted ripe black olives, drained
4-ounce jar sliced pimentos, drained
Salt to taste
Black pepper to taste

Yield: 8 servings

Important tip

Be sure to completely cool the macaroni before adding the buttermilk and mayonnaise. Otherwise, the macaroni will "melt" and lose its firm consistency.

Stuff You'll Need

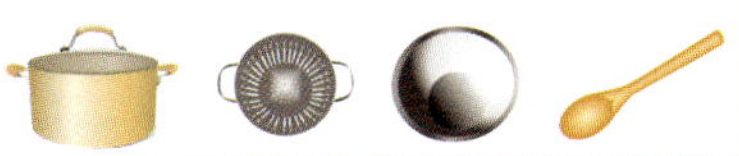

1. Cook the macaroni in a large pot of boiling water for 6 to 8 minutes, or until firm but tender. Drain in a colander, rinse under cold water, then drain well again.

2. Place the vinegar, mayonnaise, and buttermilk in a small bowl and stir until thoroughly combined.

3. Transfer the cooled macaroni to a large bowl. Add the eggs, onions, pickles, olives, pimentos, and mayonnaise mixture. Toss gently to coat. Season with salt and pepper.

4. Cover and refrigerate. Serve cold.

Perfect Potater Salad

Since the almighty potater has made it into all other types of recipes— breads, main courses, side dishes, and desserts—it may as well be in a salad, too.

Ingredients

2 russet potatoes, peeled and cubed
2 green onions, sliced
1 celery stalk, minced
4 hard boiled eggs
2 teaspoons salt
½ teaspoon ground black pepper
½ cup mayonnaise
1 tablespoon prepared yellow mustard

Important tip

The secret to making perfect potato salad is cooking the potatoes to perfection—in other words, they should be tender. To test for doneness, after the potatoes have been cooking for 30 minutes, remove a cube every 2 or 3 minutes, let it cool, then bite into it. If it's hard or crunchy, the potatoes are undercooked; if it's mushy, the potatoes are overcooked; and if it's tender, the potatoes are ready.

1. Cut the potatoes into ½-inch slices, then cut each slice into ½-inch cubes.

2. Slice the green onions.

3. Cut the celery lengthwise into ⅛-inch strips, then cut each strip into ⅛-inch pieces.

4. Place the eggs in a large bowl and loosely chop with a fork.

5. Fill a 2-quart pot about two-thirds with water, add the potatoes, and bring to a boil. Reduce the heat to medium and simmer the potatoes 30 to 45 minutes until tender (see the important tip on the previous page). Drain in a colander.

6. Place all of the ingredients in a large bowl and mix gently with a wooden spoon until thoroughly combined.

Try This Variation!

German Potato Salad

- Substitute 4 unpeeled red potatoes for the russets, and cut them into ¼-inch slices instead of cubes.
- Substitute 4 crumbled strips of bacon and the bacon fat for the eggs.
- Substitute ¼ cup white wine vinegar for the mayonnaise.

Important tip

When stirring the ingredients in Step 6, it is best to use a wooden spoon. The sharp edge of a steel spoon can cut or chop the cooked potato cubes.

7. Serve immediately or place in a covered container and refrigerate.

Chicken Pasta Salad

I like to use rotini or farfalle (bowtie) pasta for this salad, but feel free to use any shape that suits your fancy— it's all good!

Ingredients

8 ounces boneless, skinless chicken breasts
14.5-ounce can chicken broth
¾ cup chopped red bell pepper
2 green onions, sliced
20 to 30 snow peas
½ cup mayonnaise
1 teaspoon minced fresh dill
2 cups farfalle or rotini pasta

Yield: 4 servings

Important tips

- The chicken and pasta must be cool before combining them with the mayonnaise. Otherwise the mayonnaise will melt and turn oily.
- While cooling the cooked pasta under running water, stir it to keep it from sticking together.

Stuff You'll Need

1. Place the chicken and broth in a pot and bring to a boil. Reduce the heat to medium-low and simmer the chicken 20 minutes or until it is no longer pink inside when cut with a knife.

2. Remove the chicken from the broth and refrigerate for 30 minutes or until cool. Cut into bite-size pieces and place in a large bowl.

3. Chop the bell pepper.

4. Slice the green onions.

5. Cook the pasta according to package directions or as shown on page 236. Drain in a colander and rinse under cold running water while stirring with your hands. When the pasta is cold, drain it again.

6. Place the cooled pasta and all the remaining ingredients in the bowl and stir with a wooden spoon until thoroughly mixed.

Try These Variations!

Ranch Chicken Pasta Salad

Substitute ranch dressing for the mayonnaise.

Shrimp Pasta Salad

Substitute 8 ounces peeled, cooked medium shrimp (40 to 60 count) for the chicken.

Sundried Tomato Pasta Salad

Substitute 2 cups sundried tomatoes for the chicken; use Italian dressing instead of mayonnaise; and add ¼ cup grated Parmesan cheese.

7. Spoon the cold pasta salad into bowls and serve.

Green Energy

The salad can be an impressive start to a meal, a simple side dish, or a spectacular main-course feast. Here are some fun facts about this versatile dish.

Tennis Ball Salad

Ever hear of Amish Deer Tongue? How about Grandpa Admire's? What about Tennis Ball, Drunken Woman Frizzy Head, or Devil's Tongue? Believe it or not, they are all types of lettuce!

100-Year-Old Vinegar

Did you know that balsamic vinegar isn't a wine vinegar? It's made from the condensed slow-cooked juice of unfermented fresh grapes that's aged in wooden barrels. True traditional balsamic comes from one of two Northern Italian provinces (Modena or Reggio Emilia). It must be aged at least twelve years and can be very pricy – as much as $100 an ounce!

No Longer a Side

I love the story of the first Cobb salad – an on-the-spot creation by Bob Cobb, owner of The Brown Derby restaurant in Hollywood. One night in 1936, Cobb found himself foraging through the restaurant kitchen in search of leftovers for a midnight snack. He chopped up some bacon, tomato, celery, and a hard boiled egg; cubed some chicken, avocado, and blue cheese; and then arranged the ingredients in rows over a bed of watercress, iceberg, and romaine lettuce. Cobb's main-dish salad became a signature dish at the restaurant and soon evolved into an American classic.

Salt, Anyone?

The word "salad" comes from the Latin *salata,* which means "salted herbs."

That's a Lotta Green!

The average American eats approximately thirty pounds of lettuce a year – mostly in salads. Interestingly, during the 1930s, about one-third of the salad recipes in most cookbooks were for Jell-O salads!

Early Grazers

The first salads – grasses and herbs sprinkled with salt – can be traced to the ancient Romans. It wasn't long before vinegar and olive oil were also used to dress raw greens and vegetables.

No Anchovies for Me

Restaurateur Cesare Cardini has been largely credited with creating the Caesar salad, which was first served at his popular Tijuana restaurant. During the Fourth of July weekend in 1924, the restaurant had an exceptional number of patrons. By Sunday, the only food left was romaine lettuce, a few dozen eggs, a block of Italian cheese, lemons, and some dry bread. Cesare came up with the idea to create a full-meal salad from the ingredients, which he instructed the waiters to prepare tableside in an elaborate ceremony. The guests were made to feel as if they were getting a house specialty, which it was. Word of the dish spread and was soon adopted by restaurants throughout the U.S. Although many versions of the Caesar salad use raw eggs and anchovies, Cardini's original creation called for coddled eggs and Worcestershire sauce, which gave the salad a slight fishy flavor.

10. Soup Is Hot!

Making soup without a can opener . . .

Whether it's light and brothy or thick and hearty, soup is always a welcome choice. Best of all, real homemade soup is "souper" delicious and "souper" easy to make. Personally, I don't know how people eat soup from a can. The only time I *might* break down and have some is when I'm really sick. But that's only because I don't have the energy to cook.

Soup also lends itself to creativity, which is why making it can be so much fun. You can add a little of this and some of that to come up with new twists on the same basic recipe. Making your own soup is also a great way to stretch your food budget. You can often find a leftover or two lurking in the refrigerator to toss in. And don't throw out those onion skins and carrot peelings. Save them! They're great for making flavorful broth – the base for most soups. Many food remnants like ham bones, chicken skin, and fish heads also make sensational broths, and in this chapter I'll show you just how easy it is.

Another advantage to homemade soup is that you can use your own fresh ingredients, which have better taste, texture, and nutritional value than canned, packaged, or ready-to-eat varieties. Most commercial soups are also highly processed and loaded with sodium (even the low-sodium varieties). Now that I've whetted your appetite for soup, let's make some. On the following pages you'll find classic chicken, hearty vegetable, savory bean, and many more. There's even a Mexican-inspired soup complete with tortilla chips!

So pull out the soup pot. It's time to get simmering!

Soup warms the bones on a cold winter day, but isn't so great during the hot days of summer. That's probably why you don't see a lot of soup stands at the beach. As you will see, there are many different kinds of soup and soup products available at your local market. Of course, nothing beats the taste of homemade, but when you're serving store-bought varieties, the "Souping It Up" suggestions at right will show you how to dress them up.

Canned soup

Canned soups are available in ready-to-eat and condensed varieties. Condensed soup, which requires the addition of water, usually contains less meat and vegetables than ready-to-eat varieties. They also tend to be less expensive.

Packaged dry soup

Available in packets and microwaveable containers, these mixes are dehydrated soup ingredients that require only boiling water. Although they are not as fresh-tasting as prepared varieties, they *are* very convenient, which makes them popular choices to take to the office or on camping trips. Some dry soups, especially those flavored with bits of onion or mushrooms, are often used to season foods like pot roast and meat loaf. Dry vegetable, onion, and bean soups are favorite choices for flavoring dips and sauces.

Prepared broth

Chicken, beef, and vegetable broths are available in cans and resealable cartons. Used as the base for soups, broth also adds flavor to a variety of savory foods like stews and rice dishes.

Bouillon

Bouillon (dehydrated broth concentrate) comes in powder or foil-wrapped cubes and is available in beef, chicken, and vegetable flavors. Often added to gravies and sauces, bouillon can be mixed with water and used as a base for many soups.

Canned soup

Bouillon

Dry soup mix

Souping It Up!

You can "soup up" prepared soup from a can or package by adding fresh or even leftover ingredients. Here are some suggested additions to make an ordinary store-bought soup less ordinary. (For extraordinary soup, it has to be homemade!)

Broth and simple soups

- Sliced green onions
- Chopped chives
- Egg noodles
- Pasta
- Rice
- Minced parsley
- Freshly ground black pepper

Bean and potato-based soups

- Bacon bits
- Chopped chives
- A dollop of sour cream

Spicy soups

To make hotter:

- Minced hot chili peppers
- Tabasco or other hot sauce

To cool down:

- Shredded or grated mild cheese
- Dollop of sour cream
- Dollop of plain yogurt

Tomato and vegetable soups

- Grated or shredded Romano or Parmesan cheese
- Freshly ground black pepper
- Minced fresh basil, oregano, tarragon, or dill

Broth Basics

Chicken, turkey, beef, ham, fish, and vegetable broths are typically used as bases for soup, although they are also used to flavor sauces, gravies, and various dishes. Broth is made from parts of the animal that you would normally consider inedible, like bones, fat, skin, and, in the case of poultry, the giblets (a nicer term for the heart, liver, and other internal organs). Making your own broth is an excellent way to stretch your food dollar and to use up all the parts of the meat, chicken, or fish.

In this homemade broth recipe, the photos show the steps for making chicken broth, but the instructions are pretty much the same for all types of broth. The suggested ingredients for the different broths are listed in the inset below.

Important tip

When making chicken or turkey broth, carefully check for small bones that may have fallen off as the broth simmered. And be sure to remove them—unless you like your soup extra crunchy!

Stuff You'll Need

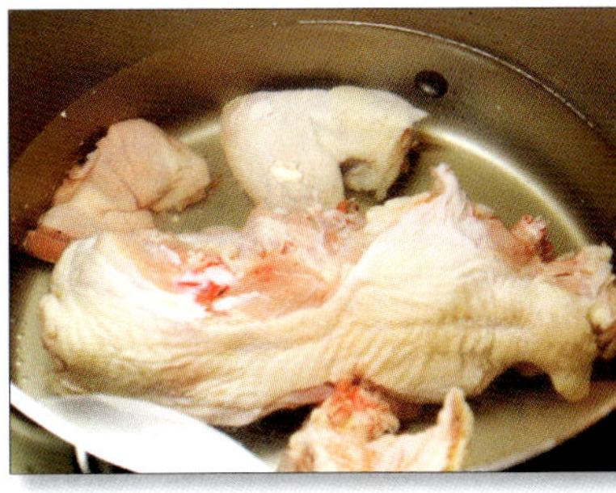

1. In a pot, place the broth ingredients (see inset below) and enough water to cover. Bring to a boil over high heat, then reduce the heat to low.

2. Simmer uncovered for at least an hour, and always keep enough water in the pot to cover the ingredients. When making beef, ham, or poultry broth, the meat will easily fall off the bones when it has been cooking long enough.

3. Strain the solids from the pot. Place any edible parts in a bowl and discard the rest. Unless you want a clear broth, cut up the edible meat or vegetables into small pieces and return them to the broth. Add salt, about ½ teaspoon at a time, until the broth is seasoned as desired.

Homemade Broth Ingredients

Use the following suggested cuts of meat or types of vegetables to make broth:

Beef broth
Shank bones and/or pieces or scraps of fatty beef.

Chicken and turkey broth
Neck, back, carcass, bones, skin, fat, giblets, and/or extra meat.

Fish broth
Bones, head, tail, and pieces or scraps of fish.

Ham broth
Ham bone and pieces or scraps of ham.

Vegetable broth
Carrots, celery, leeks, and onions, including peelings, skins, and other scraps.

Mama's Chicken Soup

This soup is so flavorful it may even be better than the one your mom used to make (no offense, Ma). Mom was right about one thing, though—chicken soup is "good for whatever ails ya'." So eat up!

Ingredients

2 medium carrots, sliced into 1/8-inch rounds
1 large onion, chopped
8 cups chicken broth
1 large boneless, skinless chicken breast, cut into 1/2-inch cubes
1 tablespoon minced garlic
1 tablespoon dried thyme
1 tablespoon salt, or to taste
1 teaspoon black pepper
1/2 teaspoon chili powder
1/4 teaspoon curry powder

Yield: 4 to 6 servings

Important tips

- Instead of using canned broth, I usually make this soup with homemade chicken broth (previous page) for the best flavor.
- Chicken soup can be served over cooked rice, noodles, or orzo pasta.

Stuff You'll Need

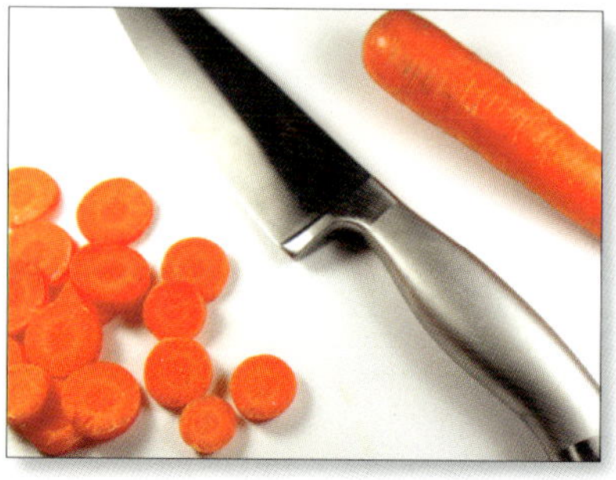

1. Cut the carrot into 1/8-inch-thick rounds.

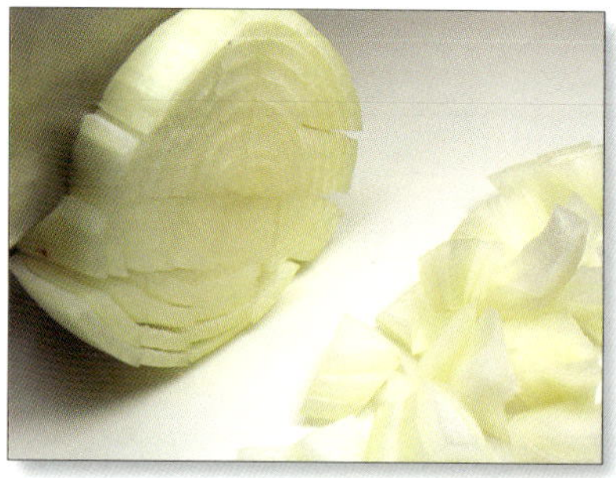

2. Chop the onion.

3. Bring the broth to a boil in a large pot, add all the ingredients, and stir. Reduce the heat to medium-low and simmer for 1 hour or until the chicken is cooked and tender.

4. Ladle the hot soup into bowls and serve.

Chicken-Tortilla Soup

What is that special spice that makes this soup taste sooo good? It's cumin, which is contained in many savory spice blends, including curry.

Ingredients

8 ounces boneless, skinless chicken breasts, cut into bite-size pieces
1 large onion, chopped
2 cans (14.5 ounces each) chicken broth (about 3½ cups)
1 cup chunky salsa
1 tablespoon lemon juice
1 cup corn kernels
1 tablespoon minced garlic
1 teaspoon chili powder
½ teaspoon ground cumin
2 cups coarsely crumbled tortilla chips
½ cup shredded Monterey Jack cheese (optional)

Yield: 4 servings

Important tip

The tortilla chips will begin to soften as soon as you ladle the hot soup on top, so be sure to serve the soup right away. For the best crunch, buy the thickest tortilla chips you can find.

Stuff You'll Need

1. Cut the chicken into bite-size pieces.

2. Chop the onion.

3. Stir all the ingredients together in a large pot. Bring to a boil over high heat, then reduce the heat to low and simmer for 1 hour or until the chicken is cooked and tender.

4. Place an equal amount of tortilla chips in the bottom of four soup bowls. Ladle the soup on top.

5. Serve immediately either as is or topped with some shredded Monterey Jack.

Creamy Tomato Soup

I'm not a big fan of most tomato soups. I don't care for ketchup or raw tomatoes, either. But I do like dishes with cooked tomatoes if they are flavored right—and this soup fills the bill. It's creamy, delicious, and very filling. Great when paired with a sandwich or some crusty French bread.

Ingredients

1 onion, minced
28-ounce can whole, peeled tomatoes
2 cans (14.5 ounces each) chicken broth (about 3½ cups)
1 cup heavy cream
1 tablespoon minced garlic
1 tablespoon dried thyme
1 teaspoon salt
Black pepper to taste

Yield: 4 to 6 servings

Stuff You'll Need

1. Mince the onion.

2. Purée the tomatoes in a blender or a food processor and transfer to a large pot over medium-low heat.

3. Stir the remaining ingredients into the pot and blend well. Simmer for 45 minutes or until the onions are soft.

4. Serve with some freshly ground black pepper.

Italian Vegetable Soup

Remember that fresh herbs, which are usually available in the produce section of most grocery stores, are preferred over dried, especially for vegetable soups. When using dried herbs, use one-third of the fresh amount.

Ingredients

1 small zucchini, quartered and sliced
1 small yellow squash, quartered and sliced
1 medium onion, chopped
2 cans (14.5 ounces each) beef broth (about 3½ cups)
16-ounce can diced tomatoes
1 tablespoon olive oil
1 tablespoon minced fresh oregano
1 tablespoon minced fresh dill
2 teaspoons minced garlic
½ teaspoon salt
½ teaspoon black pepper
Grated Parmesan cheese for garnish (optional)

Yield: 4 servings

Important tip

Although most soup tastes better the longer it simmers, this soup is an exception. Cook it only until the onions are soft. If you cook it much longer, the other vegetables will get mushy (and that's not good).

Stuff You'll Need

1. Cut the zucchini and yellow squash lengthwise into quarters. Reassemble the quarters and cut into bite-size pieces.

2. Chop the onion.

3. Bring the broth to a boil in a large pot. Stir in all of the remaining ingredients, reduce the heat to medium-low, and simmer for 45 minutes or until the onions are soft.

4. Serve immediately as is or topped with a sprinkling of Parmesan cheese.

Minestrone!

Ay. You wonna try soma good soup, ah? I-a love this-a soup. I donna know why, but I always-a think in an Italian accent when-a I-a think of … Minestrone. You gonna love it!

Ingredients

3/4 cup chopped zucchini
1 small russet potato, cubed
1 large carrot, diced
8 cups chicken broth
15-ounce can kidney beans, drained
15-ounce can diced tomatoes
2 teaspoons minced garlic
2 teaspoons salt
1 cup rotini pasta
Grated Parmesan cheese (optional)

Yield: 6 servings

Important tip

The pasta will absorb a lot of liquid, so have some extra chicken broth on hand in case more is needed. And because much of the liquid can boil off as the soup cooks, keep the pot covered during the first 30 minutes.

Stuff You'll Need

1. Chop the zucchini into 1/2-inch pieces.

2. Cut the potato into 3/4-inch cubes.

3. Dice the carrot into small 1/8-inch cubes.

4. Place all of the ingredients except the pasta and Parmesan in a large pot, stir, and bring to a boil. Reduce the heat to medium-low, cover, and simmer for 30 minutes, or until the potatoes are tender.

5. Remove the cover, increase the heat to medium-high, and bring the soup to a low boil. Add the pasta and continue to cook, stirring occasionally, for 10 to 12 minutes or until the pasta is al dente. Serve the soup as is or with a sprinkling of Parmesan cheese.

Lentil Soup

Lentils helped feed me when I was going to college and tight on funds. You can still buy a pound for next to nothing. I used to make this soup with the homemade chicken broth on page 185. There's another great thing about lentils . . . unlike most other dried legumes, they don't need to be presoaked.

Ingredients

1 large onion, chopped
1 large carrot, diced
2 medium tomatoes, diced
2 cans (14.5 ounces each) chicken broth (about 3½ cups)
1 cup dry lentils
1 teaspoon minced garlic
1 teaspoon dried oregano
1 teaspoon salt
½ teaspoon black pepper
Sour cream for garnish (optional)

Yield: 6 to 8 servings

Important tips

- ▶ Keep the pot covered unless you are stirring the soup.
- ▶ After making the purée (Step 5), if the soup is too dry, add more broth, ½ cup at a time, until it reaches a soupy consistency.

Stuff You'll Need

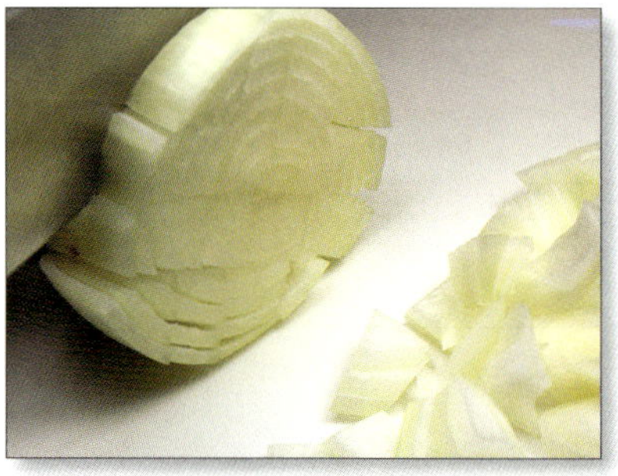

1. Chop the onion.

2. Dice the carrot into small ⅛-inch cubes.

3. Dice the tomatoes into ¾-inch cubes.

4. Place all the ingredients in a large pot, stir, and bring to a boil. Reduce the heat to medium-low, cover, and simmer for 1 hour, stirring occasionally.

5. Remove 2 cups of mostly solids from the soup, place them in a food processor or blender, and purée.

6. Stir the purée back into the pot and simmer another 30 minutes or until the lentils are melt-in-your-mouth soft.

7. Serve as is or topped with a dollop of sour cream.

Navy Bean and Bacon Soup

This was my "go to" soup in my college days. It is inexpensive, easy to make, rich, hearty, and very satisfying.

Ingredients

6 cups water
16-ounce package dried navy beans, rinsed
2 ½ cups chicken broth
14.5-ounce can diced tomatoes
1 medium onion, chopped
2 teaspoons minced garlic
12 ounces ham, cut into small cubes
1 tablespoon Worcestershire sauce
2 tablespoons dried parsley
1 teaspoon salt
1/2 teaspoon black pepper

Yield: 4 to 6 servings

Stuff You'll Need

1. Place the beans and water in a large pot and bring to a boil over high heat. Reduce the heat to medium-low and simmer, stirring occasionally, for 2 hours or until the beans are tender.

2. Add all of the remaining ingredients to the pot. Cook another 30 minutes or until the onions are soft.

3. Remove 2 cups of mostly solids from the soup, place in a blender, and purée until smooth.

4. Return the puréed soup to the pot, and stir well.

5. Ladle the piping hot soup into bowls and serve immediately.

(Thick as) Pea Soup

Split pea soup is an excellent choice for the novice cook because it's so easy to make. The dried peas don't need to be soaked before they're cooked and the cooking itself requires very little attention. Traditional split pea soup has a wonderful smoky flavor – adding pieces of ham or a leftover ham bone as it simmers is one way get this great taste. For this recipe, I use bacon.

Ingredients

4 ounces thick bacon slices, cut into ½-inch strips
2 tablespoons olive oil
1 cup minced onion
½ cup diced carrots
1 teaspoon minced garlic
1 tablespoon ground cumin
1 pound green split peas
6 cups chicken broth

Yield: 4 to 6 servings

Important tip

If you prefer this soup a bit chunkier, you can skip puréeing the peas in Step 4.

Stuff You'll Need

1. Cook the bacon in a skillet over medium heat until brown and crisp. Remove with a slotted spoon and place on paper towels to absorb the excess fat.

2. Place the olive oil, carrots, onions, and garlic in a large pot over medium heat. Sauté about 5 minutes or until the onions and carrots are soft.

3. Add the peas and broth to the pot, bring to a boil, then reduce the heat to low. Simmer covered, stirring occasionally, for 1 hour or until the peas are soft.

4. Transfer 4 cups of the cooked peas to a blender and purée. Return the purée to the pot along with the bacon. Stir well.

5. Ladle the piping hot soup into bowls and serve immediately.

Chickpea and Spinach Soup

Nutrient-rich chickpeas — also called garbanzos or ceci beans — are spotlighted in this savory soup. Not only is this soup satisfying and delicious, it's good for ya'!

Ingredients

¼ cup extra-virgin olive oil
1 large onion, chopped
1 tablespoon minced garlic
3 cans (15-ounces each) chickpeas, rinsed well and drained
15-ounce can chopped tomatoes
2 teaspoons paprika
1 teaspoon ground cinnamon
1 teaspoon ground cumin
Pinch cayenne pepper
4 cups chicken or vegetable broth
1 cup baby spinach, tightly packed

Yield: 4 to 6 servings

Stuff You'll Need

1. Heat the olive oil in a large pot over medium heat. Add the onions and garlic, and sauté 3 to 5 minutes or until soft and translucent.

2. Add the chickpeas, tomatoes, paprika, cinnamon, cumin, and cayenne pepper to the pot, and stir well.

3. Add the broth and bring to a boil over medium-high heat. Reduce the heat to low, and gently simmer for 45 minutes.

4. Remove 2 cups of mostly solids from the soup, place in a blender, and purée until smooth.

5. Stir the purée back into the pot and simmer another 20 minutes.

6. Add the spinach to the soup, and cook 2 to 3 minutes or until the leaves have wilted.

7. Ladle the piping hot soup into bowls and serve immediately.

Soup for the Soul

Just about every culture in the world enjoys soup in one form or another.

Soup Can Painter

When asked why he painted those famous Campbell Soup cans, noted artist Andy Warhol claimed he ate the soup for lunch – every day for twenty years.

Go Cornell!

Campbell's, a name synonymous with soup ("Mmm Mmm Good"), began as a small canning company in 1869. Among its products, ready-to-serve tomato soup was its bestseller. Although inexpensive to make, the canned soup was costly to ship. When chemist Dr. John Dorrance joined the company in 1897, he developed a formula for condensing soup – this reduced can size, slashed shipping costs, and made Campbell's a household name by the 1920s. Today, Campbell's soup, with its signature red and white label (inspired by the colors of Cornell's football team) is very much an American icon.

Chowder Legislation

The number-one spot for the soup served most in the U.S. is shared by chicken noodle and New England clam chowder. New Englanders take their cream-style chowder very seriously. So much so that in 1939, State Assemblyman Seeder of Maine proposed a bill to make the addition of tomatoes (the base for Manhattan-style clam chowder) illegal!

10 Billion Bowls

Americans eat about 10 billion bowls of soup a year. (I wonder how many spoonfuls that is.) And women eat more soup than men.

Spoon Away!

When eating soup, most Americans dip the spoon into the broth and bring it toward themselves. The proper way to fill the spoon is to place it in the bowl and move it away from you.

Army Soup

Near the ancient Chinese capital of Xi'an, archeologists dug up a bronze cooking pot from the tomb of a soldier in the famed terra cotta army. The 2,400-year-old soup inside the pot had oxidized from the bronze and turned green, but it was still liquid because the tomb had been sealed so tightly.

It's Made of What?

In China, bird's nest soup has been considered a delicacy for hundreds of years. Unlike most bird nests, which are made of twigs and leaves, these prized varieties are made from the dried saliva of tiny male cave birds called *swiftlets.* Built primarily on cave walls, the nests vary in color and value depending on a number of factors. A bowl of bird's nest soup, in which the nest is gently simmered in broth, can cost anywhere from $30 to $100. The nests themselves can sell for as much as $5,000 a pound.

Are You Going to Eat That?

You might be surprised at what some cultures put in their soup.

- *Menudo.* A Mexican soup made with cow stomach (tripe).
- *Kiburu.* A mixture of bananas, beans, and "earth" (dirt) – a staple of Tanzania's Chagga tribe.
- *Chicken testicle soup.* Need I say more about this Chinese/Taiwanese favorite?
- *Fruit bat soup.* Served in the Palau Islands, with the fur still on!

11. Show-Stopping Sides

My sides are splitting!

Although the entrée is meant to be the star of a meal, the side dish can play an all-important supporting role. As long as it has the right combination of ingredients, the simple side dish can be just as tantalizing and inspiring as the main dish. (And if you're not crazy about the entrée, you can usually count on a side dish or two to fill the bill – or the belly!) The best side dishes are the ones that *complement* the main course — as in "go well with it." Not a *compliment* — such as a potato telling a steak, "My, you're looking juicy today!" (*Although it's always nice to hear.*)

While many chapters in this book focus on entrées, this chapter is all about the sides. Kicking it off are some basic easy-to-make potato, rice, and bean dishes along with helpful preparation and cooking guidelines. Next comes the veg-o-rama — a parade of your favorite fresh veggies and the popular ways to cook them. Rounding out this chapter are instructions for making amazing Yorkshire pudding and a flavorful garlic bread to accompany many of your delicious meals.

One thing is certain, no matter what type of meal you're serving, this chapter offers plenty of sides from which to choose.

By the way, did I mention how juicy you look today?

Baked Potatoes

The always versatile and ever-popular potato can be baked in a conventional oven, a convection oven, or a microwave, as well as on a grill or over an open fire. Just follow a few simple steps and you'll be bakin' 'taters in no time!

1. Wash the potatoes thoroughly, then prick them with a fork in several places. These holes allow steam to escape from the interior as they cook. Without them, the potatoes will explode.

2. Wrap the potatoes in foil if you want the skin soft, and leave them unwrapped if you want them crisp. If you're cooking on a grill, wrap them in foil.

3. Place potatoes on the rack of a 425°F oven. Bake 45 to 70 minutes (depending on their size). To bake on a grill, wrap the potatoes in foil and turn them a few times as they cook. To test for doneness, gently squeeze the middle of the potato (use a potholder)—it will give easily when done.

4. To serve, cut a slit along the top of the potato, then pinch it together to open. Add your favorite toppings and enjoy.

Important tip

Microwaving a potato takes only about 6 to 10 minutes, depending on its size. The problem is that the skin is wet, not crisp and dry. For this reason, whenever I have the time, I microwave the potato for 4 to 5 minutes, then place it in a preheated 425°F oven for 20 minutes or so. This method cuts down on the conventional baking time and results in a nice crisp skin. Remember not to use foil in a microwave!

To Top It All Off

Every baked tater needs some good toppings.

- Bacon bits
- Butter
- Shredded cheddar cheese
- Chili
- Chopped chives
- Grated Parmesan cheese
- Salsa
- Sour cream

Twice-Baked Potatoes

The only thing better than a potato baked once is . . . you guessed it!

Ingredients

2 small russet potatoes
¼ cup sour cream
½ teaspoon garlic salt
¼ cup shredded sharp cheddar cheese
2 slices cooked bacon, crumbled
1 small green onion, sliced or 1 tablespoon chopped chives (optional)

Yield: 2 servings

Important tip

The beauty of twice-baked potatoes is that you can make them the day before serving. Just cover them tightly with plastic wrap or place in an airtight container and store in the refrigerator. Heat in a 450°F oven for 20 minutes or until they are heated through.

Stuff You'll Need

1. Bake the potatoes as instructed on page 200. A dry, crisp skin is best for this recipe, so don't wrap the potatoes in foil as they bake.

2. When the potatoes are cooked, cut them in half. (You may have to hold them with a potholder for this.) Leaving the skin intact, carefully scoop out the insides into a mixing bowl.

3. Set aside 1 teaspoon of the crumbled bacon and 1 tablespoon of the cheddar cheese. Add the remaining bacon and cheese to the potatoes along with the sour cream and garlic. Whip with an electric mixer until smooth and fluffy.

4. Spoon the potato mixture into the hollowed-out skins, and top with the reserved cheese and bacon. Place in a 450°F oven for 10 minutes or until thoroughly heated. Enjoy as is or topped with sour cream and sliced green onions.

Mashed Potatoes

This is a traditional recipe for mashed potatoes. Sometimes, I make them without the milk, which has thicker results. No matter which type you try, both are delicious.

Ingredients

3 large russet potatoes (about 2 pounds)
¼ cup butter or margarine
¾ cup milk
1 tablespoon minced parsley
½ teaspoon minced garlic (optional)
Salt to taste
Black pepper to taste

Yield: 6 to 8 servings

Important tips

- You can use a potato masher or ricer instead of an electric mixer.
- After mashing the potatoes, inspect for lumps. If you find some, mash a little more.

Stuff You'll Need

1. Cut the potatoes into ½-inch-thick slices.

2. Place the slices in a large pot with enough water to cover by an inch or so. Bring to a boil, then reduce the heat to medium-low. Cover and simmer about 30 minutes, or until the potatoes are very tender. Drain in a colander.

3. Transfer the potatoes to a large mixing bowl, add the butter, and blend well with an electric mixer. Add the remaining ingredients and whip for 1 or 2 minutes until smooth and fluffy. If too thick, add more milk a little at a time.

4. Serve hot as is or topped with gravy.

Hungarian Fries

I call these Hungarian fries because the French don't eat French fries (they call them "pommes frites" or fried potatoes) and the Hungarians are known for using paprika. If that didn't make any sense to you, then you're paying attention

Ingredients

1 large russet potato
¾–1 cup vegetable oil
½ teaspoon paprika
Salt to taste

Yield: 20 to 24 fries

Important tips

- Be patient. These fries won't cook as quickly as processed frozen fries, which have had most of the starch and moisture removed.
- For crispier fries, cut smaller wedges or julienne the potato.

Stuff You'll Need

1. Cut the clean, unpeeled potato in half lengthwise. Then cut each half into 10 to 12 wedges. Pat the wedges with paper towels to absorb some of the starchy moisture.

2. Add enough oil in a small pot to cover the potato wedges, and place over medium-high heat. When the oil is hot, carefully add the potatoes. (The oil should bubble around the wedges. If it bubbles too furiously, reduce the heat a bit.) Stir to keep the wedges from sticking together.

3. Fry for 10 to 12 minutes, or until the wedges are light brown and crisp. Remove with a slotted spoon and drain on paper towels.

4. Shake on the paprika and salt. Enjoy hot!

Potatoes au Gratin

The best compliment I ever got for my Potatoes au Gratin was from a baby. He not only wolfed down the first serving (after I was told he was a fussy eater and not feeling well), he also spit his pacifier three feet across the room when he saw that a second helping was coming.

Ingredients

4 large russet potatoes
¼ cup minced onion
1 cup breadcrumbs
¼ cup grated Parmesan cheese
1 tablespoon minced garlic
⅓ cup heavy cream
1 pound sharp cheddar cheese, shredded
2 tablespoons butter

Yield: 8 to 10 servings

Important tip
When boiling the potatoes in Step 3, don't let them get too soft or they will fall apart when you layer them.

Stuff You'll Need

1. Cut the potatoes into slices about ⅜-inch thick.

2. Finely mince the onion.

3. Place the potato slices in a large pot with enough water to cover by an inch or so. Bring to a gentle boil and partially cook for 20 minutes or until tender but firm.

4. Transfer the slices to a bowl of cold water. When cool, drain them well and pat dry. Arrange the slices in a single layer in a 13-x-9-inch casserole or baking dish.

5. Mix together the breadcrumbs, garlic, onions, and Parmesan cheese in a small bowl.

6. Sprinkle about a third of the breadcrumb mixture over the layer of potatoes. Next add a layer of cheddar cheese (about a third). Top with dots of butter. Repeat the layers.

7. Bake in a preheated 350°F oven for 1 hour. Let rest about 10 minutes before serving.

Throw the Rice

Rice is considered one of the world's numero uno staple foods. Popular as a side dish, rice is also the perfect foundation for main dishes like stir-fries, stews, and paellas, and a popular addition to stuffings, meatloaves, and even some desserts. As explained in Chapter 2, rice is generally classified by grain size. Long-grain rice is long, slender, and fluffy, making it the perfect choice for most side dishes. Medium-grain rice is shorter, plumper, and stickier, so it's good for dishes like paella. Short-grain rice is very round and sticky and the best choice for rice pudding and rice balls. Most rice varieties are sold as either brown or white.

For a description of popular rice varieties, including those in the Rice Cooking Chart at right, see page 31.

Packaged Rice Choices

Although rice is pretty easy to prepare from scratch, there are also plenty of quick-cooking packaged options.

Boil-in bags

This is my favorite way to make rice . . . no muss and no fuss. You don't even have to measure anything. Just put enough water in the pot to cover the rice by an inch or two, bring to a boil, then add the bag of rice. Boil for the specified time, which is usually under ten minutes. The cooking time is so short because the rice is partially cooked.

Instant rice

Also labled "quick" or "minute" rice, instant rice is partially cooked and takes just a few minutes to prepare on the stovetop. Bring the water to a boil and add the rice. Reduce the heat to low and simmer for the amount of time specified on the package.

Premade rice dishes

Nothing can be simpler to prepare than these rice dishes, which are practically ready-to-eat. Just pop the package into the microwave for just a few minutes.

Rice mixes

Dry mixes for rice pilaf, rice and beans, curry rice, and dozens of other rice dishes are readily available in most grocery stores. They contain the seasonings, spices, and other ingredients needed to turn plain rice or rice blends into flavorful side dishes.

Rice Cooking Chart

Per 1 cup of rice

Type of Rice	Water	Cooking Time	Yield
Basmati	2 cups	45–60 minutes	3 cups
Brown, short-grain	2 cups	45 minutes	3¼ cups
Jasmine	2 cups	25 minutes	3 cups
Red	2 cups	45 minutes	3 cups
Texmati	2 cups	45-60 minutes	3 cups
White, long-grain	2 cups	20 minutes	3 to 3¼ cups
Wild	3 cups	35–55 minutes	2¼ to 3 cups

Stovetop Rice

This is the most basic method for cooking just about any type of rice. Use the Rice Cooking Chart on the left page to determine the amount of water and cooking time, which will depend on the variety of rice you are making.

Preparing Stovetop Rice

- Make sure the water comes to a rolling boil before adding the rice.
- After adding the rice, stir it only once, then reduce the heat to low, cover the pot, and simmer for the allotted time.
- As the rice cooks, do not lift the lid, which releases the steam needed for proper cooking. And don't stir the rice, which will affect its texture.
- Cook the rice until the liquid is absorbed and the rice is tender. If there is still too much liquid at the end of the specified cooking time, cover the pot and continue to cook for another few minutes.
- To make sure you don't overcook the rice, which can result in a burnt mass that sticks to the bottom of the pot, set a kitchen timer.
- To make a more flavorful rice, cook it in broth instead of water.

1. Bring the water to boil in a pot.

2. Add the rice.

3. Stir once, reduce the heat to low, and simmer covered for the required time. Don't stir the rice as it cooks or you'll wind up with a sticky mass.

4. If the rice is not fully cooked, it will be wet and won't fluff up. Cover and cook a few more minutes.

5. Let the cooked rice sit about 5 minutes, then fluff with a spoon or fork and serve.

Rice-otto

This is my simplified version of risotto, but my editor said it's not properly made so I can't call it risotto (and she's a New York/Italian—so I don't mess with her). I personally can't taste much difference between this and "the real thang" . . . and this is a heck of a lot easier to make.

Ingredients

1 tablespoon butter
$\frac{1}{3}$ cup chopped onion
$\frac{2}{3}$ cup medium- or short-grain white rice
2 cups chicken broth
$\frac{1}{3}$ cup canned early peas, drained
$\frac{1}{3}$ cup grated Parmesan cheese
Black pepper to taste

Yield: 2 to 3 servings

Important tip

Rice-otto is supposed to be thick and creamy. If it's soupy, cook it a little more; if it's dry, add a little more broth or water.

Stuff You'll Need

1. Melt the butter in a pot over medium heat. Add the onions and cook 3 to 5 minutes, or until soft and translucent. Add the rice and cook for 2 minutes, stirring occasionally.

2. Add the broth and stir. Increase the heat to high and bring to a rapid boil. Cover the pot, reduce the heat to low, and simmer 20 minutes or until the broth is absorbed and the rice is tender.

3. Add the peas and cheese, and stir until well mixed.

4. Serve as is or topped with a sprinkling of freshly ground pepper.

Fried Rice

Although this recipe can be made with leftover rice, you can cook some up fresh with the Stovetop Rice recipe on page 207.

Ingredients

2 eggs
2 tablespoons olive oil
3 cups cooked rice
8-ounce can early peas, drained
3 green onions, finely chopped
1 teaspoon minced garlic
2 tablespoons soy sauce, or to taste

Yield: 4 servings

Important tip

Keep the pan hot but not too hot. If it's too hot, the rice will snap, crackle, and pop when you add it. Expect some crackling, but if rice projectiles start flying from the pan, remove the pan from the burner and turn down the heat a bit.

Stuff You'll Need

1. Beat the eggs.

2. Heat the olive oil in a deep frying pan or wok over medium-high heat. Add the rice and stir to coat with the oil. Cook while stirring frequently for 2 minutes.

3. Add the eggs, peas, green onions, and garlic. Stir rapidly until the eggs are cooked and the ingredients are well combined.

4. Pour the soy sauce over the mixture and stir well.

5. Serve immediately.

Spanish Rice

I'm not sure whether this is Spanish rice or Mexican rice but it sure is good. Try it as a side for any Mexican . . . or, I guess, Spanish dish!

Ingredients

½ cup chopped onion
2 tablespoons chopped fresh cilantro
2 tablespoons vegetable oil, margarine, or butter
1 cup long-grain white rice
1¾ cups water
1 cup chunky salsa
2 tablespoons chili powder
1 teaspoon minced garlic
1 teaspoon salt
½ teaspoon ground cumin

Yield: 4 servings

Important tip

This rice dish requires frequent stirring in the beginning to keep it from sticking to the pan. Once it is covered and simmering, stir it every 10 minutes.

Stuff You'll Need

1. Chop the onion.

2. Chop the cilantro

3. Heat the oil in a deep frying pan over medium-high heat. Add the rice and stir to coat with the oil. Fry for 2 minutes while stirring frequently.

4. Add the water and the remaining ingredients, stir well, and bring to a boil. Then reduce the heat to medium-low.

5. Cover and simmer 20 to 25 minutes, stirring every 10 minutes, until the water is absorbed and the rice is tender. Serve the rice as is or topped with shredded cheddar cheese.

Couscous Parmesan

I prefer couscous to rice. It cooks up faster and soaks up sauces just as well.

Ingredients

2 tablespoons minced parsley
2 cups water
2 tablespoons olive oil
1½ cups couscous
¼ cup grated Parmesan cheese

Yield: 3 to 4 servings

1. Mince the parsley.

2. Place the water in a pot and bring to a rolling boil over medium heat. Add the oil and couscous. Stir once and remove from the heat. Cover and let sit for 5 minutes, or until the liquid is absorbed and the couscous is tender.

3. Fluff the couscous with a fork, stir in the parsley and Parmesan, and serve hot.

Stuff You'll Need

Baked Polenta

Polenta is cornmeal that is boiled with water or a flavorful broth. In this recipe, it is also baked, which gives it a firmer texture. This is an excellent side dish, especially when topped with sauce, buttered with jam, or drizzled with syrup.

Ingredients

1 cup cornmeal
½ teaspoon salt
3 cups cold water, divided
Pizza, spaghetti, or other tomato-based sauce (optional)
Grated Parmesan cheese (optional)

Yield: 4 to 6 servings

Important tip

Do not add the cornmeal mixture to the boiling water all at once or it won't thicken properly. Add it slowly, a little bit at a time.

Stuff You'll Need

1. Place the cornmeal, salt, and 1 cup of the water in a bowl and mix well.

2. Bring the remaining 2 cups of water to a rolling boil in a medium pot. Slowly add the cornmeal mixture a little at a time, stirring constantly for about 5 minutes or until the mixture thickens. Cover the pot, reduce the heat to low, and simmer for 20 minutes.

3. Transfer the pot to the refrigerator for 30 minutes. Spread the cooled mixture in an oiled 8- or 9-inch square baking pan in an even layer. Bake in a 350°F oven for 30 minutes or until the top is golden brown. Cut into squares and remove with a spatula.

4. Enjoy the polenta plain, topped with sauce, or sprinkled with Parmesan cheese.

Beans, Beans . . . the Musical Fruit

Like rice, protein-rich beans (legumes) are a staple food throughout the world. They are impressive in both variety and versatility. Along with enjoying beans as a side dish, you can toss them into soups and salads, add them to stews and casseroles, combine them with vegetables and grain dishes, and mash them to create dips and spreads.

I usually buy canned beans because they're already cooked—it's a lot quicker than preparing them from scratch. Dried beans are, however, a better value! When you're in the mood to prepare beans from scratch, the guidelines on the following pages will show you just how easy it is.

All Beans Line Up for Inspection!

You wouldn't believe what I have found in bags of dried beans over the years. The picture above shows what I recently found in a one-pound bag of white beans. The beans on the right are what the beans are supposed to look like. The "stuff" on the left includes some of the debris that was also in the bag, including shriveled, broken, and discolored beans; empty shells; and pebbles. And these beans were nicely packaged and bought at a clean, high-quality grocery store.

The point I'm making here is obvious. Always make a visual inspection of any dried beans you purchase. Spread them out in a pan or colander and pick through them. Remove and discard anything that looks questionable.

Soak It Up

With the exception of lentils and split peas, dried beans benefit from presoaking before they are cooked. Soaking shortens a bean's cooking time; it also reduces its gas-producing compounds. For this reason, never cook beans in their soaking water.

One soaking methods is slow and takes at least eight hours or overnight; the other quicker method takes only an hour or so. The advantage of overnight soaking is that the beans are soaked in cold water, which allows them to retain more of their flavor and texture.

For both soaking methods, use four cups of water for every cup of beans.

Overnight soak

After rinsing the beans, place them in a bowl or pot and cover with cold water. Let them soak for eight to twelve hours.

Quick soak

After rinsing the beans, place them in a pot and cover with cold water. Bring to a boil, reduce the heat to low, and simmer about ten minutes. Then turn off the heat, cover the pot, and let the beans soak for an hour or two.

Bean Cooking Chart

Per 1 cup of beans

Type of Bean	Water	Cooking Time	Yield
Black	4 cups	1½ hours	2 cups
Black-eyed peas	3 cups	1½ hours	2 cups
Chickpeas	4 cups	3 hours	2 cups
Kidney	3 cups	1½ hours	2 cups
Lentils	3 cups	20 minutes	2¼ cups
Lima	2 cups	1½ hours	1¼ cups
Navy	3 cups	1½ hours	2 cups
Pink	3 cups	1½ hours	2 cups
Pinto	3 cups	1½ hours	2 cups
Red, small	3 cups	1 hour	2 cups
Split peas	3 cups	20 minutes	2¼ cups

Cooking Guidelines

After soaking the beans (see page 214), rinse them and place in a pot of fresh water (see the chart at left for the water amount). Generally, one cup of dried beans yields two to three cups cooked—so make sure you use a large enough pot.

Bring the pot to a boil, reduce the heat to medium-low, and cover. Simmer gently until the beans are plump and tender. Avoid boiling, which will cause the skins to burst and result in mushy beans.

Don't add salt or any acidic ingredients (tomatoes, lemon juice) to the pot until the beans are tender and nearly cooked. Acidic foods cause beans to become tough, resulting in longer cooking time.

If you're making the beans to use in another recipe, cook them until they are tender but firm (not soft). This will help maintain their texture when cooked a second time.

For a description of popular dried bean varieties, including those in the Bean Cooking Chart above, see pages 32–33.

Baked Beans

Preparing this picnic favorite is a little time consuming, but it makes a lot and beats any canned variety by light years.

Ingredients

2 cups dried navy beans
6 cups cold water (for cooking)
1 cup minced onion
8 ounces bacon
1 cup catsup (or is it ketchup?)
⅓ cup maple syrup
⅓ cup packed brown sugar
1 tablespoon minced garlic
1 teaspoon dry mustard

Yield: 10 servings

Stuff You'll Need

1. Soak the dried beans according to the instructions on page 214.

2. Drain the soaked beans.

3. Mince the onion

4. Cut two-thirds of the bacon into ¼-inch strips, then separate the strips.

5. Place all of the ingredients in a bowl and mix together well.

6. Spoon the mixture into an oven-safe covered casserole dish or Dutch oven. Bake in a preheated 350°F for 3 hours or until the beans are tender.

7. Serve the baked beans as is or topped with crumbled bacon.

OMG! Refried Beans

If the only refried beans you've ever had came from a can, you really don't know what you're missing! Try this recipe and you'll understand what I mean.

Ingredients

2 cups dried pinto beans
6 cups cold water (for cooking)
1 cup chopped onion
½ cup bacon drippings
(see "Important tip" below)
1 teaspoon salt, or to taste

Yield: 8 to 10 servings

Important tips

- You'll have to fry up about a pound of bacon to produce a half-cup of drippings. You can refrigerate the cooked bacon and use it at another time (like for breakfast) or add it to another recipe.
- If the beans run out of water as they cook, don't be afraid to add more.

Stuff You'll Need

1. Soak the beans according to the instructions on page 214.

2. Chop the onion.

3. Rinse and drain the soaked beans, then place them in a large pot along with the onions and water. Bring to a boil, then reduce the heat to low and simmer covered for 2 hours, or until the beans are very tender.

4. Drain the cooked beans and onions.

5. Coarsely mash the beans with a wooden spoon or potato masher.

6. Place the bacon drippings and mashed beans in a skillet over medium-low heat. Cook for 8 to 10 minutes or until all the drippings are absorbed. Stir in the salt.

7. Serve as is or topped with shredded cheddar cheese.

There are so many ways to prepare vegetables—you can steam 'em (my favorite), boil 'em, bake 'em, sauté 'em, grill 'em, and deep-fry or stir-fry 'em. You can also eat 'em raw. You should eat at least one or two servings of vegetables a day if you know what's good for ya.

Fresh, Frozen, and Canned

When it comes to produce, we have lots of options. For the most part, fresh varieties are the recommended choice. They are superior in appearance, texture, and nutritional value, especially when freshly picked.

But when fresh produce is not available or frequent trips to the grocery store are not always possible, you can still choose frozen and canned varieties. The vegetables are already washed, cut up, and fully or partially cooked, which means they are convenient, requiring little or no preparation.

Frozen vegetables, which are packaged shortly after harvest, are close to fresh in nutrients, taste, and appearance. Canned varieties go through an extensive heating process during canning that compromises their nutrient content. It also results in an appearance and texture that are not as desirable as fresh or frozen.

Overcooking Veggies

The longer you cook fresh vegetables, no matter what cooking method you use, the more nutrients will be lost. So from a health standpoint, it is best not to overcook them. Overcooking also robs many vegetables of their appetizing texture and appearance.

Steaming Is Soooo Easy!

To steam vegetables, add an inch of water to a pot, place a steamer basket on top, then add the vegetables. Bring the water to a boil, then cover the pot and steam the vegetables according to the time listed in the chart below.

Steamed Vegetable Cooking Chart

Some people consider vegetables overcooked if you can't break a tooth on them; others like them as soft as pudding. This chart gives approximate cooking times for popular veggies that are somewhere in the middle—tender, yet firm.

Vegetable	Cooking Time
Artichoke	40 to 50 minutes
Asparagus, thin stalks	3 to 4 minutes
thick stalks	6 to 7 minutes
Beets, whole	30 to 35 minutes
Broccoli flowerets	4 to 5 minutes
Brussels sprouts	7 to 11 minutes
Carrots, ¼-inch slices	6 to 8 minutes
whole baby	4 to 5 minutes
Cauliflower flowerets	4 to 6 minutes
Green beans	4 to 5 minutes
Peas	2 to 3 minutes
Potatoes (new), ½-inch slices	12 to 15 minutes
Spinach	4 to 5 minutes
Sweet potatos, 1-inch slices	12 to 15 minutes
Zucchini, ¼-inch slices	4 to 5 minutes

Corn On and Off the Cob

Who doesn't love corn? When it's in season, there is nothing better.

Grilled Corn

To grill corn, follow the instructions in Step 1 and then wrap the ears in foil. Place on the hot grill (or on the coals), and turn with tongs every 2 minutes for 6 to 8 minutes.

Off the Cob

If you prefer eating your fresh corn with a fork, remove the kernels from the cob. Hold the cob firmly at an angle with one end in a bowl. Using a sharp knife, cut the kernels off the cob (they will fall into the bowl).

Stuff You'll Need

1. Husk the corn and trim the top. Rinse under running water to remove the stringy fibers.

2. Pour enough water in a deep pot to cover the corn by a few inches. Bring to a rolling boil, then carefully add the corn. Cook for 3 to 5 minutes if you like crunchy kernels and 6 to 10 minutes if you like them softer.

3. Remove the corn from the pot with tongs. Serve plain or smothered with butter and seasoned with salt.

Sautéed Veggie Medley

This is my "everything but the kitchen sink" vegetable recipe. I use whatever vegetables I have in the fridge. I sauté them in butter with garlic and basil, or oregano, or sage.

Ingredients

½ small yellow squash, cut into ½-inch slices.
½ small zucchini, cut into ½-inch slices.
½ cup chopped red or green bell pepper
1 small onion, cut into slices then halved
1 tablespoon butter
2 teaspoons dried basil
1 teaspoon minced garlic
½ teaspoon salt
¼ teaspoon black pepper

Yield: 2 servings

Stuff You'll Need

1. Slice the yellow squash.

2. Slice the zucchini.

3. Chop the bell pepper.

4. Slice the onion, then cut the slices in half.

5. Melt the butter in a large frying pan over medium heat. Add the vegetables and all of the remaining ingredients. Stirring occasionally, sauté the vegetables for 5 minutes or until they are tender-crisp.

Steaming on the Grill

Instead of sautéing the vegetables in a pan, place all of the ingredients in a foil pouch. Place the pouch on a hot grill and cook for 5 to 7 minutes, flipping it once or twice as it cooks. The sealed pouch will steam the vegetables inside.

Green Beans and Mushrooms

When shopping for green beans, look for the smallest, thinnest ones you can find. The larger, thicker beans tend to be tough and fibrous.

Ingredients

8 ounces fresh green beans
$^3/_4$ cup sliced mushrooms
2 tablespoons butter or margarine
$^1/_2$ teaspoon garlic salt

Yield: 2 servings

Stuff You'll Need

1. Cut off the stems from the beans, then cut the beans into 3-inch lengths.

2. Melt the butter in a frying pan over medium heat. Add the mushrooms, sprinkle with garlic salt, and sauté, stirring occasionally for 5 minutes, or until the mushrooms are soft.

3. Place an inch of water in the bottom of a pot, set a steamer basket on top, then add the beans. Bring the water to a boil, then cover the pot and steam the beans 4 to 5 minutes, or until tender-crisp.

4. Transfer the beans to a bowl, top with the sautéed mushrooms, and serve.

Asparagus with Mustard Dressing

The dressing for this recipe may be a snap to make, but it adds incredible zing to the asparagus.

Ingredients

1 pound asparagus
¼ cup mayonnaise
2 teaspoons Dijon mustard

Yield: 3 to 4 servings

1. Trim an inch or two from the stalky end of the asparagus.

2. Place an inch of water in the bottom of a pot, set a steamer basket on top, then add the asparagus. Bring the water to a boil, then cover the pot and steam the asparagus for 5 minutes, or until tender-crisp. Transfer to a serving platter.

3. Mix the mayonnaise and Dijon mustard in a small bowl, spoon over the hot asparagus, and serve.

Acorn Squash

This dish is so sweet and delicious, you can serve it as a dessert.

Ingredients

1 acorn squash
2 tablespoons butter
¼ cup brown sugar
Sprinkle of cinnamon

Yield: 2 servings

1. Cut the squash in half and remove the seeds and stringy fibers with a tablespoon.

2. Add ¼-inch water to a baking pan, then place the squash halves cut-side down in the pan. Bake in a preheated 400°F oven for 30 minutes.

3. Remove the pan from the oven and turn the squash halves right-side up. Drop 1 tablespoon of butter in the center of each and sprinkle with brown sugar.

4. Place the pan under the broiler for 5 minutes. Before serving, sprinkle the squash with a little cinnamon.

Stuff You'll Need

Yams 'n Apples

The apples really complement the flavor of the yams in this dish, which also makes a great dessert!

Ingredients

2 medium yams or sweet potatoes
2 medium McIntosh or Granny Smith apples
¼ cup brown sugar
¼ cup butter (half stick), cut into chunks
1 teaspoon cinnamon
1 teaspoon salt

Yield: 3 to 4 servings

Stuff You'll Need

1. Peel the yams, then cut into ½-inch slices.

2. Place the slices in a large pot with enough water to cover by an inch or so, and bring to a boil. Reduce the heat to medium, then gently boil for 15 minutes, or until the yams are tender but firm.

3. Peel, core, and thinly slice the apples. In a 9-inch round casserole dish, alternate layers of yams, apples, brown sugar, and chunks of butter until all the ingredients are used up.

4. Bake uncovered in a preheated 375°F oven for 45 minutes, or until the yams and apples are tender. Serve hot.

Veggie Tempura

Tempura is a Japanese specialty of batter-dipped, deep-fried pieces of vegetables or seafood. It is also a good way to prepare some fruits.

Ingredients

1 pound assorted vegetables (zucchini, carrots, broccoli, cauliflower) cut into bite-size pieces
2 cups vegetable oil
Soy sauce or tempura sauce for garnish

EZ Tempura Batter

1 egg
1 cup ice water
1 cup flour

Yield: 2 to 3 servings

Stuff You'll Need

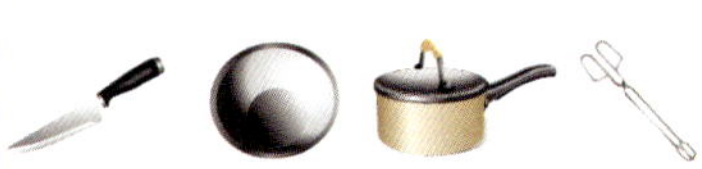

1. Slice the zucchini and carrots into long, flat pieces. Cut the cauliflower and broccoli into flowerets. Pat with paper towels to absorb any moisture.

2. To make the batter, beat the egg in a medium bowl, then add the ice water and stir. Add the flour and stir to form a thin, slightly lumpy batter.

3. Dip the vegetables in the batter. Let the excess drip back into the bowl. Place the coated vegetables on a platter.

4. Heat the oil in a pot over medium-high heat. (The oil is ready when a drop of batter sizzles in the pot.) Add the vegetables, but don't crowd the pot. Cook for 1 to 2 minutes or until the batter is golden brown.

5. Drain the vegetables on paper towels.

Fun with Tempura!

Tempura is also good with fruits, such as apples, apricots, bananas, and pears. This picture is of tempura-fried bananas with some powdered sugar sprinkled on top.

6. Serve the vegetables plain or with a sprinkling of soy sauce.

Garlic Bread

Whatsa a good Italian meal without some delicious garlic bread, eh? It's easy to make, and great as an appeteaser, too.

Ingredients

1 loaf French or Italian bread
1 stick butter, softened
1 tablespoon minced garlic
¼ cup shredded Parmesan cheese

Yield: About 20 pieces

Important tip

Check your bread right before, during, and after the suggested cooking time. It can go from being undercooked to burned to a crisp in less than a minute.

Stuff You'll Need

1. Cut the loaf in half lengthwise, then cut each half into 1½-inch slices. Cut almost but not all the way through the bottom of the crust.

2. Mix together the butter and the garlic in a bowl until soft and spreadable.

3. Using a spatula or pastry brush, coat the bread halves with the garlic/butter spread. Place the halves on a baking sheet, and then sprinkle with Parmesan cheese.

4. Bake in a preheated 350°F oven for 20 minutes, or until the top of the bread is golden brown. Serve immediately.

Yorkshire Pudding

A cross between a popover and a soufflé (and not at all like pudding), Yorkshire pudding is a natural accompaniment to any meal that has gravy. (Perfect with roast beef.) In this recipe, the "pudding" is made in a muffin tin, which results in light and airy puffs; however, you can also prepare it in a 13-x-9-inch pan as a single-layered dish.

Ingredients

3 large eggs
1 cup lowfat milk
½ cup flour
Dash salt
6 tablespoons vegetable shortening, lard, or meat drippings

Yield: 6 servings

Important tip

When baking the "puddings," do not open the oven before 20 minutes—not even a little—or they will drop.

Stuff You'll Need

1. Place the eggs, milk, flour, and salt in a bowl, and whisk or beat with an electric mixer to form a smooth batter. Let sit for at least 30 minutes.

2. Place 1 tablespoon of the shortening in each cup of a large (6-cup) muffin or popover tin. Place in a preheated 450°F oven for 10 minutes.

3. Remove the tin from the oven. Gently stir the batter, then pour or ladle it into the hot cups, filling them halfway. Return to the oven for 20 to 25 minutes or until golden brown.

4. Serve piping hot, topped with gravy or au jus.

A La Carte

Thank goodness for side dishes.
If you're not thrilled with the main course, they can make for a good backup.

Poison Potatoes?

Sir Walter Raleigh, famous for bringing tobacco and other items to Europe from the New World, was the first to introduce potatoes to Ireland. At one time, potatoes were considered poisonous.

Wild, But Not Rice

Authentic wild rice isn't rice at all. It is actually a type of marsh grass. Much of what is sold as wild rice today is actually cultivated paddy-grown rice that has been harvested and processed by machine – not true wild rice.

Green, Snap, or String

The common green bean was once called a *string bean* because of a stringy fiber that ran along its seam. (Thanks to hybridization, most beans no longer have this "string.") Green beans are also called *snap beans* because of the mild snapping sound that occurs when breaking off the tips.

French Fry Fight

When people in the United States think of French fries, it's a good bet that McDonald's will come to mind. The fast-food chain uses about 7 percent of the country's potatoes for its signature fries, and sells more than one-third of the French fries sold in U.S. restaurants each year. But who came up with the idea of deep-frying small pieces of raw potato? Both France and Belgium have long claimed to be the originators, but evidence points to France as the victor. Numerous historical documents verify that frying potatoes in hot oil was a common cooking method in France before 1830, the year Belgium gained its independence.

Rice Eaters

Rice, of which there are over 100,000 varieties, is a common side dish in the United States. It is also the main dietary staple for over half the world's population. More than 9 million acres of land are devoted to growing rice in the United States alone.

Poppin' Popovers

Ah, the popover . . . that puffy, light-as-air roll that's crisp on the outside and hollow on the inside. While most rolls are made from dough, popovers are made with a liquid egg batter, which is poured into muffin cups. As the popovers bake, the liquid within the batter creates steam. This causes the batter to rise up and "pop over" the sides of the cups, while remaining hollow inside.

That's Very Corny

Every continent with the exception of Antarctica produces corn, with about 40 percent produced in the United States. Here's more interesting trivia about this versatile crop:

- Originally cultivated in Mexico over 8,000 years ago, corn is actually a hybrid of different grass varieties.
- The average ear of corn has sixteen rows and about 800 kernels.
- One pound of corn contains approximately 1,300 kernels.
- After fresh corn on the cob is stored at room temperature for six hours, nearly half the sugar content will turn to starch.
- Corn is an ingredient in over 3,000 food products and beverages, and used in the production of such items as soaps, paints, plastics, and ethanol fuel.

You're Full of Beans

The average American eats about fifteen pounds of beans (legumes) a year.

12. Everyone Loves Pasta!

Pasta is sooo easy!

Making pasta is about as easy as it gets. You boil some noodles, add some sauce, and you've got a tasty meal in just a few minutes. I call pasta a "sauce delivery system." Its mild flavor and hundreds of different shapes makes pasta the perfect vehicle for sauce, which also comes in a wide range of luscious varieties.

Cooking pasta perfectly, however, can be a bit of a challenge, so on the next few pages, I'll show you a few simple rules for getting it just right. You'll discover the amount of water to use, how often to stir the pasta as it cooks, and how to test for doneness — because nobody likes sticky, soggy, or (even worse) crunchy noodles.

This chapter also includes an overview of the most common pasta varieties and sauces that you'll find at your local supermarket. Although you may find it easiest to top your pasta with commercial sauce from a jar, there may be times when you'll want to make your own. For those adventurous moments, you'll find a nice selection of sauce recipes that are as easy to make as they are delicious. I've also included recipes for some of my favorite pasta dishes. There's Mama's Lasagna, Stuffed Manicotti, and Baked Spaghetti, as well as a couple of good ol' American favorites like Chili Mac and Macaroni 'n Cheese. Whatever you're looking for, you'll find it here.

You'll think you've died and gone to pasta heaven!

Mama Mia! Atsa Lotta Pasta!

Made from semolina wheat, pasta comes in hundreds of different shapes and sizes. Some, like lasagna noodles, work best in baked dishes; others, like manicotti, are stuffed with a luscious filling; still others, like orzo, are perfect in soup. But the majority of pasta goes well with just about any sauce. It's one of the beauties of this versatile food. Fresh pasta is also available. It's more expensive than dry, but worth it, especially stuffed varieties like ravioli and tortellini.

Elbow "macaroni"

America's favorite pasta. Perfect for macaroni salad, macaroni and cheese, and chili mac.

Lasagna noodles

These long, flat, wide noodles are used to create layers for baked lasagna.

Cellentani

This curly pasta is similar to elbow macaroni, only longer and larger with a few more twists.

Farfalle (Bowties)

A good choice for cold pasta salads, farfalle has a bowtie shape that adds a little fun to the dish.

Manicotti

This large, tube-shaped pasta is usually stuffed with a meat or cheese filling, and then baked in the oven.

Conchiglie (Shells)

Small shell-shaped pasta is good in soups; medium shells are best in pasta salads or topped with sauce; large shells are stuffed like manicotti.

Gemelli

Two intertwined pieces of pasta, gemelli is good with most pasta sauces. It's also good in baked casseroles because it maintains its firmness.

Orzo and Acini de pepe

These tiny pastas are used primarily in soups, although the larger orzo is sometimes served as a savory rice-like side dish.

Penne

This diagonally cut, tube-shaped pasta is very popular with most tomato-based, cream, pesto, and meat sauces.

Rigatoni

These bite-sized tubes work well with most tomato-based or cream sauces.

Rotini

This bite-sized spring-shaped pasta works well with most tomato-based sauces.

Ravioli

Pillow-shaped ravioli is often filled with cheese, meat, or vegetables. Fresh varieties are best.

Rotelle (Wagon wheels)

This pasta is fun for kids of all ages. Good in soup or topped with most sauces.

Tortellini

These little pasta "doughnuts" are often filled with meat or cheese. Fresh varieties are best.

Angel hair

The thinnest of the long pasta noodles, angel hair—also called capellini—is somewhat translucent when cooked.

Spaghetti

This pasta "staple" is a long, solid, round noodle that comes in thin and thick versions.

Linguini

This long, thin noodle resembles flat spaghetti.

Fettuccine

This flat noodle is a wider, thicker version of linguini.

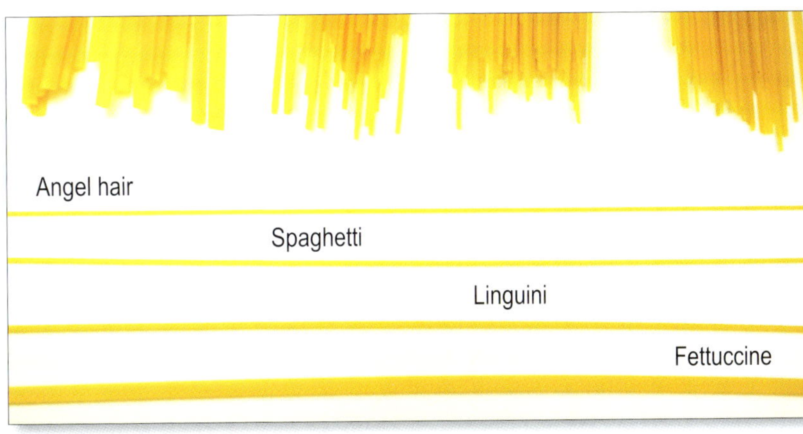

Some long pasta and sauce combinations are more popular than others. Spaghetti and angel hair are usually topped with a tomato-based sauce, while linguini is a seafood sauce favorite (linguini with clam sauce is classic). Wide fettuccine noodles are often tossed with a cream sauce, like Alfredo. And be aware that long pasta has a greater surface area than short varieties, so it tends to require more sauce.

Cooking Pasta

Pasta is quick and easy to prepare. Just follow these simple rules for perfect pasta every time.

Gimme a break!

The proper way to eat long pasta is to twist it around a fork (with the aid of a spoon if you like) and then put it delicately into your mouth . . . or "pasta hole." Pasta purists believe that long pasta noodles should never be broken in half before they are cooked. And as long as your pot is large enough, there is no reason to do so. However, twirling those long noodles around a fork can be a little difficult, especially for kids and even some adults. In such cases, breaking the noodles in half is probably a good idea because it makes them easier to eat.

How much water?

Each pound of pasta you cook requires about four to five quarts of water. So be sure the pot is big enough. Don't fill the pot too high or the boiling water will splash onto the stovetop.

Adding salt

Adding a teaspoon of salt to the water for every pound of pasta serves a number of purposes. Salt increases the temperature at which water boils, which means the pasta cooks more quickly. It also prevents the pasta from sticking to the pot as it boils. Finally, salt adds a little flavor to the pasta.

The rapid boil

Do not add the pasta until the water comes to a rapid boil. As soon as you add the pasta, the temperature of the water will drop and it will stop boiling for about a minute. When it starts to boil again, reduce the heat to medium-high to prevent the cooking pasta from boiling over.

Stirring the pasta

As soon as you add the pasta to the pot, stir it constantly and gently until the water returns to a boil. This is a critical time during the cooking process when the pasta tends to stick together. Stirring the pasta at this time will prevent it from sticking. Once the water returns to a boil, continue to stir the pasta every minute or two until it is done.

Testing for doneness

There are many theories on how to test pasta, from squeezing it until it breaks easily to throwing it against the wall until it sticks (ever see the movie *The Odd Couple*?). Mine is the most basic—take a piece from the pot, blow on it to cool, and then bite it. You'll know immediately if it is undercooked (crunchy), *al dente* (tender but still chewy), or completely cooked (soft). I usually test pasta at the suggested cooking time and every minute thereafter until it's the way I like it. Then I rush the pot to the sink, pour the pasta into a colander, and drain the water.

Draining the pasta

Once pasta is cooked, it must be removed from the water to stop the cooking. There are two tools for draining pasta—a colander and a strainer.

The colander, which is seen in the top photo, is the more popular choice. This bowl-shaped utensil made of metal or plastic has fairly large holes or slots and is able to stand on its own in the sink. You can hold the pot with two hands when emptying it into a colander. Very convenient.

Instead of having a bowl with slots like a colander, the strainer, as seen in the bottom photo, has a mesh screen. It also has a long handle, which must be held with one hand while emptying the pot with the other hand. Some strainers have brackets that hold them over the sink so you can use both hands to empty the pot.

Unless it is for a cold pasta salad, don't rinse drained pasta! As pasta cooks, it releases starch, which helps the sauce cling to it.

Adding the sauce

After draining the cooked pasta, some people transfer it to a plate or serving bowl, and then cover it with sauce. I add sauce the way my Italian friends do it . . . once the pasta is drained, I return it to the empty cooking pot. Then I add a ladle or two of the sauce and toss the pasta until it is well coated. This keeps the pasta from sticking together, and ensures that it is evenly coated. Then I serve the pasta with additional sauce on the side.

Pasta Cooking Times

*The approximate cooking times in the chart below are for pasta that is cooked **al dente**—tender, yet firm and chewy. For softer pasta, add another minute. If the pasta will be used in a dish that requires further cooking—like lasagna, manicotti, or a noodle casserole—undercook the pasta by a third of the specified time. Also be aware that cooking times are provided on the packaging.*

Long pasta	
Angel hair	4 to 5 minutes
Thin spaghetti	6 to 7 minutes
Spaghetti	9 to 10 minutes
Fettuccine	12 to 15 minutes
Linguini	12 to 15 minutes
Short pasta	
Conchiglie (small)	8 to 9 minutes
Rotini	8 to 9 minutes
Elbows	9 to 10 minutes
Cellentani	10 to 11 minutes
Rigatoni	10 to 11 minutes
Farfalle	11 to 12 minutes
Gemelli	11 to 12 minutes
Penne	11 to 12 minutes
Rotelle	11 to 12 minutes
Soup pasta	
Acini de pepe	8 to 9 minutes
Orzo	8 to 9 minutes
Pasta for baking	
Manicotti	10 to 11 minutes*
Lasagna	13 to 14 minutes*

Fresh pasta

Follow package directions for cooking fresh pasta, which takes less time than dry varieties. Ravioli, tortellini, and other stuffed pasta typically cooks in 5 to 7 minutes.

* Reduce this cooking time by one-third if the pasta will be part of a dish that requires further cooking.

Let's Get Saucy!

Now that you know how to cook pasta, it's time to add some sauces. I must confess that I often buy premade sauce, which I use either straight from the container or as a base to which I add other flavorful ingredients.

A wide variety of premade sauces is readily available in most grocery stores.

Sauce Varieties

Many sauces are available fresh in the refrigerated section of most grocery stores, usually near the fresh pasta. They also come in bottles, cans, or jars that are found in the dry pasta aisle. Although these sauces are for pasta, many varieties go well with meat, poultry, and fish.

Tomato sauces

There are many different types of tomato-based pasta sauces from a simple marinara to a hearty meat sauce. In many countries, marinara refers to a tomato sauce with seafood (marinara means "of the sea"), but here in the United States, we think of it as a fresh-tasting, often chunky, tomato sauce with garlic and herbs. Plum tomatoes (fresh or canned) are usually used as its base.

Another popular tomato sauce that is commonly referred to as "spaghetti sauce" is made from tomato purée or paste, which are thicker than plum tomatoes and pulp-free. These sauces are cooked longer than marinara and usually smoother. They often contain added ingredients, like meat, mushrooms, bell peppers, and/or onions.

Vodka sauce, another tomato-based pasta topper, contains Parmesan cheese, cream, and, of course, vodka. But don't worry (or, sorry about that) you can't get drunk on it. The alcohol burns off during the cooking process.

Pesto

Traditional pesto is essentially a ground mixture of basil, garlic, Parmesan cheese, and olive oil. If you want to enjoy it fresh, try the easy recipe on page 244. In addition to basil pesto, other varieties are appearing on store shelves, including those made with sun-dried tomatoes, spinach, arugula, and roasted red peppers.

Cream sauces

As far as a cream-based pasta sauce, Alfredo is the most common. It is a blend of heavy cream, butter, and Parmesan cheese. Originally, these ingredients were simply added to hot fettuccine noodles and then tossed. As the cheese melted, it thickened the cream to a luscious sauce. I definitely prefer to make this sauce myself (see the recipe on page 243) because it's very easy and there's nothing like the flavor of the fresh ingredients. If you do buy Alfredo, I recommend the fresh sauce, which is found in the refrigerated section, rather than a jarred variety.

Meat sauces

Most meat sauces have a tomato base and are made with ground beef or sausage. Commercial varieties, however, often don't contain much meat, so I usually make my own. Try the recipe on page 240.

Special Touches

I usually buy premade marinara or spaghetti sauce, and then doctor it up with flavorful herbs and other ingredients. Here are just a few recommendations:

- Cooked sausage, ground beef, or ground turkey
- Sliced mushrooms
- Chopped onions
- Minced fresh parsley
- Minced fresh garlic
- Fresh basil, whole leaves or chopped
- Oregano, fresh or dried
- Thyme, fresh or dried
- Freshly ground black pepper
- Fresh or canned diced tomatoes

Also, it's nice to serve pasta with some grated, shredded, or shaved cheese like Parmesan, Romano, or Asiago.

Marinara Sauce

This classic pasta sauce is easy to make. It is also easily doubled, so you can use what you need and freeze the rest for later use.

Ingredients

3 tablespoons minced shallots
2 tablespoons olive oil
2 tablespoons minced fresh parsley
28-ounce can peeled whole tomatoes
1 tablespoon minced garlic
1 teaspoon dried oregano
1 teaspoon salt

Yield: About 4 cups
(enough for 1 pound of pasta)

Recommended with:
All pasta varieties.

Stuff You'll Need

1. Mince the shallots.

2. Heat the olive oil in a medium pot over medium-low heat. Add the shallots and sauté about 3 minutes, or until they begin to soften.

3. Mince the parsley.

4. Add the tomatoes (and juice) to a blender or food processor and blend until smooth. For a chunky sauce, crush the tomatoes with your hand or coarsely chop them with a knife.

5. Transfer the tomatoes to the pot along with the parsley, garlic, oregano, and salt. Bring to a boil, then reduce the heat to low. Simmer, stirring occasionally, for about 20 to 30 minutes.

Tomato Meat Sauce

The key to a great dish of spaghetti is a great meat sauce. I learned this lesson from my mother who made the only "pasegetti" I liked as a kid.

Ingredients

1 medium red or green bell pepper, chopped
1 large onion, chopped
10 large mushrooms, sliced
1 pound ground beef
8 ounces sweet Italian sausage, removed from casing
24-ounce jar spaghetti sauce or Marinara Sauce (page 239)
1 tablespoon minced garlic
1 tablespoon dried tarragon
1 tablespoon dried basil
1 teaspoon salt

Yield: About 4 cups (enough for 1 pound of pasta)

Recommended with:
All pasta varieties.

Important tip
The longer this sauce simmers, the thicker and richer it will become. Stir every 5 to 10 minutes to keep it from sticking to the bottom of the pot.

Stuff You'll Need

1. Chop the bell pepper.

2. Peel and chop the onion.

3. Slice the mushrooms.

4. Brown the ground beef and sausage in a frying pan and drain off the excess fat. Transfer the meat to a large pot.

5. Stir the remaining ingredients into the pot and bring to a boil. Reduce the heat to low and simmer covered for a minimum of 1½ hours, stirring occasionally.

Vodka Sauce

*Here's a sauce that's **really** saucy. The vodka gives it a kick—one that is non-alcoholic though. The hard stuff is burned off during the cooking process.*

Ingredients

3 cups Marinara Sauce (page 239), or commercial variety
$^{3}/_{4}$ cup vodka
1 cup heavy cream
1 teaspoon minced garlic
$^{1}/_{4}$ teaspoon salt
Dash black pepper
1 cup grated Parmesan cheese

Yield: About 4 cups (enough for 1 pound of pasta)

Recommended with:
Tortellini and other filled pasta; Penne, rigatoni, and other short pasta.

Stuff You'll Need

1. Heat all of the ingredients except the cheese in a medium pot over low heat until it begins to simmer.

2. Add the cheese and gently stir for about 5 minutes, or until the cheese melts and the sauce is somewhat smooth.

Terrific with Tortellini!

Cream Sauce

I recommend trying this rich sauce with the "optional" cinnamon ingredient. That's how I first had it. I was in a restaurant in Miami's South Beach, and found the touch of cinnamon to be a flavorful, intriguing addition to the sauce.

Ingredients

2 tablespoons minced fresh parsley
1½ cups heavy cream
½ teaspoon dried basil
½ teaspoon dried tarragon
½ teaspoon cinnamon (optional)
½ cup shredded Parmesan cheese

Yield: About 2 cups
(enough for 1 pound of pasta)

Recommended with:
Ravioli and other filled pastas;
Fettuccine and linguini;
Bowties and shells.

Important tip

Do not leave a cream sauce unattended. It takes very little time to heat the sauce, and if it is left to boil, it will be ruined.

Stuff You'll Need

1. Mince the parsley and place in a medium pot.

2. Add the remaining ingredients to the pot, stir, and place over low heat. Simmer while gently stirring for 5 minutes, or until the cheese melts and the sauce is somewhat smooth and thick. *Do not boil the sauce.*

Radical with Ravioli!

Alfredo Sauce

This classic sauce for fettuccine is also great with chicken. Add some cooked cut-up chicken to the pasta or serve the sauce over chicken pieces. You'll be glad you did!

Ingredients

5-ounce block Parmesan cheese or 1 cup grated
1 stick butter
1 cup heavy cream
2 tablespoons minced fresh parsley
1 teaspoon minced garlic (optional)
¼ teaspoon salt
Dash pepper

Yield: About 2 cups (enough for 1 pound of pasta)

Recommended with:
Fettuccine and linguini;
Rotini and shells;
Ravioli and other filled pastas.

Stuff You'll Need

1. Cut the cheese into small cubes.

2. Heat all the ingredients except the cheese in a medium pot over low heat. Simmer for about 2 minutes, or until the butter melts.

3. Add the cheese and gently stir for 5 minutes, or until the cheese melts and the sauce is smooth. *Do not boil the sauce.*

Fantastic with Fettuccine!

Pesto

Here is a homemade pesto recipe that requires fresh basil leaves, which you can find in the produce section of most grocery stores. Of course, you can buy premade pesto, but fresher is always better (and it doesn't take long to make).

Ingredients

2 cups fresh basil leaves
½ cup pine nuts
½ cup olive oil
1 garlic clove
½ cup grated Parmesan cheese

Yield: About 1½ cups (enough for 1 pound of pasta)

Recommended with:
All pasta varieties.

1. Place all of the ingredients in a food processor or blender.

2. Blend for 2 minutes or until relatively smooth. Use a rubber spatula to scrape down the ingredients that stick to the sides of the bowl, and return them to the mixture.

Perfect with Penne!

Stuff You'll Need

Clam Sauce

Here is a quick and easy sauce that's loaded with flavor. Even without the clams, this recipe makes a terrific garlic-butter sauce.

Ingredients

2 garlic cloves, minced
2 cans (6 ounces each) minced clams, with juice
1 stick butter
½ cup olive oil
½ cup grated Parmesan cheese

Yield: About 3 cups (enough for 1 pound of pasta)

Recommended with:
Linguini, spaghetti, and other thin long pasta.

1. Mince the garlic.

2. Heat all the ingredients in a medium pot over medium-low heat. Simmer for 5 minutes or until heated through.

Luscious with Linguini!

Tortellini with Roberto Sauce

What makes this sauce so special is the Gruyère cheese, which is from Switzerland and the most common cheese used in fondue. Yeah, I know it's not Italian, but it's perfect for a sharp cheese that melts well.

Ingredients

2 tablespoons minced shallots
2 cups shredded Gruyère cheese
2 tablespoons olive oil
2 tablespoons minced garlic
1 cup heavy cream
½ teaspoon pepper
12 ounces tortellini (fresh is recommended)

Yield: 2 to 3 servings

1. Finely mince the shallots.

2. Shred the cheese.

3. Heat the oil in a medium pot over medium-low heat. Add the shallots and garlic, and sauté about 3 minutes or until soft. Add the cream, cheese, and pepper. Gently stir until the cheese is fully melted. *Do not boil the sauce.*

4. Cook the tortellini according to package directions. Drain well and transfer to a large serving bowl.

5. Add the sauce to the tortellini and toss well to coat. Enjoy as is or topped with some grated Parmesan cheese.

Baked Spaghetti

I learned about baked spaghetti (my favorite) from a Mexican friend of mine. The addition of mozzarella cheese on top is delicioso. Although you can use jarred meat sauce for this dish, I strongly recommend using homemade, which is far superior and makes this dish SO much better.

Ingredients

12 ounces spaghetti
Tomato Meat Sauce (page 240)
1 pound shredded mozzarella cheese

Yield: 6 to 8 servings

Important tip

Unless you are cooling off your freshly cooked pasta for a salad, don't rinse it with water after draining it. Pasta releases starch while it cooks—and it is this starch that actually helps the sauce cling to the pasta.

Stuff You'll Need

1. Partially cook the spaghetti 6 to 7 minutes, or until slightly firmer than *al dente*. Drain well and either return it to the pot or place it in a large mixing bowl.

2. Add the sauce to the spaghetti and toss well to coat.

3. Transfer the pasta to a 13-x-9-inch baking dish and top with mozzarella. Bake in a preheated 350°F oven for 30 minutes.

4. Cut the baked spaghetti into squares (as you would lasagna), remove it from the dish with a spatula or serving spoon.

Manicotti . . . You Stuff It!

The first time I made manicotti, I tried to add the filling with a spoon . . . and did a lot of cursing in the process. Then I figured out that I should fill the pasta like a cannoli—by squeezing the filling from a bag. My "Super Special Tip" on the next page will show you how.

Ingredients

1-pound box manicotti shells
16-ounce jar spaghetti sauce, or Marinara Sauce (page 239)
½ cup shredded Parmesan cheese

Filling

2 cups finely chopped mushrooms
2 cups chopped fresh spinach
2 tablespoons olive oil
1 tablespoon minced garlic
15-ounce container ricotta cheese
2 eggs
1 tablespoon dried basil
1 teaspoon salt

Yield: 4 servings

Important tip

It's very important not to overcook the manicotti—because once they're stuffed, they're going to continue to cook in the oven. Besides, if the noodles are too soft, they will be limp and hard to fill, and once baked, they will be mushy.

Stuff You'll Need

1. Finely chop the mushrooms.

2. Chop the spinach.

3. Heat the oil in a frying pan over medium heat. Add the mushrooms and sauté 5 minutes or until soft.

4. Add the spinach and garlic to the pan and cook another 5 minutes, or until the spinach is wilted. Remove from the heat.

5. Thoroughly mix the ricotta and eggs in a large bowl.

6. Add the mushroom-spinach mixture, basil, and salt, and stir until well combined.

7. Partially cook the manicotti 5 or 6 minutes, or until slightly firmer than *al dente*. Drain, run under cold water to stop the cooking process, and drain again.

8. Place the filling in a quart-size freezer bag, as shown in the "Super Special Tip" at right, and fill the noodles. (If the noodles are wet before filling them, pat them dry with paper towels.)

Super Special Tip

You can make your own disposable filling bags for stuffing pasta and pastry!

1. Place the filling mixture in a 1-quart (or gallon) freezer bag.

2. Push the mixture to one corner of the bag and seal the top. Cut off about a half inch from the corner, then squeeze the mixture into the shells.

9. Spoon half the sauce on the bottom of a 13-x-9-inch baking pan and arrange the stuffed manicotti on top. Add the remaining sauce, sprinkle with Parmesan cheese, and bake in a preheated 350°F oven for 30 minutes.

Mama's Lasagna

Although this recipe may be a bit more involved than the others in this book, the results are well worth the effort. The good news is that it serves a lot of people, so as long as you don't invite too many guests for dinner, you'll be sure to have leftovers . . . and lasagna is better the second time around.

Ingredients

1-pound box lasagna noodles
8 ounces sliced mozzarella cheese
1 cup shredded mozzarella cheese

Sauce

8 ounces ground beef
8 ounces sweet Italian sausage, removed from casing
24-ounce jar spaghetti or marinara sauce
1 cup chopped mushrooms
$\frac{3}{4}$ cup minced onion
1 teaspoon minced garlic
1 tablespoon dried basil
1 tablespoon dried oregano
1 tablespoon salt
1 teaspoon black pepper

Filling

15-ounce container ricotta cheese
$\frac{1}{2}$ cup grated Parmesan cheese

Yield: 12 squares (approximately 3-inch)

Stuff You'll Need

1. Brown the ground beef and sausage in a large pot over medium heat. As the meat browns, break it into small pieces with a wooden spoon. Drain off the excess fat.

2. Add the remaining sauce ingredients to the pot and stir until thoroughly mixed.

3. Bring the sauce to a boil, then reduce the heat to low and simmer covered for 30 minutes. Stir occasionally as it cooks.

4. While the sauce simmers, place the ricotta and Parmesan in a bowl and stir until well blended.

5. Partially cook the noodles for 8 or 9 minutes, or until slightly firmer than al dente. Drain, run under cold water to stop the cooking process, and drain again.

6. Spoon a third of the sauce on the bottom of a 13-x-9-inch baking pan and follow with a layer of noodles. (If the noodles are wet, pat them dry with paper towels before placing them in the pan.)

7. Top the layer of noodles with half the filling.

8. Cover the filling with half the mozzarella slices.

9. Repeat the layering, ending with a layer of noodles. Top with the shredded mozzarella. Bake in a preheated 325°F oven for 45 minutes.

10. After removing the lasagna from the oven, let it sit about 10 minutes. This will help it set, making it easier to cut into squares and serve.

Macaroni 'n Cheese

There is an easy way to make this classic American pasta dish without having to open up a box full of chemicals. This simple recipe, which is easily doubled, will show you how.

Ingredients

2 cups shredded cheddar cheese
1 cup heavy cream
½ teaspoon minced garlic
½ teaspoon paprika
8 ounces elbow macaroni

Yield: 2 servings

Important tip

Be sure to simmer the sauce over low heat. Don't let it boil, which will cause the cream to curdle. Cheddar cheese melts at a low temperature, so there's no need to boil the sauce.

Stuff You'll Need

1. Shred the cheese.

2. Heat the cream, garlic, paprika, and cheese in a small pot over low heat.

3. Simmer the mixture while gently stirring for 5 minutes, or until the cheese melts and the sauce is smooth and uniform in color. *Do not boil the sauce.*

4. Cook the pasta about 9 minutes, or until *al dente*. Drain well and transfer to a large mixing bowl.

5. Add the sauce to the pasta and stir until thoroughly mixed. Serve hot.

Easy Cheesy Chili Mac

This dish is easy to make and reheats well in a pan, a microwave, or the oven.

Ingredients

2 cups shredded sharp cheddar cheese
2 cups elbow macaroni
15-ounce can of your favorite chili

Yield: 4 servings

Important tip

This is a good dish to make if you have any leftover macaroni and cheese. Just reheat the pasta and add the chili!

Stuff You'll Need

1. Shred the cheese.

2. Partially cook the pasta about 6 minutes, or until slightly firmer than *al dente*. Drain well and transfer to a large mixing bowl.

3. Add the chili and half the cheese to the pasta and mix together well.

4. Transfer the pasta to a 13-x-9-inch baking pan and top with the remaining cheese. Bake in a preheated 325°F oven for 20 minutes. Serve hot.

Everybody Loves Pasta!

Over 75 percent of Americans eat pasta every week! Now that's a lotta pasta!

French-American Pasta

The first U.S. pasta plant opened in 1848 in Brooklyn, New York. Interestingly, the founder was a Frenchman named Antoine Zerega, who spread his spaghetti strands on the roof to dry in the sun. Large-scale pasta production didn't begin until the early 1900s – by 1929, there were over 500 pasta factories in the United States.

Jewelry for Pasta

The world's first pasta factory, Il Pastificio Buitoni, opened in 1927 in Tuscany. It was started by Giulia Boninsegni Buitoni, who sold some of her jewelry for the start-up money. Still in existence today, the company is now part of the Nestlé Group.

Sorry, Italy!

Whether today's modern version of pasta was first invented by the Italians or the Chinese has long been debated. Recently, however, a 4,000-year-old bowl of noodles was unearthed in China, the earliest example of this food. The noodles were long, thin and made from millet (unlike modern pasta, which is typically made from wheat). The discovery suggests that Asia, not Italy, is where this food originated. There is no doubt, however, that the Italians are largely responsible for popularizing pasta and introducing it to the world.

1 = 42

One bushel of wheat makes about forty-two pounds of pasta.

Mangia!

According to the American Pasta Association, 77 percent of the U.S. population eats pasta once a week – an average of about twenty pounds per person each year. The average Italian eats three times that amount.

Five Hundred Shapes and Counting

Pasta comes in all shapes and sizes – over 500 worldwide. Stuffed pasta varieties like ravioli, tortellini, and agnolotti hail from different Italian regions. Vegetable-filled versions were traditionally served in Italy during Lent and on "meatless" Fridays.

Wait Your Turn

Puttanesca sauce – a favorite over pasta – is literally translated as "in the style of the whore." Made from tomatoes, olives, capers, garlic, onions, and oregano, the briefly cooked sauce, which hails from Naples, has quite an interesting history. Because it was quick, easy, and inexpensive to make, the *puttana* (Italian for "ladies of the night") often served it to the customers awaiting their turn at the brothel.

Pasta . . . in a Swimming Pool?

To date, the world record for the largest bowl of spaghetti was set in March 2010 by the Buca di Beppo restaurant in Garden Grove, California. Restaurant workers formed a bucket brigade to fill a portable 4,000-gallon swimming pool with more than 13,780 pounds of pasta, which was then topped with 120 gallons of marinara sauce.

13. Something Fishy

Fruit of the sea.

Ah, seafood . . .

In France, this "fruit of the sea" is called *fruit de la mer*; in Italy, it's *frutto del mare* — which is how it often appears on restaurant menus. I love seafood — there are so many varieties to choose from. And talk about a food that lends itself to different preparation methods! Most types can be poached, fried, boiled, broiled, grilled, stir-fried, baked, steamed, and even eaten raw. You can even eat shark (which I hear is a lot better than having one eat you!).

Before getting to the recipes in this chapter, I'm going to tell you just about everything you need to know about freshwater and ocean fish, including how they differ from farm-raised varieties. Not only is fish quick and easy to cook, it's also rich in vitamins, minerals, and valuable omega-3 fatty acids, making it a healthy choice. Next, you'll learn all about shellfish, which fall into two main categories — crustaceans such as crabs and shrimp, and mollusks like clams and oysters. You'll discover how to select, handle, and store all of these "fruits" of the sea, along with their recommended cooking methods.

You're gonna love the recipes! There's a nice variety of basic fish dishes like pan-fried sole, grilled salmon, and shark kabobs, as well as flavorful fish tacos and tuna burritos. And if you're in the mood for shellfish, there are some boilin' hot recipes for shrimp and crab, and a saucy French recipe for mussels. *Ooh-la-la!* Fish is great on its own, but it can be even better when paired with the right sauce. That's why I've also included a few classic "boss sauces" – like a rich tartar and a spicy cocktail — that go with just about any type of fish.

So come on. Let's make some "sea fruit."

Something Fishy

Whether from freshwater lakes and streams or salty ocean waters, fish is one of our favorite foods. Not only is it a healthy choice—it has lots of vitamins, minerals, and valuable omega-3 fatty acids—it is also quick and easy to cook. Unlike poultry and red meat, fish doesn't have much muscle, so it doesn't take long to tenderize.

Fish ranges in texture and taste. When cooked, some varieties have flesh that is light and flaky, while others are firm and meaty. When it comes to taste, they range in flavor from very mild tasting to a strong natural fishy taste.

The next few pages present some culinary fish basics—including how to buy, store, and prepare these tasty little devils.

How Much Fish?

Depending on the cut, the amount of fish to purchase per serving will vary. As a general rule:

Cut	Amount per Serving
Filets	4 to 6 ounces
Steaks	4 to 6 ounces
Whole fish (dressed)	8 to 12 ounces
Whole fish (pan-dressed)	6 ounces

Steaks, Filets, or Whole Fish?

Along with being freshwater or saltwater, fish are considered either round or flat. Round fish have rounder bodies and one eye on each side of the head. Flat fish are flatter with both eyes on one side of the head. Depending on whether they are round or flat, fish is sold whole or cut into steaks or filets.

Steaks

Most fish steaks are cut from larger, firm-fleshed round fish like tuna, halibut, salmon, and swordfish. Steaks are cross-section slices (usually about an inch thick and weighing between five and eight ounces) that are cut perpendicular to the backbone. They contain part of the backbone and often the outside edge has skin.

Firm and meaty, fish steaks are perfect for grilling and broiling. Baking and poaching are also good cooking methods. You can also cube them for fish stews and kabobs.

Filets

Unlike steaks, which are cut through the backbone, filets are cut parallel to the backbone. Any type of fish— round or flat—can be filleted. Filets are largely boneless, weigh between two and twelve ounces, are generally thinner than fish steaks, and may or may not have skin.

Filets are popular because they are boneless and lend themselves to most cooking methods. You can even roll them up (with or without stuffing).

Whole fish

Both round and flat fish are available in their whole form. The skin on a whole fish acts as a protective covering that helps the fish maintain its moisture and natural flavor better than filets and steaks. Whole fish, which have the head, tail, fins, and scales, are also the most economical; but they must be gutted and scaled before cooking. This is generally done before purchasing.

You can buy a whole fish *dressed*, which means it has been gutted and scaled, but still has the head, tail, and fins. A *pan-dressed* fish has been gutted and scaled with the head and tail removed (so it fits in a pan). When cooking a whole fish, make several shallow cuts on both sides (in the thickest part) to allow for even cooking.

Farm-Raised or Wild?

Although a "farm-raised" fish might sound like a better choice than a "wild" one, it isn't, and for many reasons. Farmed fish are raised in small pens that are kept in the ocean or ponds (depending on the type of fish). The crowded environment leaves little swimming room and because disease in the pens can spread quickly, the fish are regularly fed antibiotics. Their diet consists of food pellets, not algae, which is a wild fish staple. It is algae that helps build those healthful omega-3 fatty acids. Not only do farmed fish have lower levels of omega-3s, they also have higher levels of harmful mercury. Of course, farm-raised fish are much lower in price than wild; but their health benefits are also much lower.

Meet Some Fish

	Fish	Characteristics	Best Cuts	Best Cooking Methods
	Catfish	Medium to firm texture; mild tasting.	Filets	Bake, broil, fry, grill, poach.
	Cod	Delicate texture; mild flavor.	Filets	Bake, broil, fry, grill, poach.
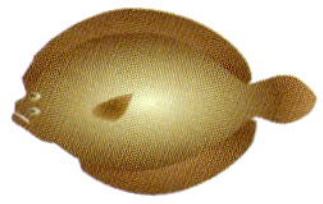	Flounder	Delicate texture; mild flavor.	Filets	Bake, broil, fry, grill, poach.
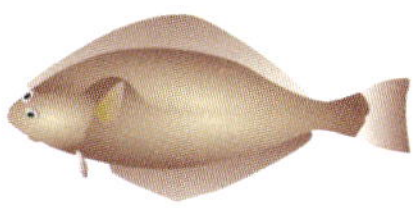	Halibut	Medium texture; mild flavor.	Filets Steaks	Bake, broil, fry, grill, poach. Broil, grill, poach.
	Mahi-Mahi (dolphin fish)	Medium to firm texture; mildly sweet flavor.	Filets Steaks	Bake, broil, fry, grill, poach. Broil, grill, poach.
	Orange roughy	Medium to firm texture; mildly sweet flavor.	Filets	Bake, broil, fry, grill, poach.
	Red snapper	Medium to firm texture; mildly sweet flavor.	Filets Whole fish	Bake, broil, fry, grill, poach. Bake, fry, grill.
	Salmon	Medium texture; mildly rich flavor.	Filets Steaks	Bake, broil, fry, grill, poach. Broil, grill, poach.
	Shark	Medium to firm texture; medium to strong flavor.	Steaks	Broil, grill, poach.
	Sole	Medium to firm texture; mild flavor.	Filets	Bake, broil, fry, grill, poach.
	Swordfish	Firm meaty texture; mild flavor.	Steaks	Broil, grill, poach.
	Tilapia	Medium to firm texture; mildly sweet.	Filets	Bake, broil, fry, grill, poach.
	Trout	Medium to firm texture; mild to strong flavor.	Filets Whole fish	Bake, broil, fry, grill, poach. Bake, fry, grill.
	Tuna	Firm texture; medium to strong flavor.	Steaks	Broil, grill, poach.

Fish Facts

Now that you have met the different types of fish on the previous page, it's time to learn how to buy 'em, store 'em, and cook 'em.

Buying and Storing Fish

- Buy fish from a reliable and busy fish store. The faster the turnover rate, the fresher the fish is likely to be.
- Make sure that the fish is displayed on ice. This helps keep it at its freshest.
- Use your nose to select the best fish. All seafood should smell fresh and clean—not strong or "fishy."
- When buying fish whole, select those with eyes that are bright, clear, and full, not cloudy or sunken. Make sure that the scales are shiny and tightly packed, and the flesh is firm and springy when touched. Also look for gills that are bright pink or red, not dull and brown. Finally, check the tail; if it's dried out, the fish is not as fresh as it should be.
- When selecting fish filets, look for firm cuts that are moist and dense without any visible gaps. The flesh should be translucent, not opaque.
- When buying packaged fish, carefully examine the package to make sure that it contains no visible liquid. Keep in mind, though, that it's best to avoid packaged fish, as the plastic can lead to bacterial growth. Whenever possible, have filets cut fresh for you.
- As soon as you get your fish home, place it in the coldest part of the refrigerator. Many experts even suggest placing it on ice. Whenever possible, use fish within twenty-four hours of purchase.

Cook 'em Up!

What follows next are the most popular ways to cook fish.

Baking

Baking is good for small steaks and filets, which cook very quickly. Place the fish on an oiled baking dish (you can add a little lemon juice, wine, or broth) and bake in at 400° to 450°F. For even cooking, try to use similar size cuts. If the ends are much thinner than the thickest part of the fish, tuck them underneath. You can also bake a whole fish—be sure to add a little liquid to the pan.

Broiling

Broiling under direct heat is a good choice for steaks and thick filets like salmon and halibut. Arrange the fish in a single layer on a broiler pan and place under the broiler unit—about one to two inches below for pieces less than an inch thick, and five to six inches below for thicker pieces. Turn over pieces that are thicker than a half-inch when cooked halfway. Thinner pieces don't need to be turned.

Seasonings and Finishing Touches

The following herbs, seasonings, and other ingredients are popular choices for enhancing the flavor of fish.

- Chives, parsley
- Dill, oregano, thyme, basil, garlic
- Lemon and lime juice
- Butter
- Salt, pepper, paprika
- Splash of red or white wine
- Capers
- Old Bay seasoning blend

Frying

Frying is a popular cooking method for fish, especially filets. Using a heavy pan with high sides is best. You can pan-fry fish in a little hot oil, or deep-fry it in an inch or two of oil. For both, it's best to coat the fish to protect its delicate flesh. Simply roll it in flour, or dip it in beaten egg and coat it with breadcrumbs, crushed crackers, or corn flakes.

Heat the oil over medium-high heat, then add the fish (don't crowd the pan). The oil should bubble moderately around the fish. (If it doesn't, it's not hot enough; if it boils furiously, it's too hot and the heat should be lowered). Cook the fish until brown on the bottom, which should take about two minutes, then turn and cook the other side.

Grilling

Grilling over medium-high to high heat is ideal for firm, meaty fish like salmon, tuna, and swordfish—steaks and thick filets are best. It's also good for whole fish, like trout and snapper.

Make sure the grill is very clean and lightly oiled (to keep the fish from sticking) before adding the fish, which should also be coated with oil. To keep fish moist, baste it with oil or marinade as it cooks. Turn it once when halfway cooked. Use a wide spatula to turn steaks and filets. When cooking a whole fish, don't flip it. Instead, use two spatulas and gently roll it onto the uncooked side. You can also wrap the fish in a foil packet along with some herbs and a little olive oil before grilling.

Poaching

Poaching—simmering fish in liquid—keeps the fish moist throughout cooking. It is the method used primarily for steaks and filets, and generally done in a covered pan on the stovetop.

Simply place the fish in a pan and just barely cover it with liquid, which can be water, fish stock, vegetable broth, or wine, and can be flavored with herbs and other seasonings. Bring the liquid to a boil, then reduce the heat to low. Cover and simmer until the fish is cooked (see "Ready or Not?" below). Don't let the liquid boil, which will quickly overcook the outside of the fish.

Poached fish is sometimes served cold or at room temp with an accompanying sauce, like sour cream-dill.

Ready or Not?

To test a fish for doneness, slip a fork into the thickest part of the flesh and gently separate it a bit. If the flesh is completely opaque and easily separates (called "flaking"), it is done.

When using a meat thermometer to determine doneness, look for a reading of 145°F at the thickest part of the flesh.

Crustaceans and Mollusks

For the most part, shellfish fall into two categories—crustaceans and mollusks. Crustaceans have elongated bodies with jointed, external shells that are shed periodically. Shrimp, lobster, and crab are examples of crustaceans. Mollusks, which include clams, oysters, mussels, and scallops, have soft, tender bodies that are covered by a shell. On the following pages, you'll get to know more about shellfish, including how to select the best varieties, how to store them properly, and how to cook them.

Crustaceans

Blue/soft shell crabs
Soft shell crabs are blue crabs that have shed their shells. They are often deep-fried or sautéed and eaten in their entirety.

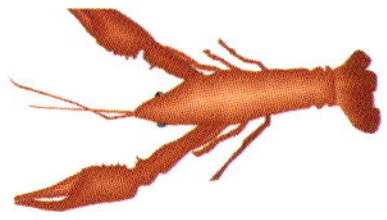

Crayfish (crawfish, crawdads)
These freshwater shellfish are related to lobsters—and look like smaller versions. Often steamed or boiled, they are popular in Southern-style cooking.

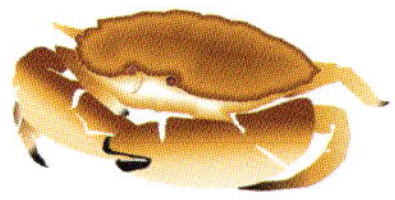

Dungeness crabs
This prized crab variety, which can grow to about ten inches, is found on the Pacific Coast. It has tender, sweet meat and is best boiled or steamed whole.

Lobsters
Found on both Pacific and Atlantic Coasts, clawed lobsters can weigh as much as forty pounds. Usually boiled or steamed, they have sweet, succulent meat.

King crabs
The largest of the crab varieties, king crabs can measure up to ten feet in length. The leg portions contain sweet, succulent meat that is excellent hot and cold.

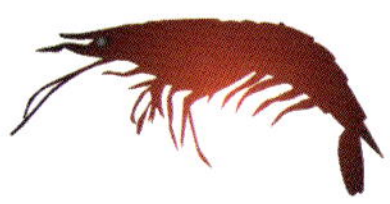

Shrimp
Shrimp, of which there are many sizes and varieties, is one of the most popular ingredients in seafood dishes. They are sweet-tasting and lend themselves to most cooking methods.

Stone crabs
Only the large meaty claws of this crab variety are harvested. The tender meat is white, flaky, and sweet-tasting. The claws are always sold precooked and can be served hot or cold.

Mollusks

Clams
Available in many sizes, clams have a sweet, chewy meat that is popular in chowders, pasta sauces, and dips. They are also baked, fried, steamed, and eaten raw.

Mussels
Mussels have black oblong shells and meat that is somewhat tender yet slightly chewy. They are often boiled, steamed, or cooked in a flavorful sauce.

Oysters
Often eaten raw on the half shell, oysters can also be fried, smoked, boiled, and stewed. The meat is moist and slippery when raw and a little chewy when cooked.

Scallops
Ranging in color from creamy white to tan to light pink, scallops are delicate and firm with a succulent sweet flavor and moist velvety texture.

Ready or Not?

Raw shrimp and other crustaceans are usually grey or light brown in color and translucent. When cooked, they turn pink and become opaque. The shells of raw clams and other mollusks should be tightly closed. When cooked, the shells will open—discard any with shells that don't.

Steam or Boil Away

Whether it's a crustacean or a mollusk, two popular ways to cook these fruits of the sea is by boiling or steaming them. This insures rapid cooking or heating of the delicate flesh—usually just a minute or two will do the trick.

Buying and Storing Shellfish

- When choosing shrimp, keep in mind that, depending on the variety, raw shrimp can be light gray, brownish-pink, or red in color. For this reason, do not use color as an indication of freshness. Do, however, choose shrimp that are dry and firm. And when buying shrimp with shells, the shells should be shiny, not dull.
- Choose scallops that are firm, free of cloudy liquid, and sweet smelling. An ammonia- or sulfur-like odor is a clear sign that the scallops are not fresh.
- Fresh clams, mussels, and oysters are purchased live in their shells. Make sure the shells are tightly closed. If they are slightly open, tap them. If they don't close when tapped, they are dead. And again, use your nose to avoid any strong smelling mollusks.
- Place fresh shellfish in the coldest part off the refrigerator, and use them as soon after purchase as possible, within two or three days. Do not store live shellfish—clams, oysters, mussels, crabs, lobsters—in any type of airtight container, which will cause them to suffocate. And don't keep them in water. Salt water will shorten their shelf life, fresh water will kill them. It is best to place mussels, oysters, and clams in an open container and cover them with a clean, damp cloth.

Shrimp Counts

Shrimp are the most popular of all the crustaceans. They have thin shells, sweet tender flesh, and are always available. You can buy them fresh or frozen, raw or cooked, and with or without shells.

Shrimp range in size from Tiny (about ½-inch in length) to Colossal (over 6 inches). They are sold by the "count," which is the approximate number of shrimp per pound.

Size	Count
Colossal	10 to 15
Jumbo	16 to 20
Large	21 to 30
Medium	31 to 40
Medium-small	41 to 60
Small	61 to 80
Tiny	up to 500

Deveining Shrimp

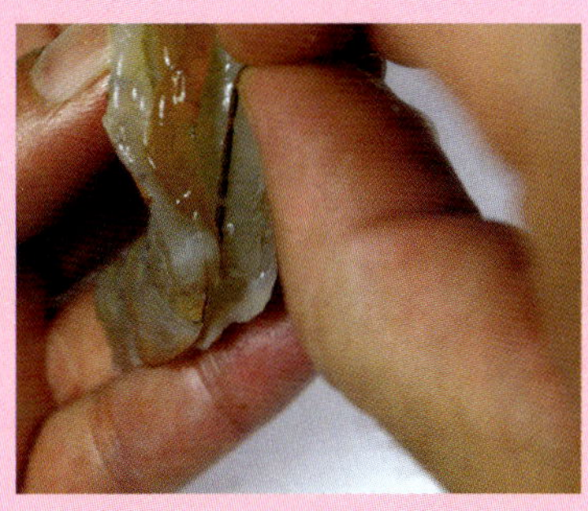

Although it is not necessary to devein shrimp, I recommend it.

Actually, the "vein," which runs along the shrimp's back, is its digestive tract and contains "you know what." Although safe to eat, it can be a little gritty. Much of the shrimp you buy has already been deveined. To devein shrimp yourself, make a shallow cut through its back from the top to the tail with a sharp knife. (You can do this with shrimp that are peeled or still in the shell.) Open the cut with your fingers and easily remove the vein. A special tool for deveining shrimp in one quick swipe is also available.

Tartar Sauce

This classic sauce is a favorite addition to most any type of fish.

Ingredients

¾ cup mayonnaise
1 tablespoon chopped fresh parsley
1 tablespoon minced onion
2 tablespoons sweet relish

Yield: About 1 cup

Stuff You'll Need

1. Mince the onion.

2. Mince the parsley.

3. Place all of the ingredients in a bowl and mix well. Use immediately or cover and store in the refrigerator.

Cocktail Sauce

This spicy sauce is great with shrimp, raw clams and oysters, and most other seafood.

Ingredients

1 tablespoon minced fresh parsley
1½ teaspoons lemon juice
¾ cup ketchup
1½ tablespoons horseradish

Yield: About ¾ cup

Stuff You'll Need

1. Mince the parsley.

2. Place all of the ingredients in a bowl and mix well. Use immediately or cover and store in the refrigerator.

Black Bean Salsa

Here's a great recipe for a fish salsa that requires just the opening of a few cans. It's so easy yet sooo good. The beans add rich flavor while the pineapple adds a touch of sweetness to the fish. This salsa is best served with any type of white fish. It even makes a dry, overcooked fish moist and delicious.

Ingredients

12-ounce can black beans, drained
8-ounce can chopped pineapple, drained
8-ounce can whole corn kernels, drained
2 tablespoons fresh cilantro, chopped
2 tablespoons Mexican salsa

Yield: About 2 cups

1. Open the cans and drain the excess liquid.

2. Place all of the ingredients in a bowl or container and stir well. Cover and refrigerate at least 2 hours.

3. Serve generously over any white fish.

Stuff You'll Need

Deep-Fried Mahi-Mahi

Deep-frying results in fish that's crisp and moist. It is a good method for cooking most white fish filets.

Ingredients

12 ounces mahi-mahi filets, or any mild white fish
2 cups vegetable oil (or enough to fill the pan ¼ inch deep)

Batter

1 cup flour
½ cup milk or beer
1 teaspoon salt
½ teaspoon black pepper

Yield: 2 servings

Important tip
To test if the oil is hot enough, drop a bit of batter in the pan. If the batter sizzles, the oil is ready.

Stuff You'll Need

1. Cut the fish into 1-x-3-inch slices.

2. Place all the batter ingredients in a bowl and stir to form a thick batter (it can be a little lumpy). Add the fish and coat each piece well.

3. Heat the oil in a deep skillet over medium-high heat. Add the coated fish but don't crowd the pan. Cook for 2 minutes or until the bottoms are golden brown. Carefully flip the pieces over with tongs, and cook another 2 minutes or until the other side is golden brown. Drain on paper towels and serve hot.

Pan-Fried Sole Almondine

This is a quick and easy way to cook filet of sole or any other thin fish filet. I use the "shake and bake" method to coat the fish with seasoned flour.

Ingredients

12 ounces sole filets, or any mild white fish
½ cup flour
1 teaspoon salt
½ teaspoon black pepper
2 tablespoons olive oil
2 tablespoons butter
½ cup sliced blanched almonds
1 teaspoon lemon juice

Yield: 2 servings

Stuff You'll Need

1. Place the flour, salt, and pepper in a gallon-size resealable plastic bag. Add the fish, seal the bag, and shake gently to coat well.

2. Heat the oil in a frying pan over medium heat. Add the coated fish but don't crowd the pan. Cook for 2 minutes or until the bottoms are golden brown. Turn the pieces over, and cook another 2 minutes or until the other side is golden brown. Transfer to a platter.

3. Add the butter, almonds, and lemon juice to the same pan used to cook the fish (don't clean the pan). Cook the almonds over medium heat for about 2 minutes, or until they begin to brown.

4. Spoon the almonds over the sautéed fish and serve.

Baked Cod

This recipe calls for a bake/fry method that I prefer to stovetop frying. The fish is less likely to dry out and I don't have to deal with the inevitable splashes that come from frying food in a pan.

Ingredients

2 thick cod, tilapia, or sole filets (6 to 8 ounces each), or other white fish
½ cup milk
½ cup breadcrumbs
¼ cup vegetable oil
Lemon wedges for garnish

Yield: 2 servings

1. Pour the milk into a bowl. Add the fish and coat each piece well.

2. Place the breadcrumbs in another bowl. Add the fish and roll in the crumbs until completely coated.

3. Add the oil to the bottom of a casserole dish or baking pan, and add the fish. Bake in a preheated 325°F oven for 7 to 10 minutes. Remove from the oven, turn the fish over with a spatula, then return to the oven. Bake for another 5 to 10 minutes, or until the fish is opaque and flakes easily with a fork.

4. Serve with lemon wedges.

Stuff You'll Need

Grilled Salmon

Grilling is my absolutely favorite way to cook fish steaks and thick filets. The only problem is that they can dry out quickly, so I always prepare a simple marinade to help keep the fish moist.

Ingredients

2 salmon steaks or thick filets (4 to 6 ounces each)

Marinade

2 tablespoons olive oil
2 tablespoons lemon juice
½ teaspoon chopped garlic (optional)

Yield: 2 servings

Stuff You'll Need

1. Place all the marinade ingredients in a bowl and stir well.

2. Brush the fish with some marinade and place on a medium-hot grill. Cook 3 to 4 minutes, brush with more marinade, and turn over with a spatula.

3. Brush the remaining marinade on the fish and cook another 3 to 4 minutes, or until the fish is opaque and flakes easily with a fork. Serve hot.

Shark Kabobs

I like the idea of eating a shark instead a shark eating me!

Ingredients

1 medium onion
1 medium red bell pepper
10-ounce can sliced pineapple, drained
1 pound shark, swordfish, halibut, or any firm fish steak

Yield: 4 servings

Important tip

Make sure the grill is very hot to cook these. It's important to cook the fish quickly so it stays moist. When it's done, remove it from the grill immediately.

Stuff You'll Need

1. Cut the onion in quarters, then peel apart the layers.

2. Cut the bell pepper into 1½-inch squares.

3. Cut the pineapple slices into quarters.

4. Cut the fish into 1½-inch cubes.

5. Thread the fish, onions, and peppers (alternating them) on two 12-inch or four 6-inch skewers.

6. Place the skewers on a very hot grill, turning them every minute or so until cooked on all sides. Remove when the fish is opaque and flakes easily with a fork. Serve immediately.

Fish Tacos

I prefer using grilled or deep-fried cod or mahi-mahi for these tacos, but any mild white fish will do.

Ingredients

12 ounces cod or mahi-mahi filets, or any mild white fish
½ cup chopped white cabbage
6 corn tortillas

Sauce

½ cup sour cream
1 tablespoon lemon juice
½ teaspoon garlic salt

Yield: 6 tacos

Stuff You'll Need

1. Place the sour cream, lemon juice, and garlic salt in a small bowl and blend well.

2. Chop or shred the cabbage.

3. Deep-fry or grill the fish (page 259).

4. Wrap the tortillas in aluminum foil and place in a preheated 250°F oven for 20 minutes, or until soft and warm.

6. Place even amounts of the fish and cabbage on the tortillas. Top with the sour cream sauce (you can also add salsa or guacamole), then fold the tortillas in half over the filling and enjoy!

Salmon with Cilantro Sauce

Creamy cilantro sauce pairs beautifully with the salmon in this dish.

Ingredients

1 pound skinless salmon filets

Cilantro Sauce

½ cup chopped fresh cilantro
1 cup sour cream
1 medium lemon, juiced
1 teaspoon minced garlic

Marinade

2 tablespoons lemon juice
2 tablespoons olive oil
½ teaspoon minced garlic

Yield: 3 to 4 servings

Stuff You'll Need

1. Chop the cilantro.

2. Place the cilantro, sour cream, lemon juice, and garlic in a bowl, stir, and refrigerate at least 30 minutes.

3. Combine the marinade ingredients in a bowl and brush over both sides of the fish.

4. Place an inch of water in the bottom of a large pot, set a steamer basket on top, then add the salmon. Bring to a boil, cover the pot, and reduce the heat to medium-low. Simmer the fish 5 to 8 minutes, or until it is opaque and flakes with a fork.

5. Transfer the filets to a platter. Spoon the cilantro sauce on top and serve with lemon wedges.

Ahi Tuna Burritos

I had a friend who could catch his limit in fish when the tuna were running. Every week for several months, he would give me at least two pounds of fresh tuna. So I became very creative with my tuna recipes . . . this is one of my favorites.

Ingredients

¼ cup chopped fresh cilantro
1 medium onion, minced
1 pound ahi, albacore, yellow tail, or bluefin tuna
2 tablespoons olive oil
2 tablespoons chili powder
1 tablespoon garlic salt
12-ounce can black beans, drained
8 ounces shredded Monterey Jack cheese
8 flour tortillas

Suggested Toppings

Avocado slices
Guacamole
Salsa
Shredded Monterey Jack cheese
Sour cream

Yield: 8 burritos

Stuff You'll Need

1. Chop the cilantro.

2. Mince the onion.

3. Cut the fish into small pieces.

4. Heat the olive oil in a large frying pan over medium heat. Add the onion, fish, chili powder, and garlic salt.

5. Stir the ingredients with a wooden spoon. As the fish begins to cook, use the spoon to break it into flakes.

6. Lay each tortilla on a sheet of foil (make the sheets a few inches wider than the tortillas). On top of each tortilla, place 2 tablespoons fish, 1 tablespoon black beans, 2 tablespoons cheese, and 1 teaspoon cilantro. Roll up the burritos and seal with foil.

7. Place the foil-wrapped burritos directly on the rack of a preheated 350°F oven for 20 minutes or until heated through. Serve immediately.

Boiled Shrimp

Like most shellfish, shrimp cooks in a matter of minutes, no matter what method you use. Boiling in water is one of the most basic ways. If you want to spice things up with a down-home Southern-style "shrimp boil," just add a few seasonings to the cooking water. For a real authentic shrimp (or crawfish) boil, add ears of corn as well as whole unpeeled new potatoes, onions, and heads of garlic to the pot . . . then invite a bunch of friends over to share it!

Ingredients

1 pound large raw shrimp, unpeeled and deveined (see page 261 for deveining instructions)
1 tablespoon dried oregano
1 tablespoon salt (sea salt is preferred)
2 teaspoons dry mustard
1 teaspoon cayenne pepper
1 teaspoon black pepper
Lemon wedges for garnish

Yield: 2 servings

Stuff You'll Need

1. Fill a large pot or Dutch oven halfway with water. Add the spices, bring to a boil, then immediately reduce the heat to medium.

2. Add the shrimp and simmer for 2 or 3 minutes, or until they turn pink.

3. Remove the shrimp with a slotted spoon or drain in a colander.

4. Transfer the shrimp to a bowl, add some lemon wedges, then peel and eat!

Shrimp Gumbo

Everybody loves this spicy, flavorful Cajun dish. If you can't find andouille sausage, use a spicy smoked sausage instead.

Ingredients

8 ounces andouille sausage
1 pound large shrimp, peeled and deveined (see page 261 for deveining instructions)
4 tablespoons butter
⅓ cup all-purpose flour
14.5-ounce can diced tomatoes, with juice
10-ounce package frozen sliced okra, thawed (about 2 cups)
2 cups chopped onion
1 tablespoon minced garlic
¼ teaspoon cayenne pepper
2 cups water

Yield: 6 servings

1. Cut the sausage into ¼-inch thick rounds.

2. Melt the butter in a large pot over medium heat. Add the flour and cook, stirring often, for about 2 minutes, or until it begins to brown.

3. Add the tomatoes, okra, onions, garlic, cayenne pepper, and water, and stir until well mixed. Cook uncovered for 15 minutes.

4. Add the sausage and shrimp to the pot and cook another 10 minutes.

4. Spoon the piping hot gumbo into bowls as is or over rice.

Stuff You'll Need

Greek Shrimp

The addition of feta cheese gives this dish some tang . . . and tang is good!

Ingredients

2 medium tomatoes, diced
1 large onion, chopped
1 tablespoon chopped basil
1 tablespoon minced garlic
1 tablespoon olive oil
12 ounces medium to large shrimp, peeled and deveined (see page 261 for deveining instructions)
⅓ cup crumbled feta cheese

Yield: 2 to 3 servings

1. Dice the tomatoes.

2. Chop the onion.

3. Place all of the ingredients except the shrimp and feta cheese in a medium saucepan over medium-low heat. Simmer for 5 minutes.

4. Arrange the shrimp in the bottom of a casserole dish. Spoon the tomato sauce on top and sprinkle with feta cheese. Bake in a preheated 325°F oven for 30 minutes or until the sauce is hot and bubbly.

Stuff You'll Need

Shrimp Scampi

This dish came from a houseguest who made dinner one night. He said it was the only recipe he knew. If you know only one recipe, this is a good one.

Ingredients

- ¾ cup breadcrumbs
- ¼ cup shredded Parmesan cheese
- 1 tablespoon minced garlic
- ¼ cup olive oil
- 12 ounces medium to large raw shrimp, peeled and deveined (see page 261 for deveining instructions)
- 2 tablespoons butter, cut into small pieces

Yield: 2 to 3 servings

Stuff You'll Need

1. Place the breadcrumbs, Parmesan cheese, and garlic in a small bowl and mix well.

2. Cover the bottom of a casserole or baking dish with olive oil and arrange the shrimp on top.

3. Cover the shrimp with the breadcrumb mixture and top with the butter. Bake in a preheated 325°F oven for 25 minutes, or until the shrimp is cooked and the breadcrumbs are golden brown.

4. Stir the mixture before serving.

King Crab with Butter Sauce

Most crab is cooked before you buy it—especially varieties like king crab and stone crab—so all you have to do is heat it up.

Ingredients

1½ to 2 pounds precooked king crab legs
Lemon wedges

Butter Sauce

1 stick (½ cup) butter
1 teaspoon minced garlic
1 teaspoon lemon juice

Yield: 2 servings

Important tips

- For this dish, you will need a nut or seafood cracker to break the shells.
- Although using a small fish fork to remove the meat from the shells is recommended, it isn't necessary.

Stuff You'll Need

1. Heat the butter, garlic, and lemon juice in a saucepan over medium-low heat. Stir until well blended.

2. Place an inch of water in the bottom of a large pot, set a steamer basket on top, and bring to a boil. Reduce the heat to medium and add the crab legs. Cover and steam 3 to 5 minutes or until heated through. Remove the crab from the pot with tongs.

3. Serve with lemon wedges and the flavored butter sauce.

Mussels au Currie

The French love "moules" and they prepare them in hundreds of different ways. I discovered this dish when I was in Northern France. It's easy and flavorful.

Ingredients

1 pound fresh mussels, scrubbed well
8 ounces coconut milk or heavy cream
1 tablespoon mild curry powder
1 teaspoon salt

Yield: 2 servings

Important tip

When buying live fresh mussels, make sure the shells are closed. Discard those that are open. (If the shells are open a little, give them a tap, which should cause them to close. If they don't, throw them out.) When the mussels are cooked, the shells will open—throw out any that don't.

1. Place the coconut milk, curry powder, and salt in a saucepan over very low heat. Stir and simmer about 2 minutes, or until the sauce is hot.

2. Bring 2 inches of water to boil in a large pot. Add the mussels, cover the pot, and cook about 1 minute, or until the shells open.

3. Using a slotted spoon, transfer the mussels to a serving bowl. Cover with the curry sauce and serve.

See-Food Diet

My favorite diet throughout the years has always been the "see-food diet." I see food, and I eat it!

Mudbug Madness

Every Memorial Day weekend, the Mudbug Madness Festival is held in Shreveport, Louisiana. Dedicated to mudbugs, also known as *crayfish* or *crawdaddys,* the four-day street fair is home to Cajun music, regional cuisine, and lots of fun-filled competitions. Featured are mudbug-eating contests for men, women, and children. For the adult competitions, the first entrant to eat fifteen pounds of crayfish within thirty minutes is crowned the winner.

Lobsters, Beware!

Held in Rockland, Maine, the annual five-day Maine Lobster Festival attracts crowds of more than 70,000. On average, about twelve tons of these "bugs" are consumed there each year!

That's a Big Snail

The conch (pronounced *konk*) is the second-most consumed snail after escargot. It's very popular in the Caribbean, where conch chowder and fritters are traditional island favorites.

Does That Come with Tartar Sauce?

In January 2013, a 489-pound bluefin tuna was sold during the first auction of the year at Tsukiji Market – Japan's largest wholesale fish mart. One of the country's popular sushi restaurant chains bought the fish for the record-breaking price of $1.76 million (155.4 million yen) – that comes to nearly $3,603 a pound (or $225 an ounce)!

Popular Fish

Salmon is the most popular fish in the United States. Shrimp ranks as the country's favorite shellfish.

That's a Lotta Tuna

To date, a 1,500-pound bluefin tuna caught off Nova Scotia in 1979 is the largest tuna on record.

Not So Shrimpy

The world consumes an average of 5 billion pounds of shrimp each year. The U.S. alone accounts for over 1 billion pounds – of which 80 percent is served in restaurants.

The Oldest (Formerly) Living Animal

In October 2007, a team of British marine biologists found what was possibly the world's oldest living animal – an ocean quahog clam that turned out to be over 405 years old. Unfortunately, the team realized the clam's extreme age only after cutting through the shell to count its growth rings. The largest clam ever recorded was found in Okinawa in 1956 and weighed 750 pounds.

I Vote for Mr. Mussels

During elections in ancient Greece, votes were cast by scratching the names of candidates inside mussel shells.

Sexy Oysters

Oysters are among the most prolific of all creatures, with females producing hundreds of millions of eggs in a lifetime!

14. Chicken Tonight

Chickening out . . .

Taking any big step in life — like choosing a college or taking a job or committing to a relationship — can be a little intimidating. Hopefully, once you've made your decision and taken that step, you're glad you didn't "chicken out." Speaking of chicken (*nice transition, huh?*), this chapter is all about this poultry variety, which kinda gets a bum rap. Take its name for example. Why do we call it "chicken" when it's anything but timid? If you've ever met one up close you'd understand. I learned this fact the hard way (*awww, look at the cute little chicken . . . OW!*). Chicken also falls into a category of birds that people call "fowl." Now that's not very nice, is it?

In this chapter, you'll discover all things chicken — the different types, the various parts, and even the proper way to cut up a whole bird. You will also learn the many delicious ways to prepare chicken, as well as safe handling guidelines and cooking practices.

And the recipes are great. They will take you on an international tour of delectable chicken delights. Traveling "chicken-style" through Greece, Italy, France, India, and, of course, the good ol' US of A, you'll learn to barbecue, roast, fry, poach, and sauté this versatile bird. The dishes are easy to prepare and really delicious, so be sure to give them all a try.

Don't "chicken out" on me (*bawk, bawwwwwk*) and don't worry — you can't "fowl" things up, even if you're being "henpecked" to hurry and get dinner on the table!

Fowl Play

Chicken belongs to a group of domestic birds (or "boyds" if you come from Brooklyn) known as "fowl" or "poultry." Some of these boyds are game for hunters while others are farmed. Here are some poultry varieties you can find in most markets and on restaurant menus. The more exotic types are often available at gourmet markets.

Cornish (not) Game Hens

Although their name implies that they are wild, Cornish game hens are actually farm raised. Looking like miniature chickens, these birds are a hybrid of the very small Cornish and White Rock breeds. Often found in the freezer section of most supermarkets, Cornish hens are best roasted or broiled.

Duck!

A popular choice in French and Chinese cuisines, duck or duckling has dark, fatty meat that is stronger tasting than chicken. (Because ducks are waterfowl, they have an extra layer of fat under their skin for warmth.) In the United States, Peking duck, which is of Chinese origin, is the most popular type. Because most of this breed is farmed in Long Island, New York, it is often called "Long Island duck." Ducks typically weigh between three and five pounds, and are usually roasted or broiled.

Goose Me

Like ducks, geese are a type of waterfowl only much larger (between five and eighteen pounds). Popular in Europe, goose is traditionally served on Christmas in many countries. Most geese that are marketed in the US are frozen, although a specialty butcher can order them fresh. Because they are so fatty, roasting is the preferred cooking method.

Ostrich?

These big birds are farmed all over the world, including the United States. The meat, which is closer in taste to red meat than it is to chicken, is mild tasting and low in fat. Have you ever tried an ostrich burger? I have!

Pleasant Pheasants

Usually caught in the wild, pheasants are mild flavored, low in fat, and, yes, they taste like chicken! Farm-raised varieties are not as flavorful. The male pheasant is larger than the female, but the female's flesh is plumper and juicier. Weighing from two to five pounds, pheasant is sometimes sold in specialty butcher shops and occasionally appears on the menu of upscale restaurants. Roasting is the common cooking method for this bird.

Quintessential Quail

A small, mid-sized bird of the partridge family, quail is both farmed and hunted in the wild. Its meat is mild, sweet, and delicious, and best when roasted or broiled. Its eggs are considered a delicacy. Quail can usually be ordered through a specialty butcher.

Jive Turkey

In the United States, turkeys provide the fourth most popular meat after chicken, beef, and pork. Did you know that the average American consumes about seventeen pounds of turkey per year? That means there's a Tom with your name on it somewhere. Turkey is available in many forms, including a few you wouldn't normally expect, like burgers, hot dogs, and bacon. Mild and low in fat, the white meat found in the breast and wings tends to be more prized than the dark meat, which is found in the leg quarters. Dark meat is fattier and has a gamey flavor. (Some people prefer it for this very reason.) For most families, Thanksgiving dinner would be unthinkable without a roasted turkey. (For a great holiday feast with turkey and all the delicious trimmings, see Chapter 17, beginning on page 345.)

A whole chicken is equal to . . .

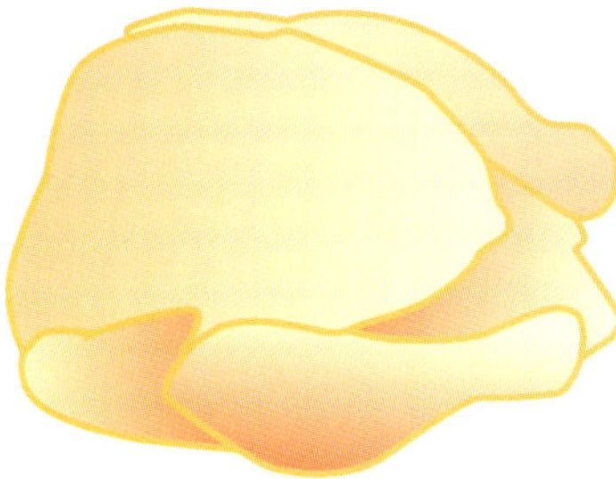

Whole chickens come in many varieties. *Fryers* and *broilers* are young chickens and very tender. *Roasters* are older, meatier, and more flavorful that broilers or fryers. They are also higher in fat. *Capons* are male chickens that have their (*ahem*) "nuggets" removed when they are a few weeks old. They are then fed a high-fat diet for many months, and become full-breasted birds with tender, flavorful meat. Most whole chickens come with *giblets*, which are the edible innards (liver, gizzard, heart, and neck). Giblets are usually placed in a little packet and tucked into the bird's empty cavity.

. . . the sum of its parts.

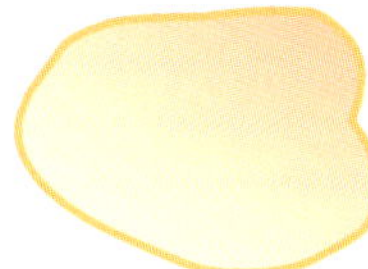

Breasts contain white meat and are available whole, halved, or quartered. They come with or without skin and with or without bones. Whole breasts are often fried, barbecued, or roasted. Low in fat, breast meat also comes in variety of cuts, such as uniformly sliced *cutlets*, thin strips or *tenders*, and bite-size *nuggets*. These boneless cuts are often grilled, sautéed, or breaded and fried.

Wings contain white meat, but there isn't a lot of it. They are popular when barbecued or fried.

Legs, also called *drumsticks*, are the bottom portion of the leg quarter and attached to the thigh. They consist of dark meat and are famously good when barbecued or fried. Also very convenient to pick up and eat on the run.

Thighs contain dark meat, which is juicier than white meat (and higher in fat). Like legs, thighs are often fried or barbecued.

For information on safe handling and storage, see page 44–45

Testing for Doneness

The cooking time for chicken varies, depending on the thickness of the cut, the amount of bone that is present, and the cooking method used.

- To test cutlets, tenders, and other thin cuts, cut into the meat with a knife. If the inside is white with no sign of pink, the meat is cooked.
- To test chicken parts or a whole chicken, stick a fork into the thickest area (on a whole chicken, this is the inner thigh). If the juices run clear, it is done; but if the juice is pink or red (as shown above) it's not ready.
- To test a whole roasted chicken, place a meat thermometer in the thickest part of the thigh. The chicken is done at 180°F. You can remove the bird at 170° to 175°F, as it will continue to cook as it "rests" for a few minutes.

Cutting Up a Flippin' Bird

Smaller fowl like quail and Cornish hens are best roasted whole in the oven. Larger birds like turkeys and chickens can also be roasted whole, but are often cut up into individual parts and cooked in lots of different ways. You can buy individual chicken and turkey parts in most grocery stores, but if you want to save a few pennies and cut up the whole bird yourself, the steps on the right will show you how. And oh, if you need to cut apart a really big bird like an ostrich, either consult your ostrich cooking manual or call a trained, licensed professional.

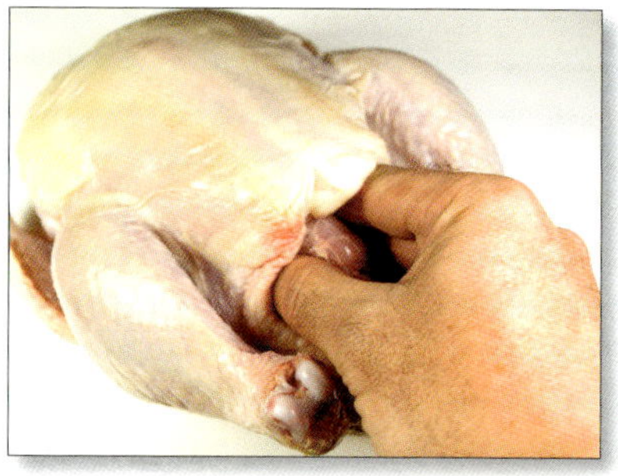

1. Check the cavity between the legs of the prepared bird. Often, the giblets (heart, liver, gizzard, neck) are placed in a small packet and stored there. Remove the packet.

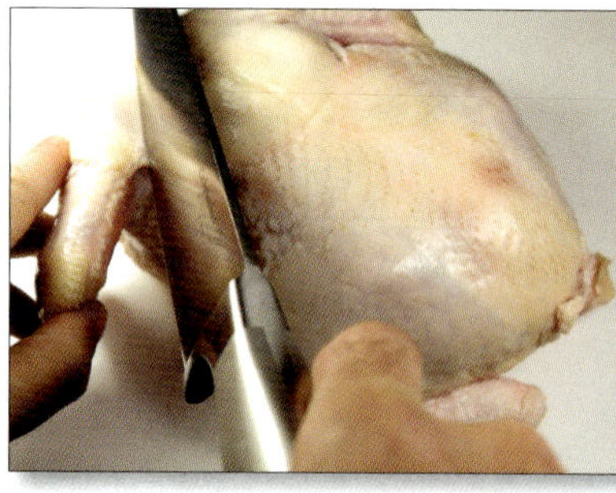

2. Find the wing joint, and cut the flesh all the way around it.

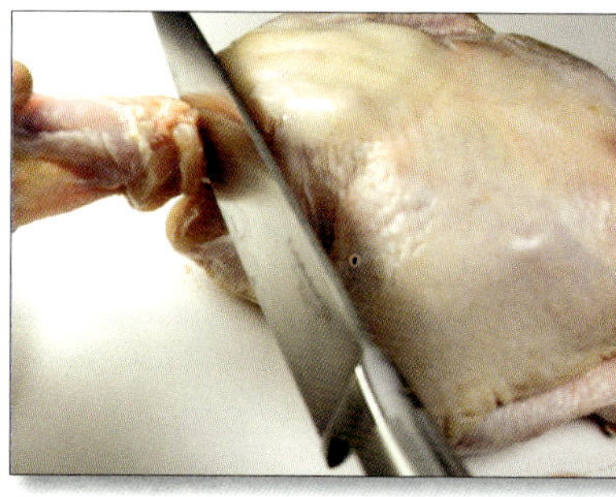

3. Bend the wing back to dislocate the joint—you'll hear a pop (*ewwww!*). Cut through the joint to remove the wing.

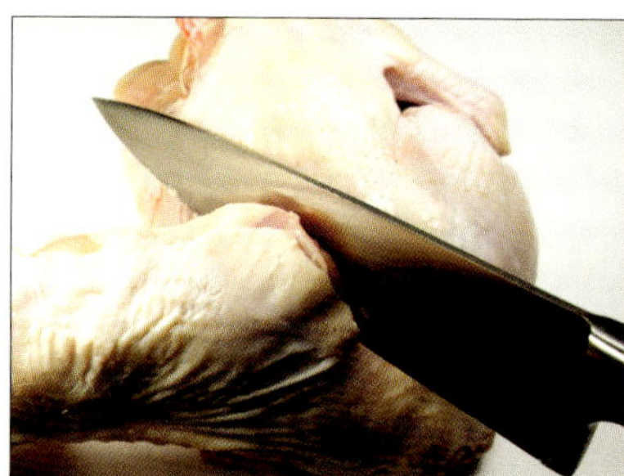

4. To remove the leg quarter (thigh and leg), cut around the thigh joint, pop it, then cut this section from the body. To separate the leg from the thigh, first flex the leg. Then cut through the joint between these two sections.

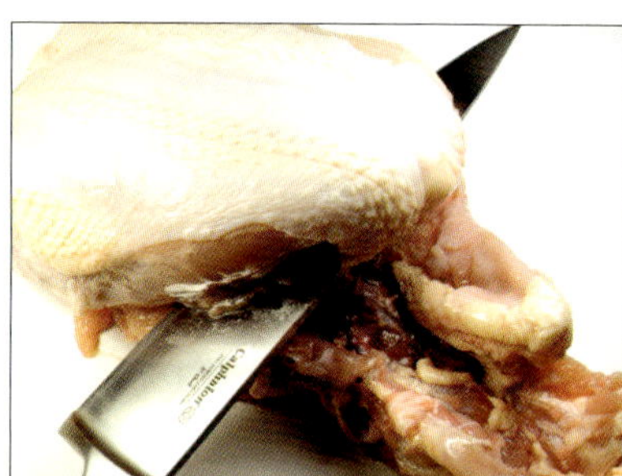

5. To separate the breasts from the backbone, cut through the thin portion of flesh and ribs that connects these two areas. Discard the back or use it to make stock (see page 185). Leave the breasts together or cut them apart.

To Rinse or Not to Rinse?

Is it necessary to rinse off the raw chicken before preparing it? Although it may surprise you, the answer is no. As the chicken cooks, the heat will destroy any bacteria that may be present on the raw meat. Many cooks, however, still prefer to rinse off the chicken first.

BBQ Chicken

A great barbecue sauce makes a great barbecued chicken. Store shelves are stocked with lots of different kinds. Along with the popular tomato-based varieties, be sure to check out the more exotic blends. I once tried raspberry-chipotle sauce, which may sound strange, but was really fantastic.

Ingredients

2 pounds chicken legs and thighs
$^{3}/_{4}$ cup barbecue sauce

Yield: 4 servings

1. Place the chicken on a medium-hot grill or barbecue. If you are using a barbecue, close the lid and cover the chicken.

2. As the chicken cooks, turn it over every 3 or 4 minutes. Depending on the thickness of the pieces, cook between 15 to 25 minutes, or until the juices run clear from the thickest part when poked with a fork.

3. When the chicken is nearly done, brush the top with barbecue sauce, then turn the pieces over and brush sauce on the other side. Cook for 1 or 2 minutes, turn the pieces over, and brush on more sauce. Cook for another minute, then remove from the heat and serve.

Important tips

- Grills can develop hot spots where the grease drips on the flames. Be sure to monitor your chicken as it cooks, and move the pieces around if hot spots develop. Closing the lid of a barbecue and shutting down the air vent will also reduce flame-ups.
- Most barbecue sauce has a high sugar content, which will burn black if put on the chicken too early. For this reason, it is best to add the sauce during the last few minutes of cooking time. A little burning is to be expected and even adds flavor, but too much is not desirable.

Fantastic Fried Chicken

Like some fast-food restaurants, I also use a blend of "seven herbs and spices" to coat my fried chicken. But trust me, mine tastes a lot better than any chicken you can pick up from a drive-through window. My coating has a lot more flavor . . . and flavor is good.

Ingredients

3–4 pound fryer, cut-up
$^{3}/_{4}$ cup flour
1 tablespoon salt
1 teaspoon black pepper
1 teaspoon garlic powder
1 teaspoon chili powder
1 teaspoon thyme
1 teaspoon paprika
$^{1}/_{4}$ teaspoon cayenne pepper
2–3 cups vegetable or canola oil

Yield: 4 servings

Stuff You'll Need

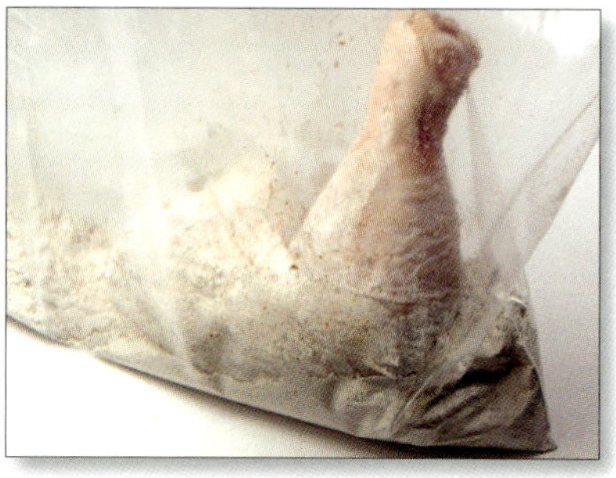

1. Put the flour and all the spices in a gallon-size plastic zip-lock bag. Add one or two pieces of chicken, seal the bag, and shake until fully coated. Repeat with the remaining chicken.

2. In a large pot or deep frying pan, add 1 inch of oil. Place over medium-high heat until the oil is hot but not smoking. Carefully add the chicken, one piece at a time. If the oil splashes violently, turn down the heat a bit (but not too much).

3. As the chicken cooks, turn it every 3 to 5 minutes. Depending on the thickness of the pieces, cook between 20 to 30 minutes, or until the juices run clear from the thickest part of the chicken when poked with a fork.

4. Drain the chicken on paper towels, transfer to a platter, and serve.

Extra-Crispy Fried Chicken

You want crunch? I got crunch. The trick for making this crisp, batter-dipped chicken is keeping an eye on it as it cooks.

Ingredients

3–4 pound fryer, cut-up
2 cups flour
1 tablespoon paprika
1 tablespoon garlic salt
2 teaspoons black pepper
1 egg
1 cup milk
2–3 cups vegetable or canola oil

Yield: 4 servings

1. Place the flour and all the spices in a gallon-size plastic zip-lock bag. Shake to mix, then transfer 1 cup of the seasoned flour to a medium mixing bowl.

2. Add the egg and milk to the flour, and stir to form a smooth batter. Coat the chicken pieces.

3. Place the battered pieces (one or two at a time) in the plastic bag with the remaining seasoned flour. Toss to coat.

4. In a large pot or deep frying pan, add 1 inch of oil. Place over medium-high heat until the oil is hot but not smoking. Carefully add the chicken, one piece at a time. If the oil splashes violently, turn down the heat a bit (but not too much).

5. As the chicken cooks, turn it every 3 to 5 minutes. Depending on the thickness of the pieces, cook between 20 to 30 minutes, or until the juices run clear from the thickest part of the chicken when poked with a fork.

6. Drain the chicken on paper towels, transfer to a platter, and serve.

Oven-Fried Chicken

Love fried chicken but hate cleaning up oily pans and greasy stovetops? Then try frying your chicken in the oven. Although the skin may not be quite as crisp as stovetop fried chicken, the meat will be just as tender and juicy.

Ingredients

3–4 pound fryer, cut up
½ cup milk
1 cup seasoned breadcrumbs
½ –1 cup vegetable or canola oil

Yield: 4 servings

Stuff You'll Need

1. Pour the milk in a medium-size bowl. Add the chicken and coat each piece.

2. Place the breadcrumbs in a gallon-size plastic zip-lock bag. Add one or two pieces of milk-dipped chicken, seal the bag, and shake until fully coated. Repeat with the remaining chicken.

3. Pour ½-inch oil in a casserole dish or baking pan, then add the coated chicken pieces. Bake in a preheated 325°F oven for 20 to 30 minutes, or until the top is golden brown.

4. Remove the dish from the oven, turn the pieces over, then return to the oven. Cook another 15 to 20 minutes, or until the juices run clear from the thickest part of the chicken when poked with a fork.

5. Drain the chicken on paper towels, transfer to a platter, and serve.

Rowbear's Cordon Bleu

Here's an oven-baked chicken dish that is bound to please. I made it for some of my friends in France and they fought over the last piece. The French can get pretty ugly when they fight over food.

Ingredients

- 2 boneless, skinless chicken breasts (about 8 ounces each)
- 4 slices (1/8 inch thick) ham or Canadian bacon
- 4 slices (1/8 inch thick) Gruyère or Swiss cheese
- 1 cup milk
- 1 cup seasoned breadcrumbs
- 1/4 cup vegetable or canola oil

Yield: 2 servings

Important tip

Select large breasts for this recipe and be sure you make the pocket large enough to hold the cheese and ham. It is okay if this stuffing sticks out of the pocket slightly, but 90 percent should be inside the breast.

Stuff You'll Need

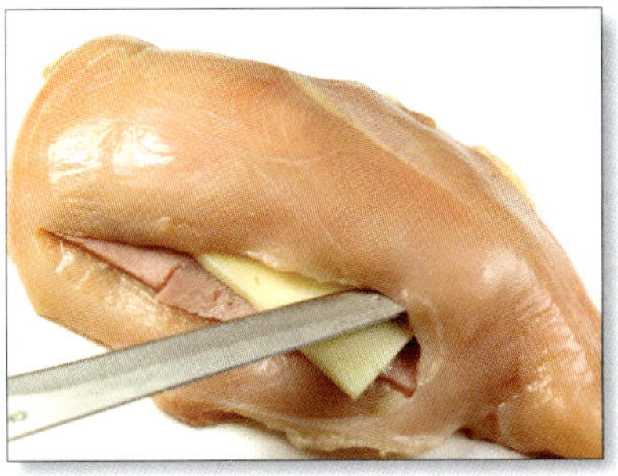

1. Cut a pocket into each breast (but do not cut all the way through). Place 2 slices of ham and cheese in each pocket.

2. Pour the milk in a medium-size bowl. Roll each stuffed breast in the milk.

3. Place the breadcrumbs in another bowl. Roll the breasts in the crumbs until fully coated.

4. Pour the oil in a casserole dish or baking pan, add the coated breasts, and bake in a preheated 350°F oven for 20 minutes. Turn the chicken over and cook another 20 minutes, or until no longer pink inside when cut with a knife.

5. Serve hot from the oven.

Easy Roasted Chicken

A whole oven-roasted chicken is very easy to prepare and makes a beautiful presentation (so it's a good choice when guests are coming for dinner). For this basic roasting method, I'm a little unconventional . . . I mostly cook the chicken "breast side down." This allows the breast meat, which is the driest, to cook in the juices and stay moist. It also eliminates the need for basting.

Ingredients

4–6 pound whole chicken
1 tablespoon garlic salt
2 teaspoons dried thyme
1 teaspoon black pepper

Yield: 4 to 6 servings

Chicken Roasting Chart

At 350°F:

2½ – 3 pounds	1¼ – 1½ hours
3 – 4 pounds	1½ – 1¾ hours
4 – 6 pounds	1¾ – 2¼ hours

Poultry is cooked when its internal temperature reaches 180°F. When the thermometer reads 170°F to 175°F, you can remove the bird from the oven. It will continue to cook as it "rests" for a few minutes.

Stuff You'll Need

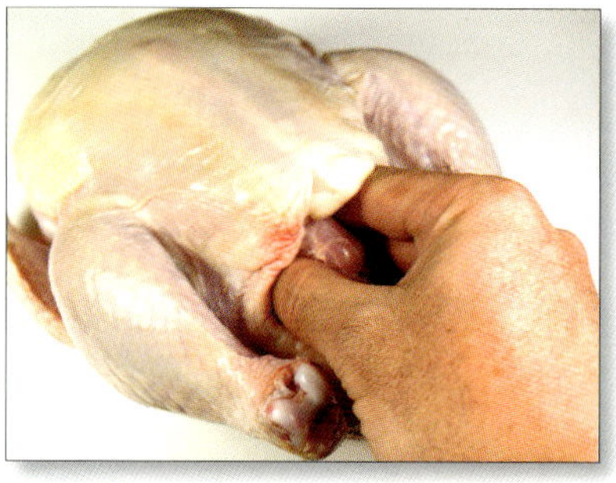

1. Remove the giblet packet.

2. Sprinkle the garlic salt, thyme, and pepper over the chicken. With your hands, rub the spices over the entire chicken, front and back.

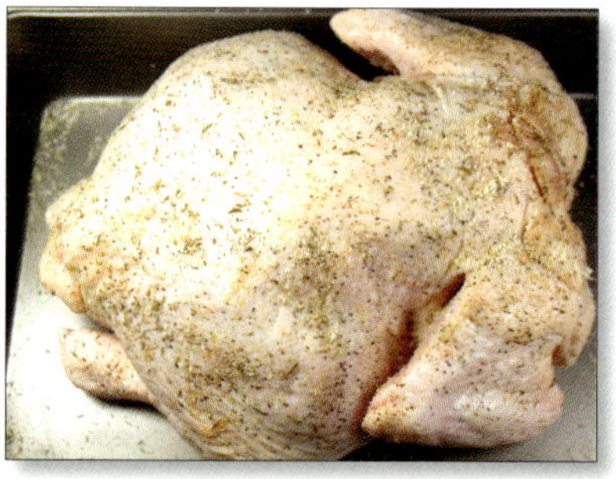

3. Put the chicken in a baking pan breast side down. Place in a preheated 350°F oven, and cook according to the roasting chart at left. During the last 15 minutes, turn the chicken over, insert the meat thermometer into the inner thigh, and continue roasting according to the chart.

4. Let the bird sit about 5 minutes before cutting and serving.

Greek Chicken

This recipe will give your chicken a bit of zing and some zang! The flavorful marinade makes the chicken more tender, juicy, and delicious. And there is no need to roast it breast side down (as in the Easy Roasted Chicken at left).

Ingredients

4–6 pound whole chicken

Marinade

½ cup olive oil
⅓ cup lemon juice
2 tablespoons honey
1 tablespoon minced garlic
2 teaspoons salt
1 teaspoon dried rosemary
1 teaspoon dried oregano
½ teaspoon black pepper

Yield: 4 to 6 servings

Stuff You'll Need

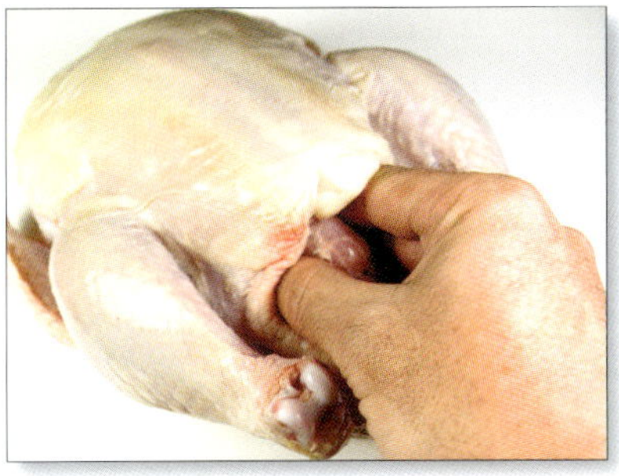

1. Remove the giblet packet.

2. Juice enough lemons to yield ⅓ cup.

3. Place all of the marinade ingredients in a medium-size bowl and stir.

4. Pour the marinade in a sturdy gallon-size plastic bag with a zip-lock top. Add the chicken, shake to coat, and refrigerate from 1 to 8 hours.

5. Place the marinated chicken in a baking pan breast side up. Cook in a preheated 350°F oven according to the chart on page 290. Let the cooked bird sit about 5 minutes before cutting and serving.

Cutlets in Lemon Caper Sauce

Chicken cutlets are so versatile. I often sprinkle them with seasonings and cook them on the grill or coat them with breadcrumbs and fry them in a pan. Along with tasting great, cutlets cook in no time!

Ingredients

12 ounces thinly sliced chicken cutlets
½ cup breadcrumbs
¼ cup olive oil
2 tablespoons capers
¼ teaspoon minced garlic
2 tablespoons lemon juice

Yield: 2 servings

1. Place the breadcrumbs in a pie plate or shallow bowl. Press each cutlet into the crumbs and coat well.

2. Heat the oil in a large frying pan over medium-high heat. Add the capers and garlic, then add the cutlets. Cook 3 minutes or until the bottom of the cutlets are golden. Turn over and cook 2 minutes, or until no longer pink inside when cut with a knife. Transfer to a platter.

3. Reduce the heat to low and allow the pan to cool a bit. Add the lemon juice and stir with the seasoned bits of food and juices that are left in the pan to make a sauce.

4. Spoon the sauce over the cutlets and serve hot.

Making Cutlets

Cutlets are simply boneless, skinless chicken breasts that have been sliced and/or pounded to a uniform thickness (typically, less than ½ inch thick). Although you can buy cutlets from the butcher or most grocery stores, you can also make them yourself. Simply take a boneless chicken breast and cut it horizontally into two or three slices. Voila! You have just made cutlets! To make them thinner, place the slices between two pieces of wax paper and pound them with a rubber mallet.

Stuff You'll Need

Chicken Tenders in Cream Sauce

This dish is easy and quick to make, but tastes like you really slaved over it. Serve over rice or pasta along with some fresh bread to soak up the delicious sauce. If you can't find chicken tenders, you can cut up a boneless, skinless chicken breast into small 1½-inch strips.

Ingredients

8 ounces chicken tenders
2 tablespoons butter
1 teaspoon minced garlic
½ teaspoon salt
¼ teaspoon black pepper
½ cup heavy cream
1 tablespoon minced fresh basil

Yield: 2 servings

1. Melt the butter in a pan over medium heat, then add the garlic, salt, and black pepper. Add the chicken tenders and cook about 2 minutes on each side.

2. Reduce the heat to medium-low and add the cream and basil. Simmer the chicken for 2 or 3 minutes, turn the pieces over, and continue to simmer another 2 or 3 minutes.

3. Spoon over rice or pasta, and serve hot.

Stuff You'll Need

Indian Chicken Curry

I originally made this dish with beef, but I like it better as a chicken dish. The cucumber-yogurt sauce helps cool down the spicy curry.

Ingredients

1 pound boneless, skinless chicken breasts
2 cups shredded carrots
1 large onion, chopped
2 tablespoons olive oil
1 tablespoon minced garlic
¼ cup curry powder
1 tablespoon chili powder
1 tablespoon salt
¼ teaspoon cayenne pepper

Sauce

1 small cucumber, peeled and chopped
2 cups plain yogurt

Yield: 4 servings

Stuff You'll Need

1. Cut the chicken into bite-size cubes.

2. Shred the carrots.

3. Chop the onion.

4. Place the olive oil in a 4-quart pot. Add the chicken, carrots, onion, and the remaining spices. Cover and set over medium-low heat. Stir every 2 or 3 minutes for the first 10 minutes, and then once every 10 minutes or so. Cook for 1 hour.

5. While the chicken and vegetables are cooking, peel the cucumber and cut it into ¼-inch cubes.

6. Place the yogurt and cucumbers in a bowl and stir until well mixed.

Important tip

Stirring the ingredients several times during the first few minutes of cooking will prevent them from sticking to the bottom of the pot. After about 10 minutes, there should be enough moisture from the carrots and onions to keep the ingredients moist. If not, add a little water.

7. Serve the chicken with 1 or 2 heaping spoonfuls of cucumber-yogurt sauce. White rice and crisp, cool cucumber slices are other recommended accompaniments. And don't forget to have plenty of water in your glass.

Chicken Fajitas

I think of this dish as a Mexican stir-fry. I recommend cooking it in a sizzling hot wok, which has a lot of surface area for fast cooking. Before you start cooking, be sure to have all the ingredients ready, because everything cooks up fast!

Ingredients

12 ounces boneless, skinless chicken breasts
1 medium onion, chopped
1 red bell pepper, cut into strips
1 avocado, sliced
2 tablespoons olive oil
1 tablespoon minced garlic
1 packet taco seasoning or ¼ cup chili powder and 2 teaspoons salt
4–6 flour tortillas

Optional fillings

Guacamole
Sour cream
Shredded cheese
Salsa
Hot sauce

Yield: 4 to 6 fajitas

Stuff You'll Need

1. Cut the chicken into strips about 2 inches long and ½ inch wide.

2. Thinly slice the onion. Cut each slice in half, then break them apart.

3. Cut the bell pepper into strips.

4. Slice the avocado.

5. Heat the oil in a wok or deep frying pan over high heat. Add the chicken and cook, stirring constantly for 3 minutes.

6. Add the onions, peppers, garlic, and taco seasoning. Stirring constantly, cook about 3 or 4 minutes, or until the peppers and onions have softened.

7. To soften the tortillas, wrap them in paper towels and heat in the microwave for about 20 seconds. (You can also steam them in a covered pot.)

Important tips

- Everything cooks up very fast for this recipe, so before you start cooking, be sure to have all the ingredients cut up and ready to go.
- Frequently stirring the ingredients in the hot pan will prevent them from sticking.

8. Serve when the filling is still sizzling hot. You can even bring the pan to the table and set it on a trivet. Also place bowls of additional toppings and fillings on the table. Spoon some chicken mixture down the center of a warm tortilla along with the fillings of your choice. Roll up the tortilla and enjoy! Have plenty of napkins ready!

Chicken Paprikash

I discovered this recipe at a family reunion in San Francisco. We had a bet to see who would be the last person to spill something on their clothes. I won, but as I pointed to my cousin, who was my final contender, my sleeve dipped into some of the paprika sauce.

Ingredients

1 bell pepper, chopped
1 medium onion, chopped
14.5-ounce can chicken broth
1 pound boneless, skinless chicken breasts or thighs
3 tablespoons paprika
2 tablespoons minced garlic
1 teaspoon salt
1 teaspoon black pepper
8 ounces sour cream

Yield: 4 servings

Stuff You'll Need

1. Chop the pepper.

2. Chop the onion.

3. Place the broth in a large pot over medium-low heat. Add all of the ingredients except the sour cream and stir. Simmer for at least 1 hour, occasionally stirring and flipping the chicken until the broth is reduced by half. Stir the sour cream in the pot right before serving.

Pesto Chicken Rolls

Super easy and super delicious. If you like pesto, Asiagio cheese, and chicken, you've found your dish!

Ingredients

- 4 chicken cutlets (about 3 ounces each), $\frac{1}{4}$ to $\frac{3}{8}$ inch thick
- 4 tablespoons Pesto (page 244), or commercial variety
- 4 tablespoons grated Asiagio or Parmesan cheese
- $\frac{1}{4}$ cup olive oil

Yield: 2 servings

Stuff You'll Need

1. Top each chicken cutlet with 1 tablespoon pesto, then sprinkle with 1 tablespoon cheese. Roll up the cutlets like jelly rolls.

2. Place the olive oil in the bottom of an 8-inch square baking pan. Add the cutlets, seam side down.

3. Bake in a preheated 325°F oven for 45 to 50 minutes, or until the chicken is no longer pink inside when cut with a knife. Serve immediately.

Chicken Enchiladas

This is a fast and easy recipe that everyone loves. Be sure to check the chili label to determine if the peppers are mild, medium, hot, or very hot. If you don't, you could be in for a big surprise!

Ingredients

8 ounces boneless, skinless chicken breasts
1 tablespoon olive oil
1 tablespoon canned diced chili peppers
1 teaspoon minced garlic
5 ounces shredded Monterey Jack cheese
4 or 5 corn tortillas
15-ounce can enchilada sauce

Yield: 4 or 5 enchiladas

1. Cut the chicken into ½-inch cubes.

2. Heat the oil in a large frying pan over medium-high heat. Add the chicken, chilies, and garlic, then reduce the heat to medium-low. Sauté the chicken about 5 minutes. As it cooks, use a spoon to break up the cubes and prevent them from clumping together.

3. To soften the tortillas, heat them in a microwave for about 30 seconds, or steam them in a covered pot. Spoon the chicken mixture and half the cheese down the middle of the tortillas. Fold over the sides to form the enchiladas.

4. Pour half the sauce in the bottom of an 8-inch square baking dish. Add the enchiladas and top with the remaining sauce and cheese. Cover the dish (you can use aluminum foil) and bake in a preheated 325°F oven for 20 minutes, or until the enchiladas are heated through.

Stuff You'll Need

Cajun-Style Buffalo Wings

These five-alarm wings are sure to make you sweat; but if you like steam coming out of your ears, add more cayenne!

Ingredients

20 chicken wings, separated at the joints (tips discarded), to yield 40 pieces
1 ¼ cups tomato sauce
½ cup melted butter
⅓ cup Louisiana hot sauce or Tabasco
2 tablespoons honey
2 tablespoons chili powder
1 teaspoon cayenne pepper

Yield: 4 to 6 servings

Cutting Wings

Chicken wings have three sections — a tip, a flat midsection, and a drummette — that are held together by two joints. To separate the sections, place the wings on a cutting board, and with a sharp knife, carefully cut through the two joints, where the cartilage is easier to penetrate than the bone. (You can discard the tips or save them for soup.)

Stuff You'll Need

1. Arrange the wings on a parchment-lined cookie sheet. Bake in a preheated 375°F oven for 30 minutes or until lightly browned and crisp. Set aside to cool.

2. Place the remaining ingredients in a medium bowl and stir until well combined. Dip the cooled wings in the sauce to cover and return to the cookie sheet.

3. Reduce the oven to 225°F, and bake the wings another 15 minutes or until the sauce has set.

4. Serve the wings as is or with a dip, like the Blue Cheese or Sour Cream Ranch dressings on page 168.

Greek Stuffed Chicken Breasts

Chicken breasts are low in fat, high in protein, and very versatile. In this recipe, they're stuffed with a delectable filling! A great choice for dinner parties.

Ingredients

3 tablespoons olive oil, divided
¾ cup chopped onion
1 teaspoon minced garlic
2 cups chopped fresh baby spinach
⅓ cup crumbled feta cheese
2 tablespoons pine nuts (optional)
2 boneless, skinless chicken breasts (about 6 ounces each)

Yield: 2 servings

Important tips

Use a very sharp knife when cutting the breasts, and be careful. Raw chicken is slippery!

Stuff You'll Need

1. Heat 1 tablespoon of the olive oil in a medium-size pot over medium-low heat. Add the onions and garlic, and sauté 3 to 5 minutes or until soft and translucent.

2. Add the spinach to the pot and sauté for 2 to 3 minutes or until the leaves have wilted.

3. Transfer the spinach mixture to a medium bowl. Add the cheese and pine nuts (if using), and stir until well combined. Set aside.

Making a Butterfly Cut

To butterfly the chicken breasts for this recipe, do the following:

1. Lay the breast on a flat cutting surface and place your non-cutting hand on top (to keep it steady). Starting at the thicker side, begin slicing the breast in half horizontally, keeping the thickness of the two halves about the same. Cut almost, but not all the way through.

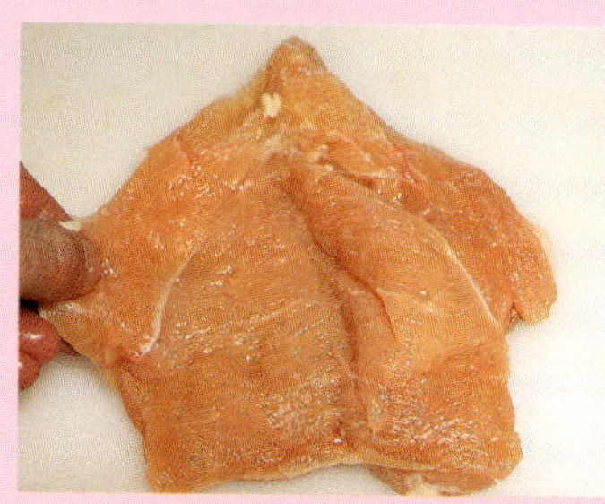

2. Open the two sides of the breast as if you are opening a book and flatten a bit. (The flattened piece will sort of resemble a butterfly, which explains how this cut got its name.) The chicken is now ready for the filling.

4. Butterfly cut the breasts (see instructions on previous page), open, and flatten. Spoon an equal amount of the spinach mixture along the center of each.

5. Close up the breasts to enclose the filling.

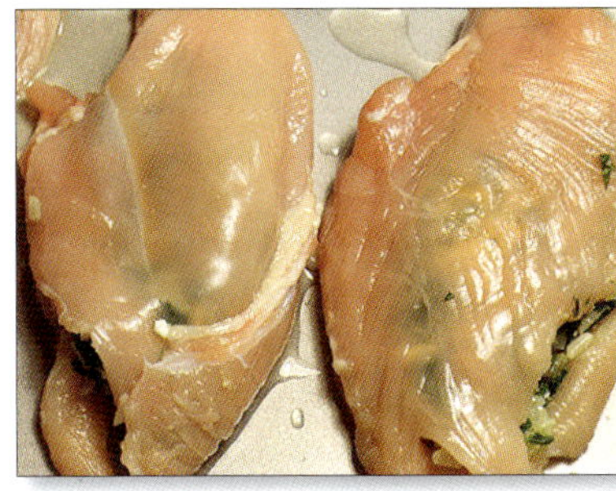

6. Place the remaining oil in the bottom of a small casserole dish or baking pan, and arrange the stuffed breasts on top.

7. Bake in a preheated 325°F oven for 40 to 45 minutes, or until the chicken is no longer pink inside when cut with a knife. Serve immediately.

We Love Birds

*It's ironic that we love the chicken,
yet we disrespect it by using the word "chicken" as an insult!*

Fowl Fit for an Emperor

Peking duck – a culinary masterpiece prized for its crisp skin and moist flesh – originated in Beijing during the Ming Dynasty. Once served only to Chinese royalty, the dish requires a unique preparation process. After the specially bred duck is plucked and cleaned, it is dropped into boiling water, which loosens the skin. Air is then blown between the skin and the flesh, allowing the skin to become extra crisp as the bird roasts.

Wings on a Buffalo?

Buffalo wings – that Super Bowl favorite – were first served at the Anchor Bar in Buffalo, New York. According to the son of owners Frank and Teressa Bellissimo, one busy Friday night in 1964, Frank decided to serve a post-midnight snack to the mostly Catholic patrons (who observed "meatless" Fridays). Teressa came up with the idea of deep-frying chicken wings (normally used for soup) and serving them with a spicy sauce she created. The wings cooked quickly, were inexpensive, and very tasty – the perfect snack and an instant hit. From that night on, Buffalo wings were on the Anchor menu. Today, they are served throughout the world.

Chicken Eunuchs

A capon is a young male chicken (rooster) that has been castrated (*ouch!*) and fattened up to twice its normal size. Lack of sex hormones also makes the meat less gamy.

Eat Your Fingers Off!

When Kentucky Fried Chicken first came to China, its famous slogan "It's finger lickin' good" was translated in Chinese as "Eat your fingers off." No wonder it took awhile for the chain to succeed there.

The Loser Was Delicious

Cock-a-leekie is a Scottish version of chicken soup that dates back to the Middle Ages. By tradition, the loser of a cock fight would be thrown into a pot of water and cooked with leeks, barley, and prunes.

Fun Chicken Facts

Chicken is the most popular meat eaten in the United States. Here's some trivia about this bird:

- The average American eats eighty pounds of chicken every year.
- Nearly 95 percent of restaurants have chicken on the menu – about half is served fried.
- Ancient Egyptians built brick incubators that could hold up to 10,000 chicks at once.
- Because of its large number of processing plants, Gainesville, Georgia is considered the "Poultry Capital of the World." According to an unenforced law, it's actually illegal to eat chicken with a fork there!
- On record, the most eggs laid by a chicken in one day is seven.
- Some chickens lay colored eggs! The Ameraucana and Araucana breeds produce eggs in different shades of blue.

15. What's Your Beef?

The king of meats.

In my opinion, beef is the king of meats in the American diet. Without it, you can't make a real hamburger or enjoy an all-American beef frank. And grilled steak is one of the most requested choices at barbecues.

In this chapter, you are literally going to meet some meat — specifically beef. The first few pages begin with a brief overview of the different types and grades of beef, and the cuts that are commonly sold in supermarkets and butcher shops. Also included is an informative chart that lists the various cuts along with brief descriptions and recommended cooking methods.

In a section devoted entirely to steaks, you'll find helpful guidelines for preparing and cooking them to perfection. If you like roast beef, I'll show you how to make one that's juicy and delicious. How about pot roast? I've got one here that will melt in your mouth (and not in your hands). There's a hearty beef stew to warm you on cold nights, and if you're ready for nirvana, I have a meatloaf recipe that will take you there. For my Mexican-food-loving amigos, there's Upside-Down Beef Tamale Pie, Bad Boy Burritos, and Me Gusta Tacos. I will also teach you the secrets of ancient Chinese stir-fry. Once you know the proper time to add the bean sprouts, you will have learned much, my dear apprentice chef.

So come along beef lovers. It's time to sink your teeth into this chapter!

Meet Some Meat

Here are some of the most common varieties and cuts of beef—the ones you are likely to find at your local grocery store or butcher shop.

How Now, Brown Cow

Aged beef

When beef is aged—a process that breaks down muscle—it becomes more flavorful and tender. Dry-aged beef has been exposed to the air in an open, sterile environment where it forms an outer crust. When this crust is trimmed away, the tender steak is left. Wet-aged beef, the most common type, has been vacuum packed in plastic, then sits for one to four weeks in a cool environment.

Beef Grades

The USDA inspects and grades meats for quality. Butchers and grocers are likely to carry the top four grades. *Prime* is the best. The meat is rich with marbling (flecks of fat), which enhances its flavor, tenderness, and juiciness. Prime roasts and steaks are best when cooked with dry heat—roasted, broiled, or grilled. *Choice* grade beef is also high quality, but it has less marbling than prime. It is also less expensive. *Select* grade beef has less marbling than the higher grades; it may be tender, but not as juicy and flavorful. *Standard* grade beef has virtually no marbling and little flavor. It requires moist cooking, like stewing or potting.

Where's the Beef?

Chuck

A little tough, this meat is basically hard muscle. It is good for stews and pot roasts. Also good for grinding.

Flank

Muscular, lean, and a little tough, this meat is usually cut into thin steaks.

Rib

Rib meat is very tender and flavorful. I growl when I'm around a plate of ribs. Eating meat off the bone brings out the animal in me.

Round

Fairly tough, this meat is located near the cow's rear (or derrière if you're French). It is cut into steaks or roasts that are best potted, braised, or stewed. Also good for grinding.

Shank

Shank meat comes from the front legs and tends to be dry, tough, and sinewy. Good for soups and stews.

Short loin

The meat from this area is very tender. Porterhouse steak and the tenderloin (filet mignon and chateaubriand) are from this section.

Short plate

Flavorful but tough, the meat from this section is best in stews, where its rich, beefy flavor can be appreciated.

Sirloin

This loin area boasts tender cuts, but not as tender as the meat in the short loin. Sirloin is often cut into steaks or ground.

What a Grind!

Often referred to as hamburger, ground beef is labeled to let you know what area of the cow it comes from—the chuck, round, or sirloin—as well as its fat content. Packages labeled simply "ground beef" are usually made with the trimmings of less expensive cuts and can contain up to 30-percent fat. It is best to store ground beef in the coldest area of the refrigerator and use it within two days. It will also keep for three months in the freezer.

Popular Beef Cuts

Dry-cooking methods—grilling, pan-frying, broiling, and oven-roasting—are best for tender cuts of beef. Tough cuts are best prepared with wet-cooking methods, such as braising in stews or potting. Some tough cuts also benefit from marinating and can be grilled or broiled.

		Cut	Description	Best Cooking Methods
Steaks		Beef tenderloin (filet mignon)	The most tender and juicy of all steaks.	Grilled; broiled.
Steaks		Chuck mock tender steak	The most tender part of the chuck; shaped like a filet mignon.	Grilled; broiled; pan-fried.
Steaks	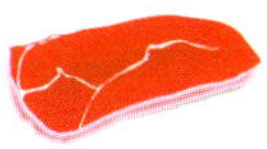	Chuck shoulder steak	Tough steak from the chuck portion.	Braised in stews; well-marinated and grilled or broiled.
Steaks		Porterhouse steak	Very tender steak that consists of both tenderloin and strip portions.	Grilled; broiled; pan-fried.
Steaks		Ribeye steak	Very tender steak from the center of the rib section.	Grilled; broiled; pan-fried.
Steaks		Sirloin steak	Somewhat tender cut from the loin area. Boneless top sirloin is the best.	Grilled; broiled.
Steaks		Strip/shell steak	Tender steak from top of short loin. Also called NY or Kansas City strip steak.	Grilled; broiled; pan-fried.
Steaks		T-bone steak	Very tender, from center of short loin. Like porterhouse but with smaller tenderloin.	Grilled; broiled; pan-fried.
Steaks	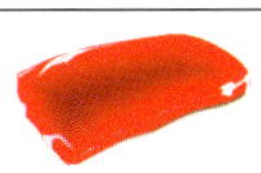	Top round steak	From tenderest part of the round, but a bit tough. Thick cuts called London broil.	Potted; braised in stews; well-marinated and grilled or broiled.
Roasts		Chuck roast	Very tough cut.	Potted; braised in stews.
Roasts		Eye of round roast	Flavorful, somewhat tough cut from the round.	Roasted.
Roasts		Rib roast	Tender, flavorful cut from rib section. Comes with or without rib bones.	Roasted.
Roasts	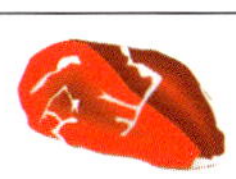	Rump roast (boneless)	Tough cut from the upper part of the round.	Potted; braised in stews.
Roasts		Tenderloin roast (chateaubriand)	Most tender cut from the short loin.	Roasted; broiled; grilled.
Special Cuts		Beef ribs	Tender, meaty rib bones found between short loin and chuck areas.	Slow-baked; braised. Can also be partially cooked, then grilled.
Special Cuts		Brisket	Fatty, very tough cut; often brined for corned beef.	Potted.

Cooking the Perfect Steak

There are several methods for cooking steak. Pan-frying, grilling, and broiling are the most popular. Thick steaks (1 inch or thicker) are best cooked on the grill or broiled in the oven, while thin steaks lend themselves to pan-frying.

Pan-Frying

This is the best way to cook a thin steak. I usually heat a little olive oil in a pan over medium-high heat, add the steaks, and sprinkle on some seasonings. The thinner the steak the quicker it cooks. A minute steak takes a minute!

Broiling

This is a good way to cook thick steaks. Set your oven to broil, place the steak in a broiling pan, and place it on a rack under the broiling unit.

Grilling

In my opinion, this is the best way to cook a tender thick steak like a New York strip or a filet mignon. For the best flavor and juiciness, the grill must be really hot. The high heat will cook the exterior quickly while sealing in the juices. The smoky grilled exterior complements the moist tender meat on the inside.

Important tips

- After cooking a steak, let it rest at least five minutes before serving. This allows the juices (which move to the center of the steak as the outside is cooked) to be reabsorbed throughout the meat.
- Any steak that is cooked too long will shrink and become dry and tough—even the most expensive cuts.

Seasoning steaks

I find that seasoning steaks before cooking brings out their flavor. Savory garlic and onion powder, black pepper, oregano, and rosemary are good choices. Salt however draws out the meat's juices; so if you add salt, do so near the end of cooking time.

Preparing filet mignon

Because filet mignon has very little fat, I always wrap it with bacon and secure it with toothpicks (as shown) to help keep the meat juicy as it cooks.

Marinades

Marinating helps tenderize tougher cuts of steak, whether whole or cubed (for kabobs or stews). Marinades have an acidic content—usually vinegar or a citrus juice—which breaks down the muscle fibers of the meat. As an added bonus, marinating meat before grilling it can reduce the formation of harmful carcinogens by 90 percent.

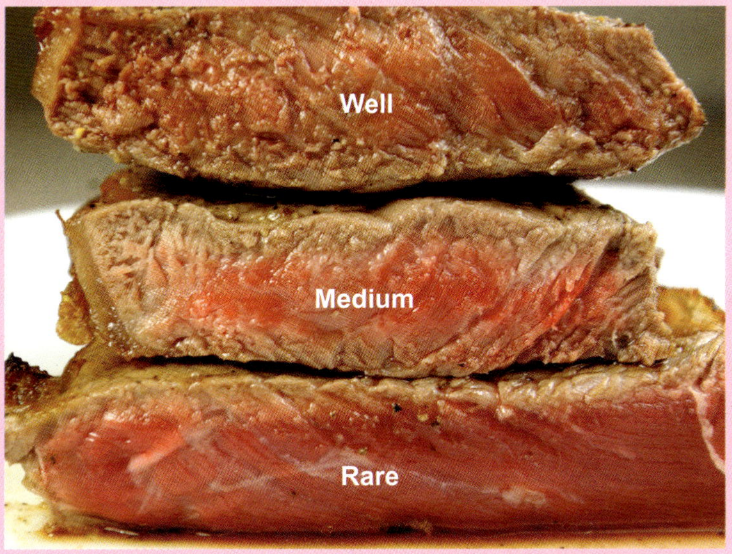

Steak Cooking Times

Cooking time for steaks is determined by thickness, not by weight. The following chart gives the approximate times for a 1-inch-thick steak that is cooked on a hot grill or under a broiler. Reduce or increase the times proportionally for steaks that are thinner or thicker.

For a 1-inch-thick steak:

Rare	Medium-rare	Medium	Well
1½ to 2 minutes per side	2 to 2½ minutes per side	3 to 3½ minutes per side	4 to 4½ minutes per side

Pan-Fried Steak with Gravy

The preferred way to cook thin steaks—those that are one-inch thick or less—is on the stovetop in a frying pan. For this recipe, I recommend top round or chuck mock tender steaks.

Ingredients

8 ounces thin steaks (¼ to ½ inch thick)
3 tablespoons olive oil
½ teaspoon minced garlic
½ teaspoon dried rosemary
½ cup water
1 tablespoon flour

Yield: 2 servings

1. Heat the oil, garlic, and rosemary in a frying pan over medium heat, then add the steaks. Cook 1½ minutes, then turn the steaks over and cook another minute. Remove the pan from the heat and let the steaks sit a minute.

2. Transfer the steaks to a platter and return the pan to the stove over medium-low heat. Add the water and flour, and stir until the flour has dissolved and the mixture has a gravy-like consistency.

Stuff You'll Need

3. Place the steaks on a plate, top with gravy, and enjoy!

Pepper Steak

This quick and easy steak dish has the veggies built right in. For color, I use a variety of yellow, green, and red bell peppers.

Ingredients

2 top round or top sirloin steaks (6–8 ounces each)
1 medium onion
1 cup sliced green, red, and/or yellow bell peppers
3 tablespoons Worcestershire sauce
1 teaspoon garlic salt
½ teaspoon black pepper

Yield: 2 servings

Important tip

Cook the steak in a hot pan set over medium-high heat. The steak will cook very quickly, so keep an eye on it the entire time.

Stuff You'll Need

1. Slice the onion, then cut each slice in half and break apart.

2. Cut the peppers into strips.

3. Heat the Worcestershire sauce in a frying pan over medium-high heat. Add the steaks, onion, bell peppers, garlic salt, and black pepper. Cook for 2 minutes, then turn the steaks over and stir the peppers and onions. Cook another 2 to 4 minutes, or until the steaks have reached the desired doneness.

4. Transfer the steaks to dinner plates and cover with peppers and onions.

Mushroom 'n Onion Topping

Here's a tasty steak topper that will amaze your friends and frighten your enemies (it's that good).

Ingredients

10 large white button mushrooms, sliced
1 medium onion, sliced
2 tablespoons butter
1 teaspoon minced garlic
½ teaspoon salt

Yield: 2 servings

Stuff You'll Need

1. Slice the mushrooms.

2. Chop the onion.

3. Place all the ingredients in a small frying pan over medium-low heat. Sauté about 7 minutes or until the onions are translucent and the mushrooms are soft.

4. Serve over your favorite grilled or broiled steak.

Béarnaise Sauce

I know this sauce is loaded with fat and cholesterol, but that's why it tastes so good! Enjoy some on your favorite steak, then eat salads for the rest of the week!

Ingredients

4 egg yolks
1 stick (½ cup) butter
1 tablespoon white wine vinegar
1 teaspoon fresh tarragon, or
  ½ teaspoon dried

Yield: About 1 cup

Important tip

The butter must be bubbling hot when added to the blender. It must also be poured in a slow, steady stream. If the butter is just warm or you pour it in too quickly, the sauce will not thicken properly.

Stuff You'll Need

1. Separate the eggs (see page 60). Discard the whites or reserve them for another use. Place the yolks in a blender.

2. Heat the butter in a small saucepan over medium heat until it is bubbling, but not burning. Be ready to use it immediately. (I usually transfer it to a measuring cup at this point, which makes the next step easier.)

3. Blend the egg yolks, vinegar, and tarragon in the blender on the lowest speed. Pour the hot butter slowly into the opening at the top of the blender in a thin, steady stream. When all the butter has been added, turn off the blender.

4. Serve immediately over your favorite grilled or broiled steak.

Roast Beef with New Potatoes

This is an excellent choice for a holiday meal. Try it with the Yorkshire Pudding on page 231.

Ingredients

3–3½ pound eye of round or tenderloin roast
3–4 large garlic cloves
2 teaspoons salt
2 teaspoons black pepper
6 medium red potatoes

Gravy

1 cup beef broth
1 cup pan drippings
1 teaspoon dried rosemary
½ teaspoon salt
¼ cup flour

Yield: 6 to 8 servings

Important tip
When making the gravy, if you don't have enough pan drippings to measure 1 cup, simply add some beef broth.

Stuff You'll Need

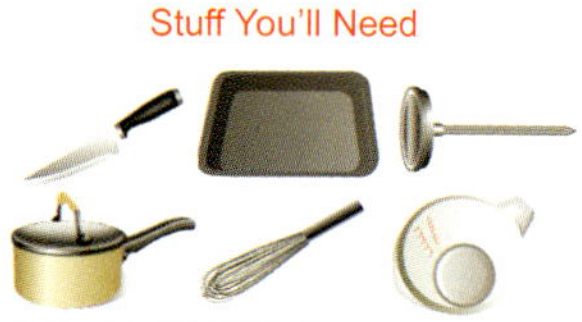

1. Cut the garlic cloves into slivers.

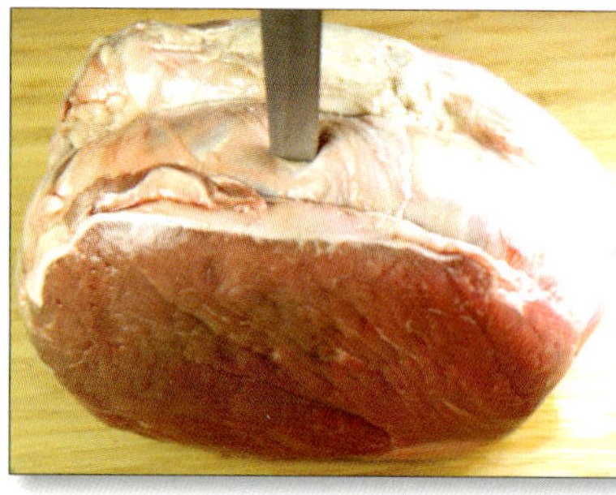

2. With a thin pointed knife, cut holes into the roast about 2 inches apart and ¾ inch deep.

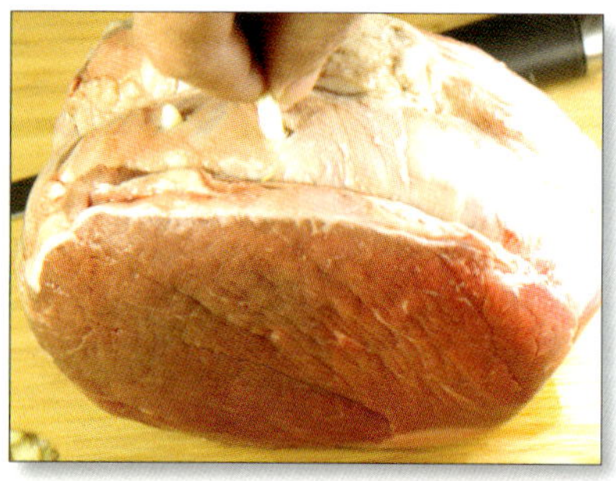

3. Insert the garlic slivers into the holes.

4. Place the roast in a roasting pan and sprinkle with salt and pepper. Put the potatoes next to the roast and cook in a preheated 325°F oven according to the chart at right. After removing the roast from the oven, let it sit 5 minutes.

5. Transfer the drippings to a saucepan. Add the broth, rosemary, and salt, and bring to a boil over medium-high heat. Slowly add the flour, stirring constantly until the liquid has a gravy-like consistency.

Roast Beef Cooking Chart

It is best to use a meat thermometer for determining a roast's doneness. Insert the thermometer into the center of the meat before placing it in the oven, and leave it in throughout the cooking process. The internal temperature at the center of the roast will read as follows:

	Rare	Medium-rare	Medium	Well
	125°–135°F	135°–145°F	145°–155°F	165°F

If, however, you are not using a meat thermometer, use the following chart for approximate cooking times. Keep in mind that the weight of the roast, along with its thickness, fat content, and whether or not it contains a bone will affect cooking time.

	Rare	Medium-rare	Medium	Well
2 pounds	35 minutes	40 minutes	50 minutes	60 minutes
3 pounds	50 minutes	60 minutes	75 minutes	90 minutes
4 pounds	65 minutes	80 minutes	100 minutes	120 minutes

6. Cut the roast into thin slices and place on a platter. Cut the potatoes in half and place around the slices. Pour the gravy over the meat or serve it on the side.

Savory Beef Stew

There's nothing more comforting than a hearty bowl of beef stew, especially on cold nights. And this simple version is not only delicious, it's also easy and inexpensive to make. This recipe calls for beef broth, but you can use red wine instead (for some added spirit!).

Ingredients

1 pound beef stew meat, cubed
2 medium russet potatoes, cut into bite-size cubes
1 large onion, chopped
1 large carrot, diced
4 strips thick bacon
15-ounce can beef broth
1 tablespoon Worcestershire sauce
1 tablespoon minced garlic
1 tablespoon dried thyme
1 teaspoon ground sage
1 teaspoon salt
½ teaspoon black pepper

Yield: 2 to 3 servings

Stuff You'll Need

1. Cut the potatoes into cubes.

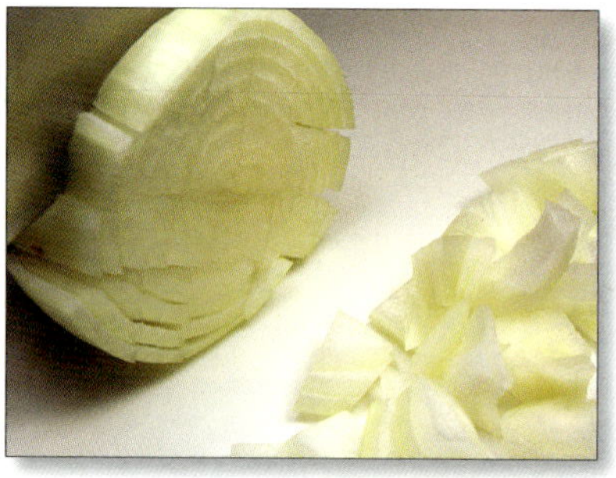

2. Chop the onion.

3. Dice the carrot.

Thickening Tips

I enjoy the consistency of this stew. For me, the natural starch from the potatoes thickens it perfectly. If, however, you prefer yours a little thicker, simply uncover the pot during the last half hour of cooking. For an even thicker stew, near the end of cooking time, mix 1 tablespoon of flour with some of the cooking liquid to form a loose paste. Then slowly stir it back into the pot.

4. Slice the bacon into ½-inch strips.

5. Cook the bacon in a large pot over medium-high heat until lightly browned. Drain the excess fat.

6. Add all of the remaining ingredients and bring to a boil. Reduce the heat to low, cover, and simmer for 2 hours or until the beef is tender.

7. Spoon the piping hot stew into bowls and dig in!

Easy Pot Roast

Slow-cooking a tough cut of meat over low heat makes it melt-in-your-mouth tender. Although beef brisket is often the recommended choice for pot roast, it may be hard to find. For this recipe, I generally use a rump roast, which is available in most grocery stores.

Ingredients

3 large carrots, sliced
2 large russet potatoes, cubed
3-pound rump roast or brisket
2 cups water
1 package dry onion soup mix
1 tablespoon minced garlic
1 tablespoon dried sage

Yield: 6 to 8 servings

Important tip

To test for doneness, stick a long fork deep into the simmering roast. If the roast slides off the fork easily, the meat is done.

Stuff You'll Need

1. Slice the carrots.

2. Cut the potatoes into ¾-inch cubes.

3. Place the roast in a Dutch oven or a heavy-bottomed pot. Add the water, soup mix, garlic, and sage. Bring to a boil, then reduce the heat to very low. Cover tightly and simmer 3 hours. Add the carrots and potatoes, and cook another hour, or until the meat is fork tender.

4. Slice the roast and serve with the carrots and potatoes. Top with some of the cooking broth.

Nirvana Meatloaf

After many attempts to combine the right ingredients for the perfect meatloaf, I knew that I finally had a winner with this one. The pleasure center in my brain started to ring after I took my first bite.

Ingredients

½ cup minced onion
1 pound fresh ground beef
8 ounces ground sausage
½ cup breadcrumbs
1 egg
1 teaspoon minced garlic
1 teaspoon dried sage
1 teaspoon dried thyme
½ teaspoon salt
¼ teaspoon black pepper
½ cup spaghetti sauce

Yield: 6 to 8 servings

Important tip

The best way to determine if the meatloaf is cooked is with a meat thermometer. When the center of the loaf reaches 160°F, it is done.

Stuff You'll Need

1. Mince the onion.

2. Place all of the ingredients except the spaghetti sauce in a large mixing bowl. Stir gently until well mixed.

3. Loosely press the mixture in an 8-x-4-inch loaf pan. Spread the spaghetti sauce on top with a spatula or the back of a spoon.

4. Place in a preheated 350°F oven and cook for about 70 minutes, or until the meat thermometer reads 160°F when placed in the center of the loaf.

4. Cut the meatloaf into slices and serve.

Me Gusta Tacos!

I generally use a taco seasoning mix to flavor the beef for tacos and burritos. In this recipe, however, I use the actual spices—chili powder, garlic salt, and cumin. But feel free to use a packaged seasoning mix if you prefer.

Ingredients

1 pound ground beef
1 cup water
½ cup minced onion
3 tablespoons chili powder
1 tablespoon garlic salt
¼ teaspoon cumin
2 cups shredded lettuce
1 cup shredded sharp cheddar cheese
16 tomato wedges

Shells

8 corn tortillas
Vegetable or canola oil

Optional Fillings

Guacamole
Sour cream
Sliced avocados
Salsa
Hot sauce

Yield: 8 tacos

Stuff You'll Need

1. Brown the ground beef in a frying pan over medium heat, then drain the fat. Add the water, onion, chili powder, garlic salt, and cumin. Simmer, stirring occasionally, for 10 minutes or until most of the water has evaporated.

2. To prepare the shells, heat ¼-inch of oil in a small frying pan over medium-high heat until hot but not smoking. Place a tortilla in the oil for about 30 seconds, turn it over with tongs, and fold in half (as shown). Cook 30 seconds, turn over, and cook another 30 seconds

3. Once cooked, transfer the crisp, golden shells to paper towels and drain.

4. Fill each shell with 2 or 3 tablespoons of meat, some lettuce, cheese, tomato wedges, and any optional fillings you choose.

Bad Boy Burritos

Burritos are easy to make. They're also great to make in batches so you can freeze them for later. For vegetarian burritos, eliminate the beef filling and add more refried beans, cheese, and rice. You can also use packaged burrito or taco seasoning mix and eliminate the chili powder, garlic salt, and cumin.

Ingredients

1 pound ground beef
1 cup water
½ cup minced onion
3 tablespoons chili powder
1 tablespoon garlic salt
¼ teaspoon cumin
1 cup white rice
15-ounce can refried beans
2 cups shredded cheddar cheese
10–12 flour tortillas

Yield: 10 to 12 burritos

Topping Suggestions

Sour cream
Guacamole
Salsa
Fresh cilantro sprigs
Hot sauce
Red or green enchilada sauce

Important tip

To heat up the burritos in a microwave, remove the foil, wrap them individually in paper towels, and cook 1 to 1½ minutes.

Stuff You'll Need

1. Brown the ground beef in a frying pan over medium heat, then drain the fat. Add the water, onion, chili powder, garlic salt, and cumin. Simmer, stirring occasionally, for about 10 minutes or until most of the water has evaporated.

2. Cook the rice according to package directions, or use the rice cooking chart on page 206.

3. Place each tortilla on a piece of foil. Spoon 3 tablespoons of the meat mixture on half of each tortilla. Top with 3 tablespoons refried beans, 2 tablespoons rice, and 2 tablespoons cheese.

4. Fold the tortilla over the filling, roll up, and seal with foil. Place directly on the rack of a 400°F oven and bake for 30 minutes. Carefully remove the foil and enjoy hot!

Stir-Fry Beef

The secret to a good stir-fry is knowing when to add the ingredients based upon their cooking times. Make sure the wok (or deep pan) is hot, and have all your ingredients cut up and ready to go before you start cooking—once you get started, there's no turning back!

Ingredients

1 medium onion, sliced
1 medium bell pepper, cut into strips
¾ cup sliced mushrooms
1 pound top round or sirloin steak, cut into strips
2 cups white rice
2 tablespoons olive oil
1 cup bean sprouts
20–30 snow peas
2 large garlic cloves, minced
¼ teaspoon black pepper
2–3 tablespoons soy sauce or oyster sauce
1 tablespoon flour or cornstarch

Yield: 4 servings

Stuff You'll Need

1. Slice the onion, then cut each slice in half and break them apart.

2. Cut the bell pepper into strips.

3. Slice the mushrooms.

4. Cut the beef into thin strips about 2 inches long and ½ inch wide.

5. Cook the rice according to package directions, or use the rice cooking chart on page 206.

6. Heat the oil in a wok or deep frying pan over medium-high heat. Add the beef strips and cook about 2 minutes, or until browned on both sides.

7. Add the onions and bell peppers. Cook while stirring for about 1 minute.

8. Add the bean sprouts, snow peas, garlic, black pepper, and soy sauce. Toss the ingredients, then sprinkle with flour and stir another minute, or until the vegetables are tender-crisp and the liquid thickens a bit.

9. Spoon a cup of rice into individual serving bowls and top with the stir-fry mixture. Serve with soy sauce and eat with chopsticks (if you're brave enough!).

Beef Stroganoff

When I was a kid my father knew two recipes. One was a horrible tuna casserole made with cream of mushroom soup and canned tuna fish that was topped with canned peas and crushed potato chips. Fortunately, he also had this great stroganoff recipe, which he made with chicken, veal, pork, day-old steak, or any type of meat we had on hand. He also served it over rice, rather than the classic egg noodles.

Ingredients

1 medium onion, chopped
1 cup sliced mushrooms
1 pound round steak, cut into thin strips
1 cup rice
2 teaspoons olive oil
2 large garlic cloves, minced
1 teaspoon salt
½ teaspoon black pepper
1 cup sour cream

Yield: 4 servings

Important tip
Cool the pan slightly before stirring in the sour cream. The ingredients should be hot, but not still cooking.

Stuff You'll Need

1. Chop the onion.

2. Slice the mushrooms.

3. Cut the beef into thin strips about 2 inches long and ½ inch wide.

4. Cook the rice according to package directions, or use the rice cooking chart on page 206.

5. Heat the oil in a deep frying pan over medium heat. Add all the ingredients except the sour cream, and cook, stirring occasionally, until the meat is thoroughly cooked and the vegetables are tender.

6. Remove the pan from the heat and let cool for a minute. Add the sour cream and stir well.

Try This Variation!

Traditional Stroganoff

Instead of serving the stroganoff over rice, try it the traditional way—over egg noodles. For this recipe, a 12-ounce package of wide egg noodles is recommended.

7. Spoon the stroganoff over rice and serve immediately.

Moo for You

The cow is one America's most versatile domesticated farm animals. It gives us milk, cheese, butter, and meat for our burgers!

$5,000 Burger Special

The Fleur de Lys restaurant in Las Vegas offers a $5,000 burger-and-wine combination. The Kobe beef burger is topped with duck foie gras and shaved black truffles, and served on brioche. It comes with a bottle of limited-edition wine that is served in expensive crystal stemware, which the diner gets to take home! Those who order the FleurBurger 5000 can bring a friend (who gets a free regular burger) to witness the "event." They also receive a certificate of proof. Incidentally, the burger can be ordered without the wine for the bargain price of $75.

Beefy Holidays

In the U.S., the day when the most beef is eaten is Memorial Day. Labor Day and the Fourth of July run a close second.

Liberty Burgers

The hamburger's name is derived from its ancestor, the Hamburg steak, which originated in Hamburg, Germany, and was brought to America by German immigrants in the late 1800s. During World War I, hamburgers were called *Liberty Sandwiches* to avoid any association with Germany.

I'll Take Mine "To Go"

In the U.S., when it comes to burgers, about 60 percent are ordered in restaurants – and 65 percent of those are from fast-food places.

A Distant Second

Americans eat lots of burgers, but beef falls a distant second to chicken as their favorite meat.

Indian Cows

If you were a cow and got to choose where to live, you should definitely pick India, where cows are considered sacred. They are allowed to roam freely and live full lives without ever taking a trip to the slaughterhouse. There are over 1 billion cows on earth, and about 200 million live in India.

Butter Cow

Every August at the Iowa and Illinois State Fairs, a full-size cow is sculpted out of over 550 pounds of butter. (I'm betting they don't display these "butter bovines" in the sun!)

Ye Olde 96er

Noted for its hamburger-eating contests, Denny's Beer Barrel Pub in Clearfield, Pennsylvania, began offering "Ye Olde 96er" on the menu in 1998. The six-pound burger is garnished with a half head of lettuce, two tomatoes, twelve slices of cheese, a cup of peppers, two onions, and plenty of mayo, mustard, and ketchup. To date, no one has been able to finish one.

Big Bertha

While the average cow lives for seven years, a bovine named Big Bertha, who lived on a farm in Northern Ireland, clobbered that statistic. She lived forty-nine years, during which time she also gave birth to a record thirty-nine calves.

First the Beef, Then the Breath Mints

Among consumers, the most popular flavors enjoyed with beef are onion, garlic, and Worcestershire sauce.

16. Pigs and Lambs

Pig and lamb public relations.

Pigs don't have very good publicists. Although they are one of the smartest animals and cleaner than most, pigs are often considered dirty because they wallow in the mud. What most people don't realize, however, is that pigs don't have sweat glands, so they lie in the mud just to cool themselves off.

Lambs, on the other hand, get very good press. They're considered sweet and pure — like Mary's little lamb, whose "fleece was white as snow." They are also thought of as calm and mild, as in the well-known phrase "gentle as a lamb." You'll never hear anyone describe a pig's skin as pink as a rose, or utter the words "gentle as a pig."

Although pigs and lambs are very different, they do have one thing in common — neither is as popular as chicken or beef in the standard American diet. Because of this, they don't have as great a presence in the marketplace. Typically, there are fewer cuts of each available. Both, however, are delicious and shouldn't be ignored. So this chapter pays tribute to these two slightly overlooked varieties of meat.

You'll learn all about pork and lamb, including the different cuts and how to cook them, as well as important storage and handling practices. I've included some easy-to-make, delicious recipes for pork chops, ribs, and ham. There are also instructions for cooking a lamb roast, as well as preparing lamb stew, chops, and kabobs.

So go ahead . . . feel free to eat like a pig (just remember to be silent as a lamb about it).

Hey, Porky!

Pork can be a healthy choice. Ounce for ounce, pork tenderloin, which is the leanest cut, is nearly as lean as a boneless, skinless chicken breast. Pork is also a very versatile meat that lends itself to a variety of cooking methods. Depending on the cut, pork is a popular choice for roasting, pan-frying, baking, and grilling. It can be smoked or cured for ham and bacon, and is also a popular ingredient in sausage and hot dogs. The following pages present the most popular pork cuts and pork products, and how to buy, store, and cook them.

Popular Pork Cuts

		Cut	Description	Best Cooking Methods
Fresh		Chops	Loin chops are lean, meaty, and resemble mini T-bone steaks. Rib chops are tender and a bit fatty. Shoulder chops are tough and chewy.	*Loin and rib chops:* Baked; pan-fried; broiled; grilled. *Shoulder chops:* Braised.
Fresh		Fresh ham (pork leg)	Available whole or halved and with or without the bone. It is the same cut used for cured or smoked hams.	Roasted.
Fresh		Loin roast	Lean, tender roast sold with or without the bone. Tends to dry out if overcooked.	Roasted.
Fresh		Rib roast (rack of pork)	Tender, somewhat fatty, and very flavorful roast.	Roasted.
Fresh	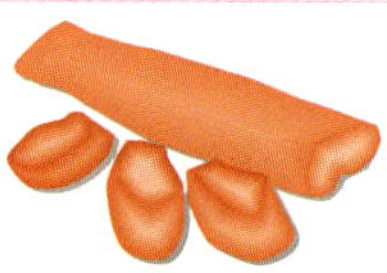	Tenderloin	Lean, boneless, and very tender roast. Mild-flavored and juicy. Sliced tenderloins are called cutlets and medallions.	*Whole roast*: Roasted; grilled; broiled. *Sliced or cut up:* Sautéed.
Fresh		Ribs (baby backs and spareribs)	Baby back ribs are smaller, not as fatty, less meaty, but more tender than spareribs.	Oven baked; grilled.
Cured	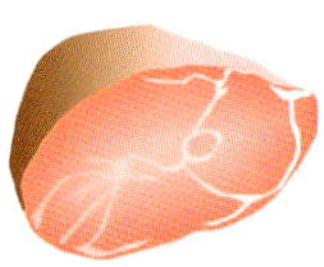	Ham	The cured hind leg. Most are fully cooked and available with or without the bone.	*Uncooked:* Requires oven baking. *Cooked:* Can be heated or eaten cold.
Cured		Bacon	A cured, smoked, fatty cut.	Pan-fried (frizzled).
Cured		Canadian bacon	Fully cooked, smoked pork loin. More like ham than bacon in flavor and texture.	Needs to be heated only.

Buying and Storing Tips

- When buying fresh pork, look for cuts that are moist and have a healthy pink color (not grey or red).
- Store prepackaged cuts in the coldest area of the refrigerator, where they will keep up to three days. Ground pork will keep a day or two.
- Use packaged hot dogs, luncheon meats, and bacon by the date on the label. If opened sooner, use within five days.
- If you don't plan to cook raw pork within two days, freeze it. It should be well wrapped and used within six months. Ground pork will keep in the freezer about three months.
- I don't recommend freezing ham because it affects the texture of the meat. You can, however, freeze leftover ham (usually chopped or cubed) to use in soups or casseroles, or to flavor cooked greens and bean dishes. It should be used within three months.

The Other Ground Meat

Traditionally made from the tough shoulder meat, ground pork is an excellent choice to use in burgers, meatloaves, and meatballs. Use it alone or mix it with ground beef.

Cooking the Pig

When it comes to cooking pork, two basic methods are used. Dry-heat methods (grilling, broiling, pan-frying, sautéing, stir-frying, roasting) are good choices for naturally tender cuts. Moist-heat methods (stewing, braising) are best for tenderizing tougher cuts.

Lean, fresh pork cooks quickly and can become dry and tough, so be careful not to overcook it. Cooking times for pork depend on the cut and cooking method. For instance, a roast's cooking time depends on its weight, if it has a bone, and the heat of the oven. For other pork cuts, like chops and cutlets, the thickness (not the weight) and the cooking methods are factors.

Cook roasts and thick chops until they should reach an internal temperature of at least 160°F (the inside may be slightly pink). Use a meat thermometer to determine doneness. Ground pork and sausage should be cooked thoroughly with no sign of pink.

Here are more cooking tips and guidelines:

- Cook roasts uncovered, fat side up, and without liquid.
- Unless otherwise instructed, cook roasts 20 to 25 minutes per pound in a 350°F oven.
- A roast keeps cooking after it's taken from the oven. So remove it when the thermometer reads 150° to 155°F. Cover loosely with foil, and let rest 10 to 15 minutes before carving.
- Grill chops, kabobs, burgers, tenderloins, and sausage over medium-low heat. Broil them about four inches below the heat source.
- Don't pierce the meat as it cooks. Use tongs or a spatula for turning.
- Stir-fry pork strips quickly over medium-high heat.
- When frying or sautéing, add a little oil to the pan. Cook uncovered over medium-high heat.

How Much Should I Buy?

When determining the amount of pork to buy, use the following general guidelines:

Type of Pork	Servings per Pound
Bone-in roasts and chops	2½ to 3
Boneless roasts and chops	3 to 4
Bone-in ham	2½ to 3
Boneless ham	3 to 4
Spareribs	1

Mediterranean-Style Pork Chops

This is a fast and easy pork recipe that tastes like you spent hours preparing it. The meat is tender and juicy, and richly flavored by the surrounding ingredients.

Ingredients

1 small onion, chopped
2 tablespoons olive oil
2 pork loin chops, 1½ inches thick
1 cup diced tomatoes
1 teaspoon minced garlic
1 tablespoon dried oregano
4 ounces feta cheese, crumbled

Yield: 2 servings

Stuff You'll Need

1. Chop the onion.

2. Heat the oil in a deep skillet over medium heat. Add the pork, onions, tomatoes, garlic, and oregano. Cover and cook for 3 to 4 minutes.

3. Turn the chops over and stir the other ingredients. Cover and continue to cook another 3 to 4 minutes.

4. Place the chops on individual dinner plates. Cover each with half the tomato-onion mixture, then sprinkle with feta cheese.

Rosemary Pork Loin

A former roommate bought a pork loin and didn't know how to cook it. I did a little research and came up with this recipe, which is actually a "merger" of two others. The pineapple came from one recipe, and the rosemary-garlic crust came from another. Turned out to be a winning combination.

Ingredients

2 tablespoons olive oil
2 tablespoons dried rosemary
1 tablespoon minced garlic
3–3½ pound boneless pork loin
8-ounce can sliced pineapple

Yield: 6 to 7 servings

Important tip

If the pork loin you buy has already been halved into two pieces, sandwich the pineapple slices between the halves, then secure all around with toothpicks.

Stuff You'll Need

1. Combine the olive oil, rosemary, and garlic in a small bowl. Set aside.

2. With a sharp knife, split the pork loin lengthwise down the middle to make a deep pocket. *Do not cut all the way through to the bottom.* Fill the pocket with pineapple slices.

3. Close the pocket and seal with wooden toothpicks. Place the roast in a baking pan, then brush the outside with the rosemary-garlic mixture.

4. Bake in a preheated 350°F oven for about 45 minutes, or until the internal temperature reaches 160°F on a meat thermometer. Let the roast rest for 10 minutes before cutting into slices.

Stuffed Pork Chops

These pork chops taste like there's a holiday party in your mouth and everyone is invited!

Ingredients

1 large apple, peeled and chopped
1 medium onion, finely chopped
2 tablespoons butter
1 cup dry bread stuffing cubes
1 teaspoon dried thyme
½ teaspoon minced garlic
½ teaspoon salt
2 boneless pork loin chops, 1 inch thick
½–1 cup beef broth

Yield: 2 servings

Important tip

Be careful not to cut yourself when making pockets in the chops. Always cut away from your hands and body.

Stuff You'll Need

1. Peel and core the apple and chop into small pieces.

2. Finely chop the onion.

3. Melt the butter.

4. Place the apples, onions, bread cubes, butter, thyme, garlic, and salt in a large bowl and mix well.

5. With a sharp knife, cut a deep pocket into each pork chop. *Cut close to but not all the way through the bottom and sides.*

6. Fill the pockets with as much stuffing as you can.

7. Place the stuffed chops in an ovenproof dish. Add about ¼ inch of beef broth in the bottom of the dish. Cover and bake in a preheated 350°F oven for 25 to 30 minutes.

Spice-Rubbed Baked Ribs

This is an easy way to prepare ribs without a lot of kitchen or barbecue mess. The meat becomes so tender it practically melts off the bone.

Ingredients

2–3 pounds baby back ribs
3 tablespoons brown sugar
1 teaspoon garlic salt
1 teaspoon paprika
½ teaspoon dry mustard

Yield: 2 to 3 servings

Stuff You'll Need

1. Cut the slabs of ribs into smaller portions, usually 4 to 5 ribs.

2. Mix the brown sugar, garlic salt, paprika, and mustard in a bowl. Rub the mixture on both sides of the rib.

3. Tightly wrap the rib portions in foil and refrigerate for 1 hour.

4. Place the wrapped ribs on a cookie sheet and bake in a preheated 300°F oven for 2 hours or until the meat is very tender.

BBQ Ribs

This recipe shows you how to finish cooking partially baked ribs on the grill.

Ingredients

2–3 pounds baby back ribs
3 tablespoons brown sugar
1 teaspoon garlic salt
1 teaspoon paprika
½ teaspoon dry mustard
½–¾ cup barbecue sauce

Yield: 2 to 3 servings

Important tip

When browning the ribs on the grill, it's okay if they burn a little. Just be careful they don't burn too much. If the grill flames up, move the ribs away from the fire until it subsides.

Stuff You'll Need

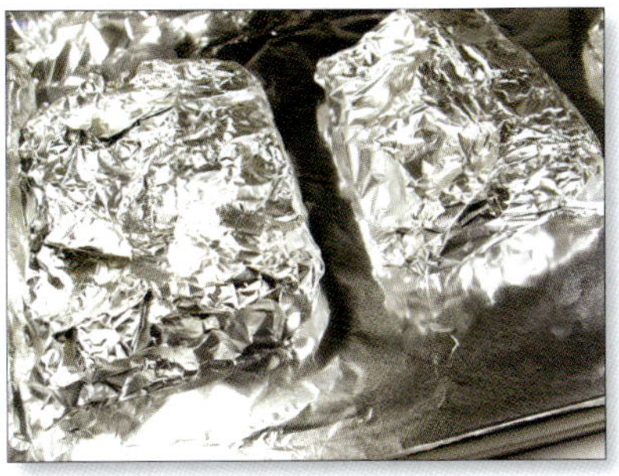

1. Follow the same steps for the Spiced-Rubbed Baked Ribs on page 334.

2. Unwrap the cooked rib portions and place on a heated grill, bone side down. Brush liberally with barbecue sauce.

3. Cook 2 minutes then turn the ribs over.

4. Brush with barbecue sauce and cook another 2 minutes.

5. Remove from the grill and serve as is or with additional sauce.

Maple-Glazed Ham

Because it is smoked and precooked, this ham is easy to prepare.

Ingredients

1 cup maple syrup (pure is best)
3/4 cup firmly packed brown sugar
8–10 pound fully cooked smoked ham

Yield: About 20 servings

Stuff You'll Need

1. Place the maple syrup and brown sugar in a small mixing bowl and stir until most of the sugar has dissolved. Set aside.

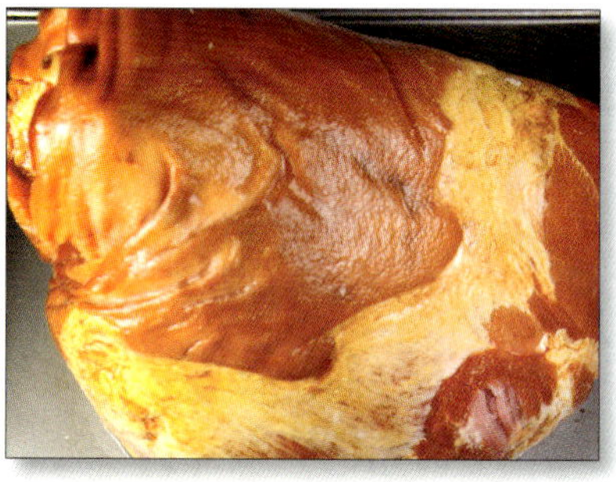

2. Place the ham in a roasting pan meat side down. Set it on the bottom shelf of a preheated 325°F oven. Bake uncovered for 2 1/2 to 3 hours, or until the internal temperature reaches 130°F on a meat thermometer.

3. Remove the ham from the oven and allow it to cool 5 minutes. Then, using a very sharp knife, cut the rind from the ham, being careful not to cut away the fat.

4. Cut criss-cross diagonal slashes into the fat (but not into the meat) every 3/4 inch. Spoon half the glaze over the top and sides of the ham.

5. Increase the oven heat to 450°F, return the ham to the oven, and bake 10 minutes. Remove from the oven, spoon on the remaining glaze, and return to the oven for another 10 minutes.

Ham Baking Chart

Hams are sold either uncooked or fully cooked. A cooked ham can be eaten as is or it can be heated up before serving. This chart gives approximate baking times for uncooked ham, as well as heating times for ham that is already cooked. It is best to use a meat thermometer for determining doneness. Simply insert the thermometer into the thickest part of the ham (without touching the bone), and bake until it reaches the internal temperature listed below.

Type of Ham	Oven Temp	Weight (pounds)	Internal Temperature	Minutes per Pound
Smoked half, bone-in (uncooked)	350°F	5 to 7	160°F	25 to 30
Smoked whole, bone-in (uncooked)	350°F	Up to 14	160°F	18 to 20
Smoked whole, bone-in (uncooked)	350°F	Over 14	160°F	25 to 30
Smoked half, boneless (cooked)	325°F	2 to 3	130°F	25 to 30
Smoked whole, bone-in (cooked)	325°F	6 to 10	130°F	20 to 30
Smoked whole, bone-in (cooked)	325°F	11 to 16	130°F	15 to 20

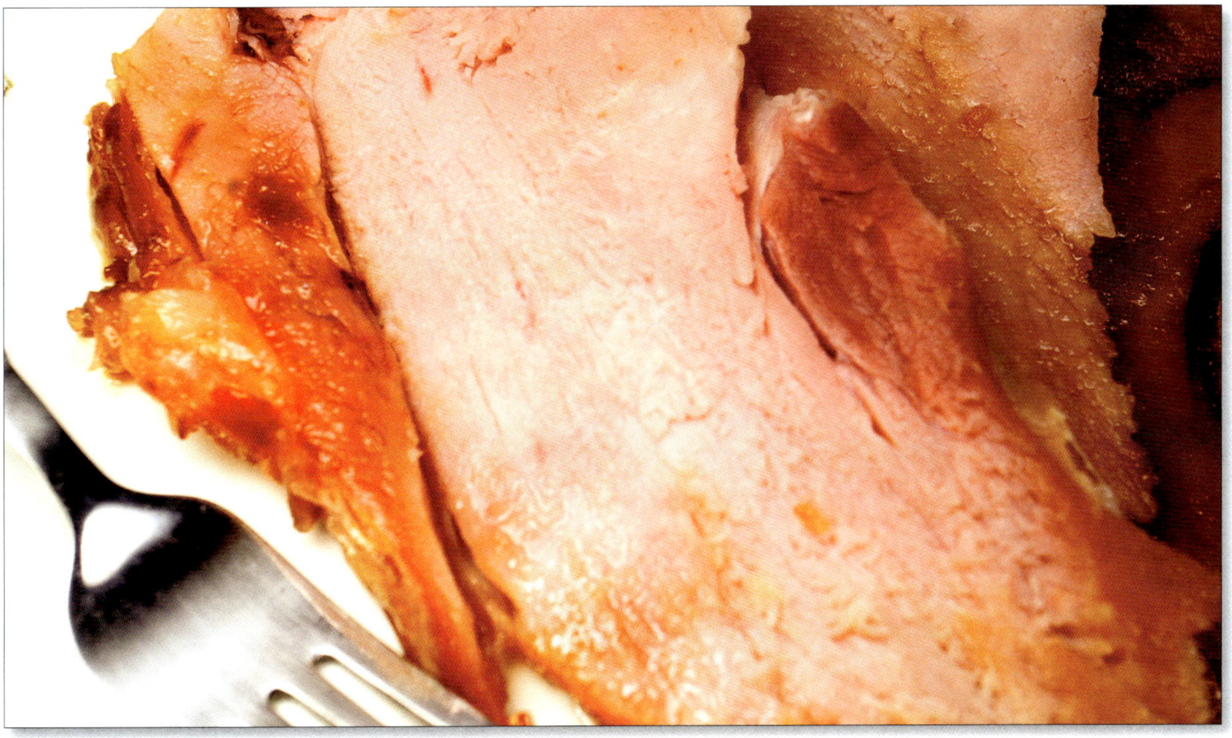

6. Let the ham rest for 20 minutes before slicing and serving. Enjoy as is or with a little Dijon mustard on the side.

Let's Talk Lamb

There are over 200 different breeds of sheep, and over the years we have used them for their wool, their meat, and their milk. Lambs are young sheep, under one year old; their meat is tender and flavorful. Meat from a full-grown sheep, called mutton, is very tough and has a strong gamey taste.

Lamb cuts—other than shoulder and loin chops—are hard to find. I once had to go to three stores to find a leg of lamb. It wasn't displayed; I had to ask the butcher for it.

Grades of Lamb

The USDA-graded lamb sold in supermarkets is labeled as prime, choice, or select. Color, maturity, firmness, texture, and the proportion of fat to lean meat are factors that determine grade. Prime lamb, which is the top grade, is flavorful and tender with a good amount of fat marbling. Choice and select grades have less fat than prime, and they are not as tender.

Buying and Storing Tips

- When buying fresh lamb, choose cuts that are moist and pinkish-red. (A dark red color indicates that the meat is older and less tender.)
- Store fresh lamb in the refrigerator in its original packaging up to four days. Ground lamb will keep a day or two.
- If you don't plan to use the raw lamb within two days, freeze it. It should be well wrapped and used within six to nine months. Ground lamb will keep about four months in the freezer.
- Defrost frozen lamb in the refrigerator, not on a countertop or in an empty sink.

Popular Lamb Cuts

		Cut	Description	Best Cooking Methods
Roasts		Leg of lamb	Usually the whole leg (with or without the bone). Meat is tender yet firm.	Roasted.
		Rib roast (rack of lamb)	Tender, somewhat fatty, and very flavorful. Often tied in a circle and called a "crown roast."	Roasted.
		Loin chop	Extremely tender cuts from the loin.	Broiled; pan-fried; grilled. Best cooked quickly and served rare to medium.
Chops		Rib chop	Extremely tender cuts from the rib (have a rib bone attached).	Broiled; pan-fried; grilled. Best served rare to medium.
		Shoulder chop	Very tough and fatty with several bones.	Stewed; or well-marinated and grilled or broiled.

How Much to Buy?

To determine how large a roast to buy, figure that each pound of an uncooked leg of lamb (bone-in) yields about eight or nine ounces of edible meat when cooked. Boneless roasts and cuts, as well as ground lamb yield a little more than ten ounces.

Cooking Lamb

Lamb can be grilled, pan-fried, broiled, roasted, braised, or stewed. The premier tender cuts like rib and loin chops cook up quickly and work with any method. Tough shoulder and shank cuts benefit from moist cooking methods such as stewing and braising. They can also be marinated and then broiled or grilled.

The more tender roasts and cuts are recommended to be eaten rare or medium-rare. Tougher cuts must be slow-cooked until they are well done before they are easy to chew.

Here are some additional cooking tips:

- Lamb meat is marbled with fat, so trim off any excess fat found on the exterior. (Leave no more than ⅛-inch.)
- Cook lamb roasts and chops to a minimum internal temperature of 135°F. Cook ground lamb to 160°F.
- Before cooking a roast, preheat the oven to 450°F. As soon as you pop the roast in the oven, reduce the heat as indicated in the Lamb Roasting Chart below.
- Because a lamb roast will continue to cook after it is taken from the oven, remove it when the temperature registers about five degrees lower than the desired degree of doneness. Allow it to rest for fifteen to twenty minutes. Smaller roasts (five pounds or less) may not rise much in temperature after being removed from the oven; let them rest only five to ten minutes before serving.

Marinating Lamb

Marinating can help tenderize tough lamb cuts like shoulder chops. It also adds flavor. Cubes of lamb for kabobs are also good marinade candidates. Most marinades have an acidic content—usually vinegar or a citrus juice—which breaks down the tough muscle fibers of the meat.

As an added bonus, marinating meat before grilling it can reduce the formation of harmful carcinogens by about 90 percent.

Lamb Roasting Chart

This chart gives approximate cooking times for lamb roasts. It is best to determine doneness with a meat thermometer, which should be inserted in the center of the roast before cooking. The internal temperatures for the various degrees of doneness appear in the chart below.

It is important to preheat the oven to 450°F. As soon as you pop in the roast, reduce the heat as indicated in the chart below.

		MINUTES PER POUND		
Type of Roast	Oven Temp	Rare (135°–140°F)	Medium (155°–160°F)	Well (165°–170°F)
Leg of lamb, bone-in	325°F	15 to 20	20 to 25	25 to 30
Leg of lamb, boneless	325°F	10 to 15	15 to 20	20 to 25
Rib roast (rack of lamb)	375°F	25 to 30	30 to 35	35 to 40

Pan-Fried Loin Lamb Chops

Here's a quick and easy recipe for stovetop chops.

Ingredients

3 tablespoons olive oil
1 teaspoon dried rosemary
1 teaspoon minced garlic
12 ounces loin lamb chops

Yield: 2 servings

1. Combine the olive oil, rosemary, and garlic in a small bowl.

2. Heat a large frying pan over medium-high heat. Add the chops and cook 1 to 2 minutes on each side until browned.

3. Add the olive oil mixture to the pan and continue to cook the chops another 3 to 4 minutes on each side.

5. Remove from the heat, let the chops rest 2 minutes, then serve.

Stuff You'll Need

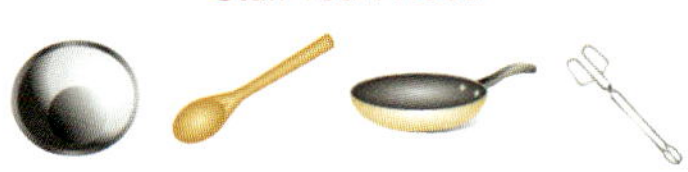

Greek-Style Lamb Stew

In my opinion, the Greeks are specialists with lamb . . . Gyros, lamb shish kabobs, and my favorite—lamb stew!

Ingredients

1 medium onion, chopped
1 pound lamb shoulder
2 tablespoons olive oil
15-ounce can diced tomatoes, or
  2 medium tomatoes, chopped
1 teaspoon dried rosemary
1 tablespoon minced garlic
1 teaspoon dried thyme
2 teaspoons salt
¼ cup sliced black olives
2 tablespoons flour
¼ cup crumbled feta cheese

Yield: 4 servings

Stuff You'll Need

1. Chop the onion.

2. Cut the lamb into bite-size cubes.

3. Heat the olive oil in a deep pot over medium-high heat. Add the lamb and brown and all sides.

4. Add all of the remaining ingredients, except the flour and feta cheese, and stir well. Reduce the heat to low, cover, and simmer for 45 minutes stirring occasionally. Add the flour and continue to cook another 10 minutes, or until the lamb is tender.

5. Spoon into individual bowls, sprinkle with feta cheese, and serve.

Bob's Kabobs

I once gave a piece of this lamb to my dog. She liked it so much, from that day forward she would sniff her dog food and walk away, letting me know that mere dog food was no longer acceptable. The battle lasted for nearly a week. The lesson—don't give any of this to your dog!

Ingredients

1 pound lamb shoulder
1 large red bell pepper
1 medium onion
2 large lemons
$\frac{1}{4}$ cup olive oil
1 tablespoon dried rosemary
1 tablespoon minced garlic
$\frac{1}{2}$ teaspoon salt

Yield: 4 servings

Important tip

It's best to use metal skewers for these kabobs because they take a while to cook. If you use wooden skewers, be sure to soak them at least 30 minutes before adding the meat and vegetables. This will help keep them from burning.

Stuff You'll Need

1. Debone the lamb, trim the excess fat, then cut the meat into bite-size pieces.

2. Cut the bell pepper into $1\frac{1}{2}$-inch squares.

3. Cut the onion in quarters, then peel apart the layers.

4. Juice the lemons.

5. Place the lemon juice, oil, rosemary, garlic, salt, and meat in a resealable container. Cover the container and shake to coat the meat with marinade. Refrigerate at least 4 hours or overnight.

6. Thread the marinated lamb, onion, and peppers (alternating them) on four 6-inch (or two 12-inch) skewers.

7. Place the skewers on a hot grill, turning them every 5 minutes or so, for 15 to 20 minutes, or until cooked to the desired degree of doneness.

8. Serve the hot kabobs as is or placed over a bed of rice.

Don't Forget These Guys!

Calling all carnivores . . . check out the following trivia tidbits on these tasty choices.

Trotting Pigs

In many cookbooks throughout the world, pigs' feet are called *trotters.*

Follow That Pig!

Sailors are a superstitious lot. Early seamen always kept pigs on board ships because they believed the animals would instinctively swim toward land in case of a shipwreck. Sailors also felt pigs had magical control over the wind. They feared just saying the word "pig" out loud while sailing would cause the wind to kick up. Killing one would result in a major storm.

Pigs and Sheep Rule!

In Denmark, known for its Danish ham, there are twice as many pigs as people. In New Zealand, sheep outnumber people nine to one – in Australia, that number is four to one.

A Symbol of Luck

In many countries, people believe that eating pork on New Year's Day will bring a year of good luck and prosperity. Why pork? Because when pigs root, they move forward, a symbol of progress. (Unlike chickens, which scratch backwards and have wings – a symbol of luck flying away.) Pigs are also plump, a hopeful sign of "plump" wallets in the coming year. Pork roasts are traditionally served in Germany; sausage is an Italian favorite; roast suckling pig is eaten in places like Spain, Portugal, Cuba, Ireland, Hungary, and Austria; pig's feet are a customary choice in Sweden; and ham is often served in the United States.

It's Number One

Pork is the most consumed meat throughout the world. In the U.S., it ranks third behind chicken and beef.

Bacon on a Stick

In Hungary, it is customary to spear a chunk of bacon with a stick and roast it over a fire. As the fat heats up, the drippings are caught on a piece of bread, which is eaten immediately (usually with a glass of wine).

I'll Have a Glass of Lamb's Wool, Please

When you hear "lamb's wool," you probably think of something warm and fleecy that lines your boots. It is also the name of a traditional English beverage that has been enjoyed during the Christmas season since the Middle Ages. The hot brew contains ale, spices, and the soft flesh of baked apples. Its name comes from the fleecy look of the apple bits that float on top.

Pork Belly Futures

In China, cooks began salting pork bellies as early as 1,500 BC. That makes bacon one of the world's oldest processed meats.

You May Be Missing Something

You'll find that the meat cases in most U.S. supermarkets dedicate very little space to lamb. Although its consumption has increased in recent years, lamb still lags behind other meats. As a matter of fact, one in three Americans (women in particular) have never even tried it.

17. Holiday Feast

Cooking for twelve!

One of the best things about the holidays and other special occasions is getting together with friends and family members you don't get to see all the time. Another highlight is the food – always a feast! I can still remember one of the first holiday dinners I made for my family. It was Christmas and I was living in Florida, where the temperature was generally around seventy degrees in December. That year, however, the temperature dropped to twenty degrees and my house lost power for six hours! Although we sat down to dinner later than expected, somehow I managed to get it all done (including the holiday turkey).

In this chapter, I'll guide you in preparing a spectacular feast for those special occasions when you want to offer your guests more than just a meal. For the main course, I've chosen turkey because it is the most popular holiday entrée served in the United States. You'll learn how to buy it, prep it, cook it, stuff it, and carve it up. By the time you're finished, you'll be making gravy out of this bird.

You can't have a feast without some scrumptious side dishes, and I've included some of my favorites. There are Candied Sweet 'Taters and a luscious Broccoli Soufflé, as well as a moist and flavorful Cranberry Bread. And when it comes to dessert . . . there's Pumpkin Pie to die for, and mouthwatering Bread Pudding.

Don't forget to put on your extra-loose holiday pants before you sit down to this feast. You'll need all the room you can get!

There are many ways to prepare a turkey—deep fry, barbecue, smoke, and roast. Most people roast their turkeys in the oven. It's the tried and true method, and the easiest for beginners.

Fresh, Frozen, or Breast Only

Most turkeys are sold frozen, but you can also buy them fresh from a butcher or even some grocery stores. Frozen turkeys are delicious, but fresh turkeys are generally moister. If you're cooking for just a few people and everyone is a fan of white meat, you might consider buying a turkey breast.

Thawing

Frozen turkeys must be thawed before they are cooked—the larger the turkey, the longer it will take. It is best to thaw a frozen turkey in the refrigerator (leave it wrapped). Never leave it out to thaw on a counter or in an empty sink.

Fridge Defrost

Size	Defrost time
4 to 12 pounds	1 to 3 days
12 to 16 pounds	3 to 4 days
16 to 20 pounds	4 to 5 days
20 to 24 pounds	5 to 6 days

If there is no time to defrost the turkey in the refrigerator, you can thaw it in a cool water bath. Place the bird (still in the packaging) in a large clean sink, then fill the sink with cool water. Allow about thirty minutes defrosting time per pound, and change the water every thirty minutes until the turkey is thawed.

1. Check inside the turkey!

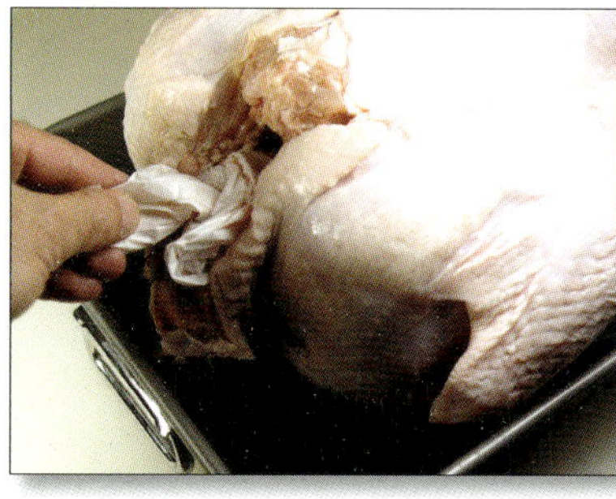

The turkey will have two cavities (one at the neck and the other between the drumsticks) that are filled with extra turkey parts. These parts include the neck and the giblets, which are the bird's edible innards—the heart, liver, and gizzard (don't ask). They are generally placed in a packet before being tucked into the cavities. Although you may want to pitch them, be aware that the neck and giblets are excellent addition to turkey soup. Whether you plan to use these parts or not, *be sure to remove them before cooking the turkey!*

If you want to stuff the bird at this point, check the instructions on page 350.

Turkey Roasting Chart

This chart gives approximate roasting times for whole turkeys and turkey breasts. Roasting times will vary depending on oven type, so begin checking for doneness about an hour before the end of the recommended time. The best way to determine doneness is by inserting a meat thermometer into the thickest area of the bird. An internal temperature of 170°F means the bird is done.

In preheated 325° F oven:

Whole Bird	Unstuffed	Stuffed	Serves
8 to 12 pounds	2¾ – 3 hours	3 – 3½ hours	Up to 4
12 to 14 pounds	3 – 3½ hours	3½ – 4 hours	4 to 7
14 to 18 pounds	3½ – 4 hours	4 – 4½ hours	7 to 8
18 to 20 pounds	4 – 4¼ hours	4¼ – 4¾ hours	8 to 10
20 to 24 pounds	4½ – 5 hours	5 – 5½ hours	10 to 15
Breast Only			
4 to 6 pounds	1¾ – 2¼ hours		4 to 6
6 to 8 pounds	2½ – 3¼ hours		6 to 8

2. Butter the bird.

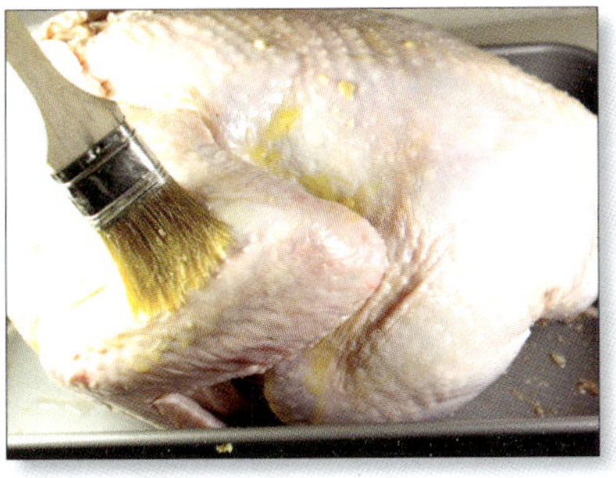

Although turkey is usually cooked breast-side up, as shown in the photo below, I like to cook it breast-side down, as shown in the photo above. This keeps the breast moist as it cooks. After placing the turkey in the roasting pan, brush the skin with butter, which will also help it stay moist and turn golden brown as it roasts. *During the last thirty minutes of cooking, turn the turkey over to brown the breast.*

3. Baste for taste.

Basting the bird as it roasts is another way to help it stay moist. As soon as there are enough drippings in the bottom of the pan, carefully remove the pan from the oven. Using a turkey baster or a spoon, take the juices from the pan and pour them over the skin. Return the turkey to the oven and continue to baste every thirty minutes or so.

4. Test for doneness.

To determine if the turkey is cooked, pierce the inner thigh with a fork. If the juices run clear, the bird is probably done. A more accurate way to check for doneness is with a meat thermometer, which should be inserted deep into the thigh without touching a bone. (When cooking a breast, insert the thermometer deep into the meatiest part.) When the internal temperature reaches 170°F, the bird is done.

To avoid bacterial contamination from the raw turkey, wash every plate, platter, utensil, and surface it has touched with hot soapy water.

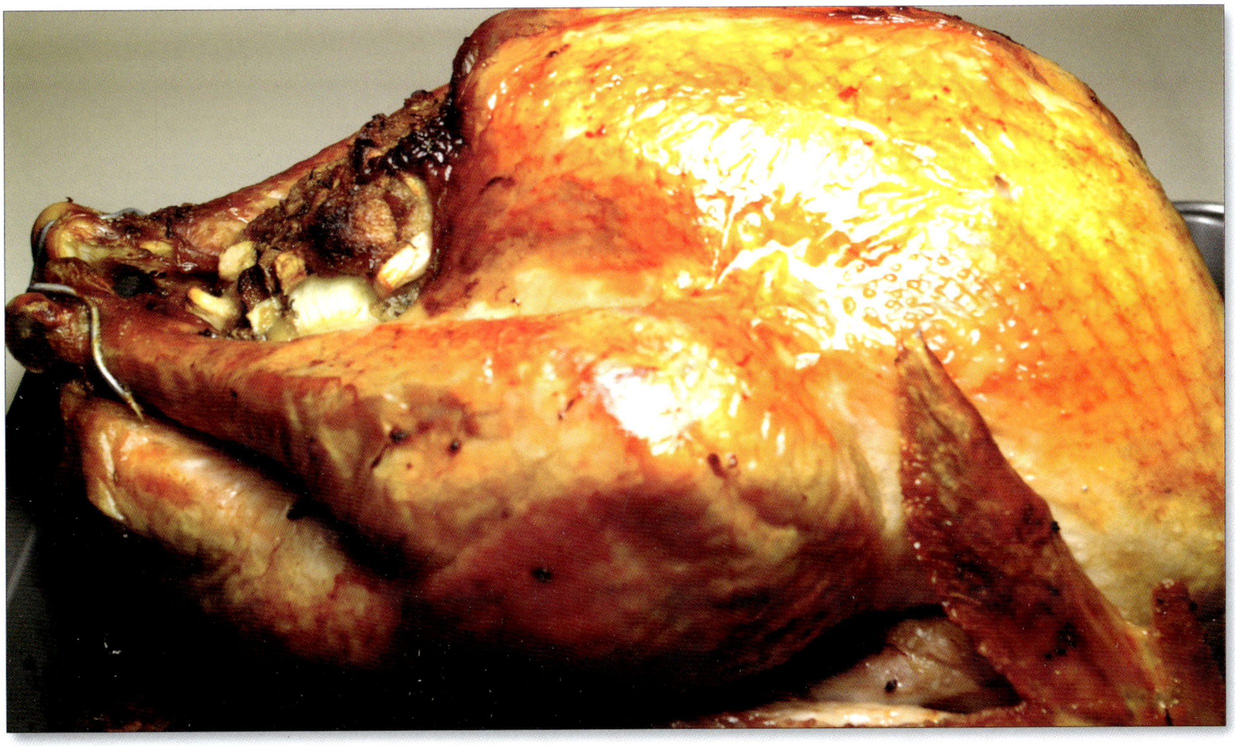

Serve It Up!

Carving a turkey is an art. In skilled hands, the bird can be cut in many ways, all of them good.

Let It Rest

I know that your lovely turkey looks ready to eat right now, but it needs to rest at least fifteen minutes before you start whittling away. Letting the bird rest allows it to cool a bit, so it is easier to handle. The meat will also slice better and produce cleaner cuts. You can remove the stuffing while you wait.

Be Sharp

Be sure to use a sharp knife when carving. The skin can be tough to cut with a dull knife. If you don't have a good carving knife, or an electric knife, use a serrated bread knife.

The Traditional Carve

This is the carving method most people use. It's very impressive when done right at the table.

First, locate the breastbone in the center of the breast and cut slices following the same angle as the breast. You can cut the pieces thin or thick. Make sure the person who loves the skin gets the first piece. Cut only as much as you need; the meat will keep better on the carcass. Once sliced, it will dry out.

In addition to removing the breast meat, you'll need to remove the wings, legs, and thighs. Start with the legs—cut the skin around the top of the leg then bend the joint with your hand until it pops. Cut the meat around the joint. Follow the same procedure for the wings and thighs.

For a detailed description of how to cut up a flippin' bird, see page 284.

The Whole Breast Carve

Instead of carving the breast in the traditional way, you can also remove it in one piece before slicing it. Start with your knife at the breastbone and follow the contour along the ribs. Remove as much breast as you can at once, set it on a platter or cutting board, then cut it widthwise into slices.

Gravy, Turkey!

Believe it or not, the juices and drippings and other bits of "stuff" on the bottom of the roasting pan are the basis for delicious gravy.

Ingredients

2 cups turkey drippings, excess fat removed
1 cup water
1 tablespoon butter
$\frac{1}{2}$ teaspoon crushed dried rosemary
$\frac{1}{2}$ teaspoon garlic salt
2–3 tablespoons flour

Yield: About 3 cups

1. Transfer the pan drippings to a pot and skim off and discard the excess fat with a spoon.

2. Add the water, butter, rosemary, and garlic salt to the pot and place over medium heat. Stir with a whisk while gradually adding the flour. Cook while constantly whisking for 5 minutes, or until the flour thickens to a gravy-like consistency. If it gets too thick, add water 1 tablespoon at a time. If it's too thin, add flour 1 teaspoon at a time, and wait about 1 minute between each addition.

3. Serve piping hot over turkey, stuffing, and, of course, mashed potatoes!

Time Saver

Instead of transferring the pan drippings to a pot, you can make the gravy right in the roasting pan on the stovetop (if it's large enough and you have the room).

Stuff You'll Need

Stuff It!

Turkey and stuffing go together like love and marriage. You can make stuffing in a pot on the stove or bake it in the oven in a casserole dish, but there's nothing better-tasting than stuffing that cooks inside the bird.

Grocery store shelves are lined with boxed stuffing mixes that are a snap to prepare and pretty tasty. However, homemade stuffings are pretty easy to make. Traditional varieties are made with bread and usually flavored with vegetables, herbs, and spices. But every family has its own special stuffing that it considers "traditional." Some have a rice or potato base; others contain sausage, chestnuts, oysters, or fruit; while vegetarian stuffings contain tofu. It's all good! My favorite stuffing has a cornbread base and is flavored with apples and sausage. The recipe is on page 351. Check it out!

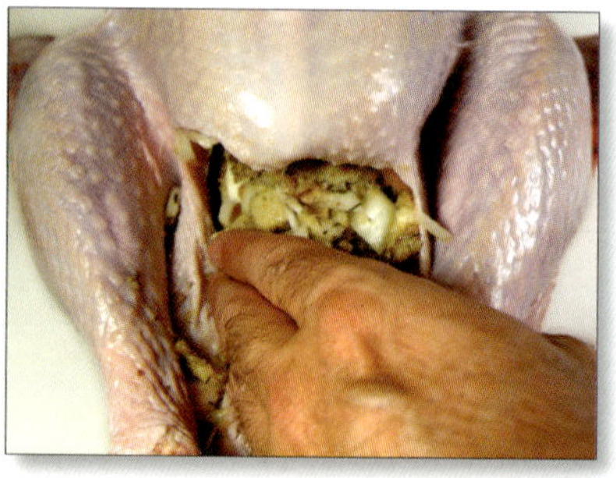

1. Fill 'er up.
With your hands, firmly pack as much stuffing as you can in the lower cavity. Try not to mash the stuffing as you pack.

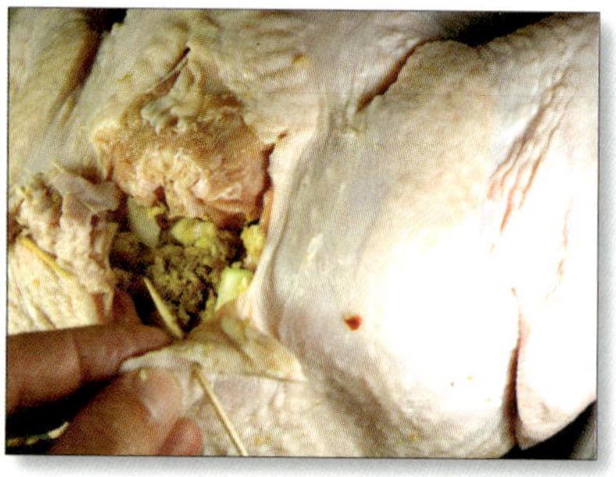

2. Don't forget the neck cavity.
If you have additional stuffing, fill the neck cavity. Lift up the flap of skin and add as much stuffing as you can. Seal the flap with wooden toothpicks.

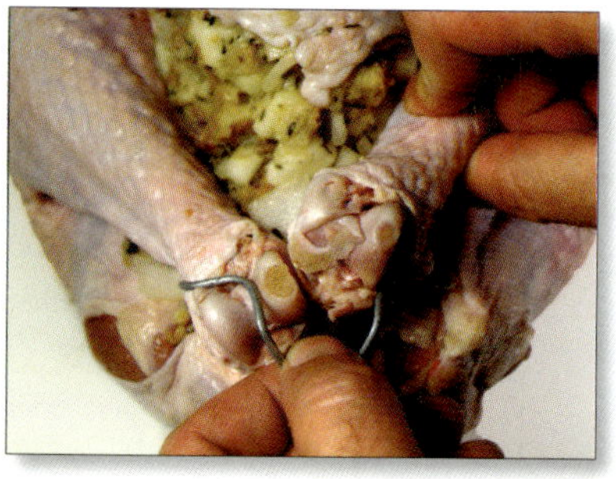

3. Secure them legs.
To hold the shape of the bird and to keep the stuffing in place, you have to secure the legs together. Some turkeys come with clips or ties for this. If your turkey doesn't come with these items, simply use a piece of string to tie the legs together.

4. Serve it up.
Before carving the bird, remove the stuffing. Using a long-handled spoon, scoop the stuffing from the cavity and place it in a serving bowl. Don't forget to remove the stuffing from the neck cavity, too.

How Much Stuffing?

The amount of stuffing you'll need is determined by amount of people you want to serve and the size of the bird. This chart offers general guidelines:

Turkey Weight	Stuffing Amount
8 to 12 pounds	6 cups
12 to 14 pounds	9 cups
14 to 18 pounds	12 cups
18 to 20 pounds	15 cups
20 to 24 pounds	18 cups

Cornbread-Apple-Sausage Stuffing

With the possible exception of dessert, this is my favorite part of a turkey feast.

Ingredients

1 pound ground sausage, removed from casing
1 medium onion, minced
1 large apple, peeled and chopped (about 1 cup)
4 cups dry cornbread stuffing cubes
$1\frac{1}{4}$ cups apple juice or cider, divided
1 tablespoon minced garlic
2 teaspoons dried sage
1 teaspoon dried thyme
1 teaspoon salt
2 tablespoons butter, cut into small pieces*

* Will need this ingredient if baking the stuffing in a casserole dish.

Yield: About 6 cups

Stuff You'll Need

1. Brown the sausage and drain the excess fat.

2. Mince the onion.

3. Chop the apple into $\frac{1}{4}$-inch cubes.

4. Place all of the ingredients, except the butter and $\frac{1}{4}$ cup of the apple juice, in a large bowl and mix until well blended.

5. Add the stuffing to the cavity of a turkey (or chicken) or place it in a large buttered casserole dish. If using a dish, dot the top of the stuffing with butter and drizzle with $\frac{1}{4}$-cup apple juice. Cover and bake in a preheated 350°F oven for 45 minutes or until golden brown.

Candied Sweet 'Taters

There are lots of recipes for sweet potatoes; most involve mashing the potatoes and adding a ton of sugar. I love this recipe because you get to experience the texture of the potato, which is topped with a sweet and buttery brown sugar crust.

Ingredients

4 medium sweet potatoes, peeled and cut into ½-inch slices
⅓ cup melted butter
¼ cup brown sugar

Yield: 8 servings

Stuff You'll Need

1. Peel the sweet potatoes and cut into ½-inch slices.

2. Line a cookie sheet with foil, add the potatoes in a single layer, and brush with half the butter.

3. Liberally sprinkle half the brown sugar on top of the potatoes. Place in a preheated 350°F oven for 15 minutes.

4. Remove the cookie sheet from the oven and flip the potatoes with a spatula. Brush with the remaining butter, sprinkle with the remaining brown sugar, and bake for another 15 minutes.

5. Let the potatoes cool a few minutes. Remove with a spatula and transfer to a platter. Serve hot.

Broccoli Soufflé

This soufflé was one of the only ways I would eat broccoli as a kid. My mother would make it for most holidays and I would greedily eat as much as I could.

Ingredients

1 ½ cups chopped broccoli flowerets
½ cup milk
½ cup grated Parmesan cheese, divided
2 tablespoons melted butter
2 tablespoons all-purpose flour
½ teaspoon minced garlic
½ teaspoon salt
4 eggs, separated*

* Instructions for separating eggs are on page 60.

Yield: 4 to 6 servings

Important tip

It is better to use a food processor than a blender for this dish. If you use a blender, the solids may get stuck above the blades. If this happens, turn off the blender and push the solids to the bottom with a wooden spoon. You may have to do this more than one time.

Stuff You'll Need

1. Place the broccoli, milk, half the Parmesan cheese, the butter, flour, garlic, salt, and egg yolks in a food processor or blender. Purée for 2 minutes or until smooth.

2. Whip the egg whites with an electric beater until stiff peaks form.

3. Fold the egg whites, half at a time, into the broccoli mixture until fully blended.

4. Transfer the mixture to an oiled 1½- to 2-quart baking dish. Bake uncovered in a preheated 350°F oven for 30 to 35 minutes, or until a toothpick inserted into the center comes out clean. Sprinke the remaining cheese on top and serve.

Cranberry Sauce

I think the first thing I ever made as a child was cranberry sauce. Well, I didn't actually make it—I opened a can, slid the cranberry goo on a plate, and cut it into 1-inch slices. This recipe is for the real thing. The sauce is fresh and flavorful with actual cranberries that give it texture. You will never look at canned sauce again.

Ingredients

1 cup orange juice
1 cup granulated sugar
4 cups fresh cranberries*

* You can also use frozen (thawed) berries.

Yield: About 2 cups

Stuff You'll Need

1. Place all of the ingredients in a medium pot.

2. Bring the mixture to a boil, stir, and reduce the heat to medium-low. Simmer about 5 minutes or until all the berries pop.

3. Remove the pot from the heat and cool completely at room temperature. Transfer the sauce to a bowl and serve warm, or refrigerate and serve chilled. The sauce will thicken as it cools.

Cranberry Bread

This easy-to-make holiday quick bread is delicious plain or topped with a little butter.

Ingredients

- 2 cups fresh cranberries, coarsely chopped
- 3/4 cup fresh orange juice
- 2 tablespoons melted butter
- 1 egg, well beaten
- 2 cups all-purpose flour
- 1 cup granulated sugar
- 1 1/2 teaspoons baking powder
- 1/2 teaspoon baking soda
- 1/2 teaspoon salt
- 1 cup chopped walnuts

Yield: 9-inch loaf

1. Coarsely chop the cranberries.

2. Place the orange juice, butter, and egg in a large bowl and stir until well blended. Add all of the remaining ingredients and stir to form a thick batter.

3. Spoon the batter into a greased and floured 9-x-5-inch loaf pan. Bake in a preheated 350°F oven for 1 hour, or until a toothpick inserted in the center comes out clean.

4. Let the bread cool for 10 minutes before removing from the pan. Allow it to cool completely before serving.

Stuff You'll Need

Pumpkin Pie

What's Thanksgiving without a classic pumpkin pie? This one is super delicious and super easy to prepare. Top it with some whipped cream. (And don't be skimpy!)

Ingredients

- 9-inch single pie crust, commercial or homemade
- 3 eggs
- 15-ounce can pumpkin purée
- 1/2 cup heavy cream
- 2/3 cup firmly packed brown sugar
- 1 teaspoon ground cinnamon
- 1/2 teaspoon ground nutmeg
- 1/2 teaspoon salt

Yield: 8 to 10 servings

Stuff You'll Need

1. Place the eggs in a large mixing bowl and beat well with a whisk or fork.

2. Add the pumpkin purée, cream, brown sugar, cinnamon, nutmeg, and salt. Stir until the mixture is smooth and well blended.

3. Pour the pumpkin mixture into the prepared pie crust.

4. Bake in a preheated 350°F oven for 50 to 60 minutes or until the center has set (it doesn't jiggle when you *gently* shake it). Cool at least 20 minutes before cutting. Serve at room temperature.

Bread Pudding

The name of this dessert doesn't sound as good as it tastes. It is actually more like a custard with a nice crispy crust. Top it with a sprinkle of cinnamon and you'll know it's holiday time.

Ingredients

- 3 cups ½-inch bread cubes (French or Italian bread)
- 2 cups whole milk
- 1 can sweetened condensed milk
- ¾ cup granulated sugar
- 6 eggs
- 1 tablespoon vanilla extract
- ¼ cup raisins
- ¼ cup melted butter
- 1 teaspoon cinnamon

Yield: 8 servings

Important tip

If you want the top of this pudding to come out crunchy, let the bread cubes dry out for a day. Like French toast, stale bread is preferable in this recipe.

Stuff You'll Need

1. Cut the bread into ½-inch cubes and place in a greased and floured 9-inch square baking pan or 2-quart casserole dish.

2. Place the whole milk, condensed milk, sugar, eggs, and vanilla in a blender. Purée for 2 minutes to form a smooth batter.

3. Pour the batter over the bread cubes. Bake in a preheated 350°F oven for 1 hour, or until a toothpick inserted into the center comes out clean.

4. Spoon the pudding into individual serving dishes. Enjoy warm or cold.

Sweet Memories

People all over the world celebrate special occasions with sweet treats.

Holy Bread

Greek Orthodox *Christopsomo,* which literally means "Christ's bread," was originally meant for the Christmas holiday. Today, it is served at celebrations of all kind. Before preparing this holy bread (made with only the finest ingredients), the baker makes the sign of the cross. Pine nuts, tangerines, and anise are favorite flavorings, and the loaf is decorated with strips of dough that form a cross.

Pan de Muertos

This Mexican "bread of the dead" is traditionally made to celebrate the country's Day of the Dead – its equivalent to Halloween. The yeast bread is shaped into skulls, corpses, bones, and other macabre forms, and then decorated with icing, sprinkled with sugar, or dipped in chocolate.

Spotted Dick or Spotted Dog?

In England, spotted dick (also called spotted dog) is a real holiday favorite – and one of the oldest English desserts. It is a thick steamed pudding made with raisins, apples, brown sugar, lemon, breadcrumbs, and shredded suet. Traditionally, this pudding is cut into thick slices and served hot with custard.

Lucky Nut

Throughout Scandinavia, rice pudding is customarily served during the Christmas season. Traditionally, a single almond is stirred into the pudding – whoever finds it in his or her bowl is believed to have good luck in the coming year.

And the Most Popular Pie Is . . .

Can you guess which pie is the country's most popular? According to a recent nationwide poll by Schwan's Consumer Brands (makers of Mrs. Smith's pies), the top ten favorites rank in the following order: apple, pumpkin, chocolate cream, cherry, apple crumb, pecan, lemon meringue, blueberry, key lime, and peach.

Crust or Coffyn?

Initially, pie crusts – known in England as *coffyns* – were not meant to be eaten. They were hard and thick and served as bowls designed to hold or preserve fillings, which were generally savory, not sweet. Sweet pies and edible crusts began to appear in America around the mid-1700s, when sugar became more readily available.

That's Some Pretty Old Pudding

In England, plum pudding is traditionally prepared a year in advance and left to mellow – it is often soaked in brandy or cognac as it "sets." On Christmas day, the pudding is doused with brandy, decorated with a holly branch, and then lit before serving.

Gingery Good

Gingerbread is a traditional holiday favorite, and very versatile. It can be formed into crunchy cookies, baked into delectable cakes, and used to create holiday houses. In England, it was customary for a single woman to eat a gingerbread man for luck in meeting her future husband.

18. Just Desserts

For the love of cake.

For many of us, dessert is, by far, the favorite, most anticipated part of a meal. (If I could eat dessert all day without getting sick, I probably would.) Think about it. What would life be like without it? From early childhood, sweet delights have provided us with happiness and comfort. They manage to make us smile, even when we're blue. That's why, when you were very young and you cried, someone offered you a lollipop instead of a pork chop.

This chapter presents all kinds of easy-to-make desserts; but first, I'm going to take you on a guided tour down the baking aisle of your grocery store. There you can check out the many available ingredients that are used in baked goods and other special treats — from aromatic spices and extracts to nuts and chips and other flavorful "bits."

When it comes to the recipes, I'll be sharing some of my favorites with you. There are rich puddings, heavenly cream puffs, and cookie classics like chocolate chip and oatmeal (complete with lots of yummy variations). There are also luscious pies, quick breads, muffins, and cakes. I've even included my secret recipe for Chocolate Almond Torte — a dessert so good it makes me happy just thinkin' about it.

Say goodbye to your toes and fasten your seatbelt —
You're going to Calorie City, Baby!
Yee haw!

A Trip Down the Baking Aisle

It's amazing how many different types of baking products are readily available at the grocery store—from flour varieties and leavening agents to sugars and spices. Many are time-saving items like premade pie crusts and cake frostings. Others are sweet or crunchy little bits and pieces that can turn a good dessert into a great one.

You probably know about some of the items on the following pages, while others may surprise you. Either way, I hope you have a sweet time with this section.

For information on the various types of flour and sugar, see pages 28 and 29 in Chapter 2.

Making Light of It

There are three primary rising agents—also called leavening or activating ingredients—that cause cakes, cookies, and breads to rise and become light and fluffy.

Baking powder

Baking powder is a mixture of baking soda and a few other ingredients, the most important of which is an acidic compound (such as cream of tarter). When this product is mixed in a batter or dough with wet ingredients, leavening occurs. Unlike baking soda, no acidic ingredients are needed, as the acid is already in the powder.

Baking soda

Also called *bicarbonate of soda*, baking soda has no leavening power when it is used alone. However, when it is added to a batter or dough that contains an acidic ingredient (such as lemon, molasses, honey, or buttermilk), it causes baked goods to rise.

Yeast

Yeast is actually a microscopic organism that comes to life and reproduces when moistened with warm (not hot) water and fed a carbohydrate (sugar, flour). When activated, yeast produces carbon dioxide, which causes batters and doughs to bubble and rise. It has a distinct flavor and aroma and is used primarily in breads.

In the Thick of It

Three main ingredients thicken the consistency of sauces, gravies, soups, puddings, and other liquids.

Cornstarch

This "flour" from the corn kernel is often used to thicken puddings, sauces, and soups. Sauces that are thickened with cornstarch will be clear, rather than opaque, as with flour-based sauces.

Flour

Flour is used to thicken hot liquids, like sauces and gravies.

Gelatin

Odorless, tasteless, and colorless, gelatin is used as a thickener for jams, jellies, and other "jelled" dishes.

Concentrated Milk

Certain recipes benefit from a concentrated form of milk—sweetened condensed or evaporated.

Condensed milk

This thick sweet mixture of whole milk and sugar is heated until about 60 percent of the liquid evaporates. It is used in some custards, puddings, pie fillings, and candies.

Evaporated milk

The same as condensed milk only without the sugar, evaporated milk comes in lowfat and skim forms. It lends a creamy texture to many dishes, including cream soups.

Extracts

Extracts are highly concentrated flavorings that come from various foods or plants. A small amount adds powerful flavor to foods without adding a lot of liquid. Although there are over sixty flavors, most grocery stores carry a dozen or so. Pure extracts are more expensive than artificial, but superior in taste.

- Almond
- Anise
- Clove
- Peppermint
- Pistachio
- Spearmint
- Vanilla
- Walnut

Chocolate—Food of the Gods

Chocolate is made from cocoa beans. The beans are roasted and ground into cocoa "solids," which are combined with cocoa butter to make chocolate. Sugar and milk may also be added. The highest percentage of cocoa is found in unsweetened chocolate varieties (also called bitter or baking chocolate). Next in line is bittersweet chocolate, followed by semi-sweet, and then sweet-dark chocolate. Milk chocolate, which gets its name from the fact that it contains milk, has the least amount of cocoa (and the most sweetener). White chocolate, which does not contain any cocoa solids, is not actually "chocolate."

Cocoa Powder

Cocoa powder comes in unsweetened and sweetened varieties. It easily dissolves in liquids, making it a good choice for hot cocoa and other chocolate beverages. It also adds chocolate richness to many baked goods and other desserts.

Bar Chocolate

Bars of baking chocolate come in individually wrapped one-ounce squares (usually eight squares to a pack). Each square is scored down the middle, so it can be easily broken in half. Baking chocolate comes in unsweetened, bittersweet, and semi-sweet varieties.

Chocolate Chips

Although they can be used in most recipes that call for chocolate, chocolate chips or morsels are best known as an ingredient in that American classic—the chocolate chip cookie. They come in many chocolate varieties, including, milk, semi-sweet, and white.

Awww . . . Nuts!

Feeling a little nutty? I do all the time. Nuts are a welcome addition to cookies, cakes, and breads, and great for topping off a bowl of ice cream or frozen yogurt. Many nuts, like Brazil nuts, are actually seeds; others, like peanuts, are legumes. Most nuts are available raw or roasted, with or without salt, and plain or flavored. They also come whole, halved, sliced, slivered, and chopped.

Keep 'em Fresh

Freshness is an extremely important consideration when cooking or baking with nuts. A stale nut will ruin any type of dish—guaranteed! Because of their high fat content, nuts get stale quickly. To keep them fresher longer, place them in an airtight container and store in the refrigerator or freezer. In the refrigerator, they will last three to four months; in the freezer, they will stay fresh up to eight months. Before adding nuts to a recipe, always, *always* taste them to be sure they're fresh.

Toasting nuts enhances their flavor; it also makes them easier to chop. You can easily toast nuts yourself. Simply spread them out on a baking sheet in a single layer, then pop them into a 350°F oven for five to twenty minutes (depending on the size of the nut). Keep an eye on them so they don't burn. Cool before storing.

Nutty Paste

Almond Paste
Made primarily of ground almonds and sugar, this paste is typically used as a pastry filling (ever had an almond croissant, strudel, or bear claw?). It is also used in some cookies like macaroons.

Marizipan
Made mostly of almond paste and sugar, marzipan is a pliable mixture that can be colored and rolled out or molded into edible decorative shapes (like ribbons or bows).

Almonds

Pecans

Cashews

Peanuts

Macadamias

Walnuts

Bits and Pieces

One trip down the baking aisle and you'll be amazed at all of the luscious little bits and pieces you can add to cookies, quick breads, and cakes, or mix with puddings, ice creams, and other frozen desserts. You can even make your own by chopping up your favorite candy bars.

Top Picks

Of the wide variety of tasty morsels found in the baking aisle, some of the more popular choices appear on this page. Chips of various flavors are typically added whole to cookies and ice cream, but they also melt well and can be used in most recipes that call for melted chocolate. Melted chips also make a great dip for fresh fruits like strawberries, and pineapple, not to mention frozen bananas.

Coconut, which is sold in cans or plastic bags, is available sweetened or unsweetened and shredded or flaked. It is popular in many dessert items, including cakes, cream pies, and macaroons. Once the can or bag is opened, store it in the refrigerator.

Light, fluffy marshmallows come packaged in regular and mini sizes. They are the perfect toppers for steaming cups of hot cocoa, the "glue" that holds S'mores and Rice Krispies Treats together, and the crowning touch to candied sweet potatoes. Toasting marshmallows on a stick over an open fire is a campfire tradition.

Rich, buttery toffee pieces add flavor and texture to cookies. They are also delicious sprinkled over ice cream and other frozen desserts.

Radical Raisins

Actually dried grapes, raisins come in golden, brown, and red varieties. In addition to being enjoyed alone (they've been called "nature's candy"), raisins are used in a variety of desserts, including puddings, cakes, cookies, and sweet dessert breads. They are also added to granola and trail mix, tossed into hot and cold cereals, and even covered with chocolate. Also available are special "baking raisins." Extra moist and plump (thanks to a special handling process), these raisins tend to maintain their moistness during baking.

Raisins have a long shelf life. Tightly wrapped, they will keep up to six months in the pantry and about a year in the refrigerator.

Butterscotch chips

Shredded coconut

Chocolate chips

Toffee pieces

White chocolate chips

Marshmallows

Easy Does It

You don't always have to make everything from scratch. Often premade ingredients are not only convenient, they are also better than most people can make on their own. An excellent example of this is frozen puff pastry. Only the most talented bakers can make this multi-layered flour and butter creation.

I have found great success with many of the prepared items found on these pages.

Whipped Cream vs Whipped Topping

Making whipped cream is easy, but not as easy as buying it ready-made in a tub or getting one of those fun dispensers that let you shoot the topping into your mouth. Just be sure to look at the ingredient label before buying. Just because it looks and tastes like whipped cream, doesn't mean that it is whipped cream. Many of these toppings contain unhealthy trans fats, as well as preservatives, chemicals, and other additives—and not a drop of cream. To make your own whipped cream, see the Strawberry Shortcake recipe on page 367.

Pie in the Sky

Pie crusts

I almost always use premade pie crusts unless I'm making a fruit pie with a lattice top. Graham cracker and cookie crusts are good for cream pies and cheesecakes. You'll find them in the baking aisle. A standard pastry crust is best for fruit pies and pies with savory fillings (like beef and chicken pot pies). It comes frozen in regular and deep-dish pie tins. Premade dough is also found in the refrigerated section—just unfold the dough and place it in a pie plate. (For a Homemade Pie Crust recipe, see page 378.)

Pie fillings

Canned fillings are available for most types of fruit pies—cherry, apple, blueberry, and peach are standard varieties. Although they may not be as fresh as a real fruit filling, they do taste pretty good and are very convenient. Along with a premade crust, you can have a pie ready for the oven in just a few minutes.

Tasty Pastry

Phyllo

Tissue-thin sheets of phyllo dough are used in layered and strudel-type desserts. Phyllo is very fragile, dries out quickly, and breaks easily, making it difficult to work with.

Puff pastry

Puff pastry is real expert stuff. I have tried to make it from scratch with limited success. When baked, the dough puffs into a light multi-layered buttery crust that is used in many desserts.

Vacuum-packed dough

Canned dough for biscuits, breadsticks, rolls, pizza crusts, cookies, and croissants is available in the refrigerated section of most grocery stores. Simply pop open the can, form the dough on a baking sheet, and bake according to the package instructions.

Frosting

Although I'm not a fan of ready-made frostings, they can come in handy in a pinch. There are many varieties from which to choose. (For a couple easy and delicious homemade frosting recipes, see page 391.)

Mixin' It Up

Boxed mixes are available for everything from cakes, muffins, brownies, and breads to puddings, custards, and flavored gelatins. These mixes still require some work on your part, but the time involved and the ingredients you'll need are considerably less than when preparing the items from scratch.

Biscuit/pancake/waffle mixes

Usually requiring the addition of water, oil, and eggs, these mixes also make a good batter for dumplings.

Brownie mixes

Because I don't find much difference between brownies made from a mix and those made from scratch, I usually opt for the mix to save time. I also add ingredients like nuts and/or chocolate chips for more of a homemade taste.

Cake mixes

Typically, these mixes contain all the necessary dry ingredients for making cakes. They usually require water, oil, and eggs for the batter.

Cookie mixes and doughs

Boxed mixes contain all the necessary dry ingredients for the cookies. Premade doughs, found in the refrigerated section, need only to be sliced, placed on a cookie sheet, and then baked.

Pudding mixes

Regular and instant pudding mixes come in a wide variety of flavors. By reducing the amount of milk, you can also use the pudding as a pie filling.

Gelatins

Boiling water is all you need to do to turn fruit-flavored gelatin powder into a quick and easy dessert.

Muffin mixes

Along with the dry ingredients for muffins, many mixes also include canned fruit, like blueberries.

Specialty mixes

Also available are mixes for special desserts like crepes, chocolate mousse, and crème brûlée.

Don't it Look Sweeeet?

Want to give your cakes, cookies, and other dessert items a special touch? Decorate them! You'll find lots of edible and non-edible decorations in the baking aisle. Here are just a few:

- Candles
- Colored icing
- Colored sugars
- Food colorings (liquid or spray)
- Glazes
- Piping gels
- Plastic and/or edible decorations (flowers, butterflies, etc)
- Sprinkles

Hot Fudge Sundae

This recipe yields about two cups of hot fudge. Use what you need, then place the rest in a sealed container and store in the refrigerator, where it will keep up to a month. Next time you want a hot fudge sundae, heat up a few spoonfuls of the sauce in a pot or the microwave.

Ingredients

Vanilla ice cream
Whipped cream (optional)
Chopped nuts (optional)

Fudge Sauce

1 cup semi-sweet chocolate chips
1 cup sweetened condensed milk
⅓ cup granulated sugar
1 tablespoon butter
1 teaspoon vanilla extract

Yield: About 2 cups fudge

1. Place the milk and chocolate chips in a medium pot over medium heat. Stirring frequently, bring to a light boil. Continue to stir until all the chips have melted.

2. Remove the pot from the heat and let the mixture cool for 2 or 3 minutes. Add the butter and vanilla and stir until well blended.

Stuff You'll Need

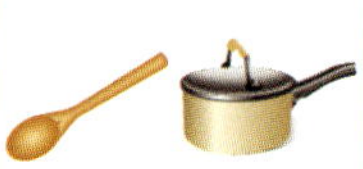

3. Place 1 or 2 scoops of ice cream in a bowl or sundae glass. Spoon on some of the hot fudge, and top with whipped cream and nuts.

Strawberry Shortcake

This dessert is a great summertime treat, especially when strawberries are in season. And since it's made with store-bought cake, it's a snap to prepare!

Ingredients

10 to 12 large strawberries, sliced

1 pound cake (8-x-4-inch loaf)

Whipped Cream

1 cup heavy cream

1 tablespoon powdered sugar

Yield: 4 servings

Stuff You'll Need

1. Remove the tops from the strawberries and slice.

2. Using a very sharp knife, slice the pound cake horizontally into three layers. Then cut the loaf vertically into four stacks.

3. To make the whipped cream, place the cream and sugar in a mixing bowl and beat with an electric hand-held mixer about 3 minutes, or until stiff peaks form.

4. Take one of the pound cake stacks and place the bottom layer on a dessert plate. Top with a layer of strawberries, followed by a layer of whipped cream. Cover with the middle layer of cake and repeat the steps with the middle and top layers.

Choco Pudding

Here's a quick and easy dessert that's chocolaty and delicious.

Ingredients

2 $\frac{1}{2}$ cups milk
$\frac{1}{2}$ cup granulated sugar
$\frac{1}{3}$ cup unsweetened cocoa
2 $\frac{1}{2}$ tablespoons cornstarch
$\frac{1}{8}$ teaspoon salt
1 teaspoon vanilla extract

Yield: 4 servings

Important tip

Keep the heat low and stir constantly to prevent the milk from forming lumpy "curds." The consistency of the pudding should be velvety smooth.

Stuff You'll Need

1. Place the ingredients in a medium pot over medium-low heat. Stir until smooth, well blended, and uniform in color.

2. Continue stirring until the mixture comes to a boil. Stir another 30 seconds, then remove the pot from the heat.

3. Pour the mixture into a large bowl or four individual serving bowls and refrigerate 2 hours.

4. Serve the chilled pudding as is or topped with whipped cream and grated chocolate.

Coconut Custard

I don't like custard normally, but once I tried this one, I was in love. The coconut floats to the top and becomes like a coconut cake. And with the flan on the bottom . . . totally heavenly!

Ingredients

1½ cups granulated sugar, divided
14-ounce can sweetened condensed milk
12-ounce can evaporated milk
½ cup whole milk
6 eggs
½ cup shredded coconut
1 teaspoon vanilla extract

Yield: 6 to 8 servings

Important tips

- Use a rubber spatula to transfer the melted sugar from the pan to the custard cups.
- After enjoying this custard, some of the sugar may stick to the cups and be difficult to clean. Simply let the cups run under very hot water, or fill them with boiling water and let sit a few minutes.
- To prevent the sugar from re-crystallizing as it melts (in Step 1), it is best to shake it in the pan, rather than stir it with a spoon.

Stuff You'll Need

1. Place 1 cup of the sugar in a small pan over medium heat. When it begins to liquify, shake the pan often until the sugar is fully melted and beginning to caramelize (turn brown).

2. Immediately pour equal amounts of the caramelized sugar into six individual ovenproof custard cups. Cool for 10 minutes.

3. Place all of the remaining ingredients in a blender and blend for 2 minutes.

4. Pour equal amounts of the mixture in the cups over the cooled sugar mixture. Carefully place the cups in a baking pan.

5. Transfer the pan to a preheated 350°F oven and bake 45 minutes, or until the center of the custards are firm. Serve warm, or refrigerate and serve chilled.

Chocolate Cream Puffs

Basic chocolate mousse is used as the filling for these heavenly cream puffs. Refrigerate any leftover filling and enjoy it as a bonus dessert!

Ingredients

$^3/_4$ cup semi-sweet chocolate chips
1 cup heavy cream
1 tablespoon powdered sugar
6 frozen puff pastry shells
Grated semi-sweet chocolate for garnish

Yield: 6 servings

Important tip

Be sure to fold the cream and melted chocolate together gently (so it is as light as possible). Stop folding as soon as the mixture is uniform in color.

Stuff You'll Need

1. Melt the chocolate chips in a saucepan over low heat. Remove from the heat and let the chocolate cool until warm—not hot.

2. Place the cream and sugar in a mixing bowl and beat with an electric hand-held mixer about 3 minutes, or until stiff peaks form.

3. Spoon the cooled chocolate over the whipped cream and fold together gently until well blended. Refrigerate at least 2 hours. (At this point, you have chocolate mousse.)

4. Remove the pastry shells from the package and place on a cookie sheet with the "top" side facing up. Bake in a preheated 400°F oven for 20 to 25 minutes, or until golden brown.

5. Remove the top of the shells and remove the soft interior with a fork. Fill the cups generously with the chocolate mousse and sprinkle with grated chocolate.

Chocolate Chip Cookies

Chocolate chip cookies are probably the most popular cookie in America. They are crunchy, sweet, and contain chocolate. They also store and travel well. Need I say more?

Ingredients

2 sticks (1 cup) softened butter
2 eggs
$^{3}/_{4}$ cup packed brown sugar
$^{3}/_{4}$ cup granulated sugar
1 teaspoon vanilla extract
1 teaspoon baking soda
1 teaspoon salt
2 cups all-purpose flour
2 cups semi-sweet chocolate chips
1 cup coarsely chopped walnuts (optional)

Yield: About 3 dozen

Important tip

For best results YOU MUST USE SOFTENED BUTTER! Do not use melted butter, hard butter, or margarine. To soften butter, place it unwrapped on a plate at room temperature for at least four hours. It should be very soft but still maintain its shape.

Stuff You'll Need

1. Place the butter, brown and granulated sugars, eggs, and vanilla in a mixing bowl. Beat with an electric mixer or wooden spoon until well blended.

2. Add the baking soda, salt, and flour half-cup cup at a time, and stir to form a smooth, fairly stiff batter. Add the chips and nuts and fold into the batter.

3. Drop rounded teaspoons of batter onto an ungreased cookie sheet, leaving about an inch or so of space between them. (For larger cookies, use a tablespoon of batter.)

Try These Variations!

Instead of semi-sweet chocolate chips, try:
Milk chocolate, white chocolate, or butterscotch chips; M&Ms; or broken-up chocolate bars.

Instead of walnuts, try:
Pecans, hazelnuts, or macadamia nuts.

Here are some of my favorite combos:

- Macadamia nuts and white chocolate chips.
- Pecans and butterscotch chips.
- Pecans and semi-sweet chocolate chips.
- Hazelnuts and milk chocolate chips.

Cool Idea!

I never plan on eating more than a few cookies at a time. So I usually bake a few, then put the remaining dough in a plastic bag and store it in the refrigerator, where it will keep for up to two weeks. That way, I can enjoy freshly baked cookies any time!

4. Bake in a preheated 350°F oven for 10 to 12 minutes, or until light golden brown. Cool for a minute before removing the cookies from the sheet with a spatula. Transfer to a wire rack to finish cooling.

Mexican Wedding Cakes

These are probably my favorite cookies. If they are served at Mexican weddings, count me in!

Ingredients

2 cups pecan halves
2 sticks (1 cup) softened butter
2 teaspoons vanilla extract
¼ cup granulated sugar
2 cups all-purpose flour
1 cup powdered sugar

Yield: About 30 to 35 cookies

Important tip

For best results YOU MUST USE SOFTENED BUTTER! Do not use melted butter, hard butter, or margarine. To soften butter, place it unwrapped on a plate at room temperature for at least four hours. It should be very soft but still maintain its shape.

Stuff You'll Need

1. Place the pecans in a food processor and finely grind.

2. Place the butter, granulated sugar, and vanilla in a mixing bowl and beat with a wooden spoon until well blended. Add the pecans and stir well.

3. Add the flour half-cup at a time, and stir to form a somewhat firm, pasty dough.

4. With your hands, roll the dough into balls that are slightly smaller than golf balls. Place on an ungreased cookie sheet, leaving an inch or so of space between them.

5. Bake in a preheated 350°F oven for 25 minutes, or until light brown. Cool the cookies about 10 minutes or until warm, then roll them in powdered sugar until completely coated.

Oat-Rageous Oatmeal Cookies

Oats add mild flavor and texture to many baked goods. What I really love about this cookie recipe is that it lends itself to lots of variations.

Ingredients

1/2 cup butter (1 stick), softened
1/2 cup firmly packed brown sugar
1/2 cup granulated sugar
1 teaspoon vanilla extract
1 egg
1 cup all-purpose flour
1/2 teaspoon baking soda
1/2 teaspoon baking powder
1/2 teaspoon salt
1 cup old-fashioned rolled oats

Yield: About 3 dozen cookies

Stuff You'll Need

1. Place the butter, sugars, and vanilla in a large mixing bowl. Cream with an electric mixer on low speed for 2 to 3 minutes or until light and fluffy. Add the egg and continue to beat until well blended.

2. Combine the flour, baking soda, baking powder, and salt in a medium bowl. Add this flour mixture to the creamed mixture a half a cup at a time, and stir with a wooden spoon to form a smooth, sticky dough. Add the oats and stir until well distributed.

3. Drop rounded teaspoons of dough onto a greased cookie sheet, leaving at least an inch of space between them.

4. Bake in a preheated 350°F oven for 10 to12 minutes or until light golden brown. Cool for a minute before removing the cookies from the sheet with a spatula. Transfer to a wire rack to finish cooling.

Try These Variations!

In addition to the variations at right, check out the following add-ins for this oatmeal cookie. Bet you can think of lots more.

Add Ins:

- Peanut butter morsels
- Chocolate morsels
- Chocolate chunks

Oatmeal-Raisin Cookies

Add

- 1 cup brown or golden raisins

Add the raisins in Step 2 of the recipe along with the oats.

Coconut-Oatmeal Cookies

Add

- 1 cup sweetened shredded coconut

Add the coconut in Step 2 of the recipe along with the oats.

Try This Variation!

Oat-Butterscotch Cookies

I bought a bag of butterscotch morsels one day and decided to try them with an oatmeal cookie recipe. Here is the very sweet result of that experiment.

Ingredients

$^3/_4$ cup butter ($1^1/_2$ sticks), softened
$^3/_4$ cup firmly packed brown sugar
$^3/_4$ cup granulated sugar
1 teaspoon vanilla extract
2 eggs
$1^1/_4$ cups all-purpose flour
1 teaspoon baking soda
$^1/_2$ teaspoon salt
3 cups rolled oats
$1^2/_3$ cups butterscotch morsels

Yield: About 4 dozen cookies

1. Follow Steps 1 and 2 of the Oat-Rageous Oatmeal Cookie recipe on page 110. Add the butterscotch chips to the dough in Step 2 along with the oats.

2. Drop rounded teaspoons of dough onto an ungreased cookie sheet, leaving at least an inch of space between them.

3. Bake in a preheated 350°F oven for 10 to 12 minutes or until golden brown. Cool for a minute before removing the cookies from the sheet with a spatula. Transfer to a wire rack to finish cooling.

Homemade Pie Crust

One of the beauties of pie making is that you can buy the crusts already made. Basic crusts come frozen and refrigerated, while special graham cracker and cookie crusts are found in the baking aisle. If, however, you want to make your own crust, here's a fairly easy one.

Ingredients

2 cups all-purpose flour
⅔ cup vegetable shortening
⅓ cup cold water

Yield: 9-inch pie crust

Important tips

- In Step 1, if the flour mixture is too dry to form into a ball, add a little more water 1 drop at a time. Just be careful not to add too much water.
- Sprinkling a little flour on the cutting board and rolling pin will help prevent the dough from sticking.

Stuff You'll Need

1. Place all the ingredients in a mixing bowl and stir with a fork or wooden spoon until it forms a crumbly mixture. Form the dough into a ball.

2. Place the ball on a lightly floured cutting board and flatten it with your hand to a ½-inch circle. With a floured rolling pin, roll out the dough (from the center outward) to ⅛-inch thickness.

3. Place the pie pan face down on top of the dough. Cut out a circle of dough that is 2 inches wider than the pan.

4. Carefully lift the dough (use a spatula if necessary) and place it in the pie pan. Gently press the dough against the sides of the pan. Trim off the excess with a knife.

5. Gather up the dough trimmings and form into a ball. Repeat Step 2, then cut the dough into ½-inch-wide strips.

6. Lay the strips across the top of the filled pie in a criss-cross lattice pattern or a sunburst pattern (above). Press the strips against the edge of the crust to seal them.

Apple-Blueberry-Walnut Pie

I love both blueberry and apple pies, so I created this pie filling, which turned out to be the perfect combination of both. The brown sugar really puts it over the top. I usually make a homemade crust for this pie, but you can opt for a premade refrigerated crust if you want.

Ingredients

2 cups sliced McIntosh or Granny Smith apples (about 2 pounds)
¼ cup firmly packed brown sugar
2 tablespoons all-purpose flour
1 cup blueberries
½ cup coarsely chopped walnuts
2 tablespoons butter, cut into small pieces
Homemade Pie Crust (page 378)

Yield: 9-inch pie

Stuff You'll Need

1. Peel and core the apples, then cut into thin slices.

2. Mix the apples, brown sugar, and flour in a bowl.

3. Spoon half of the apple mixture on the bottom of the pie crust. Add half of the blueberries and walnuts, then dot with half the butter. Repeat the layers.

4. Roll out the remaining dough in a circle and cut into ½-inch-wide strips. Also cut out a 3-inch circle of dough. Lay the strips across the pie (as shown), and place the circle of dough in the center.

5. Place the pan on a cookie sheet (to catch any drippings) and bake in a preheated 350°F oven for 45 to 55 minutes or until the crust is golden brown. Cool at least 30 minutes before serving.

Pecan Pie

Here's a holiday favorite that's easy to make, very sweet, and a little nutty.

Ingredients

1 stick (1/2 cup) butter
1 1/2 cups pecan halves
3 large eggs
3/4 cup maple syrup
1/2 cup granulated sugar
1 teaspoon vanilla extract
1/2 teaspoon salt
9-inch frozen premade pie crust

Yield: 9-inch pie

Important tip

When browning the nuts, don't let the butter get too hot or it will burn (and the nuts might burn, too). Be sure to use a medium-low heat and stir frequently.

Stuff You'll Need

1. Melt the butter in a medium pot over medium-low heat. Pour all but 2 tablespoons in a mixing bowl and set aside. Add the pecans to the pot and brown 2 to 3 minutes, stirring frequently. Remove from heat and let cool a bit.

2. Add the eggs, maple syrup, sugar, vanilla, salt, and cooled pecans to the melted butter in the mixing bowl. Stir until well mixed.

3. Pour the filling mixture in the prepared pie crust. Place on a cookie sheet (to catch any drippings) and bake in a preheated 350°F oven for 45 minutes or until the crust is golden brown and the filling is firm.

4. Cool at least 30 minutes before serving.

Chocolate Cream Pie

Here's a no-bake pie that's loaded with chocolate and whipped cream. A guaranteed crowd pleaser.

Ingredients

2 tablespoons butter
4 squares (1 ounce each) semi-sweet baking chocolate
2 cups milk
½ cup granulated sugar
¼ cup all-purpose flour
3 beaten egg yolks*
1 teaspoon vanilla extract
9-inch premade graham cracker pie crust
1 cup prepared whipped cream or topping
Grated chocolate for garnish

* Instructions for separating eggs are on page 60.

Yield: 9-inch pie

Stuff You'll Need

1. Melt the butter and chocolate in a medium pot over medium-low heat. Add the milk, sugar, and flour, and stir until smooth.

2. Remove the pot from the heat and let the mixture cool at least 5 minutes. Add the vanilla and egg yolks, and stir until the mixture is well blended.

3. Pour the chocolate filling into the prepared pie crust. Cover and refrigerate at least 2 hours.

4. Before serving, top the pie with the whipped cream and garnish with grated chocolate.

Cornbread

Simple cornbread is an American classic (and this version contains very little oil and sugar). I always serve it alongside a bowl of hearty lentil soup or crispy fried chicken.

Ingredients

¼ cup granulated sugar
1 cup milk
1 large egg
1 cup vegetable oil
1 cup cornmeal
1 cup all-purpose flour
1 tablespoon baking powder
1 teaspoon salt

Yield: 9 squares

1. Mix together the sugar, milk, egg, and oil in a large bowl with a whisk or fork. Add all of the remaining ingredients and stir until just mixed.

2. Pour the batter in an oiled 8-inch square cake pan. Bake in preheated 400°F oven for 20 to 25 minutes, or until a toothpick inserted in the center of the cake comes out clean.

3. Cut into squares and serve as is or with butter and honey (or maple syrup).

Stuff You'll Need

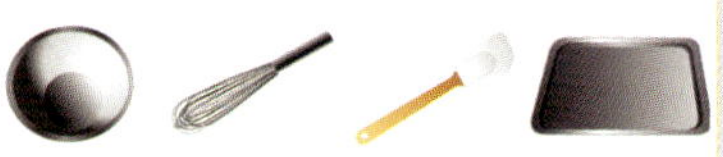

EZ Banana Bread

This is the simplest bread I know how to make. It is delicious as is, although I like it best with a little butter. I have served it at holiday feasts, both as a dessert bread and a main-course accompaniment.

Ingredients

2 very ripe large bananas
1 stick (½ cup) softened butter
2 large eggs
1 teaspoon vanilla extract
½ cup granulated sugar
1 tablespoon baking powder
½ teaspoon salt
1½ cups all-purpose flour
1 cup coarsely chopped pecans or walnuts

Yield: 8-x-4-inch loaf

Important tip

You can use bananas that are brown and overripe for this recipe. Matter of fact, the riper the bananas (within reason, of course), the more flavorful the bread.

Stuff You'll Need

1. Mash the bananas in a large mixing bowl.

2. Add the butter, eggs, vanilla, sugar, baking powder, and salt to the bowl and stir well. Add the flour half-cup at a time, then stir in the nuts.

3. Spoon the batter into a greased and floured 8-x-4-inch loaf pan. Bake in a preheated 350°F oven for 1 hour, or until a toothpick inserted in the center comes out clean. Cool 10 minutes before removing from the pan.

4. Cool the bread completely before cutting into slices and serving.

Cakes can be as simple as a pan of gingerbread dusted with powdered sugar or as complex as an ornately decorated multi-tiered wedding cake. The recipes in this section are basic and great for novice bakers.

Cake Baking Tips

- When making cakes and other baked goods, be sure to correctly measure the ingredients. (See pages 62 and 63 for helpful tips.)
- Unless otherwise specified, all ingredients—butter, eggs, liquids—should be at room temperature.
- Before starting, have all of the ingredients measured, the pans prepared, and the oven heated.
- After taking the cake from the oven, let it sit about five minutes before removing it from the pan. If you remove the cake while it's too hot, there's a good chance it will break.
- Use a dinner or butter knife to run around the edge of the pan for easy cake removal.
- To remove the cake from the pan, place a large plate or wire rack on top of the pan, then flip it over to release the cake.
- Cool the cake completely before frosting. (See page 390 for frosting instructions.)

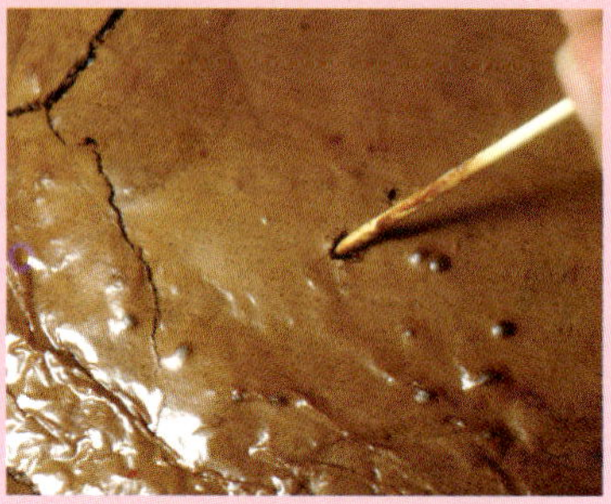

Ready or Not?

To determine if most cakes, batter breads, and cupcakes are done baking, simply insert a wooden toothpick into the center. If the toothpick comes out clean, the cake is done; but if it comes out with batter (as shown above), more baking time is needed.

Rich 'n Delicious Chocolate Cake

If you've only eaten chocolate cake from a mix, you're in for a big treat with this one.

Ingredients

2 cups all-purpose flour
2 cups granulated sugar
$^3/_4$ cup unsweetened cocoa
1$^1/_2$ teaspoons baking powder
1$^1/_2$ teaspoons baking soda
1 teaspoon salt
1 cup milk
1 cup hot water
$^1/_2$ cup vegetable oil
2 eggs
1 teaspoon vanilla extract
Rich Chocolate Frosting (page 391)

Yield: 9-inch double-layer cake

For complete step-by-step photo instructions on how to frost a double-layer cake, see page 390.

Stuff You'll Need

1. Place the flour, sugar, cocoa, baking powder, baking soda, and salt in a large mixing bowl and stir until well blended.

2. Add the milk, water, oil, eggs, and vanilla, and beat with an electric hand-held mixer for 2 minutes on medium speed.

3. Spoon the batter into two greased and floured 9-inch round cake pans. Bake in a preheated 350°F oven 30 to 35 minutes, or until a toothpick inserted into the center comes out clean.

4. Cool the cakes about 5 minutes before removing from the pans, then cool completely before adding frosting.

Carrot-Pineapple Cupcakes

For certain cakes, I confess that I sometimes use a box mix. But not carrot cake! Because it calls for fresh ingredients, homemade is the only way to go. This version is especially moist and delicious thanks to the crushed pineapple.

Ingredients

- 2 cups shredded carrots (2 to 3 large carrots)
- 2 cups granulated sugar
- 1 cup vegetable oil
- 4 large eggs
- 1 teaspoon vanilla extract
- 2½ cups all-purpose flour
- 2 teaspoons baking soda
- ½ teaspoon salt
- 8-ounce can crushed pineapple, drained
- 1 cup chopped walnuts
- 1 recipe Cream Cheese Frosting (page 391)

Yield: 12 standard (3-inch) cupcakes or 6 large (4-inch)

Important tip

This is an extremely moist cupcake because of the crushed pineapple, so it doesn't rise very much. That's why you can fill the cups to the top with batter.

Stuff You'll Need

1. Grate the carrots.

2. Place the sugar, oil, eggs, and vanilla in a large mixing bowl and stir until well blended. Add the flour and baking soda, mix well, then stir in the carrots, pineapple, and walnuts.

3. Spoon the batter into the cups of a greased or papered muffin tin. Bake in a preheated 350°F oven for 20 to 25 minutes, or until a toothpick inserted in the center comes out clean.

4. Cool the cupcakes at least 5 minutes before removing from the tin. Cool completely before frosting.

Almond-Poppyseed Muffins

Whoa! I love these muffins. The crunchy almond crust that forms on the top makes me go bananas!

Ingredients

2 cups granulated sugar
1 stick (½ cup) butter, softened
1 cup milk
2 large eggs
2 teaspoons almond extract
4 teaspoons poppyseeds
2 cups all-purpose flour
1 teaspoon baking powder
½ teaspoon salt
½ cup sliced almonds

Yield: 12 standard (3-inch) muffins or 6 large (4-inch)

1. Mix together the sugar, butter, milk, eggs, almond extract, and poppy seeds in a large bowl. Add the flour, baking powder, and salt, and stir until just mixed.

2. Spoon the batter into a greased or papered muffin tin. Fill the cups about ¾ full, then sprinkle with sliced almonds. Bake in a preheated 350°F oven for 20 to 25 minutes, or until a toothpick inserted in the center comes out clean.

3. Cool the muffins at least 10 minutes before removing from the tin.

Stuff You'll Need

Chocolate Almond Torte

This has become my favorite chocolate dessert, and that says a lot. The outside is like the lightest brownie you've ever eaten, and the center is like a rich chocolate mousse. It doesn't get much better than this!

Ingredients

- 1½ cups whole almonds
- 1 stick (½ cup) butter
- 8 squares (1 ounce each) semi-sweet baking chocolate
- 7 eggs, separated*
- 1 cup granulated sugar
- ⅓ cup all-purpose flour
- ½ teaspoon salt

* Instructions for separating eggs are on page 60.

Yield: 8 to 10 servings

Stuff You'll Need

1. Place the almonds in a food processor and finely grind.

2. Melt the butter and the chocolate in a pan over medium heat, stirring until smooth. Remove from the heat and let cool at least 5 minutes until warm.

3. Separate the eggs into two large bowls. Stir the yolks, then add the warm chocolate, sugar, flour, salt, and almonds. Stir until the mixture is smooth and well blended.

4. Beat the egg whites with an electric hand-held mixer for about 5 minutes, or until stiff peaks form.

5. Spoon the egg whites over the chocolate mixture and gently fold until well blended and uniform in color.

6. Line a 9-inch square disposable aluminum pan with wax paper, coat liberally with cooking spray, then add the batter. Bake in a preheated 350°F oven for 40 minutes, or until a toothpick inserted into the center of the cake comes out clean. Remove from the oven and let cool about 5 minutes.

7. With your hands, gently separate the flexible sides of the pan from the cake. Place a large plate on top, then flip the pan over. The cake should fall out easily. Let cool.

8. Serve the cake as is or sprinkled with powdered sugar.

The Frosting on the Cake

Frosting a cake is easy if you know how. Just remember that if you don't do a beautiful job, the cake will still taste good.

Frosting Tips

Frosting a cake, like anything else, takes practice, but here are a few helpful tips to make your frosting experience more enjoyable:

- Make sure that the cake is completely cool before adding frosting. Otherwise the frosting will melt into the cake or it will become runny.
- If the frosting is too thick, add a drop or two of water to thin it a bit. On the other hand, if the frosting is too thin, add some powdered sugar a little at a time.
- With a pastry brush, gently brush away any loose crumbs from the cake before adding the frosting.
- Make sure that the frosting is room temperature. Cold frosting is harder to spread.
- When spreading the frosting, I recommend using a rubber spatula, although special metal spatulas are also available for this. I like the rubber spatula because it lets you spread a lot of frosting at once.
- When spreading on the frosting, try not to scrape the cake below. This can create crumbs that get mixed in with the frosting.

1. When frosting a two-layer cake, place the first (bottom) layer on a serving plate (bottom side up).

2. Spoon a mound of frosting on the bottom layer and spread it to a ¼-inch thickness.

3. Place the second layer on top (bottom side down) and make sure the two layers are aligned.

4. Spoon a mound of frosting on the top layer and spread it to a ¼-inch thickness.

5. Spread frosting on the sides of the cake. If you pick up any crumbs, wipe the spatula with a paper towel before dipping it back into the bowl of frosting. If desired, decorate the cake with sprinkles, nuts, or other goodies. Refrigerate the cake until ready to serve.

Rich Chocolate Frosting

I don't like most chocolate frostings because they contain too much butter and cocoa instead of real chocolate, like in this recipe.

Ingredients

1 stick (½ cup) butter
6 squares (1 ounce each) unsweetened baking chocolate
2 teaspoons vanilla extract
¼ cup milk
3 cups powdered sugar

Yield: About 2½ cups

Stuff You'll Need

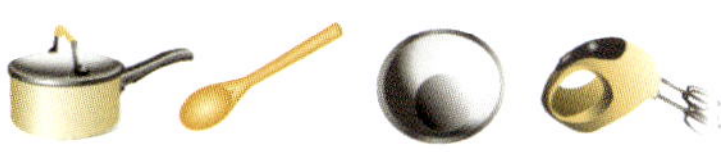

1. Melt the butter and chocolate in a medium saucepan over medium-low heat. Stir until smooth, then transfer to a mixing bowl.

2. Gradually add the sugar while blending with an electric hand-held mixer on medium speed. Blend until the frosting is smooth and uniform in color.

3. Use immediately or cover and refrigerate until ready to use. Let the cold frosting come to room temperature, stir well, and use.

Cream Cheese Frosting

This is a perfect frosting for carrot cake, but it is also great with lots of other cakes and cupcakes.

Ingredients

8-ounce package cream cheese
¼ cup heavy cream
1 teaspoon vanilla extract
3½ cups powdered sugar

Yield: About 2½ cups

Stuff You'll Need

1. Place the cream cheese in a medium bowl and mash with a wooden spoon to soften.

2. Add the cream, vanilla, and half the sugar, and blend together with a hand-held electric mixer. Gradually add the remaining sugar and blend until smooth. Use immediately or cover and refrigerate until ready to use.

METRIC CONVERSION TABLES

Common Liquid Conversions

Measurement	=	Milliliters
1/4 teaspoon	=	1.25 milliliters
1/2 teaspoon	=	2.50 milliliters
3/4 teaspoon	=	3.75 milliliters
1 teaspoon	=	5.00 milliliters
1 1/4 teaspoons	=	6.25 milliliters
1 1/2 teaspoons	=	7.50 milliliters
1 3/4 teaspoons	=	8.75 milliliters
2 teaspoons	=	10.0 milliliters
1 tablespoon	=	15.0 milliliters
2 tablespoons	=	30.0 milliliters
Measurement	**=**	**Liters**
1/4 cup	=	0.06 liters
1/2 cup	=	0.12 liters
3/4 cup	=	0.18 liters
1 cup	=	0.24 liters
1 1/4 cups	=	0.30 liters
1 1/2 cups	=	0.36 liters
2 cups	=	0.48 liters
2 1/2 cups	=	0.60 liters
3 cups	=	0.72 liters
3 1/2 cups	=	0.84 liters
4 cups	=	0.96 liters
4 1/2 cups	=	1.08 liters
5 cups	=	1.20 liters
5 1/2 cups	=	1.32 liters

Conversion Formulas

	LIQUID	
When You Know	**Multiply By**	**To Determine**
teaspoons	5.0	milliliters
tablespoons	15.0	milliliters
fluid ounces	30.0	milliliters
cups	0.24	liters
pints	0.47	liters
quarts	0.95	liters
	WEIGHT	
When You Know	**Multiply By**	**To Determine**
ounces	28.0	grams
pounds	0.45	kilograms

Converting Fahrenheit to Celsius

Fahrenheit	=	Celsius
200–205	=	95
220–225	=	105
245–250	=	120
275	=	135
300–305	=	150
325–330	=	165
345–350	=	175
370–375	=	190
400–405	=	205
425–430	=	220
445–450	=	230
470–475	=	245
500	=	260

INDEX

OTHER SQUAREONE COOKBOOK FAVORITES

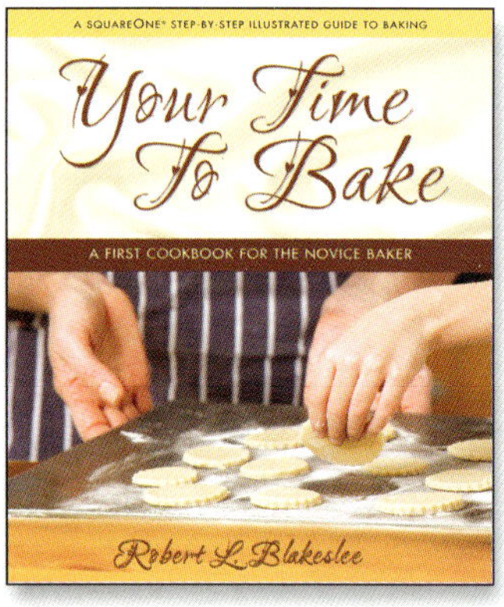

$29.95 • 400 pages • 8 x 10-inch hardback

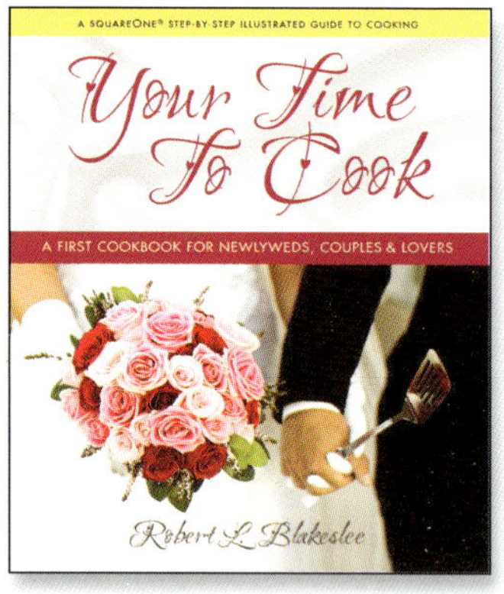

$29.95 • 416 pages • 8 x 10-inch hardback

$17.95 • 208 pages • 8 x 10-inch paperback

$17.95 • 320 pages • 7.5 x 9-inch paperback

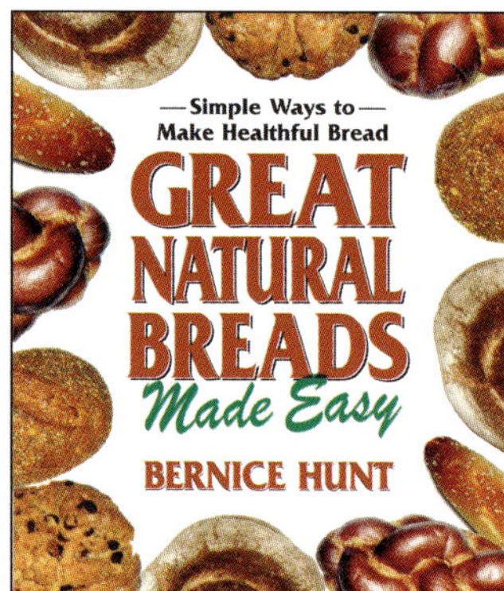

$16.95 • 160 pages • 7.5 x 9-inch paperback

$14.95 • 240 pages • 7.5 x 9-inch paperback

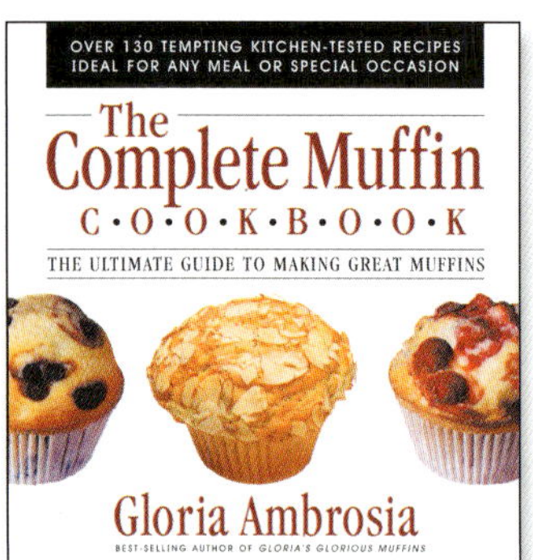

$14.95 • 216 pages • 7.5 x 7.5-inch paperback

$16.95 • 240 pages • 7.5 x 9-inch paperback

$14.95 • 156 pages • 7.5 x 7.5-inch paperback

For more information about our other cookbooks, visit us at www.squareonepublishers.com